# The Tây Sơn Uprising

Southeast Asia

POLITICS, MEANING, AND MEMORY

*David Chandler and Rita Smith Kipp*

SERIES EDITORS

## OTHER VOLUMES IN THE SERIES

HARD BARGAINING IN SUMATRA
*Western Travelers and Toba Bataks in the Marketplace of Souvenirs*
Andrew Causey

PRINT AND POWER
*Confucianism, Communism, and Buddhism in the Making of Modern Vietnam*
Shawn Frederick McHale

TOMS AND DEES
*Transgender Identity and Female Same-Sex Relationships in Thailand*
Megan J. Sinnott

INVESTING IN MIRACLES
*El Shaddai and the Transformation of Popular Catholicism in the Philippines*
Katharine L. Wiegele

IN THE NAME OF CIVIL SOCIETY
*From Free Election Movements to People Power in the Philippines*
Eva-Lotta E. Hedman

# The Tây Sơn Uprising

*Society and Rebellion in Eighteenth-Century Vietnam*

GEORGE DUTTON

UNIVERSITY OF HAWAIʻI PRESS *Honolulu*

Printed in the United States of America
11 10 09 08 07 06 6 5 4 3 2 1

**Library of Congress Cataloging-in-Publication Data**

Dutton, George Edson.
The Tây Son uprising : society and rebellion in eighteenth-century Vietnam / George Dutton.
p. cm.—(Southeast Asia—politics, meaning, memory)
Revision of the author's thesis (Ph. D.)—University of Washington, 2001.
Includes bibliographical references and index.
ISBN-13: 978-0-8248-2984-1 (hardcover : alk. paper)
ISBN-10: 0-8248-2984-0 (hardcover : alk. paper)
1. Vietnam—History—Tây Son dynasty, 1788–1802. 2. Vietnam—Social conditions—18th century. I. Title. II. Series.
DS556.7.D88 2006
959.7′03—dc22 2006000835

University of Hawai'i Press books are printed on acid-free paper and meet the guidelines for permanence and durability of the Council on Library Resources.

Designed by Richard Hendel
Printed by The Maple-Vail Book Manufacturing Group

*To Jessie, Talia, and Miranda*

# CONTENTS

# ACKNOWLEDGMENTS

This work has its origins in a doctoral dissertation I researched and wrote while at the University of Washington between 1994 and 2001. During my time at UW I benefited enormously from the assistance and encouragement of my dissertation committee members, in particular Laurie Sears and Christoph Giebel. As my adviser, Laurie was everything a graduate student could hope for: a supportive mentor and an insightful and encouraging critic. I consider myself fortunate to have been her student. Christoph was equally supportive, providing me with insightful criticisms of early drafts of this work and posing thought-provoking questions. I also benefited from the support and encouragement of fellow graduate students in Vietnamese history at UW and elsewhere, particularly Judith Henchy, Jamie Anderson, Michele Thompson, David Biggs, Liam Kelley, and Charles Wheeler.

As I subsequently revised the dissertation into the present book I was aided by the insights, suggestions, and corrections of people who read parts or all of the work in various forms. I am particularly grateful for the extensive comments offered by Victor Lieberman, Peter Zinoman, Li Tana, Nola Cooke, Liam Kelley, and David Chandler. Their comments made me rethink various elements of the manuscript and helped me to craft what I hope is a stronger final version. I also appreciated Alexander Woodside's willingness to answer some of my questions and to offer suggestions on sources and research issues. Finally, as I worked on revising the manuscript I benefited from the supportive and encouraging intellectual environment in my home department of Asian Languages and Cultures at UCLA, and especially the friendship of Thu-hương Nguyễn-Võ, Namhee Lee, and Michael Bourdaghs. While grateful for all of the suggestions and criticisms offered me in creating the current work, I of course take ultimate responsibility for the final product and its remaining shortcomings. There are many ways to write a history of the Tây Sơn; this is just one of them.

Research for this work was supported in part by a Fulbright-Hayes Dissertation Research Abroad Fellowship and by a Title VI FLAS Fellowship. This research would also not have been possible without assistance provided during my time in Vietnam, France, and Rome. In Vietnam,

Nguyễn Quang Ngọc, Phan Huy Lê, and Đỗ Bang were particularly helpful in facilitating my research, as were staff members at the Hán-Nom Institute, the Social Sciences Libraries in Hà Nội and Hồ Chí Minh City, the National Library in Hà Nội, and the Bình Định Provincial Library in Qui Nhơn. In Paris I was fortunate to have access to the indispensable holdings of missionary correspondence at the Archives of the Missions Étrangères de Paris. My use of these resources was facilitated by the archive's director, Father Gérard Moussay, and his assistant, Brigitte Appavou. I would also like to thank the staff at the Vatican Library, where I was given access to the fascinating manuscripts of the Vietnamese Jesuit Philiphê Bỉnh.

Finally, I offer thanks to my wife, Jessie Yuan, and my daughter, Talia. They put up with a lot while I researched and wrote this book, and for that I am deeply grateful. They were a constant reminder that what really matters to me does not lie in the dusty (if fascinating) records of people long dead.

# Introduction

In the spring of 1773, a small army of upland tribesmen and lowland peasants made its way down from the An Khê highlands of what is today south-central Việt Nam to attack the walled provincial capital of Qui Nhơn. At their head was a part-time betel-nut trader and minor tax collector named Nguyễn Nhạc. Lacking the resources for a direct attack on the citadel, the rebel forces employed a ruse. They feigned their leader's capture and turned him over to the provincial governor, who brought the caged Nhạc into the citadel as a prisoner. That night Nhạc released himself and opened the fortress gates to his waiting troops. The rebels made short work of the citadel's defenders, burned down its barracks, and sent its governor into panicked flight.[1] Their confidence bolstered by this success, the rebels soon moved on to other targets along the coast. As it moved about the countryside, marching under a massive red banner, its soldiers wearing red kerchiefs and making loud hissing noises to intimidate their opponents, Nhạc's army seized the goods of the uncooperative rich and distributed them among impoverished peasants, who acclaimed these new rebels as "virtuous and charitable thieves."[2]

This sequence of events marked the beginning of one of the most significant eras in Vietnamese history, one whose political and social upheaval would last for the better part of three decades and reverberate into the nineteenth century. The conflicts of the late eighteenth century played out in the rice fields and on the coastal waters of the Vietnamese territories, as well as in the centers of political power that already existed or would emerge over the course of the uprising. Before the rebel armies were finally defeated in 1802, they had overthrown two ruling families, briefly unified a territory that had long been governed as two distinct kingdoms, and brought a three-hundred-year-old dynasty to an end. Under the command of Nhạc and his younger brothers—Nguyễn Huệ and Nguyễn Lữ—the rebels also provoked and then repulsed large-scale invasions from Siam and China, even as they themselves engaged in military adventures in the neighboring Khmer and Lao kingdoms. As the uprising and its attendant wars dragged on, French, Portuguese, Chinese, and Southeast Asian mercenaries entered the fray, and hundreds of thousands of people were killed by warfare and famine. Many more were displaced from their homes and farms as Vietnamese society—from the peasantry to intellectual and political elites to religious and ethnic minorities—was confronted with a kingdom in turmoil.

The uprising came to bear the name of the hamlet from which its leaders had emerged—Tây Sơn. Meaning "western mountains," the name referred to the village's location near where the uplands rise from the coastal littoral near Qui Nhơn in a kingdom then known to the Vietnamese as Đàng Trong (the Inner Region), to the Europeans as Cochinchina. The Qui Nhơn area's population was one of transplanted Vietnamese settlers and former prisoners captured during the seventeenth-century wars between the southern Nguyễn and northern Trịnh governments, which had been contesting for political authority over the entire length of the Vietnamese territories. The Vietnamese in Qui Nhơn and its hinterlands were living in close proximity to an array of upland groups whose allegiance to the Nguyễn rulers was nominal at best. The Qui Nhơn region was also home to remnants of the mighty Cham empire that had once dominated the coastal regions of what is today south-central Việt Nam. The area became a flashpoint for hostilities that were to engulf the Vietnamese territories for more than thirty years.

The brothers who led the rebellion became known to their contemporaries by many names. The rebel chief was called "crazy biện Nhạc" by the Trịnh army commander who invaded the south in 1774, "*biện*" being a reference to Nhạc's position as a Nguyễn tax collector.[3] To others he was known as the "chief of brigands," describing his military coalition with its many bandit allies. Some European missionary witnesses called him "that apostate Nhạc," convinced he had been born into a Christian family.[4] His brother Nguyễn Huệ similarly came to bear a wide range of sobriquets. To the Chinese pirates whom he recruited for his navy, Huệ was the "big boss of Yueh-nan" and "the rebel protector of pirates."[5] To northern Vietnamese literati confronted by this larger-than-life figure who invaded their realm in 1786, he was "Chế Bồng Nga"—a reference to the fourteenth-century Cham ruler who had similarly seized Thăng Long (modern Hà Nội). For European missionaries he similarly conjured up images of ancient military adventurers, and they called him either "another Attila" or

"Alexander the Great."[6] And, as we have seen already, to some Vietnamese peasants the brothers collectively were "virtuous and charitable thieves." It was these chameleon-like figures, representing many things to many people, who led this remarkable uprising. The numerous labels applied to the rebel leaders highlight the complex and overlapping social groups involved in the events of this era. Brigands, pirates, thieves, Chams, Christians, military adventurers, and local officials were all part of the social fabric that would be severely tested by the thirty years of Tây Sơn warfare.

The Tây Sơn period is significant not merely because of the complex social dynamics that so profoundly shaped it, or its duration and enormous impact on the Vietnamese peoples. It is important for marking a point of historical rupture, even as its internal dynamics recapitulated fundamental themes that had long served to shape the trajectory of Vietnamese history. As a point of disjuncture, the Tây Sơn period is notable for representing the final drama in the gradual shift of political and economic power away from the northern Red River Delta region, southward across the Hải Vân pass and toward the Mekong Delta. This was a shift that had been under way for more than two centuries, represented by the growing strength and affluence of the Nguyễn lords and the expansion of their influence over territory south of their capital at Phú Xuân (near modern Huế). It was a shift that effectively created politically autonomous states—what Li Tana has referred to as the "two Đại Việts"—with the Nguyễn controlling the southern territories and the Trịnh family the northern region, known as Đàng Ngoài to the Vietnamese and Tonkin to the Europeans.[7] The eventual Tây Sơn conquest of Đàng Ngoài, which began in 1786, brought an end to that region's political autonomy and commenced the process whereby southern power would come to ascendance, represented first by the new rebel-created regime and then by the Nguyễn who eventually defeated them.

This period also accelerated the involvement of Europeans (most particularly the French) in Vietnamese internal politics and of the Vietnamese in mainland Southeast Asian affairs. Although European contacts with the Vietnamese had begun in the sixteenth century and were well established by the late eighteenth, the involvement of French missionaries and mercenaries in Vietnamese politics was greatly heightened during the Tây Sơn conflicts. This paved the way for future French political and military involvement throughout the Indochinese Peninsula, which would of course have enormous consequences in the mid-nineteenth century. At the same time, the Tây Sơn years also saw increased Vietnamese engagement in the

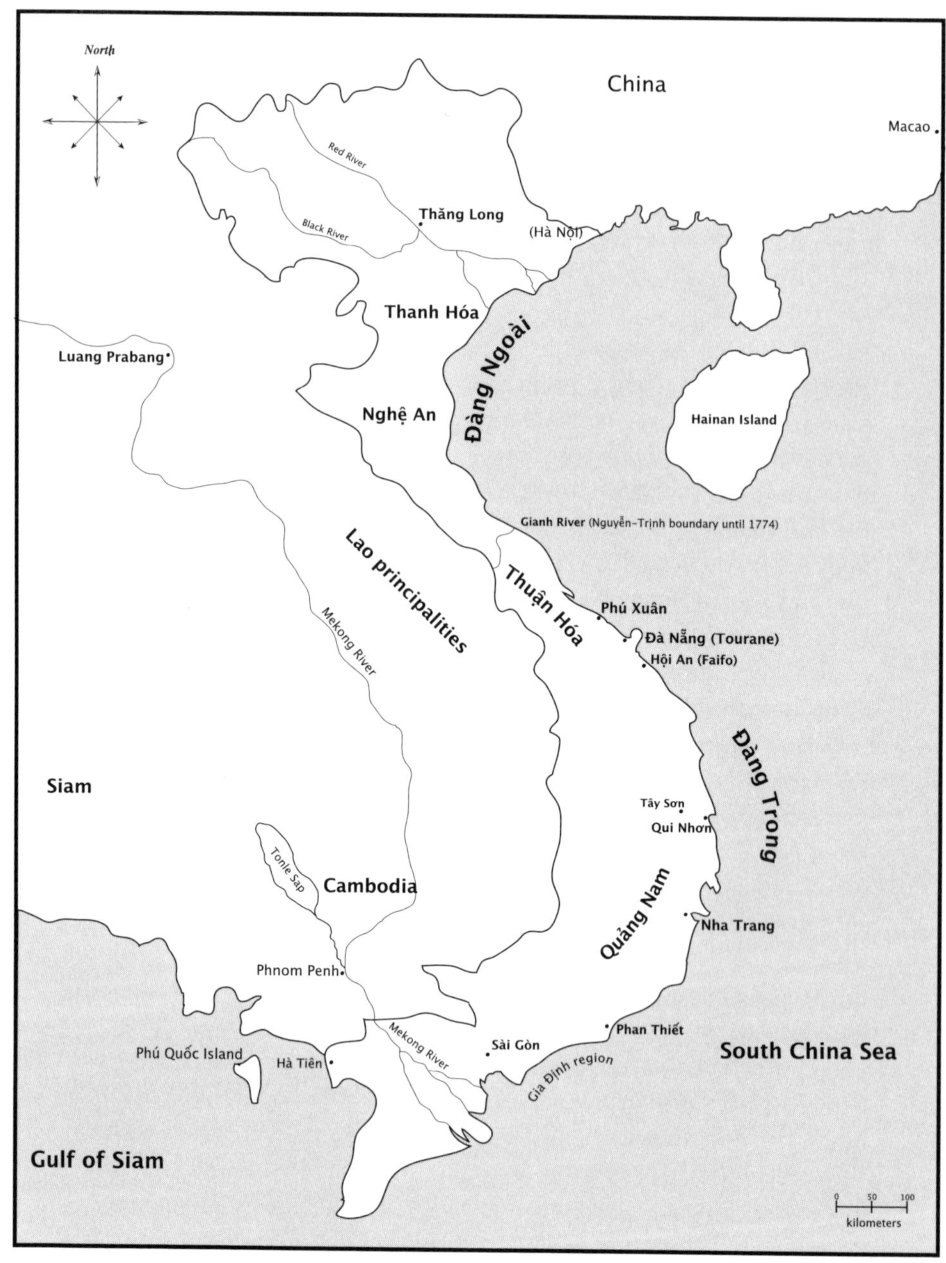


FIGURE 1. *Map of Đại Việt in the eighteenth century. Map shows major urban centers, rivers, and the division between Trịnh and Nguyễn territories that existed before 1774.*

political affairs of its neighbors, including the Khmers, the Siamese, and the Lao principalities. The Siamese became sometime allies of the Nguyễn during the struggle against the Tây Sơn, while Tây Sơn envoys sought to gain Siamese support for their own cause. Tây Sơn armies also invaded both Cambodian and Lao territories, drawing them into the Vietnamese conflicts. Consequently, the events of this era precipitated a greater Vietnamese involvement in mainland Southeast Asian politics that was to stretch well into the nineteenth century.

While one can read the Tây Sơn era as one of rupture, it nonetheless evinced numerous elements of continuity with the longer trajectory of Vietnamese history. These are to be found in the ways in which Vietnamese political leaders established their legitimacy through supernatural and institutional claims, the nature of the contentious relationship between the state and its people, lowland Vietnamese interactions with various ethnic groups, including uplanders, Chinese, and Chams, the role of Confucian precepts and rhetoric in governing the state and controlling society, and the real limitations thereof. The Tây Sơn leaders created alliances with numerous ethnic groups, and carefully appropriated elements of the historical Cham legacy, even as they made reference to Confucian principles to legitimate their rule. In these ways the Tây Sơn period can be viewed simultaneously as a transformative epoch culminating in the emergence of prominent new forces that would come to shape the Vietnamese experiences of the nineteenth and twentieth centuries and as a microcosm of fundamental aspects of long-standing Vietnamese historical experience.

This study explores the dynamics of the Tây Sơn era by analyzing the relationship between the Tây Sơn leaders and the multiple social, ethnic, and economic groups that constituted eighteenth-century Vietnamese society. The emphasis is in some ways more on continuity than on rupture as I examine the long-standing patterns that shaped interactions between political leaders and various groups nominally under their authority. And yet, some of these groups, Christians and ethnic Chinese for instance, constituted newer social categories within the greater Vietnamese territories, ones that confronted the Tây Sơn authorities with largely unprecedented challenges. Moreover, I suggest that the Tây Sơn leaders and their uprising (and later regimes) straddled the new realities of the southern realm and the long-established patterns set down when Đại Việt was still a more circumscribed place, geographically and demographically. It is clear that the Tây Sơn uprising was the product of a specific place and time in a dynamic Nguyễn realm. However, its broader impact and encounters with various groups in the realms of Đàng Trong and Đàng Ngoài revealed many elements that transcended the place and time of its origins.

The events of the Tây Sơn period were politically complex because of the wide array of political and military actors involved and because of the terrain in which they took place. What had been territories separated for more than a century were brought back into contact in the mid-1770s when a northern Trịnh army invaded the southern regions of Đại Việt. The subsequent Tây Sơn counterattack in 1786 then brought the larger Đàng Trong and Đàng Ngoài areas into still closer political contact. And yet, for political and geographical reasons, the two regions remained largely separated throughout the period. Their experiences of the Tây Sơn turmoil were frequently very different from one another, a function of different social structures and historical experiences, and of political divisions that existed both before and during the Tây Sơn era. There were, however, numerous shared experiences, ones imposed by the Tây Sơn leaders and their armies, whose demands on populations rarely respected geographical divisions. In this study I will generally treat these regions as discrete entities, highlighting aspects of their unique circumstances and experiences, though there are times when commonalities will be emphasized. The Tây Sơn era could profitably be studied from either geographical vantage point even as I have chosen, foolhardily perhaps, to examine both.

## THE TÂY SƠN IN WESTERN-LANGUAGE HISTORIOGRAPHY

In 1971 Alexander Woodside argued, in his pathbreaking study of early-nineteenth-century Việt Nam, *Vietnam and the Chinese Model*, that "modern Vietnamese history opens with the Tây Sơn Rebellion."[8] Despite the truth contained in this observation, the Tây Sơn uprising has remained a blank spot in Western scholarship, which has failed to address the complexities of this period. Woodside's own work, for instance, although it acknowledges the importance of the Tây Sơn in its preface, begins its account just after the Tây Sơn defeat, describing the manner in which the Nguyễn dynasty developed its political and administrative institutions during the first half of the nineteenth century.[9] The year 1971 also saw the publication of another pioneering work on pre-twentieth-century Vietnamese history, David Marr's *Vietnamese Anticolonialism*, which took up the historical thread in the late nineteenth century, as Việt Nam came to terms with its status as a French colony/protectorate.[10] A decade later with *Vietnamese Tradition on Trial* (1981), Marr brought the story up to the middle of the twentieth century, describing the height of the French colonial period from 1920 to 1945.[11] In each of these seminal works of English-language scholarship the Tây Sơn period lurks in the background, acknowledged for its historical and historiographical significance, but essentially unaddressed.

Recent English-language scholarship has continued the trend of studying pre– and post–Tây Sơn era events, although several works have finally started to address at least some elements of the period directly. Most notably, Li Tana's *Nguyễn Cochinchina: Southern Vietnam in the Seventeenth and Eighteenth Centuries* (1998) approaches the Tây Sơn period from the seventeenth century by examining the emergence of a Nguyễn polity in southern Việt Nam (Đàng Trong).[12] She devotes an entire chapter to the early years of the uprising, marking the first detailed consideration of the Tây Sơn in English and very importantly placing the uprising within the context of its geographical and sociopolitical origins in Đàng Trong. Li argues that this was not a "peasant movement," launched by lowland Vietnamese peasants, but rather a "provincial revolt," characterized by the substantial involvement of disaffected upland groups.[13] Her account looks only at the early years of the uprising, and thus highlights the Tây Sơn as a local phenomenon, but does not address the nature of the movement as it expanded beyond its point of origin. As I will suggest, once the uprising moved beyond its Qui Nhơn roots, its course was substantially transformed through engagement with the wider world of Vietnamese society and politics, and it became much more than a provincial revolt, both in scope and impact.

Other recent scholarship has also dealt with the Tây Sơn, though still in limited fashion. Choi Byung Wook's *Southern Vietnam under the Reign of Minh Mạng (1820–1841): Central Policies and Local Response* (2004), like Woodside's earlier account, focuses on the early Nguyễn period. Choi does open his study by looking at the late eighteenth century and exploring the emergence of a Gia Định–based polity during the course of the Nguyễn wars against the Tây Sơn. His emphasis, however, is not on the Tây Sơn, but on their Nguyễn rivals and ultimate successors, and their creation of an anti–Tây Sơn alliance within the heterogeneous realm of southern Đàng Trong. Two other recent English-language studies have also touched on the Tây Sơn. Liam Kelley's *Beyond the Bronze Pillars: Envoy Poetry and the Sino-Vietnamese Relationship* (Hawai'i, 2005) includes the Tây Sơn era and some of its prominent literati as part of a larger study that examines the representations of the greater East Asian thought-world found in Vietnamese poetry. Wynn Wilcox's recent dissertation "Allegories of Vietnam: Transculturation and the Origin Myths of Franco-Vietnamese Relations" (Cornell, 2002) is a historiographical study that looks more directly at the Tây Sơn period, using it as a lens through which to examine depictions of the relationship between Nguyễn Ánh and his European missionary supporters. Wilcox's focus, however, is less on the events of the Tây Sơn era and more on the later representations of its major historical figures. While both of these works are significant for bringing greater attention to the issues of the late eighteenth century, neither engages specifically with the Tây Sơn uprising and its larger implications for Vietnamese society.

Surprisingly, and with a few exceptions, French-language academic work on precolonial Việt Nam has similarly tended to overlook the Tây Sơn. Charles Maybon's 1919 study, *Histoire moderne du pays d'Annam (1592–1820)* devotes several chapters to the Tây Sơn period, though from a distinctly Nguyễn perspective and, unsurprisingly, with a heavy emphasis on the role played by the French.[14] In 1955, Lê Thành Khôi published *Le Vietnam: Histoire et civilisation*, which offers a sustained analysis of the Tây Sơn era within the context of a textbook history of Việt Nam.[15] Khôi describes the economic and social dislocations that provoked popular unrest in both regions of the country and then provides a balanced description of the rise and ultimate fall of the Tây Sơn regimes. Revised as *Histoire du Vietnam* (1983, 1992), Khôi's remains among the best summaries of the uprising, its course, and the dynamics that shaped it. Much more recent French-language scholarship includes Philippe Langlet's *L'ancienne Historiographie d'état au Vietnam* (1990), which although chiefly a meticulous study of the nineteenth-century Nguyễn historiographical project, also considers the Nguyễn understanding of their own historical antecedents including the Tây Sơn and the Lê.[16] Langlet demonstrates that the Nguyễn historians had to wrestle with the question of how to portray the Tây Sơn while at the same time seeking to reinforce their own legitimacy, which was clouded by their irregular path to power. Finally, Yang Baoyun's 1992 monograph *Contribution à l'histoire de la principauté des Nguyên au Vietnam méridional (1600–1775)* is another example of recent scholarship that approaches but does not directly address the Tây Sơn. As the title suggests, Yang's account stops just as the Tây Sơn began their uprising, and only briefly foreshadows what was to follow.[17]

In this manner, the Tây Sơn movement has been neatly bracketed chronologically by important scholarly work in English and examined in slightly greater detail in French, even as it has escaped detailed study by most scholars working in European languages. In some regards, the movement may have fallen victim to the systematic efforts by the Nguyễn dynasty to obliterate (to the extent that it was possible) traces of the Tây Sơn regime.[18] As David Marr has pointed out, "the Nguyễn court forbade its historians from compiling an account of the short-lived Tây Sơn dynasty (1788–1802), normally a routine function associated with maintaining for posterity chronological continuity from the distant past."[19] This prohibition inevitably rendered study of this period more difficult than of those that preceded and followed it, for which substantially more conventional historical documentation was produced and survived. Blame may also be laid at the doorstep of the colonial era itself, which has drawn much more scholarly attention, in part because it served to tie Việt Nam directly to the European world, and, of course, because it was seen as immediate prelude to the dramatic revolution and wars of the twentieth century. Whatever the reasons, Việt Nam in the late eighteenth century remains virtual terra incognita among Western scholars.

## VIETNAMESE HISTORIOGRAPHY OF THE TÂY SƠN ERA

In contradistinction to their Western counterparts, Vietnamese historians have subjected the Tây Sơn period to extensive historiographical scrutiny, even as interpretations of the uprising have generated considerable and often contentious debate. Indeed, this period and the events that defined it have been crucial to the historical narratives that were to emerge in all subsequent historiography. At issue have been questions of political legitimacy, of national division and unification, of social conflicts and confrontations. The involvement of "outsiders" in Vietnamese political struggles, from Nguyễn Ánh's alliance with the Siamese in the early 1780s to his later reliance on French mercenaries to the massive Chinese invasion on behalf of the Lê dynasty in the last years of that decade, has also sparked clashes centered on questions of nationalism. These historiographical struggles began even before the dust from the conflicts had settled and have continued to the present, and it is this contentious historiographical tradition with which my study engages. In this study, I seek to strike a balance between the two interpretive extremes that constitute existing analysis of the Tây Sơn: demonization and vilification at the hands of the Nguyễn regime that was their political successor and glorification and veneration by twentieth-century Communist historians who viewed their revolution as spiritual successor to the Tây Sơn uprising.

During the nineteenth century, the Nguyễn dynasty, whose founder fought against and eventually toppled the Tây Sơn regimes, depicted the Tây Sơn as "bandits" (*tặc*) or "rebels" (*giặc*), rejecting any notions of the Tây Sơn as having constituted a legitimate dynasty. The dynasty's court historians argued, moreover, that popular participation in the movement had been a product initially of Tây Sơn deception and later of coercion.[20] This historiographical project was explicitly designed to legitimate Nguyễn rule, which itself had emerged largely as a product of military success.[21] The Nguyễn legitimacy that emerged in their historiography combined the defeat of the Tây Sơn with what Nola Cooke has called the "myth of restoration," the idea that the new Nguyễn rulers had restored a polity established by their ancestors, rather than having continued the imperial tradition laid down by the Lê.[22]

At the official level the new dynasty was able to ensure the dominance of this interpretation, even as popular lore surrounding the Tây Sơn began to shape an idealized account of the rebel movement and as denizens of the Bình Định region sought to recuperate what were seen as local heroes.[23] Furthermore, the Nguyễn marginalization of the former Lê realms provoked some northern literati who wrote private accounts of the Tây Sơn regime that were far less critical of a short-lived dynasty officially characterized as illegitimate.[24] Consequently, the nineteenth-century historiography of the movement was already complex and conflicting, the result of differing perspectives and political purposes.

These two unofficial interpretive threads began to emerge more directly in the early twentieth century as Nguyễn political decline under French colonial domination opened a space for further reinterpretations, both those of early nationalist historians and those of later Marxist historians seeking to examine the Tây Sơn in light of the Vietnamese revolution. The early twentieth-century scholarship began to elide references to the Tây Sơn as "bandits" or "rebels." Instead, these historians, less constrained by the ideological concerns of the enfeebled Nguyễn court, suggested that the Tây Sơn brothers had made legitimate claims to political authority.[25] Even as this shift occurred, these early-twentieth-century accounts did not address the question of popular support for the movement. Indeed, references to peasants were almost completely absent in the writings of two prominent early-twentieth-century historians, Phan Bội Châu and Trần Trọng Kim, who were more comfortable in discussing the political and military leaders of the Tây Sơn period.[26] It was not until 1938 that Đào Duy Anh, in his *Việt Nam Văn Hóa Sử Cương* (An Outline History of Vietnamese Culture), ascribed the strength and successes of the Tây Sơn to peasant participation.[27] Even so, it was not until after World War II, in the wake of the Communist revolution and its strong connections to rural Việt Nam, that characterizations of the Tây Sơn as a "peasant uprising" or "peasant movement" began to emerge in Vietnamese scholarship. It is these representations, most often promulgated by Communist historians of the second half of the twentieth century, that now dominate discourse pertaining to the Tây Sơn period.

These scholars enthusiastically portrayed the Tây Sơn uprising either as a "revolution"—a *cách mạng*—or more neutrally as a "peasant movement"—a *phong trào nông dân*.[28] Both interpretations suggested that the Vietnamese peasantry supported the Tây Sơn movement's leaders and their subsequent regime. Historians working and writing under the Communist regime argued that there was eager peasant support for the Tây Sơn leaders in the uprising's early stages, followed by unified peasant cooperation in heroic efforts to unite the nation and drive out foreign invaders—the Siamese in 1785 and the Chinese in 1789. This analysis succumbed to the flawed logic of post hoc ergo propter hoc, as peasant motives were imputed from the results of their actions. Thus, the fact that peasant armies fought off Siamese (or Chinese) invasions was interpreted as representing a struggle to defend national independence. Similarly, the Tây Sơn army's crossing of the former Nguyễn-Trịnh dividing line in 1786 was characterized as having been guided by a passionate desire to see national reunification, rather than the prosaic pursuit of wealth, power, and even revenge.

In this overdetermined Communist historiography on the Tây Sơn, peasants emerged as heroic figures, marked as noble and unafraid, committed to economic and social justice and to a unified nation free from foreign interference. If this sounds suspiciously like the agenda of the Vietnamese Communist Party in the second half of the twentieth century, it is of course precisely because that is what it was. The Tây Sơn–era peasants were portrayed as forerunners of the twentieth-century peasant-supported revolution, even as their ultimate failure to transform the political and economic structures was seen as an indication of the severe restrictions placed on them by their historical moment. Only the Party, it was

FIGURE 2. *Statue of Quang Trung. A stylized rendering of the younger Tây Sơn brother situated on the grounds of the Quang Trung Museum, which was constructed on the site of the Tây Sơn brothers' family compound. Author's photo.*

argued, could ultimately overcome the conceptual limitations that had so long constrained the peasant imagination. Such characterizations of the eighteenth-century peasantry as noble and determined subalterns and loyal supporters of the Tây Sơn appear to have made them complicit in their own oppression, for the Tây Sơn era was unquestionably a time of immense hardship and difficulty for the peasantry. It was also a period in which the benefits of rising up, if they were at all discernible, rarely outweighed the staggering costs borne chiefly by this same group.

Peasants in many of these accounts were conflated with their leaders, suggesting that the motivations of the leaders (not themselves peasants) somehow represented or coincided with those of their (often reluctant) followers. Consequently, the term "the Tây Sơn" came to be used as a referent for the movement as a whole, leaders and followers alike, whose interests were assumed to have coincided, or at least largely to have overlapped, when in reality the leaders often did not address the concerns of their followers, and the supposed followers frequently came along grudgingly or under great duress, if at all. Although a few recent Vietnamese historians have begun to look somewhat more critically at the Tây Sơn period, no systematic reexamination of the period or the uprising has yet been published.[29] Writings of the late 1980s, which represented the last wave of major narrative histories of the movement, continued to characterize it as a heroic effort, strongly guided by nationalism, to defend the nation and to defend the interests of an oppressed peasantry.[30]

## SOURCES AND OBJECTIVES

This study is based on a wide range of materials, including archival and print material in Việt Nam and Europe. I have relied extensively on Vietnamese materials contemporary to the Tây Sơn and on later-nineteenth-century court chronicles for the broad outlines of the uprising and its main events. I have complemented these materials with an extensive reading of eyewitness accounts by European (primarily French) missionaries, who lived through the events of this era. Many of these accounts are preserved in the Archives des Missions Étrangères de Paris (MEP), where I spent several months reading through thousands of pages of letters from this period. The reports written by these missionaries are particularly valuable for providing a village-level perspective on events often described only in outline fashion in Vietnamese chronicles. Although

European sources have distinct biases and reflect the vantage point of an outsider, many missionaries were long-term residents who spoke Vietnamese and who had a remarkably clear sense of both village-level and national political developments. These missionary materials in particular enable me to provide a relatively detailed account of the impact of the Tây Sơn uprising on ordinary Vietnamese, and their responses to it.

Drawing on such sources, this study challenges existing characterizations of the Tây Sơn by suggesting that the uprising and the regimes it produced were extremely complex in their composition and that participants' multiple, often conflicting objectives do not allow for the oversimplified renderings that historians have heretofore presented. The uprising, which later transformed itself into a series of political regimes, involved not only peasants, but a wide range of social and political groups, each of which was in some way profoundly affected by the events set in motion in the spring of 1773. What I suggest then, is that the Tây Sơn uprising was not only about peasants, however central their participation in its long course. Indeed, the movement's leadership itself—the three brothers from Tây Sơn—were not simple farmers or rural laborers, despite their repeated claims to peasant roots. They might better be characterized as belonging to a rural lower-gentry class, with the eldest, Nguyễn Nhạc, a betel-nut trader and part-time tax collector for the Nguyễn court. Furthermore, all three brothers had received a considerable amount of education from a respected scholar who had fled the political infighting of the Nguyễn court and who later encouraged the brothers in their rebellion. Their background makes it clear that the Tây Sơn brothers, while relying on peasants to fill their armies, and addressing some peasant concerns, were not peasants themselves.

Once the uprising began, the Tây Sơn leaders quickly found themselves engaging with the broad spectrum of Đàng Trong society, and later, as the movement spread into Đàng Ngoài, its leaders were forced to deal with social complexities there as well. The Tây Sơn leaders successfully recruited supporters that ranged from lowland Vietnamese peasants and ethnic Chinese coastal merchants to members of the Cham royal family and highland tribal groups. Each of these groups had different objectives, being united primarily in their dislike for the manner in which the Nguyễn lords were mishandling the southern economy in matters of trade, taxation, and coinage. The Tây Sơn brothers were able to attract such an eclectic group of followers precisely because they appealed to the specific interests of each group and made each group's particular grievance part of their own agenda.[31] These multiple constituencies forced the Tây Sơn leadership to articulate an ambitious and frequently contradictory agenda. Consequently, it is not surprising that the Tây Sơn leadership was unable to meet the expectations of many who had initially joined their uprising.

Ultimately, the chief beneficiaries of the Tây Sơn uprising appear to have been its leaders and their elite supporters. Although some of the subaltern groups benefited at times and in certain places from the Tây Sơn actions—for example, brief periods of restored order or the possibilities of plunder offered by numerous military campaigns—these benefits were rarely systematic or enduring. The early property redistributions and ritual abolition of tax burdens that had led to the sobriquet "charitable thieves" soon gave way to demands from the rebel administration that were at least as onerous as those made by the regime it had replaced, and perhaps more so, for these demands were frequently made in the context of protracted military campaigns that rendered taxes and labor service particularly vexing.

The Tây Sơn leaders never carried out any sweeping changes that might have improved the lot of the peasantry, such as major land reforms or redistributions. Even in the movement's early days, the rebel leaders were far more likely to redistribute smaller items of value, or perhaps rice, than actually transferring titles to land. There were brief adjustments to tax rates in Đàng Ngoài and efforts to stimulate trade, but these were expedients to deal with existing crises rather than systematic reforms. Whatever convergence of interests may have existed between the movement's leaders and their followers in the very early years of the movement quickly disappeared, and what was only partly a "peasant movement" in its early days soon transformed into a more complex and diffuse political entity that increasingly represented the interests of particular political elites, seeking to gain power for its own sake. It should then be clear that the Tây Sơn uprising, like many other putative "peasant movements," cannot be read as the expression of a collective peasant will. In its very early stages the movement may have had some egalitarian strains at a time when its followers were few and its leaders still striving to establish themselves, but this egalitarianism soon gave way to conflicts between the aspirations of the leaders and the expectations of the peasants serving in their armies.

Put another way, just because an uprising is begun by (and even for) peasants, does not mean that it will remain a "peasant movement." As Michael Adas has rightly pointed out,

> A careful scrutiny of many of the rebellions that have been attributed to peasant unrest or labeled as agrarian risings often leads to the conclusion that these conflicts were, in fact, inter elite feuds or dynastic struggles in which peasant conscripts and peasant communities became unwillingly involved. . . . With important exceptions of risings in which the peasantry rallied to messianic figures or charismatic leaders struggling to overthrow inept or tyrannical rulers, the origins and outcomes of the struggles had little or nothing to do with the peasant concerns or conditions of the cultivating classes.[32]

While in some respects the Tây Sơn movement belonged to Adas' exceptional category—movements led by "charismatic leaders struggling to overthrow inept or tyrannical rulers"—it also manifested elements of what Adas termed "inter elite feuds or dynastic struggles." As will become clear in this study, the Tây Sơn became very much involved in disputed successions that took place in both Nguyễn and Trịnh territories. And although it could be said that the Tây Sơn leaders used these opportunities to their own ends, it might equally be said that they were manipulated by contestants in these power struggles and in turn manipulated the peasants to assist in their own involvement in those contests.

The emphasis of this work is on the underlying social dynamics of the Tây Sơn uprising and so is largely organized around chapters that examine different social groups in turn. To establish a context for this analytical approach, the first chapter provides a broad historical background to the Tây Sơn period, examines the major causes of the uprising, and then sketches an outline of the course of the uprising itself. Chapter 2 begins a close examination of the multiple facets of the uprising, starting with its leadership—the three brothers from the hamlet of Tây Sơn—and the ways in which this leadership defined what coherence the movement was to have. In chapter 3 I argue that the promise with which the movement began—an end to official corruption, the abolition of unjust taxation, and the redistribution of wealth—soon gave way to the gloomy realities of life under a regime almost constantly at war. I explore the question of how the peasantry, broadly speaking, were affected by and responded to this "peasant movement." Finally, chapter 4 turns to a consideration of the various peoples living at what I term the margins of Vietnamese society during this era—Vietnamese Christians, ethnic minority groups, outlaws, and pirates—and their complex relationship with the Tây Sơn leadership.

What this analysis suggests is that central to the Tây Sơn uprising was a series of interactions between the rebel leaders and various groups in Vietnamese society. Sometimes these interactions took the form of accommodations between the two sides; at others they were negotiated relationships. In yet other instances the Tây Sơn leadership co-opted certain groups or their leaders, and in many instances, depending on circumstances, the Tây Sơn relied on coercion to achieve their objectives. Thus, through accommodation, negotiation, co-optation, and coercion, the leaders of this rebel movement were able to transform themselves—to a certain degree—into rulers of "Việt Nam," even as the country remained divided and at war.

My study also challenges the notion of Tây Sơn exceptionalism which is often found in Vietnamese communist historiography, and suggests that the Tây Sơn regimes and their policies toward or treatment of the peasantry were better than those of the regimes they displaced or those that followed. There were a very few instances in which the Tây Sơn regime deviated from the actions of its predecessors—most notably in its selection of titles for various government positions, and to a lesser extent its use of the vernacular script *nôm* in some (though hardly all) government documents. But the Tây Sơn were generally not innovators, and their new regime unsurprisingly adopted the modes and forms of its predecessors, including both their administrative structures and many of their ritual trappings. The hardships that the peasants faced—corvee labor demands, increased and unpredictable tax demands, incessant military obligations—were magnified under the Tây Sơn government, but they were similar to those faced under the Trịnh and then later under the Nguyễn in the nineteenth century.

Ultimately, I argue that rather than seeing the Tây Sơn uprising as representing the triumph of a long-suffering peasantry, one should understand it as a challenge for power in the face of a vulnerable political regime, launched by men who were encouraged by indications that such a challenge might meet with success. The uprising was not an ideologically coherent movement seeking to articulate a uniform political agenda. Rather, it was an event whose course was guided by constantly changing circumstances, the whims of its leaders, and the reactions of a wide range of challengers. This study will suggest some of these complexities, though it cannot document them all.

# I

# The Tây Sơn Era and the Long Eighteenth Century in Đại Việt

In the west there is a righteous uprising,
in the north great feats are accomplished.
—Eighteenth-century Vietnamese prophecy

The best way to begin to understand the "hissing armies" whose origins lay in the hamlet of Tây Sơn is to place them into the temporal and geographical structures of what might be called the long eighteenth century in Đại Việt. The time frame that defines this period stretches from 1672, when a de facto cease-fire halted half a century of warfare between the Nguyễn and Trịnh seigneurial lords, to 1802, when the Tây Sơn conflicts came to an end. This era was one of tremendous importance for the Vietnamese people, featuring southward demographic expansion as well as shifting economic patterns, growing engagement with Europeans—merchants, mercenaries, and missionaries—and rising popular discontent sparked and compounded by political and natural forces. All of this took place within a territory that was divided politically and geographically, even as it was imperfectly united by elements of shared history, culture, and language. The Tây Sơn uprising was a product of this intersection of time and place.

The Tây Sơn leaders rose up against the Nguyễn lords (*chúa*), who governed Đàng Trong (the Inner Region), a realm comprising what is today the central and southern sections of Việt Nam. To the north lay a polity popularly referred to as Đàng Ngoài (the Outer Region), which was centered on Thăng Long and stretched from the Chinese border south to the Linh Gianh River, running through what is today the northern section of Quảng Bình Province.[1] This territory was dominated by the Trịnh clan, headed by a hereditary Chúa of their own. The entire realm of Đại Việt was ostensibly governed by the Lê emperor, whose ancestors had come to the throne in 1428, but in reality was governed by the Trịnh who controlled the imperial house. Although physically distant from the Lê court, the Nguyễn *chúa*s had also long claimed allegiance to its emperor, though by the time of the Tây Sơn outbreak they had effectively severed these putative ties. The Tây Sơn brothers took advantage of these complex political divisions to gain power themselves. While Tây Sơn armies were eventually able to stitch together long-separated Vietnamese territories, conflicts within the Tây Sơn leadership ultimately created only further political divisions.

## APPROACHING POLITICAL DIVISION IN ĐẠI VIỆT: 1509–1672

While Đại Việt reached what was arguably the height of its political, military, and cultural strength in the last three decades of the fifteenth century during the Lê dynasty's Hồng Đức reign period (1470–1497), the early sixteenth century saw a dramatic decline in its might and internal cohesion. Beginning in 1509, the Lê imperial court experienced a succession of inept or weak emperors, men who alienated many in the court and were unable to assert authority in the face of a series of popular uprisings and numerous challengers for power.[2] The result was a political vacuum at the center, which proved a tempting target for a powerful military figure, Mạc Đăng Dung. Dung was an ambitious member of a clan of fishermen that had transformed itself over the course of the fifteenth century into a prominent literary lineage, albeit one that maintained links to its coastal roots. Having worked his way through the state's military hierarchy, Dung was able to parlay a prominent military position as defender of the weakened court into one of undisputed political authority. By 1527 Dung was in a position to do away with the façade of Lê authority. He proceeded to claim the throne in the name of the Mạc family, declaring that the Lê dynasty was at an end.

In the aftermath of the Mạc seizure of power at Thăng Long, the survivors of the Lê regime fled into internal exile, eventually taking refuge in the Lao principalities. From there, aided by members of two powerful Thanh Hóa military clans, the Nguyễn and Trịnh, the Lê slowly made their way back to power. This effort continued through most of the sixteenth century, and in the course of the long seesaw struggle with the Mạc, a rivalry emerged between the two families, represented by their principal figures, Nguyễn Kim (1467–1545) and Trịnh Kiểm (?–1570). This tension developed even though the families were not merely allied militarily, but were also linked through marriage. Nguyễn Kim had married one of his daughters to Trịnh Kiểm, thus binding the two families in a time-honored fashion. Neither the military nor the marital connections, however, could forestall Trịnh Kiểm's personal ambitions. The ongoing contest for political supremacy gradually saw the Trịnh gain the upper hand, a position that was secured when the Nguyễn paterfamilias was murdered at the hands of a surrendering Mạc general in 1545.[3]

Although Nguyễn Kim's two sons were initially able to carry on their father's crusade on behalf of the Lê, their position vis-à-vis the Trịnh had been eroded. Eager to eliminate his rivals, Trịnh Kiểm arranged to have the elder Nguyễn son killed. The younger son, Nguyễn Hoàng, saw in this act his own fate unless he took measures to protect himself. Through his sister, Kiểm's wife, Hoàng requested that he be appointed governor-general of the distant southern frontier territories of Thuận Hóa and Quảng Nam. Remote exile of this political challenger suited the Trịnh overlord, and he agreed to the request. Shortly thereafter, in 1558, the thirty-four-year-old Nguyễn Hoàng entered the southern realms, marking the beginnings of a political division that would remain in effect until the Tây Sơn epoch more than two centuries later.[4] Aided by an entourage of noble families who had joined him in exile, and who now constituted the core of a ruling elite in the new territories, Nguyễn Hoàng rapidly built up political and economic strength in the territories under his control.[5]

Hoàng's departure came even as the Trịnh continued their military struggles against the Mạc, which would occupy them until the end of the century and into the next. Although Hoàng was committed to his political project in the south, in 1593 he returned to the north with a large army, and spent the next seven years aiding the Trịnh in securing a decisive victory over the Mạc. As the Trịnh began to consolidate power in the aftermath of their defeat of the Mạc, Nguyễn Hoàng returned to the south in 1600, never again to set foot in the northern regions. Some scholars have argued that this date marks an important moment of rupture between the Nguyễn and Trịnh, and thus between two increasingly autonomous political realms.[6]

Whether Hoàng's return was the defining moment in the relationship between the two sides is debatable, but his death in 1613 and the transmission of power and authority to his sixth son, Nguyễn Phước Nguyên (1563–1635), clearly accelerated the move toward independence within the southern camp. The split with the north became irreparable in 1624, when Hoàng's son declared that he would no longer send the tax revenues being collected by the Nguyễn in the provinces they were ostensibly overseeing on behalf of the Lê (Trịnh).[7] This defiance, though perhaps not unanticipated, was seen by the Trịnh lords as an act of treason, and justification for military action.

The Trịnh launched a first offensive against the Nguyễn in 1627, commencing a forty-five-year period of open conflict between the rival families. The ensuing four and a half decades saw six more large-scale military clashes, but none enabled either side to gain more than a temporary advantage over its rival. Although the Trịnh derived considerable strength from their much larger population base and the size of their armies and navies, the Nguyễn made effective use of the narrow coastal topography combined with a series of defensive walls that rendered large-scale Trịnh attacks difficult. Moreover, the Nguyễn populations were organized along military lines, contributing to their readiness for battle. The Trịnh military situation was also complicated by continuing attacks from the Mạc, who although driven out of Thăng Long in the campaigns of the late sixteenth century, continued to pose a threat from a sheltered position in the Cao Bằng region on the Chinese border. Finally, even as they confronted the Nguyễn armies across their southern frontier and Mạc holdouts to the north, the Trịnh also had to contend with popular unrest in their own territories.[8]

During this period of warfare, the ancestors of the Tây Sơn brothers came to be settled in the Nguyễn territories. The family had originally resided in the district of Hưng Nguyên, in the province of Nghệ An, in what was then territory under the control of the Trịnh family. The family surname at the time was Hồ, and according to some sources they were directly related to Hồ Quý Ly, the famous late-fourteenth- and early-fifteenth-century military official, who had seized power from the declining Trần court (1225–1400) and then briefly ruled the country before the 1407 Ming invasion.[9] Sometime between 1653 and 1657, during the height of the Nguyễn-Trịnh wars, the Tây Sơn brothers' great-great-grandfather was captured by the Nguyễn armies and forcibly resettled in the region of Qui Nhơn.[10] This was at the time a lightly settled frontier area, chiefly populated by Chams and other non-Vietnamese ethnic groups. The settlement of military prisoners into this area was part of a Nguyễn effort to increase their influence in a strategically important region, and possibly to counter the surviving vestiges of Cham political influence. The brothers' father, Nguyễn Văn Phúc, lived for a while in the hamlet of Kiên-thành before moving his family to the village of Tây Sơn.[11]

The Trịnh and Nguyễn wars dragged on through the middle of the seventeenth century, with each side launching unsustainable offensives against the other. In 1672 the Trịnh launched a final series of attacks attempting to penetrate the Nguyễn defensive fortifications, but these were all turned back. By the end of the year the Trịnh halted their offensive and pulled back their troops. Both sides then accepted the military stalemate, and a de facto cease-fire emerged. With the end of hostilities came the more rigid partition of what each side continued to recognize as a single realm, with the Linh Giang River serving as boundary between the two. During the postwar period, this border was very strictly maintained, and the Trịnh and Nguyễn had virtually no direct contact with one another. Indirect links via southern China and through merchants who traveled between both territories did continue, however, allowing at least some information to flow between the two sides.

## ĐÀNG NGOÀI AND ĐÀNG TRONG DURING THE LONG EIGHTEENTH CENTURY

The cessation of open warfare allowed each side to focus on internal matters, while the rigid separation contributed to the emergence of politically distinct states on both sides of the Linh Gianh River. Each followed a different political course, dictated by geographic and economic circumstances. Although later Vietnamese historians have insisted on the inherent unity of the Vietnamese peoples, and to some degree its territorial boundaries, it is quite clear, as Nola Cooke and Li Tana have argued, that the Nguyễn and Trịnh realms must be treated as separate states existing and developing under unique circumstances.[12] Keith Taylor, too, in an important examination of Vietnamese regionalisms, has pointed out the degree to which distinctive regional characteristics and regional historical experiences had long defined the Vietnamese peoples.[13] It was such regional differences that contributed to the emergence of two distinct political entities within the ostensibly unified Đại Việt, ones whose outlooks and orientations were markedly different. The Trịnh rulers and their society were oriented toward China and toward the cultural and trading world that lay to their north, whether overland or by sea. The Nguyễn lords looked to the south, the east, and the west, turning toward maritime and mainland Southeast Asia, and to the complex cultural and economic linkages that tied them to the Chams, the Khmers, the Siamese, and the larger commercial world of the island regions.

As the real political power in Đàng Ngoài, the Trịnh guided the course of political and economic development in that region. In the aftermath of the conflict with the Nguyễn, Trịnh rulers carried out moderate political reforms and made attempts at fiscal and economic adjustments in response to rapidly changing conditions.[14] In addition, efforts were made to promote social stability by enhancing the role and status of Confucian officials and to use civil service examinations as a mechanism for selecting them.[15] These reforms, which were but modest in the face of large-scale problems, were unable to keep pace with rapid socioeconomic changes. Moreover, the Trịnh rulers were shifting tax burdens within northern society, seeking creative solutions to the problem of chronic fiscal shortfalls. The result was increasing taxation on products that had not traditionally been subject to state exactions including salt and other mineral and agricultural products. Wealthy elites, however, were often able to avoid taxation entirely.[16] A series of natural disasters compounded the growing economic crisis in the 1730s and 1740s. So did rising official corruption. It became clear that Trịnh authority was growing more tenuous.[17] The result was dramatically increasing levels of popular unrest, fueled by these problems and by rising levels of vagabondage and landlessness. Some of these uprisings lasted for decades, including that of Hoàng Công Chất, which lasted from 1740 to 1767, and that of Lê Duy Mật, which dragged on from 1738 to 1769. This unrest consequently occupied the Trịnh armies and authorities for much of the period between the mid-1730s and 1770.

In Nguyễn-controlled Đàng Trong, on the other hand, the late seventeenth and early eighteenth centuries represented a period in which its rulers consolidated their own position and learned to tap the wealth of the southern realms. To do so, the Nguyễn continued to organize their state and populations along military lines.[18] Confucian niceties, and promotion of officials based on merit, had little place in a state that remained on a war footing.[19] Personal and clan connections were the surest path to political authority and social prestige. Moreover, the military orientation of the Nguyễn state, which had been useful in the wars with the Trịnh in the middle of the seventeenth century, continued to serve during the Nguyễn expansion southward into the Mekong Delta. This expansion took place at the expense of the remaining semiautonomous Cham princedoms still to be found in the central coastal regions and of the Khmer further to the south.

At the same time, the gradual westward expansion of Nguyễn territorial control and ambitions led to growing tensions with upland populations. These tensions eventually flared into open conflict between the Vietnamese and upland peoples during the 1750s and 1760s. Expanding Vietnamese populations and problems with poor harvests, as Li Tana speculates, may have been the trigger for this confrontation in the Quảng Nam region.[20] The upland peoples, most notably the so-called Đá Vách, regularly launched raids against Vietnamese settlements south of Phú Xuân, and efforts by the Nguyễn regime to bring the situation under control were ineffectual. The period between 1767 and 1771, immediately before the Tây Sơn uprising, saw a continuation of these attacks. The Srê rose up in Quảng Ngãi in 1770, the same year that the upland Đá Vách peoples carried out further attacks against lowland communities.[21] This continuing upland-lowland conflict was to be an important contributing factor to the early successes of the Tây Sơn movement, whose leaders found the upland regions a useful recruiting ground.

Over the course of the eighteenth century one also saw the Nguyễn gradually assuming the trappings of a more autonomous political entity. Already in 1702, the Nguyễn *chúa* sent a letter to the Chinese court via Siamese middlemen, requesting separate recognition from the Qing court as a Chinese vassal. The Qing ruler, reasoning that there was still an emperor on the throne in Thăng Long, refused to accept the letter.[22] Despite the Chinese rejection, the diplomatic overture suggests a polity attempting to redefine itself. This was reflected, among other things, in changing political nomenclature, such as the term used to designate their capital city, the titles used for officials, and the terms used to refer to members of the ruling family.[23] Eventually, in 1744, the Nguyễn formalized their break from the Lê court, marking an end to continued recognition of the northern emperor as their political superior. In that year the Nguyễn *chúa*, Nguyễn Phúc Khoát, issued an edict in which he mounted the "kingly throne" establishing himself as an equal to, rather than subject of, the northern ruler.[24]

Throughout this period, as both the Trịnh and Nguyễn consolidated their own political power, the Lê emperor remained on his throne. This once-powerful imperial family, which owed its "restoration" to the Trịnh family, was permitted to retain its titles and palaces, while real power lay with the northern *chúa*s. It was a convenient arrangement for the Trịnh, who were able to wield political and economic power without the risks inherent in displacing the Lê. The Trịnh had briefly contemplated taking power in their own name and doing away with the façade of a Lê dynasty, but they decided that the legitimacy of the Lê as well as popular memories of the golden era of that ruling house were valuable assets as they worked to restore stability in the aftermath of the civil war.[25] Ultimately, the power of the Trịnh helped to stabilize the Lê throne, and the two developed a symbiotic relationship that was widely recognized. A popular saying noted, "The Lê will survive as long as the Trịnh survive. The Lê will be lost if the Trịnh disappear."[26] This arrangement, with all of its underlying political tensions, was to last into the Tây Sơn period.

Retaining the Lê emperor on the throne proved a double-edged sword for the Trịnh, as latent loyalty to the Lê dynasty lingered well into the eighteenth century. Indeed, several of the large-scale uprisings that developed in the north during the eighteenth century played on the division between Trịnh and Lê, drawing on popular sentiment toward the Lê in their propaganda. In particular, the memory of the golden age of the early Lê served as a powerful contrast to the economic hardship affecting much of the population, who blamed the Trịnh.[27] Two of the major uprisings of this period, including one by a renegade Lê prince, Lê Duy Mật (fl. 1738–1769) used the slogan Restore the Lê, destroy the Trịnh. Some of these rebellions were even able to attract the support of scholar-officials, including most notably Phạm Công Thế, a laureate of the 1727 examinations and high-ranking official who joined Lê Duy Mật's revolt. When Thế was captured in 1738 his interrogators noted, "You are a person in the ranks of the examination laureates; why have you gone to follow this traitorous group?" To this Thế replied, "For a long time now high positions have not been clearly expressed; how is one to distinguish between loyalty and rebellion?"[28] Later in that century, this opinion was echoed by the noted literatus Phạm Đình Hổ, who in his *Vũ Trung Tùy Bút* (Random Notes from Amid the Rains) wrote, "The generation is slipping into bad habits, and the way of power is diminishing every day. [The notion of] fame is in disorder, and one no longer knows what is right and what is wrong."[29]

Given such sentiments, it might be convenient to place blame for these crises and the dramatic Tây Sơn uprising that followed on ruling houses in states of irreversible decline. Closer scrutiny suggests otherwise. Although many crises arose in the middle of the eighteenth century, particularly in the northern region, both Đàng Ngoài and Đàng Trong experienced relatively strong, centralized rule in the middle and even parts of the second half of that century.[30] In the south, the middle of the eighteenth century was one of continued geographic expansion and an increasingly assertive and independence-minded court headed by the strong and ably assisted *chúa*, Nguyễn Phúc Khoát (r. 1738–1765). His twenty-seven-year reign marked a period of territorial growth and extensive diplomatic contacts with the Siamese and Khmers.[31] Similarly in the north, while there had been an enormous amount of popular unrest in the early decades of the eighteenth century in response to the harsh rule of Trịnh Giang (r. 1729–1740), the situation improved slowly under his successors, Trịnh Doanh (r. 1740–1767) and Trịnh Sâm (r. 1767–1782), both of whom made considerable efforts to resolve the major problems they had inherited.[32] They eventually succeeded in putting down most of the uprisings and began to address some underlying issues of peasant discontent. Although they were unable to eliminate the structural problems faced by the Trịnh regime, these two rulers restored some degree of order. There is little question that these men were capable, relatively strong rulers. On the other hand, while they could suppress some of the latent problems that persisted in their respective realms, they could not eliminate them entirely.

## EIGHTEENTH-CENTURY SOCIAL AND CULTURAL DYNAMISM

The political upheaval in Đàng Ngoài and Đàng Trong helped to shape the environment in which the Tây Sơn uprising emerged, but other areas of dynamism in late-eighteenth-century Vietnamese society also contributed greatly to defining the era. Some of these factors will be taken up later, but a few are worth highlighting at this point. In particular, the influence of the West was growing, as increasing numbers of Europeans, in particular missionaries, were arriving in Đại Việt. There were also internal social changes related to growing wealth and an increasingly fluid class structure. Furthermore, this was a period of intense intellectual ferment, driven in part by efforts among scholars to find solutions to the troubles of a disturbed society.

Perhaps most notably, the influence of Europeans was beginning to be felt more profoundly and directly in this period than ever before. The chief avenues for this growing contact were commerce and religion. European traders and European missionaries were competing for the goods, markets, and souls of the Vietnamese. European missionaries had already been present in Đại Việt during the early years of the Nguyễn-Trịnh civil war, and the postwar period saw an expansion of their numbers, as well as a concomitant increase in the number of local adherents. Despite the limits to missionary successes, some important families, and some entire villages converted to the new faith, creating subgroups within northern and southern society whose interests in part lay outside accepted social and religious norms.[33] The tensions between the Vietnamese courts and Christians in the nineteenth century are much better known, but indigenous Christians and European missionaries already presented a political dilemma during the latter part of the eighteenth century, as we shall see in chapter 4. In any case, Christian Vietnamese as well as European missionaries found themselves caught up in the Tây Sơn conflicts, and the lines that were drawn in choosing sides were far from rigid or predictable.

The eighteenth century was also, as Nguyên Thanh-Nhã has argued, a period of important economic transformations, in which commercial activities and trade (both domestic and international) were shaping the distribution of wealth and the bases of social status.[34] He suggests that rising wealth in the form of mercantile activities was breaking down social barriers. Existing social divisions were less carefully observed, and certain types of occupations (actors, for example) were no longer scorned. Family connections to such people were no longer a bar to high positions. Citing Lê Quý Đôn, Alexander Woodside has also noted that in Đàng Trong "class and official distinctions had been eroded."[35] While such distinctions had never been zealously observed in the Nguyễn realms, there are clear indications that their influence in the somewhat more culturally orthodox Trịnh kingdom was also waning. Indeed, authors such as Lê Quý Đôn described some of these changes and the rise of mercantile wealth in both Đàng Trong and Đàng Ngoài.[36]

Finally, the eighteenth century was a period of intellectual ferment, particularly in Đàng Ngoài. Some of the most important intellects of Vietnamese history were active in the eighteenth century, which has been described as one of the high points in the history of Vietnamese philosophical thought.[37] The latter half of the century was the era of Lê Quý Đôn (1726–1784), among the most important writers and philosophers in Việt Nam's long history. Slightly less prominent but also formidable talents such as Ngô Thì Nhậm (1746–1803), Phan Huy Ích (1751–1822), Bùi Dương Lịch (1758–1827), Bùi Huy Bích (1744–1818), Nguyễn Thiếp (1723–1804), and others were active during the Tây Sơn period and affected by and reflecting on its events. It was also the age of Nguyễn Du (1765–1820), the noted author of the *Tale of Kiều*. With the exception of Thiếp and Du, all of these men belonged to the elite ranks of the *tiến sĩ* (lit., "advanced men"), scholars who had passed the final stage of the multilevel imperial examination system.

Confronted with the increasing social and political turbulence of their era, many of these scholars were actively seeking a remedy for this disorder. Although a part of the state bureaucratic structure, scholars of this period remained closely connected to their rural roots and consequently had a personal and concrete interest in seeing that the basic needs of the peasantry were being met.[38] Important scholars of the day, including notably Lê Quý Đôn and Ngô Thì Nhậm, recalled Confucius' maxim that "the people are the cornerstone of the state."[39] Or, as Nguyễn Thiếp phrased it in a 1791 letter to the Tây Sơn ruler, "The people are the foundation of the country; they are the stable base of the newly pacified state."[40] Thus, their concerns were guided not by any particular altruism on their part, but rather by a sense that rural stability was indispensable for the survival of the state.

To resolve such social problems, these men embarked on an effort to restore the ideals of Confucian society, as depicted in the ancient texts of the philosophical heritage they shared with the Chinese. They sought to disseminate knowledge of these texts and their proper interpretation, for only in this way could these cures have their desired effects. Combining their concern about the social crisis of their community and their belief in the ameliorative qualities of Confucian doctrine, northern scholars engaged in a flurry of activity to popularize the Confucian classics and their message. The messages from the classics that these scholars were producing appeared in various forms: abridged versions of the originals, simplified extracts from the classics, versification of these works, and, very important, efforts to translate the classics or at least parts of them into the vernacular script—*chữ nôm*.[41] Although the later Tây Sơn rulers have often been credited by contemporary Vietnamese historians for their project to produce *nôm* translations of the classics, this endeavor must be seen as merely the largest and most systematic manifestation of an existing effort to extend popular awareness of the Confucian texts through their availability in a more widely accessible form.

In short, the eighteenth century bears closer examination both for its intellectual and social climate and for the violent eruption of peasant dissatisfaction that was to emerge under the leadership of the three brothers from Tây Sơn.[42] As we shall see, the two are closely interrelated, as the climate both helped to produce the Tây Sơn uprising and then substantially shaped its direction over the more than thirty years during which it spread across the Vietnamese territories.

## FACTORS AROUSING POPULAR DISCONTENT: WHY THE TÂY SƠN MOVEMENT?

While significant as a backdrop for the Tây Sơn uprising, the social dynamism just described cannot itself explain the origins of the rebellion. For that, we must look more directly at broader patterns of demographic and economic transformation that contributed to widespread unrest and to more immediate factors, again chiefly economic but also military and political. These, as we shall see below, both contributed to and were in turn exacerbated by a series of highly contested political transitions in both regions of the country, transitions that served to enable the military and political successes of the rebel armies.

### *Demographic Change in the Nguyễn Territories*

The territories claimed by the Nguyễn lords expanded rapidly from the middle of the seventeenth century into the eighteenth. The extension of Nguyễn rule into regions ever farther from their capital at Phú Xuân had important consequences. First of all, the number of people and the amount of land controlled by the Nguyễn increased considerably, rendering the logistics of governing the kingdom much more complex.[43] Moreover, the southward extension of their political authority meant that the Nguyễn lords were to some extent physically isolated from the majority of their kingdom, the vast terrain south of the Hải Vân pass—the lands of Quảng Nam. These new territories being claimed by the Nguyễn were ones peopled by a complex, volatile mixture of groups only loosely connected to the central court in Phú Xuân. The area around Qui Nhơn, as we have seen, had been settled by northern political prisoners and was also home to remnants of the Cham state, while a variety of upland groups lived in close proximity to the epicenter of the uprising at Tây Sơn. As the Nguyễn court sought to extend its influence in the area, it impinged upon local political interests of the Chams and the upland peoples, both of whom would become early supporters of the Tây Sơn uprising.

In addition, as the Nguyễn had extended their claims farther south into the Mekong Delta region at the expense of the Khmer, they came into conflict with the remnants of the Cambodian empire. While the Khmers were not a particular obstacle to the Nguyễn armies, the move into this region brought the expanding Nguyễn polity into direct engagement with mainland Southeast Asian politics, and specifically the might of the Siamese. Over the years, the declining fortunes of the Cambodian rulers had provoked internal power struggles among multiple claimants to the throne. These in turn had attracted the attention of the Siamese court, which increasingly took on a direct role in Cambodian political affairs. The subsequent arrival of the Nguyễn inevitably drew the Vietnamese court into the intrigues of palace politics in Cambodia and then into direct confrontation with the Siamese by the 1760s.[44] By 1766, the Nguyễn found themselves engaged in armed conflict with the Siamese, mostly centered on the important coastal trade center of Hà Tiên, but also in the interior.[45]

The following year a new Siamese monarch came to the throne in the wake of a Burmese invasion. The new ruler, the Sino-Thai Taksin, quickly adopted an aggressive foreign policy that saw Siamese troops becoming active in neighboring polities. Most significant, Taksin personally led an army into Cambodia in 1771, and placed his preferred ruler on the throne at Oudong.[46] The contest over Hà Tiên also continued to simmer, flaring up periodically over the following years. Early in 1772, the Nguyễn mobilized more than ten thousand troops, which they used in confrontations with the Siamese and allied Khmer forces.[47] Although the Nguyễn troops were able to hold the Siamese at bay and to capture Cambodian territory in and around Phnom Penh, the effort left the Phú Xuân court militarily preoccupied in the far southern reaches of their realm. The Nguyễn were, consequently, significantly more vulnerable to internal disorder, even as the Tây Sơn crisis was already brewing in the An Khê highlands.

### *Economic Problems in the Nguyễn Realm*

While the Nguyễn court was militarily occupied in the far south, it also faced an economic crisis unfolding on a number of fronts. This crisis consisted of a series of wide-ranging but interrelated problems including excessive spending, increasing and geographically unbalanced tax exactions, official corruption, a sharp decline in revenue from overseas commerce, imbalances in rice production, and a coinage crisis that grew from circumstances beyond the control of the court at Phú Xuân. Indeed, of all the challenges that faced the Nguyễn at this time, these fiscal problems would ultimately provide the fuel for popular discontent. It was to this fuel that the Tây Sơn leaders would apply the spark that would set off open revolt.

*Crises in Revenue, Commerce, and Coinage.* The costs of the struggles with the Siamese, which involved the deployment of relatively large numbers of troops some distance from the Vietnamese capital, was one major source of economic strain on the Nguyễn polity. It was far from the only one, however, for there were other significant drains on the treasury. Nguyễn rulers had for some time been engaged in extravagant spending on a variety of projects to enhance their prestige, including the construction of elaborate and ornately decorated edifices at their capital of Phú Xuân. The problem of excessive spending had accelerated over the second half of the 1760s, simultaneously depleting the state treasury and encouraging corruption at the local and court levels.[48] After maneuvering himself into position as the key political figure in the Nguyễn state, the new regent, Trương Phúc Loan, raised and extended taxes, thereby greatly increasing his own personal wealth and influence.[49] Loan's reported acceptance of bribes that allowed officials to exempt themselves from military service reflected an expanding problem with official corruption at multiple levels of Đàng Trong society.[50]

At the same time, the Nguyễn court faced a precipitous decline in commercial revenue as the number of foreign trading vessels visiting the major entrepôt at Hội An (Faifo) dropped rapidly in the 1760s and early 1770s. Lê Quý Đôn reported in his 1776 *Phủ Biên Tạp Lục* (Records of the Prefectural Borders) that only sixteen foreign merchant vessels arrived in Hội An in the year 1771 and that two years later only half that number had arrived.[51] This was in contrast to a thriving port that still saw the arrival of between sixty and eighty foreign trading ships in the late 1740s.[52] The decline in trade may have been due in part to rising port duties on imported goods, taxes that may themselves have been increased to pay for the extravagant construction projects of Nguyễn Phúc Khoát beginning in the mid-1750s.[53] The ripple effects of this decline in trade were felt well beyond the Nguyễn court, and had implications for many in the region, including both peoples in the interior who provided exotic goods for export and the coastal ethnic Chinese merchants who depended on these trading vessels for their livelihood. Some of these merchants were among

FIGURE 3. *View of the Thu Bồn (Faifo) River south of Đà Nẵng, 1793. From a drawing made by William Alexander, a member of Lord McCartney's 1793 mission. From John Barrow,* A Voyage to Cochinchina in the Years 1792 and 1793 *(London: T. Cadell and W. Davies, 1806; reprint, Kuala Lumpur: Oxford University Press, 1975).*

the earliest financial and military supporters of the Tây Sơn, hoping to see an administrative change that might help to restore the profitable coastal trade centers.

Directly related to the problem of declining trade was a specie crisis with important repercussions for the Đàng Trong economy. The flow of copper coinage from Japan and China had played a critical role in sustaining the economic boom that the Nguyễn had experienced for a century and a half, facilitating both foreign and domestic commercial transactions. Without their own copper mines, the Nguyễn rulers were dependent on importing the metal, and by the early eighteenth century, as the value of copper coinage increased in Japan and China, its export to Cochinchina was largely cut off.[54] The Nguyễn dependence on external sources of copper had always been a weak link in their economy, and when this link broke the Nguyễn state's options were limited.[55] Ultimately, it took the only step open to it, minting its own currency, but casting the coins from zinc instead of copper, a shift that introduced an entirely new set of problems.

To make the transition to the new metal, the Nguyễn rulers demanded that the zinc coins be accepted at parity with the copper ones. The population, however, appears overwhelmingly to have rejected this demand. Many preferred to hoard rice rather than sell it for zinc coins, and prices for rice rose as the available supply declined, leading to food shortfalls in some areas. Furthermore, as Lê Quý Đôn reported, the new coins were easily counterfeited, further contributing to a crisis of confidence in the currency and undermining efforts to stabilize the monetary situation.[56] The Nguyễn court was not unaware of the problems that the policy had provoked; they were spelled out in a 1770 memorial by the retired Thuận Hóa official Ngô Thế Lân.[57] Lân called for the Nguyễn to produce more copper coins and to establish rice warehouses to help to stabilize prices for this crucial commodity, but his warnings were ignored, and ultimately he threw his lot in with the Tây Sơn.

A final but more immediate problem that brought direct pressures on the Qui Nhơn region was a growing appetite in Phú Xuân for the inexpensive rice being grown in the Mekong Delta.[58] There was a substantial imbalance between population and rice production in the two regions according to an assessment conducted in 1769, which showed that Quảng Nam produced 30 percent more rice taxes in kind than Thuận Hóa.[59] Although this may not directly correlate with actual rice production, it is suggestive of a wide gap between the two regions. With access to the rice surpluses being produced in the Quảng Nam area, the Nguyễn regime could provide reasonably priced rice to Thuận Hóa, a region that had traditionally grown rice only as a subsistence crop and in quantities barely sufficient to support its populations. But while the southern reaches of the Nguyễn territories could produce large amounts of surplus rice, this rice still needed to be moved the nearly nine hundred kilometers to the Nguyễn capital region. The amounts in question required the requisitioning of large numbers of vessels to transport the rice.[60]

As Li Tana has elaborated, much of the Nguyễn demand for labor service and for the boats supplying the rice from the south was placed on the nearby Qui Nhơn region.[61] This area was ideally situated as a staging area for the transport of this much-needed rice, as it was roughly equidistant from Phú Xuân and Gia Định, and featured an important harbor at Thi Nại. Qui Nhơn was also useful to the Nguyễn court because it was closer at hand, and as such it could more readily be tapped for labor and other resources than could the distant Gia Định region. Consequently, the pressures that the Nguyễn state was imposing on the south-central coast began to provoke a considerable degree of resentment there. Whether shipping vessels were coerced into transporting the grain or lured into this effort with incentives, the project was a complex one with considerable uncertainty. What was certain, however, was that the Nguyễn political center had become economically dependent upon the southern regions of the realm.

*Taxation and Popular Unrest.* These structural issues posed mounting problems for the Nguyễn court, as well as for the larger Đàng Trong society, but the most immediate source of popular economic discontent was taxation. The second half of the eighteenth century had seen both an increase in tax exactions and an expansion of tax collection efforts into areas not previously subject to such exactions. The increase in taxes, driven by some of the pressures noted above, was partly facilitated by improving and updating landholding records and information regarding nonagricultural products. In 1769, the young *chúa* ordered (perhaps at the behest of Loan) the updating of official records for cultivated fields, populations, and crop yields, as well as precise data on the collection of other natural products ranging from honey to elephant tusks. This was followed in 1770 by an order that a new survey and registration of private fields be carried out in Thuận Hóa, the northern part of the Nguyễn territories.[62]

The effect of such attempts to catalogue populations, fields under cultivation, and availability of raw materials was considerable. It is likely that over the course of time existing farms had been expanded and a large number of new farms brought under cultivation in this region. Much of this newly cultivated land would likely not have been registered in the official tax rolls. Thus, an updated land registration could bring new revenue for the central government, but at the expense of people who had previously avoided taxation altogether or were still being taxed at a lower rate for land that had been enhanced since the previous land registries had been compiled.[63]

The changes provoked widespread complaints about growing tax burdens, which the people blamed directly on the regent. Lê Quý Đôn reported of his own investigations that "when we pressed the people with questions, they all informed us that each of the types of taxes (*tạp thuế*) in the region of Quảng Nam were ones newly ordered by Trương Phúc Loan and they were not ones that had already been there since the *vương công* (i.e., the Nguyễn kings) in prior times."[64] Several accounts claim that Trương Phúc Loan introduced a head tax (*thuế đinh*), which was particularly unpopular.[65] Unlike other forms of taxation, collection of which was directly proportional to crop yields and individual status, the head tax was a flat tax levied on each registered villager, though as Nguyên Thanh-Nhã notes, the amount of tax did vary by social status and even location within the Nguyễn realm.[66] This expanded tax system, and Trương Phúc Loan's tolerance for graft, spawned widespread corruption, including the sale of village offices, coveted as sources of revenue. Those who paid for village offices recouped their investment by squeezing extra tax payments from those below them.[67] A related source of popular frustration was the complex and ever-changing system of additional fees and expenses tacked onto existing taxes, either systematically or in an ad hoc fashion, by local officials. There were "lamp and oil" fees, "presentation" fees, and "areca and betel" fees, in addition to charges for the transportation of goods and for construction and maintenance of granaries.[68] This system of additional fees was at its worst in the Qui Nhơn area, where the Tây Sơn uprising not coincidentally had its roots.[69]

Another fundamental problem and source of popular unhappiness lay in the fact that government exactions were especially burdensome in regions that were flourishing economically, for these were the ones most attractive to corrupt officials. Thus, for instance, Quảng Nam was considerably wealthier than the northern region of Thuận Hóa, and it was there that the weight of taxation fell. As Lê Quý Đôn noted, "Thuận Hóa does not have much; everything that is taken is taken from Quảng Nam, since the region of Quảng Nam has the most fertile land in the world."[70] The Lê investigator concluded, "The taxes imposed in Quảng Nam are different from those in Thuận Hóa, and the requisitions are heavier than those in Thuận Hóa. Thus, the amounts that are gathered and placed into the storehouses are very great, and the salaries and benefits of the officials are also very troublesome [to the populations]. And it is for this reason that the peoples there are the first to rise up."[71]

Lowland peasants were not the only ones upset at the changing tax regimen. Tax-related discontent was also very strong in the highland regions of Quảng Nam. Upland peoples living in these regions found themselves confronted by sharply increased tax burdens and greater attempts at direct control by the Nguyễn state seeking to enlarge its economic base.[72] Facing declining revenue from commercial activity over the course of the mid-eighteenth century, the Nguyễn and their local and regional officials appear to have turned their attention to revenue extraction from peoples living at the political periphery of Nguyễn control, in part, as Li Tana has argued, to shift the burden away from the potentially more volatile lowland populations.[73] These groups controlled a wide range of valuable commodities that any Vietnamese state needed to support its commercial export economy, from fragrant woods to various mineral and animal resources. This exchange of goods had long sustained substantial economic interaction between the upland peoples and their coastal counterparts. The Nguyễn state had already been collecting taxes from highland groups as early as the late seventeenth century, a practice that only grew over the course of the eighteenth. What appears to have changed in the Trương Phúc Loan period was an increase in Nguyễn tax extractions from these regions, with a particular focus on the resource-rich Quảng Nam hinterlands.[74]

This interaction was initially focused on trade, but it developed a growing tax dimension as well, and Li Tana estimates that by the late 1760s upland people were contributing nearly 50 percent of the secondary tax revenues (nonland and capitation taxes) collected annually by the Nguyễn regime.[75] With the southern regime imposing trade tariffs and other taxes on populations who had traditionally been exempt from such impositions, it is hardly surprising that these groups would come to support a movement that had the potential to reverse these growing pressures. Elements of the upland groups had already been engaged in anti-Nguyễn actions since the 1750s; this new uprising may have thus represented for them merely a continuation of these challenges to lowland authority. This increased state demand for tax payments was a significant factor contributing to ethnic minority support for the Tây Sơn movement during its early years. In short, as Li Tana has astutely observed, "the taxation system triggered the Tây Sơn uprising."[76]

## POLITICAL TRANSITIONS IN ĐÀNG TRONG AND ĐÀNG NGOÀI

This series of economic and demographic issues created an environment that was ripe for unrest. What ultimately served to make revolt possible and to enhance its chances of success was the emergence of volatile political situations between the 1760s and early 1780s. During this time the existing political powers were crippled by questionable legitimacy even as the continued division of Đại Việt itself raised uncertainties about political allegiances. The vulnerable political structures, first in Đàng Trong in the early 1770s and then again in Đàng Ngoài in the early 1780s, permitted potential political challengers to focus popular anger about economic problems onto particular individuals. The Tây Sơn, as we shall see, were able to exploit acute political divisions and factionalism in order to rally supporters from a range of social classes.

The first political crisis emerged in 1765 in the aftermath of the death of the long-reigning southern lord Nguyễn Phúc Khoát. The *chúa*'s death enabled Trương Phúc Loan, an ambitious official and royal confidant, to come to power. Loan's father, Trương Phúc Phan, had been one of the grand mandarins of the court, and Loan himself had been Khoát's maternal uncle. Through these connections, Loan rose through the ranks of court officialdom, and on the death of the *chúa* in 1765 he was appointed regent to the presumptive crown prince, Hưng Tổ. The later Nguyễn court histories reported that Loan "was fearful that the [new] Lord was an intelligent and capable person, and would be difficult to manipulate," and so he "immediately forged an edict leading to Hưng Tổ's being imprisoned in the palace."[77] Then, seeing that another prince, Duệ Tông (Nguyễn Phúc Thuần), was only twelve years old, "[Loan] plotted with the eunuch Chử Đức and a military commander, Nguyễn Cửu Thông, to forge a decree naming Duệ Tông as the *chúa*."[78] Loan then made arrangements to be appointed to various high court positions by the twelve-year-old Duệ Tông. The new *chúa* promoted Loan to serve as his chief adviser (*quốc phó*) and as minister of civil affairs. He also granted him several military and fiscal posts, the latter of which gave Loan considerable control over tax revenue collection, the consequences of which we have already seen.[79] To tighten his connection to the court, Loan arranged for his eldest two sons to marry daughters of the recently deceased *chúa*.[80]

Contemporary and subsequent historians have all pointed to Loan's machinations as well as his unsavory personality as a cause of popular dissatisfaction and an increasing number of uprisings.[81] The nineteenth-century Nguyễn chronicles relegated Loan's official biography to the section reserved for "Rebellious Subjects and Traitors to the Court" and, in describing the regent, emphasized his personal and political shortcomings:

> Although he was held in affection by the *chúa*, he was always drunk on wine and women, and paid no attention to matters of state. It became known that on seeing power, he immediately had no regard or consideration for anything else. He sold offices, bought titles, and took bribes to

> pardon crimes. He punished and harassed [people], [while] taxes were increased, and the people all suffered in hardship. During a period of four to five years, calamities of various types occurred, as there were earthquakes and landslides, and shooting stars, and disturbed waters, while the hundred surnames went hungry, and banditry spread everywhere.[82]

The signs—earthquakes, shooting stars, and disturbed waters—all suggested that the political situation was untenable, something confirmed by the rise in banditry and the problem with food shortages. Loan's actions, as well as his involvement in manipulating the seigneurial succession, resulted in the emergence of court factions that supported either the sitting *chúa* or the excluded brother. It was internal divisions such as these that the Tây Sơn readily exploited in the early 1770s.

Even as this crisis was brewing in Đàng Trong, another political transition was taking place in Đàng Ngoài, where in 1767 the young and energetic, if ruthless, Trịnh Sâm (1739–1782) took over from his father, Trịnh Doanh. Under Sâm the last northern popular uprisings, which had been dragging on since the 1730s, were put down, and a modicum of political order restored. Moreover, it was the energetic Sâm who, at the height of his power, would use the Tây Sơn rising to invade his southern neighbor in 1774. The succession crisis that would eventually contribute to the collapse of the Trịnh in Đàng Ngoài began only in 1780, fifteen years after the disputed succession that had helped to precipitate popular revolt in the south. Trịnh Sâm's declining health led his son, the ambitious crown prince, Trịnh Khải (also known as Trịnh Tông), to plot a coup. The plan was discovered, and a new heir—Trịnh Cán (the younger son of a beloved concubine)—was named in his place. When Sâm finally died in 1782, Cán was overthrown in a palace coup by his deposed elder brother backed by rebellious military forces.[83] The coup and its aftermath further destabilized northern society as renegade soldiers created havoc in the regions surrounding the capital.

Clearly, then, there was a marked shift from the middle of the eighteenth century, when strong leaders controlled the seats of power, to the mid-1760s (in Đàng Trong) and the early 1780s (in Đàng Ngoài), when political authority was suddenly far less clearly defined. In both regions those who claimed political power did so on questionable (and openly questioned) grounds, and the dramatic succession crises created opportunities the Tây Sơn were quick to seize. Thus, the Tây Sơn leaders made their own bid for power at a time when political leaders in neither north nor south enjoyed undivided support or loyalty. In this volatile setting, claims to authority were derived in different ways and from various sources, making it easier for the Tây Sơn to advance their own claims and for people to justify setting aside their allegiances to support the rebel movement.

## ORIGINS: THE EARLY YEARS OF THE TÂY SƠN UPRISING

The situation was ripe for rebellion, and many opportunities awaited militarily ambitious figures who might find a means by which to rally supporters. Onto this stage stepped three brothers from the tiny hamlet of Tây Sơn. The eldest brother, Nguyễn Nhạc, belonged to the very administrative machinery that he would ultimately topple, for he served as a public clerk (*tuần biện lại*) responsible for collecting taxes in the circuit of Vân Đồn. Nhạc was also a trader in betel nut, an important local commodity. Thus he had links both to the ruling authority and to the larger commercial realm, which was coming under stress during the middle and latter half of the eighteenth century. Both vocations required him to travel extensively in the region, including into adjoining highland areas, which as we have seen had experienced extensive and unwelcome taxation pressure from the Nguyễn court. These travels allowed him to learn firsthand about the degree of popular discontent throughout the area.

The sources are not in agreement as to the precise impetus for Nhạc's decision to go into rebellion, but all suggest that he was unable to account for the tax money that he had been responsible for collecting from his assigned circuit (*tuần*). Some records hint that the eldest Tây Sơn brother had developed a fondness for gambling and imply that he squandered the tax receipts in this manner.[84] Maurice Durand has alternatively, and quite plausibly, speculated that Nhạc had never been able to collect the taxes in the first place because of the economic woes of the region and popular discontent with tax burdens.[85] Whatever the particulars of his inability to account for the tax revenues, at some point in 1771 Nhạc chose to flee into the highland regions just west of his home rather than risk arrest at the hands of Nguyễn officials who were already looking for him.[86] He took with him his brothers and a small group of supporters, hoping that the remote location would protect them while he planned his next move. He was encouraged in this course of action by his teacher, Trương Văn Hiến, a refugee from the Loan-dominated Nguyễn court. Hiến urged Nhạc to see himself as destined to fulfill a long-standing local prophecy:

*tây khởi nghĩa, bắc thu công* (in the west there is a righteous uprising, in the north great feats are accomplished). The "west" in the prophecy, he suggested, was to be seen as a reference to Tây Sơn (western mountains), the brothers' home village.

The region of An Khê to which the Tây Sơn brothers retreated was an ideal location for the rebel leaders as they sought to gain strength and supporters. It was relatively remote, approachable only along a narrow and treacherous route, easily defended against potential attacks by Nguyễn troops.[87] This highland region straddled important trading routes that stretched from the coastal port at Qui Nhơn westward toward Cambodia and the southern Lao territories, providing access to goods that were carried along them.[88] An Khê was also a resource-rich area that could supply the Tây Sơn with wood, iron, sulphur, horses, and elephants.[89] Nguyễn Nhạc already had numerous contacts in the region who now provided him with shelter and, equally important, recruits for his army. For the next two years, Nhạc and his growing band of followers remained in An Khê working to consolidate their base and attract additional supporters. The strength of their position allowed the brothers to win some early victories in their immediate surroundings, gaining military experience and enhancing their prestige, while risking little. Eventually, however, Nhạc decided that his army was ready to venture into the lowlands and to challenge the Nguyễn forces directly.

Seeking to establish a foothold in lowland coastal regions of their home province, the Tây Sơn armies needed to capture the walled city of Qui Nhơn, capital of the prefecture by the same name. Lacking the manpower and the armaments to attack the citadel directly, the Tây Sơn leaders decided to take the city through subterfuge. The device they used was a variation on the Trojan horse, designed to render the citadel vulnerable from the inside. To this end, in mid-September of 1773 Nhạc feigned his own capture. He directed his supporters to construct a cage, and when it had been completed he locked himself inside it. These supporters then approached the city officials, announcing that they had captured the notorious Tây Sơn leader, and presented the Nguyễn officials with their "captive."

The officials were delighted at this good fortune, and after suitably rewarding the men who had brought the prize captive, arranged for the cage to be brought into the city. That night, with his supporters gathered outside of the citadel walls, Nhạc released himself from the cage, seized the prison sentry's sword, and began attacking the guards, even as he opened the gates of the city, allowing his soldiers to stream in. Once inside, the Tây Sơn troops made short work of the military contingent posted in the city, setting fire to its barracks.[90] The provincial governor Nguyễn Khắc Tuyên fled the city in such haste that he dropped his seal, the official mark of his right to govern.[91] The seizure of Qui Nhơn with its arms and riches greatly contributed to an expansion of Tây Sơn power and prestige. Taking the city, moreover, gave them effective control over a substantial stretch of coastline.

The initial rapid success of the rebel forces is attributable to several factors, including the creation of a broad (if unstable) military alliance, an unmotivated and perhaps unprepared Nguyễn army, and the clever deployment of ruses and other devices to shorten the odds against the Tây Sơn. During these early years, the rebels developed and encouraged their popular image as honorable fighters and men of the people, and went out of their way to avoid alienating the peasant majority of the population. A Spanish missionary, Father Diego de Jumilla, noted of the rebel troops in a 1774 letter, that they

> did no harm to either persons or property. On the contrary, they appeared to desire equality for all Cochin-Chinese; they entered the houses of the rich and, if they were offered some present, they did no damage. But if they met resistance, they seized the most luxurious articles, which they distributed among the poor, keeping for themselves only rice and victuals. . . . [Consequently, the people] began to acclaim them as virtuous and charitable thieves, with a regard for the poor commoner.[92]

The Tây Sơn, however, did not appeal merely to poor peasants who formed their core following. They also found it useful to draw support from other segments of society, including the locally influential, who could bring their own entourages, and the wealthy, who could contribute much-needed financial and other material resources. Among those recruited to join the movement in its early days were men such as Nguyễn Thung, referred to in the Nguyễn biographies as a "village bully"—suggesting a degree of local influence (however disparaged by the Nguyễn historians), and Huyền Khê, described in those same records as coming from a rich family.[93]

The Tây Sơn leaders also expanded their armies to include a broad coalition of disgruntled lowlanders, most notably Chams and ethnic Chinese. Of these two groups, the more important, financially and militarily, were the ethnic Chinese, many of whom were members of the significant coastal trading community. Ethnic Chinese traders, in particular, had grown increasingly unhappy with the downturn in trade and with Nguyễn tax policies, and hoped that the Tây Sơn might provide an improvement.[94] Members of this community contributed money and manpower to the Tây Sơn effort, with a direct and important impact on the strength of the rebel movement. The ethnic Chinese forces dramatically expanded the size of the Tây Sơn force, even as their presence eroded the fragile unity of the the rebel army. The Chinese troops were organized as autonomous military forces answerable only to their Chinese commanders, who were allies of, rather than generals in, the Tây Sơn army. Moreover, it appears that the Chinese commitment to the Tây Sơn was limited, and within two years the leaders of these autonomous armies had broken ranks with the original core of Tây Sơn supporters.

Secondly, the Tây Sơn took advantage of a Nguyễn military that was unprepared for the scope of the uprising. Nguyễn troops under Trương Phúc Loan were poorly trained, and inexperienced as a result of the relatively long peace that had endured in the region. Although Nguyễn troops had not been idle for the previous decades—they had been involved in putting down unrest among upland peoples and had been involved in skirmishes with Thai forces in the late 1760s—they were unprepared for the size and speed of the newly emerging military challenge of the Tây Sơn. Nguyễn troops apparently fled the battlefields when they could, and officers were often able to bribe their way out of service, sending others in their stead.[95] Over time, the Nguyễn armies became more effective as the surprise of the initial Tây Sơn attack wore off, but it would be some time before they were able to blunt the momentum developed by rebel armies in these early encounters.

Finally, as evidenced by the cage episode, during the early years of the uprising Tây Sơn leaders used a variety of tactics and ruses to improve odds that were still stacked against them. To frighten their enemy, for example, the Tây Sơn forces made loud hissing sounds when they moved across the countryside and into battle. It was from this tactic that they derived their popular sobriquet of *quân ó*—the hissing army.[96] The Tây Sơn also sought to intimidate their enemy by fighting under an enormous red banner that was said to be nine meters long.[97] Presumably this banner could be seen at a great distance, and along with the hissing sounds had the potential, at least, of frightening the Nguyễn soldiers. Another means of intimidation involved disguising tall highland peoples as Chinese troops, then encouraging them to become drunk and to enter the field of battle naked. These troops were said to carry sheets of gold and silver, which they would hold to the faces of fallen enemy soldiers to check for breath and kill those who were only feigning death. As a result, the later Nguyễn records commented, "There were none who could resist them."[98]

## THE COURSE OF THE TÂY SƠN UPRISING: A BRIEF HISTORICAL OUTLINE

In this manner the Tây Sơn army emerged to challenge the Nguyễn for supremacy in Đàng Trong. The rebel force rapidly grew in numbers and extended its control over ever larger expanses of territory. From its small corner of the Qui Nhơn hinterland, the Tây Sơn army spread to conquer much of Đàng Trong, and eventually all of Đàng Ngoài as well. The rest of this work will examine the manner in which the Tây Sơn leaders expanded their authority and the complex relations they developed with multiple segments of late-eighteenth-century Vietnamese society. Because my approach is not strictly chronological, I begin with an overview of the political and military trajectory of the Tây Sơn uprising's three-decade-long course. This outline will touch on the major figures and events of this period, then suggest some of the social dynamics that will be taken up again in greater detail in the subsequent analysis.

### *The Battles for Đàng Trong (1773–1785)*

After their victory at Qui Nhơn, Tây Sơn forces were able to seize several adjacent prefectures before encountering some resistance from Nguyễn forces. In the meantime, and taking advantage of the upheaval in Đàng Trong, the Trịnh invaded late in 1774, ostensibly to assist the Nguyễn in putting down the Tây Sơn, but clearly seeing a golden opportunity to overpower their long-time political rivals. As the large northern force advanced toward Phú Xuân, the Nguyễn court fled southward by sea to the Gia Định region, which was to serve as the center of its resistance until the end of the Tây Sơn period. There the Nguyễn took preliminary steps to recruit supporters for a counterattack, even as the Trịnh extended their attack to capture Phú Xuân and then cross the Hải Vân pass aiming for Tây Sơn positions in northern Quảng Nam. Caught between the advancing Trịnh and the regrouping Nguyễn forces to their south, the Tây Sơn leaders pragmatically surrendered to the Trịnh in May of 1775. The northern army's commanders readily turned over responsibility for pursuing the Nguyễn to the Tây Sơn brothers, who promptly resumed their attacks on their earlier enemy.

The next ten years were marked by a series of back and forth military campaigns between the Tây Sơn and Nguyễn forces. The focal point of this contest was Gia Định Prefecture and its strategic city of Sài Gòn. The rhythms of the war were dictated to a considerable degree by the monsoon winds, which permitted the large-scale movement of naval forces only in certain directions and at certain times. The form of the contest was also shaped by the considerable ambivalence of the Tây Sơn brothers about carrying out extended military campaigns at any distance from their base. It is clear that they always felt more comfortable in and around Qui Nhơn and were reluctant to remain far afield for any length of time. Thus, while they frequently captured Gia Định, the brothers were unwilling to oversee the occupation of that region themselves. Instead, they would quickly return to their fortress at Qui Nhơn before the winds turned against them. Each time they would leave behind an occupation force whose strength appeared sapped by the absence of its primary leaders, leaving the area vulnerable to a concerted Nguyễn counterattack.

The Tây Sơn forces captured Sài Gòn for the first time in midspring of 1776 as the youngest brother, Nguyễn Lữ, led a naval attack up the Sài Gòn River. Shortly thereafter, however, the Nguyễn forces returned, recaptured the city, and forced Lữ to retreat to Qui Nhơn. In midspring of 1777, Nhạc sent Lữ and Huệ to recapture Sài Gòn. Nguyễn Huệ led a large force by land and sea that in six months destroyed the majority of the Nguyễn armed forces and captured and then killed nearly every member of the Nguyễn royal family. Having completed his task, Huệ returned to Qui Nhơn, leaving a body of troops behind to retain control of the city. The sole survivor of the Tây Sơn massacre of the Nguyễn royal family was a young prince named Nguyễn Ánh. Ánh fled from Gia Định, spending time in the swamps of Cà Mau at the southern tip of Việt Nam before finding refuge on the island of Pulau Panjang in the Gulf of Siam. On hearing news of the Tây Sơn departure from Gia Định, he regrouped his remaining forces and advanced from the west via Long Xuyên and Sa Đéc, reentering the region in triumph in early 1778.[99]

This marked the beginning of a longer-term occupation of Gia Định, and the young Nguyễn prince used the opportunity to bolster his still questionable authority. He sent an embassy to Siam hoping to reach agreement on a treaty of friendship, which would help to reinforce his legitimacy in preparation for a campaign to retake the rest of the country from the Tây Sơn. Domestically, he restructured the three provinces under his control, named political officials, levied taxes, trained armies and a navy, and encouraged a program of land redistribution to promote agriculture in a region that had now been ravaged by several years of fighting. Then, in 1780, in an attempt to strengthen the political coalition that he was forming, Nguyễn Ánh formally proclaimed himself the new Nguyễn ruler. Two years earlier, in 1778, Nguyễn Nhạc had also taken authority in his own name, proclaiming himself emperor under the reign name Thái Đức and taking the citadel at Chà Bàn, an ancient Cham political center, as his own capital.

From early 1778 until 1781 neither side sought to challenge the status quo, as both parties were busy consolidating their respective positions. Then, in the summer of 1781, hostilities broke out again as Nguyễn Ánh launched an unsuccessful attack against the Tây Sơn coastal stronghold at Nha Trang. This was followed in May 1782 by a Tây Sơn counterattack led by Nhạc and Huệ. The two brothers assembled a hundred warships and moved south, forcing their way up the Sài Gòn River to launch an assault against the citadel at Gia Định. Having succeeded in fighting their way into the city, Tây Sơn troops burned and pillaged the shops of Chinese merchants and massacred thousands of Chinese residents. This massacre was directly provoked by the killing of one of Nhạc's key lieutenants by an ethnic Chinese general fighting for the Nguyễn, but more generally reflected Tây Sơn anger at the increasing support given by the Chinese community to their Nguyễn rivals. After this savage victory, the Tây Sơn leaders returned north in June, leaving the city in the hands of their lieutenants. Hearing that Huệ and Nhạc had left the city, Nguyễn Ánh counterattacked, recapturing the city a few months later.[100]

In March 1783, Huệ and Lữ once again attacked Sài Gòn, and again destroyed the Nguyễn army and chased off Nguyễn Ánh. Seeking to extend their triumph, the Tây Sơn commanders sent a fleet to chase after Nguyễn Ánh and his largely demoralized troops. A huge storm at sea, however, destroyed much of the Tây Sơn navy, allowing Nguyễn Ánh to escape to Phú Quốc Island, where his men were reduced to eating grasses and bananas. From there he eventually made his way to Siam, where he was given shelter by the Siamese king and plotted his next move, which came in January of 1785. Starting from his base in Siam, and backed by an additional twenty thousand soldiers and three hundred ships contributed by the Siamese ruler, Ánh and his army moved by foot across Cambodia and by sea through the Gulf of Siam in an attack on the southern

Vietnamese provinces. The Tây Sơn were ready for the Nguyễn attack, waiting in ambush along a stretch of the Mekong River near Mỹ Thọ. Nguyễn Huệ lured the overconfident Siamese navy into his trap, destroying all of the Siamese ships and killing all but a thousand of the Siamese troops. The loss was devastating for the Nguyễn forces, who joined the remains of the Siamese army in fleeing back to their refuge in Bangkok.

*Tây Sơn Forces Invade Đàng Ngoài (1786–1789)*

Having decisively defeated Nguyễn Ánh, Nguyễn Nhạc saw an opportunity to realize a long-held ambition to expand his power into the former Nguyễn territories between the Hải Vân pass and the Gianh River that were still being occupied by the Trịnh. The timing could not have been better, as the Trịnh grip on power had been substantially weakened by a series of famines and floods in the 1770s that had forced many people to leave their villages in search of food. Furthermore, the death of Trịnh Sâm in 1782 had been followed, as we have seen, by political infighting that had resulted in a palace coup. This had created political instability and the emergence of a renegade militia only loosely controlled by the new ruling faction. Finally, Nhạc's decision to go north was driven by strong encouragement from a prominent Trịnh defector, Nguyễn Hữu Chỉnh. Forced to flee Đàng Ngoài in the aftermath of the 1782 coup, Chỉnh had joined the Tây Sơn as a military leader and strategist. Over the next four years he had actively cultivated Nhạc's interest in going north, hoping that such an expedition would provide an opportunity to exact revenge on those who had forced him into political exile.

On Chỉnh's advice Nguyễn Nhạc sent an expedition north toward Phú Xuân in June of 1786. The Tây Sơn army was led by Nguyễn Huệ and Chỉnh, with Huệ commanding a naval force that sailed up the coast and then entered the Hương River and Chỉnh leading an overland attack across the Hải Vân pass. After a brief resistance, the city surrendered to the Tây Sơn army, who then slaughtered many of its Trịnh defenders.[101] Shortly thereafter, surrounding areas also submitted to the Tây Sơn force, and in a matter of days, all of Thuận Hóa as far as the Gianh River had fallen into Tây Sơn hands.

Huệ's orders from his brother had been to stop at the traditional Nguyễn-Trịnh boundary (that is, the Gianh River), but on urging from Chỉnh, Huệ decided to use his momentum to press the attack and seize the rest of the Trịnh territories. Huệ and Chỉnh attacked northward with four hundred ships, seizing public rice granaries as they went. Chỉnh passed through Nghệ An and Thanh Hóa without meeting any sustained resistance. Soon afterward, panic struck Thăng Long, and the northern ruler Trịnh Cán fled to Sơn Tây, where he was captured and committed suicide, seemingly bringing an end to the long line of Trịnh lords. His death, and the general collapse of Trịnh resistance, left the road to the capital wide open, and Nguyễn Huệ's armies marched into Thăng Long on July 21, 1786.

Once in the capital, Huệ held a solemn audience with the Cảnh Hưng emperor (r. 1740–1786) during which Huệ offered his submission and presented army and population registers to the emperor as well as a document proclaiming that the Lê dynasty had been restored to its rightful authority. The emperor, in return, gave Huệ the position of general and the title of grand duke as well as the hand of a Lê princess in marriage. Several days later, the elderly emperor died, and after some discussion the reins of authority were passed on to a nephew who took the throne as Lê Chiếu Thông. Meanwhile, Nguyễn Nhạc, jealous of Huệ's accomplishments, came north himself to have his own audience with the new emperor. A few days later, toward the end of August, the Tây Sơn brothers returned south with their armies, leaving behind their erstwhile ally Nguyễn Hữu Chỉnh. Forced to fend for himself, and unsure of his stature in Đàng Ngoài, Chỉnh chose to retreat from the northern capital and to develop a base in Nghệ An Province.

After returning south, Nhạc divided the newly expanded territory among the three brothers. The weakest brother, Nguyễn Lữ, was assigned to rule over the Gia Định region as the Đông Định Vương (Eastern Stabilization King). Nhạc took the central region for himself, continuing to rule as Emperor Thái Đức at his imperial citadel near Qui Nhơn. Nguyễn Huệ, situated at Phú Xuân, was anointed as the Bắc Bình Vương (Northern Pacification King) and was assigned to rule the recently captured area of Thuận Hóa, along with the region of Nghệ An, which he had pried away from the Lê. The divisions between the brothers were not merely geographical, but also personal. These tensions, stemming from Nhạc's concern about Huệ's increasing autonomy, boiled over into a violent internecine struggle that lasted from late February to mid-June of 1787. The conflict culminated in Huệ's besieging his older brother at Chà Bàn and winning a decisive victory after which he forced Nhạc to surrender additional territory south of the Hải Vân pass.

In the north meanwhile, Chiếu Thông proved a weak ruler, easily manipulated by more-powerful politicians. His weakness prompted survivors of the Trịnh family to stage a comeback, and they were soon able to reimpose their family's traditional influence over the court. The emperor secretly communicated news of this situation to Nguyễn Hữu Chỉnh. Seeing an opportunity to enhance his own power, Chỉnh gathered a ten-thousand-man army and marched toward Thăng Long in December of 1786. By late January he had defeated the Trịnh army and effectively established himself as the new master of the north. Huệ, angered at Chỉnh's unauthorized actions, ordered him to return, but Chỉnh refused. Supremely confident in his strength, and probably still convinced of continuing divisions among the Tây Sơn leaders, Chỉnh also counseled Chiêu Thông to demand the return of Nghệ An from Nguyễn Huệ.

Huệ angrily rebuffed the Lê ruler's request, instead ordering his aide Võ Văn Nhậm to take a body of troops to Thăng Long to seize Chỉnh. Nhậm moved north in the fall of 1787, easily taking the capital, quickly abandoned by the Lê, and capturing and then killing Chỉnh. But then Nhậm was seemingly seduced by the same ambitions that had stirred Chỉnh and, seeing no obstacles in his path, took power for himself. Ngô Văn Sở, the Tây Sơn general in the north, despised Nhậm and sent a secret message to Huệ stating that Nhậm was planning to betray him. Huệ trusted Sở and decided to launch another attack on Thăng Long in the spring of 1788, capturing and then beheading Nhậm.

Having fled his capital during the second Tây Sơn invasion of Đàng Ngoài in 1787, the Lê emperor eventually made his way to China, where he appealed to the Qing emperor for assistance in reclaiming his throne. Chiêu Thông argued that since Đại Việt was a Chinese tributary state, the Chinese court was obligated to defend it against aggressors. Although the Qing emperor was hesitant to become involved in what looked like an internal Vietnamese affair, Tôn Sĩ Nghị, the ambitious Qing governor for the southern Chinese provinces of Guangdong and Guangxi convinced him that the invasion would be a simple matter.[102] In late October 1788, a Chinese army, numbering perhaps as many as two hundred thousand men, crossed into northern Đại Việt, entered Thăng Long without encountering any resistance, and placed the Lê ruler back on his throne.

Outnumbered, the Tây Sơn forces under Ngô Văn Sở retreated to Thanh Hóa, where they sent a message to Nguyễn Huệ in Phú Xuân asking for reinforcements. Huệ decided that the Lê had lost their claims to the throne and so had himself crowned Emperor Quang Trung (r. 1788–1792). The newly crowned Tây Sơn emperor immediately assembled another army and proceeded northward. He also sent an envoy with a petition to the Chinese general, requesting that he withdraw his troops. The Chinese general's reply was to tear up the petition and execute the envoy. Meanwhile, the Chinese troops were busy celebrating the lunar New Year, with no thought to their enemy. Having foreseen this, Nguyễn Huệ had ordered his troops to celebrate the New Year early, and then timed his attack on Thăng Long for midnight of the fifth day of the holiday celebration. The Vietnamese attack caught the Qing forces completely unprepared, and the Chinese army was easily defeated as its troops and their commanders fled in disarray.[103]

*Quang Trung in Power (1789–1792)*

His victory accomplished, Quang Trung embarked on a two-pronged campaign to solidify his position. In the first instance he sought to assure himself of a lasting peace with the Chinese. To this end he employed the services of two of the foremost northern literati, Ngô Thì Nhậm and Phan Huy Ích. Both had joined the Tây Sơn after the 1788 campaign against Võ Văn Nhậm, which had effectively ended the rule of the Lê. Through a combination of supplication and veiled threats, these Tây Sơn diplomats were able to convince the Chinese court to forgo any further efforts to restore the Lê. More important still, Quang Trung's diplomats secured Qing acknowledgment of their new emperor's authority, and the Chinese ruler enfeoffed him as the An Nam Quốc Vương (National King of An Nam). A Vietnamese delegation also traveled to the Qing court in late 1789 to pay their respects. The Chinese emperor had insisted that Quang Trung come on this delegation in person. Reluctant to take such a risky journey, the Vietnamese ruler sent a double in his stead. It was this figure who was greeted by the Qianlong emperor as the new ruler of An Nam when he arrived at the Qing summer capital at Jehol.[104] By all accounts the several weeks spent by the Vietnamese delegation at the Qing court were ones of mutual amity and respect.[105] Missions such as this one and the parallel correspondence between the two sides ensured tranquil relations, and the Chinese remained on the sidelines in the continuing Vietnamese struggles between the Tây Sơn and the Nguyễn. The Chinese recognized the Nguyễn only after 1802, when all traces of the Tây Sơn court had been removed.

Having established a good relationship with the Chinese, Quang Trung turned to pressing domestic concerns. The years of political chaos and warfare had taken a dramatic toll on the economic and social welfare of the territory under Tây Sơn control. Consequently, Quang Trung placed a high priority on attempting to restore order and economic productivity. He issued a proclamation calling for displaced peasants to return to their fields and established tax levels that encouraged this return and that rewarded the cultivation of abandoned fields. In addition to mandating the return of populations to their home villages, the new Tây Sơn emperor ordered a nationwide census and the establishment of a system of identity cards. Everyone would be issued one of these cards, and those found without a card were subject to immediate impressment into the Tây Sơn armies. Also in the realm of social policy, and no doubt guided by his Confucian advisers, Quang Trung ordered the inception of a project to oversee the translation and then publication of the Confucian classics from the original Chinese into *nôm*, the vernacular script. The emperor also sought to revive the moribund educational system, including attempting to create a nationwide system of local schools to be run by local scholars and reviving the examination system. Although only one provincial-level examination was held before his death in 1792, this effort reflected Quang Trung's desire to establish an institutional base for his new regime.

Even as Quang Trung was restoring domestic order, he continued to engage in the world beyond Đại Việt's borders. Quang Trung's generals engaged in at least two invasions of the Lao territories, ostensibly as punishment for the ruler of Luang Prabang, who had failed to send a required tribute mission. The first attack in 1790 saw fifty thousand troops invade Lao territory adjacent to Nghệ An. A second campaign the following year used a smaller force of ten thousand troops but marched farther into the interior, eventually seizing Luang Prabang in the fall of 1791. After looting the Lao capital and then marching as far as the Siamese border, the Tây Sơn army withdrew. Quang Trung also engaged in diplomacy with European outposts in Macao and the Philippines. Hoping to persuade the Europeans to trade with his regime instead of that of his Nguyễn rival, he sent emissaries carrying messages requesting the establishment of trading relations to Manila and Macao. These efforts were largely unsuccessful as most Europeans had established commercial relations with the Nguyễn, which they did not wish to harm by trading with their rivals. Nevertheless, the Portuguese at Macao did make some preliminary gestures in response to the Tây Sơn regime's overtures. Finally, Quang Trung also stimulated cross-border trade with China and arranged with the Qing emperor to establish new trading markets in the border region.[106]

*The Post–Quang Trung Era*

Then, in September 1792, and on the cusp of launching a massive attack against Nguyễn Ánh's forces in Gia Định, Quang Trung died suddenly at the age of forty. The premature death of the most charismatic, ambitious, and militarily talented of the three brothers was a turning point in the Tây Sơn period. Most immediately, Quang Trung's demise threatened the survival of the regime he had only recently established. He had been emperor for a period of less than four years and had made only limited progress toward creating social and political stability in the aftermath of an extended period of war and dislocation. Moreover, at the time of Quang Trung's death his son and designated heir was only eleven years of age. Quang Toản was thus forced to commence his reign as the Cảnh Thịnh emperor under the tutelage of a regent, Bùi Đắc Tuyên, his mother's half-brother. This regency was dominated by political infighting that pitted some of Quang Trung's former lieutenants against the ambitious regent, who nurtured ambitions for his own sons, one of whom he hoped eventually to place on the Tây Sơn throne.

While the death of Quang Trung had dealt a severe blow to the long-term prospects of the Tây Sơn governments, events in the far south also contributed to an erosion of their authority. After their defeat in 1785, the Nguyễn had been forced to flee to Bangkok with their Siamese allies, and there Nguyễn Ánh and a small group of followers plotted their return. As they did so, the Nguyễn leader's young son, Prince Cảnh, was in France in the custody of a French missionary, Pierre Joseph Pigneau de Béhaine. Nguyễn Ánh had entrusted his son to the Frenchman hoping that the two could persuade Louix XVI to send military assistance in exchange for economic and territorial concessions after a Nguyễn triumph. The French ruler agreed to a treaty along these lines but left the ultimate decision to execute the treaty to the discretion of his representative in Pondicherry.[107] This official regarded the project as unworthy of French involvement and to Pigneau's dismay canceled it.[108] Undeterred, Pigneau used some of his own funds and promises of suitable reward to gather a group of French mercenaries and several European ships, with which he set sail for Đàng Trong in the summer of 1789. By this time, having taken advantage of the internecine battles between Huệ and Nhạc, Nguyễn Ánh had already departed Bangkok and retaken his old base at Gia Định. He had easily driven out Nguyễn Lữ, who had been forced to flee to Qui Nhơn, where he died a short while later.

Although not needed for this initial skirmish, the small corps of French troops and military advisers were to play an important psychological role for the Nguyễn in subsequent years. The number of European troops fighting in the Nguyễn cause was always small; in 1792 they numbered about forty men serving as ground troops, who were backed by two European ships in the Nguyễn navy.[109] Despite these modest numbers, the European presence in the Nguyễn ranks and the Western ships made a considerable impression on the Tây Sơn, who sought repeatedly to lure the French tactical experts to their side.[110] The Tây Sơn leaders frequently blamed their military losses in large measure on the involvement of the Europeans on the side of the Nguyễn and on the missionaries seen to be aiding them. This was clearly to overstate the impact of the European military involvement; nonetheless, the Tây Sơn military leadership regarded the European involvement with considerable alarm.

From 1787 until 1792, Nguyễn Ánh consolidated his position in the south, taking firm control of the area so long contested between the two rival armies. Nguyễn Nhạc appears not to have had the desire or capacity to launch an attack capable of dislodging the Nguyễn from their southern stronghold. Nhạc directed periodic attacks against the Nguyễn, but none succeeded in more than temporarily stalling the incremental Nguyễn movement up the coast. Meanwhile, the Nguyễn launched their own attack in the summer of 1792, during which they succeeded in encircling Nguyễn Nhạc at Qui Nhơn. Caught off guard, his commanders were forced to abandon their substantial navy, and its vessels were all either captured or destroyed by the Nguyễn. A second Nguyễn siege the following year was only lifted after a desperate plea from Nhạc to his nephew, Quang Trung's successor, brought sufficient reinforcements.

The humiliation he suffered at the hands of the Nguyễn drove Nhạc to despair, and he attempted unsuccessfully to surrender his territories to his young nephew in exchange for being allowed to retire in peace.[111] Shortly thereafter, in the late fall of 1793, Nhạc died at the age of fifty, only a year after his younger brother. After Nhạc's death, his young son Bảo was named by his cousin Emperor Cảnh Thịnh as Nhạc's successor, but without any imperial trappings. Bảo was only to be titled *hiếu công* (filial duke) and was to be controlled by a delegation sent to Qui Nhơn for this purpose by his cousin. As Maurice Durand has pointed out, "Everything took place as if the government of Phú Xuân was directing the kingdoms that remained in Tây Sơn hands. Moreover, the military operations against the Nguyễn . . . depended for the most part on the descendents of Huệ."[112]

*Tây Sơn Politics in the Post–Quang Trung Era (1792–1802)*

While it could be said that the post–Quang Trung period was one of decline for the Tây Sơn regime, this decline was neither precipitous nor entirely assured until the last year or so of Tây Sơn rule. Even with their two main military and political figures gone, Tây Sơn generals continued regularly to challenge the Nguyễn. Although not as ambitious as his father in terms of introducing socioeconomic changes, Quang Toản, as Emperor Cảnh Thịnh, did undertake several political initiatives. He abruptly canceled his father's unpopular "trust card" program shortly after taking power.[113] He carried out at least one census in an effort to continue his father's attempts to restore population stability.[114] Cảnh Thịnh also promoted some changes on the religious front. Probably guided by Confucian advisers, the new emperor ordered the consolidation of the countless Buddhist temples that dotted the countryside. These were to be dismantled, and larger Buddhist structures, centrally situated and serving a large area, were to be built from the gathered materials. In addition, and in response to suspicions about missionaries and their perceived allegiance to the Nguyễn, he cracked down on Christianity beginning in 1795. As numerous missionary letters attest, this crackdown was far from systematic.[115] Increasingly, however, Cảnh Thịnh found himself abandoned by the northern Confucian literati who had once eagerly provided assistance to his father. The charisma of Quang Trung could not be transferred to his young son, and even the scholars who had been optimistic that the new Tây Sơn regime might reverse the decades of decline seen under the Trịnh slowly abandoned the new government. Moreover, the growing military threat posed by the Nguyễn came increasingly to occupy the court at Phú Xuân.

*Military Campaigns of the Post–Quang Trung Period*

The military campaigns of the 1790s paralleled those of the 1770s and early 1780s, in that they were dictated by the coastal winds and were sometimes referred to as the "monsoon wars." Each side would attack when the winds favored the ready movement of their naval forces. Although each camp possessed large numbers of infantry troops, movement by sea was far more efficient. On the other hand, movement by sea also meant that without a decisive victory, neither side could sustain its attacks or easily consolidate its victories. To extend one's campaign, particularly against a distant target, was to risk missing the wind patterns that would enable a return to one's base. Instead, the attackers would be left highly vulnerable to a subsequent counterattack. It was because of this pattern that Nguyễn progress in the wars was so slow, and the despair of European advisers, who frequently lamented Nguyễn Ánh's seemingly overly cautious approach.

Though slow, Nguyễn progress was steady, gradually extending the territory under their direct control up the coast. The target of the Nguyễn in virtually all of these campaigns was the southern Tây Sơn capital near Qui Nhơn and that city's coastal port of Thi Nại. The 1792 destruction of Nhạc's fleet at Thi Nại, followed by Nhạc's death in 1793, represented major setbacks to the Tây Sơn efforts to challenge the Nguyễn for control over the south. Thereafter the Tây Sơn appear increasingly to have relied on ethnic Chinese pirates to supplement their now limited naval strength. In addition, the Nguyễn cause was strengthened by their seizure, in 1794, of the citadel at Diên Khánh, just west of the important harbor city of Nha Trang. Diên Khánh became an important base for Nguyễn operations farther to the north, and accordingly became the target for continual Tây Sơn attacks including periodic and intensive sieges in the years that followed.[116]

In the spring of 1795, Tây Sơn troops counterattacked against the Nguyễn forces and chased them back toward Bà Rịa, southeast of Sài Gòn. This was, however, to prove the last major Tây Sơn counteroffensive toward the deep south, and the Tây Sơn thrust was brief in any case.[117] Meanwhile, the Nguyễn continued to mount regular expeditions up the coast toward Tây Sơn strongholds. A Nguyễn attack in the spring of 1797 bypassed the usual target of Qui Nhơn, heading instead farther north into the heart of Tây Sơn territory. This expedition led to a Nguyễn occupation of the city of Đà Nẵng (Tourane) that lasted for two months, before it was finally abandoned. Then again in 1799 the Nguyễn commenced a two-pronged offensive directed both at the Tây Sơn political center at Phú Xuân and their southern capital at Qui Nhơn. In June of that year, Qui Nhơn was finally captured by the Nguyễn and renamed Bình Định (Pacification Established). The Tây Sơn, again heavily supported by pirate forces, initiated a siege of Qui Nhơn that was to last for an entire year.[118] The Tây Sơn forces ultimately were unable to retake the

FIGURE 4. *Remaining citadel gate at Diên Khánh. Lying eleven kilometers west of the coastal town of Nha Trang, the citadel of Diên Khánh was constructed by Nguyễn Ánh as part of his 1790s campaign against the Tây Sơn. The walled city served as a lynchpin of the Nguyễn campaigns to capture Tây Sơn–held territory. Author's photo.*

city, but they were able to seize nearby Phú Yên, which then served as a base for their counterattacks.

With the threat to Phú Xuân posed by the Nguyễn attack in 1799, the young Tây Sơn ruler, Cảnh Thịnh, had fled northward, hoping to rally support for another counteroffensive. He carried out ceremonies to rededicate his forces and changed his reign name to the more auspicious Bảo Hưng (Defending Prosperity). He issued edicts to rally the populations in preparation for a defense of the north against the expected Nguyễn invasion. In the meantime, back in the central part of the country, a spirited defense of the remaining Tây Sơn positions was being carried out by the wife-husband team of Bùi Thị Xuân and Trần Quang Diệu. They were active in the siege of the Nguyễn positions at Qui Nhơn and later moved north in an effort to defend the Tây Sơn at Nghệ An. Bùi Thị Xuân, who had been trained in the Tây Sơn region's martial arts tradition, distinguished herself as a fierce commander of several thousand troops. Fighting astride an elephant, she led repeated attacks in the face of increasingly difficult odds before being captured by the Nguyễn in 1802 and executed shortly thereafter along with her husband and daughter.[119]

Meanwhile, in early 1800 the Nguyễn had mounted a large-scale campaign hoping to raise the Tây Sơn siege at Qui Nhơn. The southern armies were poised to deal the Tây Sơn a major defeat when they suffered a double setback. First, Nguyễn Ánh's long-time confidant and liaison with the Europeans, Pigneau, died. Then, shortly after Pigneau's death a large part of the Nguyễn navy was destroyed or driven into the South China Sea by a sudden storm. In the aftermath of these setbacks, the Nguyễn offensive was canceled, and the army retreated to Gia Định. Even with the setback suffered by the Nguyễn side, the Tây Sơn were unable to counter the inexorable Nguyễn advance up the coast. The final blow came in the spring of 1802, when Nguyễn Ánh's forces unexpectedly bypassed the ongoing Tây Sơn siege of Qui Nhơn and sailed farther up the coast to attack the northern half of the country directly. Despite some Tây Sơn resistance, the Nguyễn had little difficulty making landfall at Sơn Nam and then marching quickly northwest toward the capital city of Thăng Long, where the Tây Sơn emperor Cảnh Thịnh had taken refuge in the previous year. Nguyễn Ánh entered that city on July 20, 1802, commencing the reign of the final Vietnamese dynasty. Although there continued to be sporadic pro–Tây Sơn attacks in the north, and despite deep-rooted Lê loyalism, the Nguyễn began their effort to integrate the various geographical parts of the country.

# 2 The Leaders

## Laying Claim to Power

> Those who gain power become kings,
> and those who lose it become rebels.
> —Vietnamese proverb

The uprising that originated in the hamlet of Tây Sơn was precipitated by a growing economic crisis in Đàng Trong (the southern Vietnamese realm) and ongoing struggles between the Nguyễn rulers and upland groups resisting greater integration into the lowland state. At the same time, the movement's likelihood of success was enhanced by the weakness of an internally divided regime whose power had been spread thin over the course of the eighteenth century. It was up to the Tây Sơn leaders to combine economic and political discontent with manifest opportunity to transform a small and geographically marginalized group of followers into a major military and political force. To make sense of this transformation and of the Tây Sơn uprising more generally as a political force, I begin by exploring the ways in which its leaders conceptualized their actions and their relationships with existing political structures. While the events of this era demonstrated the limits of the Vietnamese state's ability to control its populations, they also underscored the ways in which populations could be mobilized by charismatic figures able to make convincing claims to political authority.

Some mid-twentieth-century Vietnamese historians, notably Trần Huy Liệu and Văn Tân, looked at the political events of this period and saw a revolution (*cách mạng*).[1] They characterized the Tây Sơn uprising as a focused effort to overthrow corrupt political forces, to reunify the country, to defend the nation against external threats, and to promote indigenous cultural elements. This interpretation of the movement conveniently reflected the political agenda of the post-1954 state in North Việt Nam, even as it glossed over the true complexities of the Tây Sơn era. A closer examination makes it clear that the accomplishments of the Tây Sơn movement do not reveal a coherent ideological agenda on the part of its leaders. Moreover, although the uprising did result in a change of administration and some reorganization of the Vietnamese territories, its overall political impact was not revolutionary as most underlying political, economic, and social structures remained unaltered.

The Tây Sơn political leaders continued to operate largely within existing political frameworks, making use of various conflicts and points of dissension to further their political objectives while never transcending them. On the one hand, Tây Sơn leaders represented the newly emergent power of the southern Vietnamese territories, with their dynamic populations and economic resources capable of supporting the rebels' political ambitions. On the other hand, many of the patterns found in the political events of this era were ones with clear precedents in Vietnamese history, and the regimes established by the Tây Sơn looked like those they replaced. Thus, rather than characterizing the Tây Sơn brothers as revolutionaries, we would be more accurate in viewing them as additional (if formidable) actors on a crowded and expanding political stage whose players and props were already well established. To extend this metaphor, the Tây Sơn leaders were actors without a script, improvising their roles and the direction of their drama. They were guided not by long-term visions, but by short-term expedience, constantly responding to changing circumstances. This chapter will consider the ways in which the Tây Sơn leaders conceptualized their actions and the political mechanisms by which they expanded their following and legitimated their claims.

## IDEOLOGICAL UNDERPINNINGS OF THE TÂY SƠN UPRISING

In trying to comprehend the ideological impetus behind a movement as large as the Tây Sơn, observers are tempted to look for the types of religious or even overtly millennialistic indicators associated with many other East and Southeast Asian rural movements of the early modern period.[2] Such indicators are, however, almost entirely absent. The Tây Sơn armies—despite their obvious intensity and some traces of iconoclasm in their actions—did not constitute a millenarian movement. The Tây Sơn leadership was not guided by any sort of religious zeal, and its troops do not appear to have drawn sustenance or bravery from talismanic incantations or religious imagery. In this respect, the Tây Sơn uprising was similar to other Vietnamese popular movements of the eighteenth century, which were themselves little influenced by religious or millennial fervor. As Hue-Tam Ho Tai has pointed out in her important study *Millenarianism and Peasant Politics in Vietnam* (1983), Vietnamese millenarian activity was largely a phenomenon of the southern Vietnamese territories.[3] Tai does not argue that such activity was not possible in regions to the north, but rather that the conditions in lower Đàng Trong (by the nineteenth century, southern Việt Nam) were peculiarly well suited to millenarian activity. Even in the south, millennial activity did not appear until the latter half of the nineteenth century. Indeed, the Buddhism that was frequently at the heart of such movements was something toward which the Tây Sơn leaders were generally disdainful or even hostile.

The absence of religious underpinnings in the Tây Sơn uprising has attracted attention from Vietnamese scholars. In the 1965 article "Why Do Righteous Peasant Uprisings in Việt Nam Seldom Have Religious Elements?" Nguyễn Khắc Đạm argued that while Việt Nam had historically seen some popular movements led by religious figures, generally speaking Vietnamese peasant movements were neither guided by religious men nor directed against religious structures. At times, as in the Tây Sơn period, efforts were made to curtail the power of religious institutions, particularly Buddhism, but unlike their European counterparts who had periodically challenged the Catholic Church, Vietnamese peasants saw no need to attack religious structures to gain economic relief.[4] Although Đạm glosses over complicated tensions between wealthy Buddhist institutions and various popular uprisings of the seventeenth and eighteenth centuries, it does appear that anti-Buddhist attacks of the Tây Sơn period were incidental to, rather than central components of, the rebel outlook.

Vietnamese peasant thought-worlds are of course suffused with elements of folk religion—beliefs difficult to separate from everyday ritual and social practice—and these were widespread during the Tây Sơn period. Indeed, as we shall see shortly, popular beliefs in the supernatural were an important component of the Tây Sơn movement, particularly during its early phase. At the same time, elements of more institutionalized religious structures (however reinterpreted), which were strong elements in many other popular uprisings in East and Southeast Asia, were almost entirely absent in the Tây Sơn movement. While the Tây Sơn leaders' reference to and occasional manipulation of popular beliefs in the realm of spirits and other supernatural forces do in a sense link the movement to religious forces, the deployment of these forces served as a means to a material end, rather than as a unifying spiritual objective.

Since the Tây Sơn did not articulate a millennial vision to drive their movement nor unite the peasantry through promises of a common spiritual endeavor, its leaders had to establish their credibility and motivate their followers in more mundane terms. At a basic level, the movement drew energy from its dynamic and charismatic leaders, a remarkable ability to mobilize soldiers to fill their armies, and early successes against a regime divided by factionalism and hampered by a weakened military. Indeed, it was apparently a combination of the Tây Sơn brothers' charisma and claims that their uprising was the fulfillment of a local prophecy—an assertion bolstered by demonstrated links to the realm of the supernatural—that consolidated early popular support. This approach focused attention on the leaders themselves, and the movement continued to be driven by the personal objectives of its leadership (or their advisers), and the circumstances in which they found themselves, rather than by a distinct ideology. This lack of ideology suggests that the Tây Sơn leaders can best be described as opportunists rather than as visionaries and that their movement's goals were in constant flux, lacking a single, defining element.

As part of their effort to attract followers, the Tây Sơn leaders had to legitimate their political aspirations, a complex undertaking in a region with no single accepted method for establishing political credibility. Consequently, they attempted to find that legitimacy, or perhaps more specifically to claim it, in a variety of ways. As a contemporary European observer noted of the Tây Sơn leaders' wide-ranging efforts in this regard,

> [The Tây Sơn] on their part, left no measures untried, nor suffered any occasion to pass by, which might be the means of acquiring them popularity. The merchant gave sumptuous entertainments, fetes and fireworks; the general cajoled the army; and the priest prevailed on the clergy to announce to the careless multitude the decree of *Tien*, which had ordained these three worthies to be their future rulers.[5]

This observation suggests, and the rest of this chapter will make clear, that the Tây Sơn made appeals for legitimacy at multiple levels: the abstract, including both mystical and moralistic claims; the socioeconomic, including redistributive and other policies designed to address structural economic issues; and the institutional, including numerous efforts to connect themselves to the multiplicity of existing power structures. Collectively, these multiple approaches to political legitimation served to secure power and authority for the Tây Sơn leaders. Each was in response to particular circumstances, audiences, and the exigencies of the moment. Although this chapter will examine these strategies in turn, the Tây Sơn leaders did not view them in a compartmentalized way, nor did they conceptualize them in an instrumental fashion. Moreover, while these approaches are presented here sequentially, they were not developed chronologically. Some of them were used only briefly, while others were pursued throughout the Tây Sơn era.

## POLITICAL LEGITIMACY IN TRADITIONAL ĐẠI VIỆT

Despite Việt Nam's long history of dynastic succession, the question of political legitimacy has never been without its ambiguities. There had been periods of tranquil and orderly succession in which power was transferred to a designated heir, but at numerous other junctures political succession had been challenged through either subterfuge or violence. There had also been instances in which heirs were displaced by sitting rulers or political factions. And, as in the sixteenth through eighteenth centuries, there were periods during which power was divided between a sitting emperor and noble individuals or clans. Political legitimacy, consequently, could be and was derived in a variety of ways that changed in response to circumstances and the particular needs of claimants to power.

These complex realities concerning political legitimacy can be traced to the very earliest periods of Vietnamese independence, when in the eleventh century the right to rule was closely linked to the particular attributes of "virtuous kings" (*đức vương*). As Keith Taylor has pointed out, the legitimacy of the Lý dynasty (1009–1225) was very much a function of what he calls "Lý dynasty religion" whereby claims to authority derived in large measure from a ruler's connections to the many powerful spirits of the land.[6] In other words, political legitimacy was highly personal and had to be actively demonstrated by succeeding rulers. O. W. Wolters has also argued that into the thirteenth century the Vietnamese did not have a fixed system of primogeniture, or indeed any strict practices with regard to royal succession. As in other Southeast Asian states, Vietnamese rulers of this period were heroic leaders who forged alliances through marriage and loyalty oaths.[7] Although the Trần dynasty (1225–1400) introduced a system of formal succession in the thirteenth century as part of an effort to fend off potential challengers, this did not end the complex competitions for power.

Based on an analysis of these early dynasties and their successors, Ralph Smith suggested that Việt Nam had historically seen cycles in which Confucian-inspired regimes alternated with ones that drew their political strength, and indeed their legitimacy, from other sources.[8] A brief survey of Vietnamese political regimes beginning in the fourteenth century appears to bear this out. In the late fourteenth century, Hồ Quý Ly married into the ruling Trần family and seized the throne from that position. He imposed a Confucian-style government before being overthrown by a Chinese army in 1406. The Chinese were driven out by Lê Lợi, who set his new dynasty on a course of even greater Confucian orthodoxy. The high point of Confucian-based political legitimacy was then reached during the Hồng Đức reign of the fifth Lê emperor, Lê Thánh Tông. By the early sixteenth century, however, the Lê dynasty had begun to crumble and with it the prominent political role of Confucianism. In response to this political turmoil Mạc Đăng Dung seized the throne, and although he attempted a return to the Confucian standards of the Hồng Đức period, this return did not endure. Instead, Đại Việt entered an extended period in which military prowess and family connections served as the primary determinants of political authority.[9] Confucianism and attempts at legitimation in terms of that doctrine receded substantially in the aftermath of the Mạc defeat at the end of the sixteenth century.

As we saw in the previous chapter, the division of the Vietnamese territories between the Nguyễn and Trịnh regimes produced two political entities, each with its own approach to political legitimation. The Nguyễn regime continued in the non-Confucian direction that had emerged during the anti-Mạc wars, governing a realm in which political authority stemmed from military connections as well as the active sponsorship of Buddhism.[10] In the Trịnh-controlled region of Đàng Ngoài there were periods in which Confucianism was again allowed to flourish, and thus to serve as a legitimizing force, particularly during the reign of Trịnh Tạc (1657–1682). By the early eighteenth century, however, Confucianism was once again in decline, and during the reign of Trịnh Giang (1729–1740), importing Confucian texts from China was forbidden, while Buddhist texts were actively being collected. At the same time, one could purchase passing grades in the Confucian examinations, degrading their value and undermining one of the cornerstones of the Confucian political order.[11] The political structures of this era were further complicated by the continued dispersion of political authority among members of the

Nguyễn and Trịnh families even as a Lê emperor continued to sit on the throne in Thăng Long. Moreover, several strong challengers to the Trịnh emerged from within the Lê family itself during the middle of the eighteenth century, suggesting that Lê legitimacy remained an important political touchstone. Consequently, by the advent of the Tây Sơn uprising in 1771, both Đàng Trong and Đàng Ngoài had seen challenges to fixed notions of political legitimacy and had, moreover, encountered shifting ideas about the sources of that legitimacy itself.

The eighteenth-century political landscape was shaped by contested and competing claims for power. With a long and well-known history of challenges to orthodox notions of political legitimacy and orderly imperial succession, the Vietnamese territories remained open for new claimants to political authority, particularly in times of turmoil. During such times, political power was often claimed by force wielded in the form of a strong army. And indeed, this approach to claiming power had a good deal of credibility in Việt Nam during the early modern era, reflecting not least the turbulence of past dynastic transitions. The idea that political realities might not reflect idealized political structures was encapsulated in the popular saying Those who have power become kings, and those who do not become rebels. During the Tây Sơn period this sentiment was echoed by the movement's talented general, Ngô Văn Sở, who in a discussion with the Tây Sơn leader Nguyễn Huệ observed that "from ancient times until the present, that under heaven [i.e., the kingdom] has not been the private possession of a particular family; if one could take it then they went ahead and did so."[12] While not a prescription for the seizure of power, Sở's assessment reflected a certain historical reality. And yet, like their many predecessors, the Tây Sơn leadership understood that brute force was not always an effective or sufficient means of gaining followers or achieving legitimacy. Such legitimacy had to be staked on manifestations of divine or supernatural support or on more concrete signs of political authority.

## THE SANCTION OF "HEAVEN" AND SUPERNATURAL CLAIMS TO AUTHORITY

From the earliest days of the uprising, the Tây Sơn brothers relied heavily on popular beliefs concerning the supernatural, including the importance of prophecies, omens, and other demonstrations of distinctive personal powers to legitimate their political claims. This was particularly important during the early years of the uprising for it was an important means by which these "rebels" could sidestep questions about their lack of political connections. While there was great value in being able to connect oneself to established political structures, as will be demonstrated later, often of more immediate value was the ability to show that higher powers were instrumental in one's rise to prominence. Thus, among other things, the Tây Sơn leaders used and manipulated popular belief in the world of spirits and the supramundane realm more generally, including the notion of a "will of heaven," while also emphasizing prophecies and other indications of their claimed destiny. As Michael Adas has noted in his work *Prophets of Rebellion* (1979), "These revelations and the prophets' claims to be divine or divinely-appointed redeemers gave supernatural sanction to their decisions and transmitted a sense of legitimacy to their followers."[13] It was precisely this mechanism that was at work in the Tây Sơn case and that was instrumental in helping the uprising's leaders gain credibility among potential followers.

### *The Tây Sơn and the Favor of Heaven*

Throughout their campaigns, one of the central ideas that the Tây Sơn leaders repeatedly emphasized was that theirs was not merely an undertaking by a group of disaffected peasants. Rather, it was a divinely ordained mission reflecting "heaven's will" and connected to what is sometimes called the "mandate of heaven" (in Vietnamese, *mệnh trời*). It is easy to overstate the significance of this term, which has often been used either to suggest a certain fatalism about the course of future events or merely as a cynical way to speak of changing fortunes. There is no doubt, however, that this term (or variants thereof) was an important element in the thought-worlds and discourse of this era.[14] In the Vietnamese worldview, the notion of "heaven" (*thiên* in Sino-Vietnamese; *trời* in Vietnamese) combines elements of elite, Confucian ideology with populist notions of divine forces. This is not heaven in a religious sense as the realm of an afterlife, but rather a more abstract reference to an unseen divine force, sometimes understood to be dictating and shaping the course of earthly events. *Trời* more generally refers to that which is above—the sky—with attendant connections to the seasons, the weather, and all manner of other natural phenomena. Consequently, the Vietnamese understanding of heaven makes reference to a broad range of ideas related to and linking the mundane and the divine.

Although heaven was sometimes conceptualized as a force guiding the fates of human actors and institutions, it was not always understood as that which caused change. Other interpretations of heaven viewed it as a force that reflected, rather than directed, the course of events. As Alexander Woodside has pointed out, Vietnamese scholars of the eighteenth century generally did not view heaven as determining the course of events, in a fatalistic sense. Rather, they saw the sources of change and transformation as residing in the mundane realm, specifically linked to the virtue and moral character of individual leaders. Thus, heaven might manifest signs of various types, but these were not indications of a foreordained outcome, but rather reflections of the moral limitations of particular individuals. Woodside cites the noted eighteenth-century scholar Nguyễn Thiếp as observing "that the destruction of states and of families was brought about by human moral failures, by mediocre rulers and by the ministers who flattered them, not by irreversible processes beyond human reach."[15] Thiếp's view suggested then that heaven did not cause change in the mundane realm, but merely signaled it.

Other eighteenth-century scholars' articulation of this concept made clear their understanding of the complex interplay between the will of heaven and the desires of the people. Ngô Thì Sĩ, a noted scholar-official, wrote that "[t]he good and bad fortunes of heaven stem from the actions of the people, and the actions of the state thus penetrate to heaven."[16] And his son, Ngô Thì Nhậm observed that "[h]eaven sees and hears the people. When the hearts of the people are settled then the will of heaven will also turn."[17] Clearly these scholars, contemporary to the Tây Sơn movement, saw important and not easily resolved linkages between the people and heaven. Moreover, these tensions could be found within the Tây Sơn leaders' justifications for their actions as well. On the one hand, they argued that a divine force had compelled them to act—the notion of the will of heaven—while on the other they acknowledged that their chief motivation was the distress of the people, something caused by misrule.

Given the potency of "heaven" in Vietnamese thought-worlds of the eighteenth century, the Tây Sơn leadership began early in their uprising to invoke the will of heaven as supporting, and indeed encouraging, their movement and its objectives. Thus, for instance, the movement's leaders cast a military seal for their officers containing the phrase "It is by the order of Heaven that the tyrant Nguyễn Phúc is being chastised" (*Phụng Thiên phạ bạo Nguyễn Phúc*).[18] The reference was to the last Nguyễn *chúa*, Nguyễn Phúc Thuần, who had been placed on the throne by Trương Phúc Loan. Here we have the most concrete evidence that the Tây Sơn leaders were invoking the concept of a heavenly mission on behalf of the people to guide their actions. Moreover, the message contained in this seal explicitly linked the wrath of heaven—being expressed through its agents the Tây Sơn—with the misgovernance of the Nguyễn ruler.

Numerous reports by European eyewitnesses underscore the importance the Tây Sơn leaders placed on their claimed connections to heaven and its support for their movement. In February 1774, a Spanish missionary, Diego de Jumilla, reported of the Tây Sơn that "they announced to the villages that they were not bandits, but that they were carrying out a war to obey the will of heaven."[19] A French missionary writing of the movement's early days also reported that "[the Tây Sơn leaders] then spread a thousand tales of dreams and revelations of signs from heaven, which they said proved their mission."[20] Another European visitor reported that the youngest Tây Sơn brother, Nguyễn Lữ, had announced that *tien* (heaven) had decreed that the three brothers would serve as the new rulers of the kingdom.[21] These early references make clear that the rebel leaders were popularizing their interpretation of the will of heaven at the very outset of their uprising.

Such claims to having heaven's support were not without their skeptics. As will become evident below, claims had to be bolstered by demonstrations of divine support. A 1776 missionary letter revealed the difficulty the Tây Sơn leaders faced as they sought to convince a reluctant public of Nhạc's legitimacy and claims to having supernatural support: "The rebel chief has gone ahead and proclaimed himself king, but he has neither the seals nor the scepter, and it is this, among these idolaters, that is regarded as proof that heaven has not chosen him."[22] In short, claiming to be king was one thing, but proving that heaven had anointed you to such a position was quite a different matter, requiring sometimes earthly signs of office, such as official seals. The importance of seals of office will be examined in more detail below, though it is worth noting here that Nguyễn Nhạc took it upon himself to cast a golden seal of office for himself when he took the throne as king in 1776, possibly in response to the public uncertainty reflected in the missionary's letter.[23]

Although the Tây Sơn leaders' emphasis on heaven's having guided their actions was particularly prominent during the early years of the uprising, this rhetoric continued to be used even as the movement matured and eventually spread into Đàng Ngoài. In 1778, Charles Chapman, a visiting Englishman, reported that Nhạc had informed him that "it has pleased God to make him the instrument of [the people's] deliverance and to raise him to the Throne."[24] Another account contained in a 1784 letter by a Spanish missionary, Father Ginestar, cited a Tây Sơn general who told him that "heaven had confided this kingdom in them," the kingdom in question being the Nguyễn realm of Đàng Trong.[25] These reports indicate both that the Tây Sơn leaders continued to underscore the purported support of heaven and that they felt it important to make this point to European visitors. This insistence suggests that the rebel leaders saw this form of political legitimation as fundamental to their overall mission.

When the Tây Sơn armies marched into Trịnh territory in the summer of 1786, they brought with them their claims to be acting on behalf of heaven. During Nguyễn Huệ's audience in Thăng Long with the aging Lê emperor, the Tây Sơn leader described his efforts on the monarch's behalf by invoking the sanction of heaven. Huệ declared, "I have come here because this was heaven's will," and "heaven has borrowed the hand of your servant to attack and destroy the disrespectful Trịnh clan, in order to broaden the powerful authority of your majesty."[26] More elaborately, Nguyễn Huệ asserted, "My coming here at this time is entirely due to the intentions of Heaven. And as for the boats that carried my troops here, were it not for the lessening of the flood waters and the powerfully blowing southern winds, how would your servant's strength have been sufficient to accomplish this?"[27] Significantly, the Tây Sơn leader argued that he was not merely claiming to be the agent of heaven's will, but that his claim was substantiated by these manifestations of heaven's power. Were heaven not on his side, Nguyễn Huệ suggested, the natural forces, which heaven itself controlled, would not so perfectly have aided his plan and allowed him to accomplish what he had.[28] It is clear from the context—the Tây Sơn military leader's restoring the Lê throne—that the claim here was that heaven had recruited the Tây Sơn to restore order and to destroy the oppressive Trịnh, not to establish themselves as rulers in the northern realm of Đàng Ngoài, as they had in Đàng Trong.

Two years later, however, the situation had changed, and Nguyễn Huệ was prepared to extend his claimed political authority to the north, again in the name of heaven. In his 1788 edict on ascending the throne, the Tây Sơn leader declared, "The oppression of the people the world over was uniformly all around me, [and my taking the throne] was what the will of heaven had intended, and was not something that the people had put forth. I then relied on the intentions of heaven, and went along with the hearts of the people."[29] Here again, the Tây Sơn leader emphasized the idea that "heaven" had called on him in response to the "oppression of the people." More significant is that this edict contained a carefully crafted formulation produced by Nguyễn Huệ's close adviser, the noted Confucian scholar Ngô Thì Nhậm.[30] The phrase "this was what the will of heaven had intended, and was not something the people had put forth," constituted the Confucian rationalization for the Tây Sơn actions, as it distinguished between something initiated by divine forces and something merely sparked by populist pressure. For a proper Confucian scholar to sanction, much less participate in, such a movement, it had to be described as emanating from heaven's will and not simply from the desires of the people. The former was ordained by the transcendent power of the divine, while the latter constituted a direct affront to the Confucian relationship that should obtain between ruler and ruled.

Although the Tây Sơn took pains to cultivate good relations with Confucian elites (as Nhậm's careful formulation made clear) and to emphasize that their actions were in response to the will of heaven, at times they more explicitly depicted their uprising as motivated by the concrete sufferings and corresponding appeals of the people. In a 1786 proclamation to the peoples of Đàng Ngoài—issued in the course of their invasion—the Tây Sơn combined the ideas of heaven's will and the longings of the people and described their action as "consenting to the will of heaven, and responding to the hearts of the people."[31] And then, describing what was seen as the condition of the populace, the same proclamation spoke of the "miserable and scattered peoples [who] await the returning banner of righteousness."[32] Moreover, even in his 1788 edict on ascending the throne, which apparently sought to credit heaven with the impetus for his movement, Nguyễn Huệ observed, "Originally, I did not have the will to serve as king. It was only because the hearts of the people had become weary of lives of chaos, that I impatiently desired to be a virtuous king in order to save lives and provide peace for the people."[33] Thus, the Tây Sơn leaders continued to vary their claims about the precise impetus for their actions, sometimes crediting heaven and at other times the aspirations of a desperate people.

Whatever the original impetus for the Tây Sơn uprising, its rebel leaders made much of the role played by the forces of heaven. They did so precisely because such rhetoric and claims were significant ones in the Vietnamese cultural and political landscape and were employed by all sides during the political contestation of this era. Toward the end of the Tây Sơn period, when there was a widespread sense that the tides had shifted against the rebel regime and toward the Nguyễn, a European observer noted that "all of the peasants, and the tyrants as well, recognize and state loudly that it is Heaven [Ciel] which has given the [Nguyễn] prince a victory that is so rapid and complete."[34] This statement reinforces the popular idea about the role of heaven in determining the rulership of the kingdom and at the same time makes clear the fickle nature of the favor of heaven and the inherent political uncertainty that it decreed. Claims to having the support of heaven might be believed only as long as a ruler or rebel could show signs of this support. If one could no longer do so, the tide of popular sentiment might quickly shift to another. Indeed, claims to having the support of heaven had always to be reinforced by demonstrations of this support, for without such demonstrations heaven's intentions might be read very differently by one's intended audience.

*The Tây Sơn Leaders and the Supernatural Realm*

While the Tây Sơn leaders frequently cited the sanction of heaven for their actions, they also linked themselves more broadly to the realm of the supernatural, whose influence on the popular imagination was considerable. They did so in a variety of ways that included the use of prophecies, local beliefs, and other indications of supernatural favor. The Tây Sơn uprising's very origins can be traced in part to the brothers' teacher encouraging Nguyễn Nhạc to view himself as fulfilling a long-standing local prophecy: "In the west there is a righteous uprising, in the north great feats are accomplished."[35] This prophecy, and Nhạc's use thereof, is recorded in numerous accounts, suggesting its significance for propelling the movement and drawing supporters in its earliest days. Prophecies were a significant element of Vietnamese popular and elite thoughtworlds in the late eighteenth century, and so the Tây Sơn brothers would certainly have sought to ensure the wide circulation of this prophecy, their interpretation of its import, and their claims to fulfilling it.[36]

In addition to this prophecy, the Tây Sơn leaders sought other means by which to claim direct connections to the supernatural world. There are numerous folktales regarding the uprising's leaders, many of which emphasize elements of the supernatural surrounding the Tây Sơn brothers, with most concerning the early years of the movement. From a historiographical perspective, such tales are problematic because most were transmitted orally rather than textually, making it difficult to trace their origins. Some were later written down and can now be found in various archival manuscripts, but most of these texts are anonymous and undated, rendering them equally problematic. A few were recorded in datable nineteenth-century writings, suggesting that they may have circulated in the late eighteenth century. Even though many of these tales cannot readily be substantiated or dated, they form an important part of the collective popular understanding of the Tây Sơn period. Moreover, although the specifics may have been invented, these tales often fit what we do know about the Tây Sơn from other sources, and about the kinds of popular traditions that might well have surrounded the movement's leaders.

Of the surviving texts and oral traditions relating to supernatural manifestations surrounding the Tây Sơn leaders, a large number concern magical weapons discovered by or presented to the brothers. Such items have a long history in Vietnamese popular consciousness, with Vietnamese legends speaking about supernatural weapons dating as early as the second century B.C.E. A tale describing that early period speaks of a magical crossbow, about which it was said, "He who is able to hold this crossbow rules the realm; he who is not able to hold this crossbow will perish."[37] And indeed, the subsequent loss of the crossbow is said to have caused the downfall of the king who originally possessed it. Much later, in the fifteenth century, the great Vietnamese hero of the resistance against the Ming, Lê Lợi, was said to have been given a magical sword to wield in his campaign against the Chinese occupation force. When his mission was completed, the divinely presented sword had to be returned to the lake from which it had originally emerged.

Magical weapons were particularly potent ritual items in the local context from which the Tây Sơn emerged, for as Li Tana has demonstrated, the highland and lowland ethnic groups in the Qui Nhơn region had a variety of legends relating to swords and the power that they allegedly imparted to those who wielded them.[38] Consequently, it is not surprising to find magical weapons, and particularly swords, playing a prominent role in lore about the Tây Sơn. One such tale, metaphorically describing the unifying power of the Tây Sơn, tells of Nguyễn Nhạc's finding the blade of a precious sword in the coastal plains and then finding its matching handle in the highland regions. A variant of this tale, one containing a certain Arthurian echo, states that Nhạc discovered the blade embedded in a stone, and that he alone had the strength to withdraw it. Then, on visiting a Bahnar village in the uplands west of Qui Nhơn, he was presented with an enormous fowl, which when opened revealed the matching handle. Once the two pieces were joined they could no longer be separated.[39] A similar account describes his finding a sword in the plains and a golden seal in the highlands, thus signifying both military and political authority.[40] This again suggested the idea of an alliance between upland and lowland peoples, something represented to a degree by the Tây Sơn in their early years.

A more elaborate tale concerning Nhạc describes an incident in the early days of the uprising in which villagers were startled one night to see bright lights emanating from a nearby forest. The lights appeared to have no discernible source. When the lights appeared on a second night, the villagers went to investigate and discovered an enormous bow and arrow. Word of these events spread, and the next time the midnight lights appeared many villagers went out to locate their source. Following the light through the woods, the villagers came upon Nguyễn Nhạc, garbed in battle armor and standing in front of a large stone. In a thundering voice, he denounced the cruelties of the Nguyễn regent, Trương Phúc Loan, and ascribed all of their hardships to this man and his officials. Overwhelmed by his stature and the signs that surrounded him, the people joined Nhạc and his brothers to overthrow Loan and to alleviate their own poverty.[41]

Nhạc's brother Nguyễn Huệ is also the subject of several popular tales linking him to magical weapons. One such account tells of a pair of giant snakes blocking a road along which Huệ was leading his soldiers. His troops were terrified, but their commander dismounted from his horse and prayed to the snake spirit saying, "If my brothers and I are able to undertake this great task then I request that the Snake spirit move off of the road and allow my soldiers to pass. If it is my fate that this cannot be allowed, then please bite me to death but permit my troops to live and to return to their wives and children." Thereupon, the snakes cleared the path and escorted the troops to their destination. They further aided the Tây Sơn by presenting Nguyễn Huệ with "a dragon knife" featuring an ebony-black handle and a razor-sharp blade.[42] Another tale about Nguyễn Huệ describes him as having superhuman strength, which enabled him to lift and wield a particular silver lance that ordinary men could not budge. Like the sword in the stone, which only Nhạc could remove, this tale too distinguished a Tây Sơn leader as existing beyond the realm of the ordinary.

Significantly, these orally transmitted tales of magical weapons are reinforced by an account in the Nguyễn court's own nineteenth-century official biographies, the *Đại Nam Liệt Truyện*. This text records of the elder Tây Sơn brother that "on the road through the mountains of An Dương, Nhạc found a sword that he claimed was a spirit sword. He used this to delude the people, and many believed him."[43] That such a description occurs in a court history, research for which began in the first half of the nineteenth century, suggests that this tale might credibly be dated to the Tây Sơn period itself. Moreover, given the power and prestige that would come with claimed possession of a magical weapon, it is highly plausible that the Tây Sơn brothers would have sought to popularize such tales during the early years of their movement.

The Tây Sơn brothers appear not only to have encouraged the transmission of such tales, but also to have actively exploited popular belief in the mysterious and magical to further their ends. This is vividly depicted in a tale about Nguyễn Nhạc that can be found in numerous written sources. According to these accounts, Nhạc took advantage of local superstitions surrounding a nearby mountain peak to convince potential supporters of his links to the supernatural. To do this he smuggled some drums and gongs up the hill and secretly arranged for them to be sounded and accompanied by flashing lights on the night of a local festival. Feigning surprise, but also curiosity, Nhạc gathered a group of adventurous locals and led a procession up the hill. In the mists at the top they encountered a wizened old man who summoned Nhạc by name and then read from a bronze tablet on which were inscribed the words "the Jade Emperor orders Nguyễn Nhạc to serve as the country's Emperor." After reading it, the old man handed the tablet to the Tây Sơn leader and vanished into the night.[44] The old man was in fact Nhạc's teacher, Trương Văn Hiến, who, according to some versions, had advised him in arranging this stunt to enhance the rebel leader's mystical aura.[45] Unaware of the elaborate deception arranged by Nhạc, impressed local villagers eagerly offered their support to this leader who had apparently been anointed by heaven—as represented by the Jade Emperor, the paramount figure in the pantheon of Vietnamese popular deities.

Another tale allegedly recounting an instance of a Tây Sơn leader manipulating the fates describes a ritual that Nguyễn Huệ is said to have performed near his capital at Phú Xuân in late 1788. The purpose of the ceremony was to discover the destiny of his impending expedition against the Chinese, who had invaded the northern part of Đại Việt earlier that year. The story notes that Huệ ascended the altar and proclaimed,

> My fellow troops and officers! I am about to lead the armies to Bắc Hà [northern Đại Việt] to ask about the crimes of the Qing invaders and to restore peace and happiness to the hundred surnames. If there is to be a signal from heaven that our great army will be victorious in battle, heaven will cause these 200 coins to land on their backs. The backs of these coins have raised copper.... Now our troops look for a sign of that victory or defeat.[46]

Having completed his oration, Huệ and his officers performed prayers at the altar, after which the Tây Sơn leader tossed all the coins into the air. At that, the troops rushed forward, saw that indeed the coins had all landed on their backs, and were convinced that their victory was foreordained. The account goes on to note that Huệ had minted special double-backed coins for this demonstration, so while the ritual may have been designed to play to popular notions of religious practice, it may also be seen as yet another instance of the Tây Sơn manipulating the signs of the gods.

## CONFUCIAN RHETORIC IN THE TÂY SƠN UPRISING

While references to heaven and to the forces of the supernatural were useful means by which to substantiate their claims and to recruit followers, the rebel leaders also employed other rhetorical registers. In particular, like leaders of earlier peasant uprisings, they chose, probably quite consciously, to emphasize the moral dimension of their crusade in distinctly Confucian terms.[47] The decision to use the rhetoric—if not necessarily the content—of Confucian ideologies was significant both for connecting the Tây Sơn leaders to potential supporters within the ranks of literati in the Nguyễn realms (however small this potential audience) and for furthering the link between themselves and the larger populations, which in their own way responded to the language of Confucianism.

Alexander Woodside has argued that the Confucian tradition was well established in rural Đại Việt in this period, noting that "[t]he hold of the Sino-Vietnamese classical tradition on the Vietnamese peasants of the 1700's and the 1800's was... indisputable, especially those parts of it which traced change to the deposition of bad monarchs by good ones."[48] Although this was much more true in the northern part of the Vietnamese territories long exposed to Chinese ideological influence, some of the rhetoric of Confucianism had inevitably made its way into the Nguyễn realms as well, even as Confucianism itself continued to be politically marginalized.[49] In a society where scholars maintained direct contact with rural populations, either through personal ties to relatives or through residence in villages where they might establish schools, it is unsurprising that peasants would imbibe elements of Confucian ideology or at the very least its rhetorical elements. The Tây Sơn brothers themselves were certainly exposed to the basics of this ideology under the tutelage of their teacher and mentor Trương Văn Hiến, making it natural for them to invoke Confucian ideals during the course of the uprising.

*The Tây Sơn and "Righteousness"*

Of the Confucian terms most frequently invoked by the Tây Sơn leaders, "righteousness" (*nghĩa*) was particularly emphasized, beginning with the insistence that theirs was a righteous uprising, a *khởi nghĩa*. The use of this term was necessary to link the uprising to the frequently invoked prophecy regarding a "righteous uprising." This emphasis on "righteousness" tied them to this prophecy even as it allowed the Tây Sơn leaders to stake a different type of claim to legitimacy. Specifically, the failure of governments (both Nguyễn and Trịnh) to meet certain basic obligations toward their subjects opened the way to acceptable criticism along lines recognized in a landscape partially shaped by Confucian philosophy. The Sino-Vietnamese term for righteousness encompasses notions of justice and right action that are perhaps most often connected to the manner in which the ideal Confucian scholar acted. It derived from a Confucian ethos that emphasized several fundamental tenets of personal behavior, most notably righteousness, filiality, virtue, and humaneness.

Indeed, throughout many parts of East and Southeast Asia the relationship between peasants and their political and economic superiors, whether landlords or government officials, was one based at least in part on some idea of reciprocity with roots in what Confucian rhetoric described as "righteousness" and "justice."[50] The classic articulation of this notion is found in James Scott's *The Moral Economy of the Peasant* (1976). Although Scott speaks chiefly about the relations between peasants and landlords, it is clear that the state is also subject to notions of the moral economy.[51] Thus, the failures of the state to live up to expected standards rendered it liable to criticisms and protests invoking the language of righteousness. Consequently, when popular movements raised banners that spoke of righteousness, these denoted not merely the rightness or justice of the movement's cause, but by implication also criticized the government, or at least its local representatives, for failing to meet basic obligations vis-à-vis the people.

Numerous popular uprisings in Vietnamese history, including most notably that of Lê Lợi in the fifteenth century, had drawn on the idea of an uprising of righteousness, which would restore order and proper relationships. In the period just before the Tây Sơn uprising, the Lê prince, Lê Duy Mật, who rose up against Trịnh Giang in 1738, issued a proclamation in the vernacular script in which he recalled the heroic uprising of Lê Lợi against the Ming, referring to it as the *Lam Sơn khởi nghĩa*—"the righteous uprising from (the region of) Lam Sơn." In doing so Mật not only sought to link his own movement to that of his illustrious predecessor, but also to suggest that both shared a commitment to "righteousness."[52] Given such a tradition, it is not surprising that Confucian referents such as "righteousness" would be taken up by Vietnamese peasants, particularly those concerned with addressing perceived lapses in righteous behavior among their overlords. Indeed, this could be seen as a peasant demonstration of their willingness to go along with orthodox thought to the extent that they believed in the conception of a "righteous order."

Peasant reference to this concept was, in some respects, at odds with the interpretations of most Confucian scholars, reflecting what Alexander Woodside has called "a kind of combative adaptiveness" on the part of the peasants in response to Confucian doctrines.[53] While scholars might acknowledge that a particular leader (or regime) was lacking righteousness, they would not necessarily (if ever) assert that peasants should be permitted to restore that righteousness. As Ralph Smith has observed,

> It might have been possible to interpret the Confucian philosophy in a spirit of rebellion, for if the personal life of the emperor or his officials was lacking in virtue and sincerity, then surely their fitness to rule was called into question. But in practice, Confucianism was essentially conservative. It was true that a ruler might lose the "Mandate of Heaven", but if he was then deposed it was less a matter of human choice than of an impersonal decree of fate.[54]

Moreover, even scholars such as Ngô Thì Nhậm, who at times viewed heaven's actions as directed by earthly events, noted that "the rise and fall, the long and the short of fate are due to heaven, they are not produced by the strength of people."[55] In other words, people could not directly change the course of heaven's intentions, though their suffering might indirectly turn the fates.

For the Vietnamese rebel seeking to depose a ruler, it was thus essential to emphasize that his successes were indications both of the changing fates and of the righteousness of his actions. To ensure that the righteousness of their mission was understood, the Tây Sơn leaders regularly used that term to describe their movement and those who participated in it. Thus, for instance, the Tây Sơn armies comprised not merely soldiers, but *nghĩa quân* (righteous troops), who were in turn commanded by *nghĩa sĩ* (righteous officers). Those who supported the movement more generally were known as *ông nghĩa* (righteous men).[56] As the Vietnamese historian Nguyễn Lương Bích has noted, "All of the Tây Sơn generals and the masses of the ordinary people at the time called those who joined the movement the '*nghĩa sĩ*' and when referring to these people never failed to include the word *nghĩa*."[57]

While most commonly used to describe individuals fighting for the Tây Sơn side, the term *nghĩa* was also used to label other elements related to the uprising. It was used, for instance, as part of the name of the two ethnic Chinese forces that fought with the Tây Sơn during the uprising's early years, the Hòa Nghĩa (Peaceful and Righteous) and the Trung Nghĩa (Loyal and Righteous) Army. *Nghĩa* was also used in a more abstract way in numerous public proclamations, which described the Tây Sơn armies as traveling under a "banner of righteousness" in their campaigns against their enemies. Notable examples are found in Nguyễn Hữu Chỉnh's 1786 appeal to the populations of Nghệ An during the Tây Sơn invasion of Đàng Ngoài and in Tây Sơn literatus Phan Huy Ích's 1800 proclamation on behalf of the Cảnh Thịnh emperor seeking to reinvigorate support for the Tây Sơn cause.[58] Finally, when Nguyễn Huệ took steps to establish a capital in the Nghệ An region after 1789, he renamed the area Nghĩa An (Righteous Peace), explicitly linking this territory to the uprising's very origins as a *khởi nghĩa* even as he sought once again to underscore the legitimacy of his claims to power.[59]

The Tây Sơn use of the term "righteousness" was clearly calculated to engage in existing rhetorical contests, for their rivals used the same term to justify their own actions in challenging the rebel armies and their leaders. The *Hoàng Lê Nhất Thống Chí* (*HLNTC*), a near contemporary chronicle of events in Đàng Ngoài, repeatedly described supporters of the Lê emperor in the north in the late 1780s as "righteous troops" and spoke of the emperor's being urged to recruit "righteous soldiers."[60] Proclamations written by the loyalist scholar Lê Huy Dao to rally supporters to the Lê restorationist cause in the 1780s and 1790s also frequently invoked the term "righteousness" to describe those who would join the struggle against the Tây Sơn.[61] Bùi Dương Lịch's early-nineteenth-century *Lê Quý Dật Sử* (Unusual Tales of the Late Lê) similarly spoke of anti–Tây Sơn movements in 1786 as being "righteous uprisings" in defense of the sitting king.[62] Clearly, the term was a contested one, and the repeated Tây Sơn deployment of it was part of an ongoing effort to win popular acceptance of their claims.

*The Tây Sơn and "Virtue"*

The Tây Sơn also stressed their possession of virtue (*đức*), another cardinal Confucian precept. While righteousness described the movement and its objectives in broad terms, the idea of virtue entailed more specifically on individual leaders. The emphasis on virtue could be linked to Tây Sơn claims of having been called by heaven, for there existed a clearly understood connection between individual virtue and the sanction of heaven. As Lê Lợi succinctly observed in the fifteenth century, "Heaven helps those with virtue."[63] Or, in O. W. Wolters' distillation of the concept, "[Virtue], in the Chinese sense of the word, meant that its possessor could exert influence over others, and its magnet-like force is illustrated in the biographies of famous local spirits."[64] As this description suggests, *đức* functioned like a form of charisma. It enabled an individual to attract a following and to bend these followers to his will.

For the Tây Sơn, being recognized as having *đức* was almost as important as actually manifesting indications thereof. Recognizing that men perceived to have virtue would be able to make political claims while at the same time linking themselves to the supernatural realms, the Tây Sơn leaders sought repeatedly to emphasize their own claims to having virtue. A Spanish missionary letter, written during the early days of the movement, noted that the rebels were popularly described as "virtuous" thieves. While the missionary was obviously translating, he was almost certainly rendering the Vietnamese term, which was commonly used in later French missionary accounts in speaking of the Tây Sơn leaders. A short while later, it is surely no accident that when Nguyễn Nhạc gave himself his first political title in 1775, he chose the name Minh Đức Chúa Công (Shining Virtue Lord). Then, in 1778, when he took the step of naming himself emperor, Nhạc selected as his reign name Thái Đức (Exalted Virtue). This use of the term *đức* as part of a reign title was not unique to Nhạc; it had been used six times by various Lê emperors (though never before the Lê period). Nonetheless, Nhạc's choice of *đức* as part of his reign title is suggestive of the particular quality that he sought to emphasize.

Beyond Nhạc's use of such titles, the Tây Sơn brothers sought other ways to underscore their claims to virtuousness. Most frequently, they attempted to popularize appellations for themselves that incorporated the word *đức*. Thus, we find numerous European eyewitnesses who regularly referred to the brothers using the term: "virtuous elder brother" (*đức anh*) for Nhạc, "virtuous younger brother" (*đức em*) for Huệ, and "virtuous sir" (*đức ông*) more generally to refer to either of them.[65] The missionaries' frequent use of these terms, which undoubtedly reflected common parlance, suggests that the Tây Sơn leaders had been highly successful in planting this term in the popular imagination. When the two Tây Sơn leaders arrived in Thăng Long in 1786, missionaries in Đàng Ngoài were already referring to them collectively as "les deux *đức ông*" and to Nguyễn Huệ as the "premier *đức ông*."[66] These terms are even found in a Cambodian historical record compiled in the 1930s, where the words *duc ong an* and *duc ong em* are used to refer to the Tây Sơn brothers. This reference, at some distance from the uprising itself, reveals just how widespread the use of these appellations had become.[67]

## SOCIAL CAPITAL AND TÂY SƠN POPULISM

While such rhetorical references, in conjunction with claims of heavenly or supernatural sanction, were a useful form of legitimation, the Tây Sơn leaders also pursued more concrete methods of gathering followers. Being from a rural area adjacent to the upland regions, the brothers were certainly aware of both lowland peasant and upland tribal grievances and of the ways in which they might (at least in a limited fashion) attempt to address these concerns. Chief among these complaints, as we have seen, were high or expanded taxation, currency problems, and the ripple effects of a decline in foreign trade. Although in the uprising's early days the Tây Sơn were not in a position to implement substantial reforms in any of these areas, they did set out to address economic injustices more generally.

One of their earliest and most important initiatives in this regard was the redistribution of wealth as they moved about the countryside with the slogan Take from the wealthy, and give to the poor.[68] According to European accounts of the period, the Tây Sơn armies appear to have focused on winning the support of rural populations through such redistribution of property.[69] The Vietnamese nineteenth-century sources, despite using less generous language, described their actions in similar terms: "At this time the rebels rose up and stole from the rich distributing their goods among the poor, and deceitfully carried out petty favors in order to buy the hearts of the people."[70] While these initiatives might be seen as a means (garnering popular support as the Nguyễn records suggest) rather than an end, the broader idea of promoting economic justice appears to have been central to the early movement. In any case, it was such actions that earned the Tây Sơn brothers the label of "charitable thieves," as well as widespread popular support.

This redistribution of wealth did not constitute a major transformation of local economic relationships, but such actions did mark the rebels as champions of the economically disadvantaged. Moreover, the idea of the redistribution of goods, and particularly of food, was not merely popular, but also supported by official sanction and historical precedent, at least in Đàng Ngoài. In times of crisis governments might send officials to make requisitions of food from wealthy inhabitants of drought- or flood-stricken regions.[71] While the effectiveness of the requisitioning was often limited, since the wealthy would frequently barricade themselves in their compounds or bribe the officials, the principle existed and was thus popularly known.[72] Trương Bửu Lâm has argued that in many instances the government could defuse local tensions and protests by making concessions or granting relief in some form. It was only when "the government did not grant relief, or because the relief came too late or too skimpily, [that] protest might linger on and develop into a force to be reckoned with nationally."[73] From this perspective, the Tây Sơn efforts to redistribute goods might have been understood as a justifiable attempt to carry out actions that the government was not undertaking for whatever reason. Indeed, the persistence and success of their uprising was as much an indictment of the state for its failure to respond to popular discontent as it was a tribute to the actions of the Tây Sơn themselves.

Although most Tây Sơn redistributive actions appear to have taken place early in the movement, several later incidents also speak to the ongoing nature of Tây Sơn attempts to use economic measures to encourage popular support. During their 1786 campaigns into Đàng Ngoài, the Tây Sơn were entering a region that had been devastated by famine for several years. Thus, when the Tây Sơn troops were able to capture the Trịnh coastal outpost at Vị Hoàng south of Thăng Long, with its important government granaries, they quickly acted to open the warehouses to distribute food among the populations of that area.[74] Later, when the Tây Sơn troops entered Thăng Long, they also opened a government storehouse there, and distributed some of the materials they found among the local inhabitants.[75] Such actions would have served both to garner goodwill and to alleviate popular concerns regarding Tây Sơn intentions during their sojourn in the north.

In addition to the seizure and redistribution of property and food supplies, once the Tây Sơn brothers captured Qui Nhơn in the fall of 1773 and effectively took control of a growing amount of coastal territory, they began to carry out other economic measures, both symbolic and substantive. The first measures centered on tax issues, with Tây Sơn leaders holding public burnings of tax registers. As a Spanish eyewitness reported,

> In the smallest hamlets, they took the official papers and burned them in a public place, especially the ancient manuscripts that fixed the tributes and the taxes imposed by the kings and their mandarins. They promulgated an edict that abolished all tributes, with the exception of the antique customs going to Tonkin, which demanded that each family holding fixed goods give a quan and a half each year. The people rejoiced at this measure and took the oath, offering their liberators infinite numbers of gifts. They placed in the cangue the soldiers and mandarins whom they captured, taking revenge on this class of society.[76]

These were acts no doubt calculated for their dramatic effect and their overt destruction of symbols of a hated government, but they were also ones that might have been read as indications of coming economic improvements. In another largely symbolic act, Nguyễn Nhạc relentlessly pursued and eventually killed two central-government tax collectors who had fled Qui Nhơn in the aftermath of the Tây Sơn attack on that provincial capital.[77] Clearly, the issue of taxation was a volatile one among the Quảng Nam populations, and one that was carefully exploited by the Tây Sơn commanders in their early campaigns.

Another area of economic concern gradually addressed by the Tây Sơn was the issue of coinage. As was noted in the previous chapter, in the middle of the century the Nguyễn court had begun to mint coins mixed with zinc to replace the older copper currency. The zinc coinage had been poorly received by the general public and appears to have contributed to the economic instability that developed in the late 1760s and early 1770s. Merchants were hoarding goods and refusing to sell them for the new coinage, while those who had the older copper coinage were reluctant to part with it. In response to this situation, the Tây Sơn began to mint new copper coinage, possibly as early as 1775, but certainly by 1778 when Nguyễn Nhạc took the title of Emperor Thái Đức.[78] The minting of new coins had a positive and concrete effect on the popular image of the Tây Sơn, for these durable coins came to replace the extremely unpopular zinc coinage.[79] Since the initial decision to shift to zinc had been prompted by a copper shortage, the only way the Tây Sơn could resolve this shortage was to melt down cultural artifacts—including ceremonial urns, drums, gongs, and bells—collected not only from the Nguyễn palaces, but also from Buddhist temples. Whatever the origins of its materials, the Tây Sơn coinage proved so popular that it remained in wide circulation well into the nineteenth century despite repeated Nguyễn attempts to suppress and replace it.[80]

In still another effort to burnish their image and bolster their popularity, the Tây Sơn brothers depicted themselves as having close connections to the ordinary people they claimed to lead. In particular, both Huệ and Nhạc represented themselves as being commoners of little wealth and without land. Specifically, they referred to themselves as people of cotton cloth (*người áo vải*)—in other words, not garbed in the finery of officialdom. Nhạc first used this term to describe himself in a memorial written to the invading Trịnh generals in 1776, which began with the phrase "I am in origin a person of cotton cloth from the area of Tây Sơn."[81] Huệ began to use the phrase in 1786, beginning with his first meetings with the Lê emperor, during which he allegedly employed exactly the same phrasing that Nhạc had earlier used.[82] Huệ then used the phrase again when writing as Emperor Quang Trung to the Qing court between 1789 and 1791.[83] Clearly, the Tây Sơn brothers' use of the term in their interactions with political superiors suggests that it was not merely directed at their potential peasant followers. Instead, it appears to have been used as a form of deference, suggesting modesty and a lack of potentially threatening ambition, but also as an indication, perhaps, of a basic purity, as such seeking to underscore the justness of their actions.

Although these references are chiefly found in communications with their political superiors, the Tây Sơn brothers' effort to propagate this image more widely appears to have succeeded, and the "cotton cloth" phrase took root in the popular imagination. Perhaps most famously, Quang Trung's young widow, the Lê princess Ngọc Hân, composed an ode to her husband on his death in 1792 in which she referred to him using the term "cotton cloth."[84] But even more tellingly, the two brothers were referred to in this manner by a Nguyễn official in 1799 as he assessed the reasons for their early success and meteoric rise:

> The brothers Nhạc and Huệ were people of cotton cloth, who did not have an inch of land to poke a stick into. Despite this, they raised their arms and voices as one, and people followed them by the tens of thousands, and it was not more than five or six years but that they had seized all of the rivers and mountains.[85]

That a Nguyễn official would thus reproduce almost verbatim the rhetoric being used by the Tây Sơn brothers themselves suggests the degree to which they had been successful in planting this notion in the popular imagination. Indeed, the image continues to have a resonance in the modern era, as the Tây Sơn brothers are still commonly referred to in Việt Nam as the *anh hùng áo vải*—the cotton cloth heroes. While on the one hand this link to the common person seems in direct contradiction to their supposed ties to the will of heaven, it is clear that they saw a dynamic that necessitated their straddling this not insuperable divide.

## ESTABLISHING POLITICAL CONNECTIONS

For all their effectiveness, supernatural manifestations, demonstrations of economic generosity, and personal prowess were insufficient fully to establish the political status of parvenus such as the Tây Sơn brothers. They had also to develop more direct connections to existing political structures, and ideally to individuals and families already holding formal power. Consequently, even as the Tây Sơn leaders used the range of legitimating techniques already described, they also sought to link themselves to the ruling powers of their time. They did so both through the establishment of formal political and military connections and through calculated attempts to marry into the families of ruling elites. In both respects, the Tây Sơn strategy was in keeping with long-standing Vietnamese patterns of political advancement. Developing connections to existing institutions, prominent political figures, and historical legacies was indispensable for enhancing one's claims to authority. Formal connections to established political authorities constituted a significant type of legitimation, even as the simultaneous formation of informal and personal links to several ruling families was also crucial to Tây Sơn success.

*The Tây Sơn and the Nguyễn (1773–1775)*

During the early years of their uprising, the Tây Sơn leaders sought to portray themselves not as a political alternative to the ruling Nguyễn family, but rather as defenders of the existing, but corrupted, order. Once they had captured the prefectural capital of Qui Nhơn, the brothers declared their support for the "legitimate ruler" of the kingdom—the young son of the previous *chúa*—an heir displaced through the machinations of Trương Phúc Loan.[86] Announcing his intention to oust both the sitting *chúa* and the corrupt regent Loan, Nguyễn Nhạc publicly observed,

> Now the evil official Trương Phúc Loan is greedily and publicly taking bribes [and] creating muddied disorder at the court. . . . The crown prince Dương, the son of the Thái-Bảo [the long-reigning *chúa*'s son] is a person of deep intelligence and we have to establish him to serve as the king in order to calm the house of the [Nguyễn] *chúa*.[87]

In other words, the "evil" regent, responsible for the political chaos that was endangering the ruling house, had to be replaced by the legitimate heir, the crown prince of "deep intelligence," and the Tây Sơn armies would be the force to effect this change.

The Tây Sơn leadership clearly recognized that slogans supporting a legitimate heir would resonate more strongly with skeptical political elites than an open challenge to the Nguyễn government. By giving their backing to the prince, the Tây Sơn leaders were also hoping to take advantage of schisms within the court that had emerged in response to the regent's actions. As Trương Bưu Lâm has pointed out,

> Loan, as regent . . . proceeded to dismantle some of the institutions and power blocks that the Nguyen had built up for almost two hundred years in the south. His actions meant that a number of scholars suddenly found themselves ejected from political power. As a consequence, the people in the south, due no doubt to these now bitter scholars, came to identify Loan with much that was amiss in the physical, social, and moral order.[88]

Among these embittered scholars was the Tây Sơn brothers' teacher, Trương Văn Hiến. Hiến's elder brother had been loyal to the late *chúa* and had been killed by Trương Phúc Loan when he resisted the regent's efforts to manipulate the succession.[89] Hiến had settled in the Qui Nhơn region, where he had opened the school attended by the Tây Sơn brothers. It is possible that Hiến, in his capacity as an informal adviser to the brothers during these early years, suggested the strategy of supporting a legitimate heir to the throne, both as a useful political gambit and as a means of gaining some measure of personal revenge against Loan.[90]

While Tây Sơn claims to be "rescuing" the king might have been most important to Confucian scholars forced to choose between "virtuous" peasant rebels and corrupt but "legitimate" dynastic kings or their attendant lords, such claims would also have been important to potential peasant supporters. Indeed, appeals for assistance in rescuing a king ultimately had to work with peasants who would constitute the bulk of the armies needed in any such effort. By portraying their movement in this manner, the Tây Sơn connected themselves to a long tradition of popular support for legitimate rulers struggling against other claimants. The Trịnh and Nguyễn clans' defense of the Lê against the Mạc fell into this tradition, as did the more recent actions of Lê family members seeking to free their emperor from domination by the Trịnh. In any case, by suggesting that they were loyalists and not rebels, the Tây Sơn hoped to gain popular support without creating ethical dilemmas for those committed to the Nguyễn seigneurial house.

The Tây Sơn efforts to associate themselves with the crown prince by claiming to be his champions soon proved successful. A popular slogan emerged at this time drawing distinctions between the competing forces: "Soldiers of the court are the soldiers of the *quốc phó*, Hissing soldiers are the soldiers of the crown prince."[91] The *quốc phó* (regent) was Trương Phúc Loan, and the phrase about "hissing soldiers" was a reference to the loud hissing sounds made by Tây Sơn armies as they moved about the countryside.[92] A similar slogan appeared around the same time, explicitly naming the political figures in question: "Attack and topple Trương Phúc Loan, aid and support crown prince Nguyễn Phúc Dương."[93] The emergence of such slogans indicates that the Tây Sơn restorationist calls resonated among the populations of Đàng Trong.

To further enhance their legitimacy as champions of the rightful Nguyễn heir, the Tây Sơn brothers took on their mother's surname, Nguyễn.[94] Their paternal surname, Hồ, while connecting them to the lineage of Hồ Quý Ly, the powerful late-fourteenth-century northern leader, had no particular resonance in the southern territories. The Nguyễn name would be far more advantageous in the course of their campaigns. Not only did this name connect them in the popular consciousness to the then ruling house, providing a cover of legitimacy, but it could also more generally be seen as auspicious. Loyalists of the ruling family were periodically granted permission to change their surname to Nguyễn as a boon from the rulers.[95] This meant that to bear the surname Nguyễn was either to be related to the royal family or to have been recognized by it for services rendered to the state. Finally, the decision to adopt the Nguyễn surname may have been calculated to connect the brothers to another contemporary prophecy: *Phù Nguyễn trì thống* (The Nguyễn clan shall protect and govern.)[96] Adopting the Nguyễn surname served to connect the Tây Sơn brothers not merely to the ruling family but, what is equally important, to this prophecy that appeared to dictate that rule should be by a Nguyễn clan.

Not satisfied with merely using the Nguyễn name, Nhạc sought to create a more direct link to the ruling family by attempting to marry one of his daughters to the young crown prince whom the Tây Sơn were championing.[97] The significance of this effort to create a marriage connection cannot be overemphasized. Since the earliest days of an independent Vietnamese state, marriage alliances had been critically important in tying together a territory divided among powerful regional lineages. From the eleventh through the late fourteenth centuries, the Lý and Trần dynasties had exercised authority over the Vietnamese realms and indeed held them together through a web of marriage linkages to largely autonomous regional families. In subsequent centuries, such alliances had continued to serve as a means to connect political families at various levels, including the Trịnh and Lê during their long political symbiosis. In a region where kinship ties determined political status and legitimacy, one of the best ways for political outsiders such as the Tây Sơn brothers to establish themselves was to marry into political prestige.[98] In this respect, their use of marriage connections was similar to that of their Nguyễn predecessors, who in the seventeenth century had developed marital ties both to rulers of adjacent kingdoms (Khmer and Cham) and to prosperous merchants as a means to reinforce their own political base.[99]

To create this marital link, however, Nhạc first had to capture the prince, who initially eluded his putative champions' efforts to track him down. Although the Tây Sơn claimed to be fighting on behalf of the crown prince, most indications are that he did not particularly welcome this assistance, and sought to maintain a safe distance from his would-be rescuers. However, after a reward was offered for his capture, the prince was finally tracked down and brought to the Tây Sơn leader at Hội An in May or June of 1775.[100] At this point, Nhạc "offered as a gift, his daughter Thọ Hương, to the Crown Prince and many times requested the Crown Prince to ascend the throne as the Lord, [but] the Crown Prince did not agree to this."[101] Most surviving evidence suggests that the prince continued to reject these overtures until he was able to flee Tây Sơn captivity in late 1776 and make his way to the Gia Định area, where Nguyễn resistance was centered. For his part, however, Nhạc believed, or wished to believe, that the marriage had been consummated, for according to the *Hoàng Lê Nhất Thống Chí*, Nhạc later presented himself to the Lê court as being a member of the (formerly ruling) Nguyễn clan by virtue of this marriage.[102]

With the crown prince's flight from Tây Sơn captivity, the usefulness of the Nguyễn connection largely evaporated. His departure left the Tây Sơn leadership with no usable remnants of the Nguyễn court, survivors of which had by now regrouped in the Gia Định region, soon to be led by another young prince, Nguyễn Ánh (a grandson of Nguyễn Phúc Khoát). Thus, in the aftermath of the crown prince's departure, the Tây Sơn abandoned any pretense of serving the Nguyễn cause, and indeed the following year rebel troops massacred virtually the entire Nguyễn family during one of their raids into Gia Định. The Tây Sơn had, in any case, continued to maintain some distance between themselves and those whose cause they were allegedly championing. As was noted earlier, the Tây Sơn had cast military seals that criticized the young Nguyễn *chúa* as a tyrant. To further extend their critique, the Tây Sơn leaders formally banned use of the character for *phúc*, which was part of the name of the regent, Trương Phúc Loan; of the recently ousted *chúa*, Nguyễn Phúc Thuần; and of the entire lineage of Nguyễn lords.[103] Their strained relationship with the young prince Dương, and awareness that their claimed support for the ruling Nguyễn clan was of only limited value, led the Tây Sơn to look for additional political connections. They did not have to look far, for a large Trịnh army had became a very immediate presence in the southern region.

### *The Tây Sơn and the Trịnh (1775–1786)*

While the Tây Sơn uprising had constituted disaster for the Nguyễn rulers, it represented a spectacular opportunity for the Trịnh lords observing events from Thăng Long. Taking advantage of the turmoil in the south, the northern *chúa* Trịnh Sâm ordered an invasion into Nguyễn territory in the summer of 1774, his declared objective being to assist the Nguyễn in their battles against the Tây Sơn.[104] Sâm mobilized an army of thirty thousand, which he rapidly marched toward the south. Trịnh forces entered the famine-weakened Nguyễn territory of Thuận Hóa in late 1774, and early the following year entered Phú Xuân, a city in considerable internal turmoil, with some officials actively assisting the Trịnh invasion.[105] Having taken the Nguyễn capital without difficulty, the Trịnh continued their advance southward, crossing the Hải Vân pass and pushing deep into Quảng Nam.

While their early advance met little resistance from the Nguyễn, and while they initially scored some important victories over the Tây Sơn, the Trịnh soon ran into trouble. Their troops were ill-prepared for the geography and climate in the south, and they found their supply lines stretched beyond sustainable limits. These problems were compounded by an epidemic that swept through the Trịnh army, and although it initially felled rank-and-file troops (killing six hundred and infecting another three thousand), it soon came to drastically reduce the Trịnh military leadership as well. In the short period between January and March 1775, three of the key Trịnh generals died.[106]

Although it had run into difficulties, the Trịnh advance of late 1774 and early 1775 represented a major threat to the Tây Sơn position, which was already imperiled by a Nguyễn counterattack developing to the south. Caught between two military forces, and without sufficient resources to fight on two fronts, Nguyễn Nhạc pragmatically offered to surrender to the Trịnh in late spring of 1775. As Nhạc characterized it in a later message to the Trịnh, "I heard that the great army was coming to attack and to reconquer its former territory. I immediately thought to myself: I am in the land of the king and I am a subject of the king, and I will bring my heart to request to follow his commands."[107] Given their own strained circumstances, the Trịnh leaders readily agreed to the Tây Sơn surrender offer, and named the Tây Sơn brothers as generals in the Trịnh army. Now the eldest Tây Sơn brother, whom the Trịnh had earlier scornfully derided as "that crazy biện Nhạc," was being referred to as "general" with the grand title of Tây Sơn Hiệu Trưởng Tráng Tiết Tướng Quân (Tây Sơn Firmly Regulating Strong and Temperate Troop General).[108] Initially, the Trịnh had granted a title only to Nhạc, but he pressed them further, and they agreed to bestow a similar title on his younger brother, naming Huệ the Tây Sơn Hiệu Tiền Phong Tướng Quân (Tây Sơn Firm Vanguard Troop General). Consequently, even as Nhạc was ostensibly still acting as an agent for the Nguyễn prince, he was a general in the Trịnh army whose mission was to topple that very Nguyễn regime.

The Trịnh bestowed not only military titles, but also highly symbolic

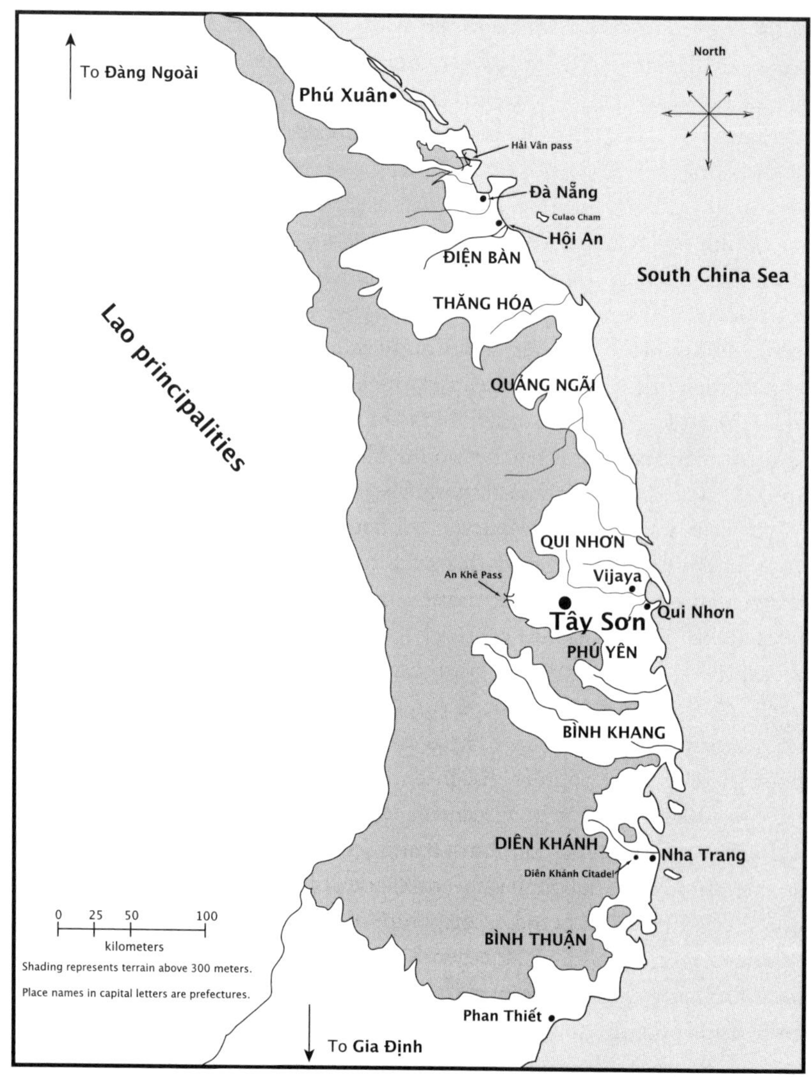


FIGURE 5. *Map of central Đáng Trong. Map shows key sites associated with the uprising. Prefectural names are given with their general geographical distribution as borders are uncertain.*

material rewards on their new Tây Sơn allies. These objects, representing emblems of both political and military power, included swords, military garb, banners, and official seals.[109] Such items held enormous political significance and were of greater value than the titles alone, which were easily claimed, but less easily substantiated. With possession of these objects reflecting their new rank and affiliation, it would have been easier for the Tây Sơn to make their claims to power. Most potent among these objects would have been the seal, the official emblem of political or military office. These were used in Việt Nam, as in China, to validate official documents, but even more important to serve as symbols of power and position. Possession of such a seal was the ultimate indication of one's authority. As was noted above, a missionary reported in 1776 that because Nhạc did not have a royal seal in his possession, the popular view was that he did not have the favor of heaven. The importance of the seal is also demonstrated in an episode involving a Nguyễn loyalist who later journeyed to the Tây Sơn capital as a translator for a 1778 English mission led by Charles Chapman:

> Our poor unfortunate Mandarine, who was now on board incog., and the better to conceal himself dressed in an English dress, his beard shaved, his teeth cleaned and, what distressed him most of all, his nails reduced to three or four inches, desiring to see the paper [an imperial order from Nhạc to Chapman] told me with tears in his eyes that the seal affixed was the ancient seal of the Kings of Cochin China, which the villainous possessor had stolen.[110]

Indeed, the importance of seals within the realm of Vietnamese political symbols is suggested by the fact that theft of a mandarin's seal was punishable by decapitation, as was the crime of forging a seal.[111]

The Tây Sơn leaders clearly understood the value of the items given them by the Trịnh and went out of their way to secure as many as their benefactors were willing to grant. Nhạc repeatedly sent gift-bearing envoys to his northern patrons offering valuable products reflecting the wealth and natural resources of the south: horses, elephants, precious eaglewood, jade, and gold.[112] These missions eventually became so persistent that the Trịnh began to refuse some of the Tây Sơn offerings.[113] Among these gift-bearing missions was one in which Nguyễn Nhạc formally offered the Trịnh lords control of the three prefectures then under his authority: Quảng Ngãi, Qui Nhơn, and Phú Yên. Since these prefectures lay in the areas south of Hải Vân, from which the Trịnh forces had already retreated, the offer was made with the full knowledge that this gift would also not be accepted. Or rather, the Tây Sơn leader was confident that even if the Trịnh accepted this gift, they would do so only in ceremonial fashion, allowing Nhạc to continue to exercise direct control over the territories, which in fact proved to be the case.

Armed with new titles and numerous objects of symbolic weight, the Tây Sơn brothers turned their attention to attacking the Nguyễn in the south, for they were now officers in the Trịnh army, ostensibly serving as the vanguard of the northern armies.[114] No longer threatened by the Trịnh to their north, the Tây Sơn forces were able to mount an effective counterattack against the Nguyễn and to push the conflict farther to the south. Yet even as his troops fought the Nguyễn, Nhạc continued to harbor further political ambitions that he hoped his Trịnh patrons could fulfill. Consequently, in early 1777 Nhạc requested that the Trịnh recognize his political authority over (as opposed to mere military responsibility for) the territories south of Phú Xuân. The Trịnh, whose authority over this region was purely nominal, readily granted his request. They appointed Nhạc as the governor-general (*trấn thủ*) of Quảng Nam and also enfeoffed him as a commandary duke (*quận công*), the third-highest of the traditional ducal titles. Not coincidentally, this was the same title that had been carried by Nguyễn Hoàng, the founder of the Nguyễn polity in Đàng Trong, suggesting that the Trịnh viewed Nhạc in similar terms.[115] These additional titles in hand, Nhạc was now a Trịnh noble and political official.

After this further set of promotions, interactions between Nhạc (and the Tây Sơn more generally) and his northern patrons appear largely to have been suspended. The Vietnamese historical record is virtually silent on contact between 1777 and 1786, and perhaps given the circumstances this is not surprising. The period saw the Tây Sơn leadership involved in an intensifying struggle with their Nguyễn foes in the south, and they had little opportunity, and not much need, for further interactions with the Trịnh. When the two sides encountered one another again it would be in the course of the massive 1786 Tây Sơn attack on their erstwhile political and military superiors.

### *The Tây Sơn and Local Political Connections: Uplanders and Chams*

In addition to their early efforts to connect themselves to the distant (if more powerful) political centers at Thăng Long and Phú Xuân, the Tây Sơn also established links to local political forces and institutions. One of the most significant aspects of the Tây Sơn uprising was its connection to various non-Vietnamese ethnic groups, including both highland dwellers and residents of the coastal plains. Through his trading connections, Nguyễn Nhạc had already established valuable relationships with the highland ethnic groups, including most notably the Bahnar. Some accounts report that Nhạc took a Bahnar woman as a wife, something that seems borne out in later European documentation, which noted that his wife and some children appeared to be from upland groups.[116] Bahnar groups, among others, offered soldiers, supplies, and protection during the early years of the movement when it was most vulnerable to attack and extermination by Nguyễn forces. The Bahnar involvement in particular may have been a continuation of their support for anti-Nguyễn actions in the 1750s and 1760s.[117] Such groups continued to offer some support to the Tây Sơn, though as will be seen in chapter 4, others also chose to side with their Nguyễn rivals.[118]

While political and personal connections developed in the uplands were clearly important, particularly in the movement's early stages, as the Tây Sơn spread into the coastal plains they came increasingly to rely on lowland political institutions, most notably those of the Chams. The region in which the Tây Sơn brothers rose up was the center of what had once been the mighty kingdom of Champa. Forebears of the eighteenth-century Chams had once controlled most of the central region of what is today Việt Nam, with their power periodically extending north toward Thăng Long and south and west toward Angkor. Champa had been a formidable political and military force rivaling the early Vietnamese state but had suffered increasing territorial losses and political decline at the hands of the Vietnamese beginning in the fifteenth century. During the sixteenth and seventeenth centuries, the Cham political entities and populations had borne the brunt of the Nguyễn southward expansion, and by the Tây Sơn period the Cham polity had been drastically reduced in size and influence. Nonetheless, Champa continued to retain a degree of political autonomy, and the landscape was still dotted with Cham temples and citadel walls, reminders of the power once wielded by Cham rulers. Because of this continuing Cham presence, the region was commonly referred to as *xứ Chiêm* (the Cham territory) or simply Cham by European visitors.[119]

Given what they had suffered at the hands of the Nguyễn, it is perhaps not surprising that the Chams would be ready to ally themselves with the Tây Sơn. Among the earliest supporters of the Tây Sơn movement were a Cham princess, Thị Hỏa, and her entourage. The Tây Sơn did not look to the Chams merely for physical support, though they certainly enrolled Chams in their armies, but also for less tangible, though equally important, political symbols. According to nineteenth-century Nguyễn court historians, Cham leaders presented numerous symbolic items to the rebel leaders: "The Cham *Chưởng Cơ* of the Cham principality of Thuận Thành [a tributary of the Nguyễn court], joined the Tây Sơn and brought with him all of the court regalia to present it to them."[120] In effect, such an act would appear to have constituted a transfer of Cham political hopes to the Tây Sơn. Perhaps the Cham ruler reasoned that the Tây Sơn might assist them in preserving their remaining autonomy or might at least permit them to exact a measure of revenge on the Nguyễn. As with the ceremonial objects presented by the Trịnh, the Cham imperial artifacts provided further ritual and material support for the Tây Sơn in their continuing effort at political legitimation.

A very different and perhaps more plausible account of the regalia transfer is contained in a letter written by a French missionary, Jean-Pierre-Joseph D'Arcet, the only Frenchman living in Tây Sơn–controlled territory between the mid-1770s and 1786:

> The other day, having retreated from his war in Đồng Nài, [Nhạc] visited a small king who was along his route between the two kingdoms. He found no one at this court but a young man of ten to twelve, who had been placed on the throne. He [Nhạc] declared himself [to be] the young man's father and elder brother, and demanded to be shown the most precious objects in the court. Among the other things he was shown, was a golden scepter admirably crafted using 14 horns to mark all of the generations of the father and sons since the founding of the kingdom. He took this admirable work and said to his pupil: "I will return it to you." [The prince] had to accept the compliment and allow the pillaging of his court by this charitable and compassionate tutor. The poor pupil now finds himself well content to remain still alive.[121]

This account indicates that the Tây Sơn seized the Cham regalia, rather than having it gifted to them, and as such suggests less about Cham aspirations than it does about possible Tây Sơn motivations. Whether the Cham regalia was offered or seized, it ended up in the hands of the Tây Sơn leadership, which no doubt used it to great effect. Such items held a powerful mystical significance whose resonance would have lent considerable weight to Tây Sơn political and ritual claims.

Perhaps the most symbolically significant Tây Sơn connection to the

Chams lay in Nguyễn Nhạc's selecting the ancient Cham capital of Vijaya to serve as his imperial capital. Known in Vietnamese as Chà Bàn (or Đồ Bàn), this citadel was slightly inland from the port city of Qui Nhơn and had fallen into disrepair over the centuries. Nguyễn Nhạc made a considerable effort to restore it, reinforcing its walls and reconstructing some of the interior palaces.[122] The Englishman Charles Chapman visited the city in 1778 and left a useful contemporary description (see below). Chà Bàn was to serve as Nhạc's capital from 1776 until his death in 1793, at which point his nephew and successor continued to use the city as a political center. Although there is no explicit evidence that the Tây Sơn selected this site because it was a former Cham capital, it is almost certain that this was an important part of Nhạc's calculus. One source, the *Nguyễn Thị Tây Sơn Ký*, does note that the site was selected for its good omens, and it was, in any case, usefully sited and relatively easily defended.[123]

The Tây Sơn–Cham connection was established in the first few years of the Tây Sơn uprising, and was a valuable one. The Cham state, after all, remained an alternative site of political power. From this site, the Tây Sơn could contest for authority with the Nguyễn, not as the direct successors of that ruling clan, but as successors to the Cham political tradition. It is perhaps not entirely an accident that when Nguyễn Huệ arrived in Thăng Long in 1786, some northerners referred to him by the name Chế Bồng Nga, recalling the powerful fourteenth-century Cham ruler who had similarly sacked the capital of Đại Việt.[124] And it is symbolically significant that like Chế Bồng Nga, Nguyễn Huệ was given, as we shall see, an imperial princess in marriage as a gesture designed both to appease the southern warrior and to connect the northern and southern political realms. While the Cham empire, which may have reached its height under the rule of Chế Bồng Nga, was by the late eighteenth century politically insignificant to the point of being virtually nonexistent, to northerners, far removed from that part of Đại Việt, the Cham might as well have remained a vital political and military force.

## BECOMING LORDS, KINGS, AND EMPERORS: THE TÂY SƠN LAY CLAIM TO POWER

Despite making important connections to existing political forces, the Tây Sơn had their own political ambitions and did not embrace the Nguyễn, Trịnh, or Cham causes unreservedly. Thus, even as they depicted themselves as defenders of the Nguyễn house, the rebel armies destroyed the sacred objects of the Nguyễn court, most notably setting ablaze the nine ancestral temples (of the Nguyễn lords beginning with Nguyễn Hoàng) in the capital city of Quảng Nam province in mid-1774.[125] While it is unclear whether this was a calculated act of political retribution or merely the uncontrolled destruction of a military campaign, it highlights the tension that already existed in the Tây Sơn relationship with their putative allies. The following year, Nhạc gave the first indication of his own (perhaps newly developed) political ambitions. This took the form of his establishing an official Tây Sơn government, which mimicked in titles, if perhaps not in functions, the major elements of an imperial administration. Most significant, Nhạc named himself the Minh Đức Chúa Công (Shining Virtue Lord)—effectively taking on the position once held by the Nguyễn lords—and then bestowed titles on his brothers.[126] He also organized, at least nominally, six administrative "boards," the ministries that handled the principal aspects of traditional Vietnamese governments: Public Works, Interior, Rites, Military, Justice, and Finance, and appointed officials to them.[127] As the *Bình Nam Thực Lục* described it, he "established positions according to the system of the Nguyễn family."[128] This act would seem a clear indication that the Tây Sơn were well on their way to dispensing with a Nguyễn figurehead, even as (at this time) they continued to hold the recalcitrant Prince Dương as a political hostage.

In 1776, to the annoyance of their Trịnh patrons, the rebel leaders pushed their political independence with Nhạc taking for himself the imperial title of Thiên Vương (Heavenly King).[129] Li Tana points out that this was the title the Nguyễn *chúa*s had used in their interactions with indigenous populations in this region.[130] This appears to have been an effort to claim an indigenized political title as part of Nhạc's attempt to further consolidate his standing among local populations. It was also at this time that he formally established his royal capital at Vijaya, cast a golden seal (as we have already seen, a very powerful symbol of authority), created new political divisions in Qui Nhơn, and announced a conscription requiring one out of every five villagers to report for military service.[131]

Nhạc's political aspirations were not yet satisfied however, for two years later in 1778 he lay claim to the pinnacle of political authority, naming himself emperor (*hoàng đế*), and inaugurating the first year of the Thái Đức reign.[132] This was symbolically an extremely important step, for in adopting a new reign name, Nhạc had made a complete break with the Lê imperial order, a step that even after nearly two hundred years the Nguyễn had been unwilling to take.[133] In the traditional Vietnamese political system, reign titles were used to date events, serving as a chronological touchstone. The Nguyễn use of the Lê imperial reign eras in their calendars and other documents had constituted their ongoing acknowledgment of Lê suzerainty.[134] For Nhạc, lacking the vested interest that the Nguyễn had in perpetuating the idea of Lê authority over the southern region, this step was probably seen as a logical personal claim rather than as a profound political challenge to the Lê rulers. Through his adoption of a new reign title, Nhạc was declaring the establishment of an independent southern state, rather than challenging the Lê emperor's claims to authority over all of Đại Việt. The documentary evidence on this point is sketchy, though it is likely that Nhạc was making claims only to former Nguyễn domains. When detailing his plans for further territorial conquests to the British envoy Charles Chapman in the same year, Nhạc spoke only of conquering the former Nguyễn territories at that time under Trịnh control, making no mention of challenging Lê authority north of the Gianh River.[135]

That Nguyễn Nhạc strove to mimic the finery of imperial courts is evidenced in Chapman's account of his visit, in July of 1778, to the Tây Sơn court at the former Cham citadel. As Chapman noted,

> Upon the whole, the appearance was a fine one, and, altho' the scene wanted some of the requisites which constitute grandeur and magnificence amongst other Eastern Princes, as a profusion of jewels, carpets, attendants &c, the regularity and decorum observed here presented one with some adequate ideas of a powerful sovereign surrounded by his Court.[136]

Chapman also reported of Nhạc's appearance that

> the King was clothed in a robe of silk of a deep yellow upon which dragons and other figures were wrought in gold; upon his head he wore a kind of close cap turned up behind, the front ornamented with some jewels and on the top of it was a large red stone through which passed a wire raising it a few inches. It shook and sparkled as he moved himself.[137]

It is possible that Chapman was visiting Nguyễn Nhạc shortly after Nhạc's enthronement as Emperor Thái Đức. While the Vietnamese sources on this point are ambiguous, the *Nguyễn Thị Tây Sơn Ký* notes that "in the spring, the first month of the year *mậu tuất* [1778], our [Nguyễn] troops advanced to attack Sài Gòn, and the group of the *Tổng đốc* Nhung were defeated and fled. *At that time*, Nhạc established himself as the Minh Đức emperor."[138] The rest of the description, including the ritual prostrations performed by the mandarins to Nhạc, suggest that his status by this time was already that of emperor, rather than mere king (*vương*).

With Nhạc's naming himself emperor, the Tây Sơn had cut their putative political and military alliances with the Nguyễn and the Trịnh as they staked out an autonomous political authority. For the next eight years this political situation held in Tây Sơn–controlled territory, even as military conflicts with the Nguyễn continued in the south. Thereafter, however, the situation changed dramatically, profoundly shaping the course of the movement and dividing its leaders.

## THE LIMITS OF COHESION: TÂY SƠN POLITICAL DIVISION

As late as 1785 the Tây Sơn leaders had continued to develop their political claims and legitimacy within the context of the former Nguyễn-held territories to the south of the Hải Vân pass. By the following year, however, circumstances had altered, and 1786 marked a watershed for the Tây Sơn movement as underlying tensions within its leadership surfaced in dramatic fashion. The source of these changes was the long-deferred expansion of Tây Sơn military and political influence into Đàng Ngoài, highlighted by Nguyễn Huệ's seizure first of Phú Xuân and then of the northern capital of Thăng Long in a lightning campaign. In essence the movement divided in the summer of 1786, and the dividing line was drawn between the more cautious and perhaps less ambitious Nhạc and his dynamic, military genius younger brother, Huệ.

Prior to this point the Tây Sơn brothers had fought together as part of what appears to have been a relatively cohesive leadership, under the ultimate control of Nguyễn Nhạc. There is, unfortunately, little information on the inner dynamics of the Tây Sơn leadership during the period between 1775 and 1786, so it is difficult to determine the nature and extent of any preexisting tensions between the brothers. One account in a missionary letter, describing the two brothers at odds over the treatment of Christians in 1784, suggests that tensions did exist. In this episode, Huệ is said to have forcefully attacked his brother's policy of cracking down on

Christians, arguing that it was too divisive at a time when they needed social unity in the ongoing struggle against the Nguyễn. The letter describes considerable anger on the part of Huệ and a reluctant acquiescence to his younger brother's arguments on the part of Nhạc.[139] Other than this, we can only speculate that whatever tension might have existed between the two was mitigated by regular military campaigns, which kept the brothers frequently apart and busy in the south. At the same time, as Huệ achieved repeated victories in the south while his brother remained largely immobile at Chà Bàn, the younger brother may have begun to develop political ambitions of his own. In any case, their relationship changed in 1786 with the campaign to recover Thuận Hóa from the Trịnh.

*The Tây Sơn Move North*

Several factors made 1786 a propitious time in which to attack the Trịnh. Of paramount importance was the decisive Tây Sơn defeat of a joint Nguyễn-Siamese force in the Mekong Delta region in late 1785. This crushing blow forced Nguyễn Ánh and his supporters into exile in Siam, where they would remain until 1787. With the Nguyễn out of the way and the southern region seemingly firmly under their control, the Tây Sơn brothers could finally look to the north. Nhạc hoped to recapture the territory that the Trịnh had seized from the Nguyễn during their 1774–1775 campaign, an ambition he had nurtured since at least 1778.[140] Secondly, Đàng Ngoài had been devastated by an extended famine that had wreaked havoc in the region and had become particularly intense in early 1786. Finally, Nhạc had the advice and expertise of a northern defector, Nguyễn Hữu Chỉnh, who had joined the southern force in 1782. Chỉnh had fled Đàng Ngoài after finding himself on the losing side in the coup following Trịnh Sâm's death.[141] Chỉnh's connections to the north had persisted even after his departure. In the spring of 1786 he was visited by an acquaintance, a Trịnh emissary who had been sent to discuss border issues with the Tây Sơn leaders. The envoy provided Chỉnh with details of the northern famine and openly encouraged his friend to organize an attack, reflecting considerable discontent with Trịnh administration and the enormous hardships that had befallen the northern realm.[142] Chỉnh's detailed knowledge of the situation in his home region thus gave the Tây Sơn information they needed to prepare and advance their attack.

Encouraged by Chỉnh's assessment that the time was ripe for an attack, Nhạc dispatched the northerner and Nguyễn Huệ to seize the

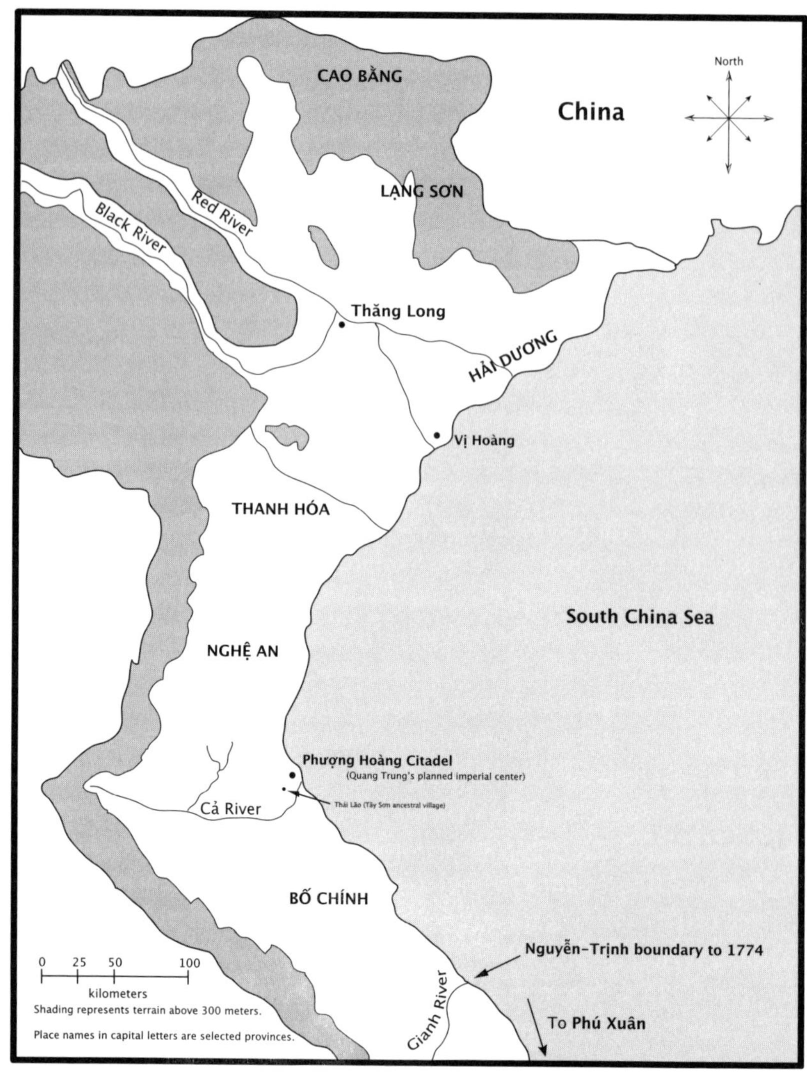


FIGURE 6. *Map of Đàng Ngoài. Map shows key sites associated with the Tây Sơn involvement in the northern region. Provincial names are given with their general geographic distribution.*

Trịnh-occupied territories as far north as the Gianh River. Already weakened by the famine, the strength of the region's defenders had been further sapped by having just observed a one-week period of fasting ordered by the local governor as part of a healing ritual.[143] A brief assault on the city of Phú Xuân overcame its defenders, and most of the Trịnh army garrisoned there was killed by the Tây Sơn force. Sources reported that the battle had amounted to a massacre with virtually none of the city's defenders left alive.[144] The governor-general was also killed in this attack. Having dispatched the primary Trịnh defenses at Phú Xuân, the southern army was quickly able to advance northward toward the Gianh River.

Rather than halting his campaign at this river, which had long served as a boundary between the Nguyễn and Trịnh, Huệ decided to exceed his brother's instructions and to extend his campaign across the river and toward the northern capital of Thăng Long. Many Vietnamese historians have credited Nguyễn Huệ with the decision to seize Đàng Ngoài in the 1786 campaigns instead of stopping at the Gianh River. Some have cited what they see as Huệ's desire to unify the country, while more cynical analysts have chosen to interpret his decision as reflecting merely a personal sense of adventure.[145] In fact, virtually all contemporary sources, both Vietnamese and European, suggest that the impetus to expand the campaign came not from Huệ, but rather from Nguyễn Hữu Chỉnh.[146] The *Hoàng Lê Nhất Thống Chí*, among the most important sources for this period, recounts an extended conversation between the two, in which Chỉnh urged Huệ to seize the opportunity to extend his offensive toward Thăng Long, noting that there were no men of great strength or intelligence in the north that might organize a resistance.[147] Although Chỉnh argued that restoration of the Lê should serve as the official justification for this venture, it is clear that his eagerness to go north was fueled by a combination of personal ambition and a desire for revenge against the Trịnh who had forced him into exile.

Based on Chỉnh's recommendation, the Tây Sơn armies carried banners emblazoned with the phrase Destroy the Trịnh, aid the Lê, suggesting that theirs was a campaign to liberate the Lê rulers.[148] Thus, as with the earlier campaigns during which they had fought in the name of the "true" Nguyễn heir, the Tây Sơn advance on Thăng Long took place under the banner of the Lê. They were not rebels, but restorationist forces coming to "aid the king." But even as the Tây Sơn were using the Lê name in this manner, there are some indications that they may also at this time have revived their use of the Nguyễn name, claiming to be *the*

Nguyễn, coming to liberate the north from the Trịnh and to assist the Lê. The *Sử Ký Đại Nam Việt Quốc Triều* (Historical Records of the National Court of the Great Southern Việt), an undated (but certainly nineteenth-century) work, reports this deception in some detail:

> First of all they sent out a letter telling the people that "the Nguyễn House has already defeated the Tây Sơn soldiers, and has also taken and pacified all the areas of Đàng Trong; now we are entering Đàng Ngoài, first, to rescue the people and to destroy the Trịnh family, because in the past they have made great difficulties for the people; second, to help rescue the Lê family; and third, because formerly the Nguyễn family acted as *chúa* governing all of the regions of Đàng Ngoài and assisted the Lê house, and thus we wish once again to take up that position." Thus some of the soldiers carried banners on which was written "The Nguyễn court undertakes to destroy the Trịnh and assist the Lê."[149]

This passage suggests that in 1786 the Tây Sơn once again emphasized their supposed connections to the Nguyễn, viewing these as having considerable political capital in the north. Moreover, a French missionary reported that during the Tây Sơn campaigns word was spread of the Nguyễn *chúa*'s imminent arrival, making the assumption that the Tây Sơn armies were those of the anticipated Nguyễn lord a natural one.[150] In all likelihood, the Tây Sơn leaders were seeking to encourage the belief that they were themselves the formerly ruling Nguyễn coming to rescue the Lê. Although northern populations might have been expected to hold some antipathy toward the Nguyễn *chuá*s, it makes sense to think that they would have been more likely to welcome them than the perceived peasant rebels represented by the Tây Sơn.

Whatever the guise in which he advanced on the north, Nguyễn Huệ led his armies on a highly effective campaign that lasted only a few weeks. The Tây Sơn force once again encountered only light Trịnh resistance, the famine coupled with political infighting at the capital having reduced the northern regime's capacity to mount a coordinated defense. Consequently, the southern armies entered Thăng Long on July 21, 1786, without any resistance, the Trịnh *chúa* having already fled the city. Once in the imperial capital, Nguyễn Huệ followed through on his promise to restore the Lê rulers. He arranged for an imperial audience in which he made a great show of returning the reins of power to the Lê emperor, Cảnh Hưng. In return the emperor bestowed titles on the Tây Sơn commander, including the lofty Đại Nguyên Soái Uy Quốc Công (Generalissimo and Mighty

Grand Duke). The granting of the title Đại Nguyên Soái is particularly significant because it was precisely this title that the Trịnh rulers had held, and so by implication Nguyễn Huệ was viewed by the Lê as having supplanted the Trịnh. In all likelihood the Lê ruler saw the Tây Sơn offer of political autonomy as a ruse, and assumed that the status quo ante would resume, only with the Tây Sơn now playing the part of the ousted Trịnh.

Despite the welcome he had received from the Lê emperor and the titles he had been granted, Nguyễn Huệ was apparently not content, and even somewhat insulted by his reception. He reportedly complained of this to his confidant Chỉnh:

> I have brought tens of thousands of troops, fought a single battle and pacified the region north of the river. As for any inch of land or any person here they are all mine; if I wish to establish myself as emperor or king, there is nothing that would prevent this. And as for the decree naming me as a generalissimo and grand duke, does this really matter to me? Is this an attempt by the northerners to use heroic titles in order to corrupt me? Do they think that I am a barbarian who on receiving these titles of enfeoffment will immediately take them to serve as sufficient honor and glory![151]

Unsatisfied with these titles and accolades, the Tây Sơn leader sought a more substantive reward. Specifically, he requested the hand of one of the imperial princesses in marriage.[152] In no position to refuse, the Lê emperor offered Nguyễn Huệ his favorite daughter, Princess Ngọc Hân.

Like the granting of the title generalissimo, the Lê ruler's marital offer continued a pattern that had been established during the long symbiotic relationship between the Lê and the Trịnh, namely the marriage of royal princesses to members of the Trịnh family. The Trịnh lords had periodically married Lê princesses to renew and deepen their relationship to the imperial house. By marrying into the Lê royal family the Tây Sơn brothers were emulating the Trịnh whom they had displaced and further extending their connections to the ruling political powers. First it had been Nguyễn Nhạc attempting to force a marriage between his daughter and the young Nguyễn heir to the throne, and now his younger brother was following a similar course, though under somewhat different circumstances. By concluding this marital alliance with the Lê, the Tây Sơn brothers had, in a little more than ten years, created or attempted to create political or familial connections to all of the ruling powers of the period and even, in the case of the Chams, marginalized local powers. Moreover, the marriage alliance between Nguyễn Huệ and Ngọc Hân is reminiscent, as was noted earlier, of the fourteenth-century marriage between the Cham ruler Chế Bồng Nga and another Vietnamese princess. Once again, a southern political-military figure came from a base in the Cham territories and was appeased by the offering of a royal princess in marriage.

Having married into the northern royal family, Nguyễn Huệ soon found himself embroiled in court politics when the elderly Lê emperor died just a few days after his audience with the Tây Sơn leader. There was some debate within the court as to which Lê relative should inherit the throne, as there was no direct male heir. Nguyễn Huệ was directly involved in the discussions about who could best succeed the Cảnh Hưng emperor and eventually settled on the emperor's nephew, Lê Mẫn Đế, who came to rule under the reign name Chiêu Thống. Although this nephew had been the leading candidate, he was also quite young and not much more politically savvy than his predecessor, leaving him vulnerable to the manipulations of more powerful political figures. It would be fewer than six months before he found himself at the mercy of surviving members of the Trịnh family.

### *A Falling Out: Division in the Tây Sơn Ranks*

With the Lê restoration and then succession settled, it would appear that Nguyễn Huệ had firmly consolidated Tây Sơn authority over territory now stretching from Hà Tiên in the Gulf of Siam to the Chinese border. Instead, his actions in the north marked the onset of open political discord within the Tây Sơn ranks. Two factors contributed to this rift. The first was Nguyễn Huệ's overt challenge to his brother's political authority. While this was not the first time that Huệ had challenged Nhạc's decisions, it was the most blatant violation of the authority emanating from Qui Nhơn. Although Huệ had sent a letter informing his brother of his intentions to press ahead with the campaign and attack Thăng Long, he had not waited for a reply before commencing his attack.[153]

The second factor contributing to the tension emerging between the brothers was simply that the territory under Tây Sơn influence had more than doubled virtually overnight. In thus becoming the largest stretch of Vietnamese lands ever controlled by a single political authority, it also became that much more difficult to govern. While Huệ had formally transferred authority in the north to the Lê, he continued to maintain an active interest in that region's affairs, particularly in the important area of Nghệ

An, which Huệ had taken from the Lê court and placed under his own authority. As a consequence of Huệ's attack on Đàng Ngoài, Tây Sơn political might had been stretched thin, particularly considering the relative remoteness of Qui Nhơn from territories north of the Hải Vân pass.

Nhạc responded to this series of events in two ways. First, after receiving Huệ's letter in the middle of August, Nhạc immediately gathered a small army and raced northward to bring his brother home. After spending only four days in the north, during which he conducted his own audience with the new Lê emperor, Nhạc took his brother and their combined armies and headed south in late August. They left Chỉnh behind ostensibly to represent their interests in Nghệ An, though there was considerable contemporary speculation that he was simply being abandoned by his one-time allies.[154] Secondly, in response to the dramatic expansion of Tây Sơn territorial control—and perhaps also to clarify his relationships with his brothers—Nhạc divided the territories among them. As noted earlier, he named Nguyễn Huệ as Northern Pacification King and placed him in control of Thuận Hóa, the territory that Huệ had just recaptured from the Trịnh, and Nghệ An, which he had taken from the Lê. Nhạc himself remained Emperor Thái Đức, though now with the added designation Trung Ương Hoàng Đế (Central Emperor), asserting immediate control over all of Quảng Nam, with the exception of the Gia Định region. That key southern area he granted to his other brother, Nguyễn Văn Lữ, as Eastern Stabilization King. The sequence of events that began in 1786 was thus one that brought the Vietnamese territories toward a state of heightened political disunion (greater even than that which had existed during the Trịnh-Nguyễn schism).

The subsequent political relationships among these three rulers is not clear from the existing sources. There was now technically only one emperor for all territory south of the Nghệ An border, Nguyễn Nhạc. We also know from official documents composed during this period by Nguyễn Huệ that he continued to acknowledge his brother's reign as the Thái Đức emperor.[155] It appears that the political relationship between the brothers was similar to that which had existed under the Lê in their dealings with the Trịnh. The Lê emperor had been the titular imperial authority, with the title of *hoàng đế*, while the Trịnh lords had also been titled kings. Whatever the precise nature of the relationship that existed between the three brothers, the reality is that there were now three high-ranking political figures controlling territory encompassing most of Đại Việt.

The division of political responsibility could not, however, suppress the growing animosity between the brothers, and in early 1787 Huệ and Nhạc became embroiled in a civil war. Some accounts suggest that Huệ was angered at not having received a suitable share of the plunder from the campaigns to the north.[156] Others indicate that Huệ was outraged by his brother's sleeping with one of Huệ's wives. In any event, war broke out between the two, culminating in Huệ gathering an army of more than eighty thousand soldiers and laying siege to Chà Bàn. After enduring a three-month siege, Nhạc was finally forced to surrender to his younger brother.[157] The terms of the surrender further complicated the territorial divisions among the Tây Sơn leaders, as Nhạc ceded two northern districts of Quảng Nam to Huệ. This created a geographically awkward configuration in which Huệ's territories straddled the Hải Vân pass, which had long served as a natural geographical dividing line. On the other hand, it provided Huệ with control that extended into the vital Quảng Nam region and potential access to regions farther south.

The discord between the brothers continued in more subtle ways after this open conflict was resolved, and manifested itself in Nguyễn Huệ's ongoing efforts to ensure his authority over the northern territories. While Huệ had been pulled back to the south by Nhạc in the late summer of 1786 and had established himself at Phú Xuân, Nguyễn Hữu Chỉnh had been abandoned in the north and had decided to remain in Nghệ An, ostensibly to protect Tây Sơn interests there. Thus, when a Trịnh survivor attempted to reestablish his family's political dominance late in 1786, it was the nearby Chỉnh whom the Lê emperor summoned to help fend off this challenge. Once back in the north, Chỉnh began to assert authority over the Lê ruler, directly impinging on Huệ's own political claims. Chỉnh had already been suspect in Huệ's eyes because of his considerable stature and influence in Đàng Ngoài.[158] Perhaps just as significantly, Chỉnh was viewed by Huệ as a close ally of Nhạc, for it was Nhạc who had developed a strong relationship with the Trịnh defector between 1782 and 1786. In this light, Huệ's decision to remove Chỉnh from power in the summer of 1787 can be viewed as an indirect attempt to reduce Nhạc's influence in the north.[159] Huệ's armies entered the north again in pursuit of Chỉnh; they eventually captured and beheaded him late in 1787, even as the Lê emperor who had relied on Chỉnh's assistance fled the capital and went into hiding.

To supervise the now leaderless north, Chỉnh was replaced as the Tây Sơn lieutenant in that region by Võ Văn Nhậm, who was Nhạc's brother-in-law and a high-ranking general in the Tây Sơn armies. Upon his arrival in Thăng Long, Nhậm had to contend with a deteriorating political situation as elements of the Lê and Trịnh regimes were still seeking to organize armies to retake the capital. Nhậm's heavy-handed exercise of political power in the north provoked widespread popular discontent, word of which reached Nguyễn Huệ in Phú Xuân.[160] Huệ quickly decided to act, partly to quell a source of popular unhappiness and partly to dispense with a man who was emerging as yet another potential political rival. Huệ led an army north in the spring of 1788 and executed Nhậm as he had Chỉnh before him. By eliminating Nhậm, Huệ was taking steps to reduce Nhạc's real or imagined influence in the north.[161] Huệ's killing of these men was not motivated solely by an attempt to reduce Nhạc's influence in the north, but this factor must be considered as part of Huệ's calculus in taking these steps. With the Lê emperor gone and the two erstwhile Tây Sơn generals eliminated by Huệ, the region fell under the direct control of the northern Tây Sơn leader. Huệ then recruited a group of highly respected Đàng Ngoài scholar-officials to oversee the area with the backing of a Tây Sơn military force, while he returned to Phú Xuân.

## THE CHINESE INVASION AND ITS AFTERMATH

As this internal division in the Tây Sơn camp developed, external concerns came to the fore as China became embroiled in the Vietnamese contest for political supremacy. When Nguyễn Huệ had come north in 1787 to oust Chỉnh, the Lê emperor Chiêu Thống had fled Thăng Long. After some time in an internal exile, during which he tried unsuccessfully to rally domestic support for an effort to retake his throne, Chiêu Thống crossed the border into China and requested assistance from the Qing court. The Qing emperor, Qianlong, urged on by Tôn Sĩ Nghị, the ambitious governor-general for the south China provinces bordering on Đại Việt, assented to this request. In November 1788 a large Chinese army began its invasion of Đại Việt in support of the Lê ruler.[162] The Tây Sơn military commander stationed in the north reasoned that it would be foolhardy to resist the large-scale Chinese invasion and so instituted a strategic retreat southward into the limestone hills and caves of Tam Điệp in the heart of Thanh Hóa.

From his vantage point at the former Nguyễn palaces in Phú Xuân, Nguyễn Huệ concluded that the best way to unify his military forces and the populations generally in advance of an attack against the Chinese was to name himself emperor, a role he considered the Lê ruler to have abdicated upon his flight to China. Consequently, on December 22, 1788, Huệ held a coronation ceremony at the former Nguyễn capital, issuing an edict declaring himself emperor with the reign name of Quang Trung and explaining his decision to take the throne. As he noted in his edict, "I restored power to the Lê dynasty, but instead of looking to the affairs of state [the emperor] ran to a foreign country for protection. The scholars and people of the north no longer esteem the Lê family. They simply rely on me."[163] With Nguyễn Huệ's assumption of the throne as Quang Trung there were now two Tây Sơn emperors ruling territory stretching from the edges of Gia Định as far north as Nghệ An.

At this point, the confusion over political authority in Đại Việt had reached its zenith. Lê Chiêu Thống, who still considered himself the emperor of Đại Việt and who retained a loyal group of followers, was on the verge of being reinstalled by a large Qing invading army. To his south was Nguyễn Huệ, now ruling as the Quang Trung emperor, with actual political control over territory stretching from the Sino-Vietnamese border as far south as upper Quảng Nam. To Huệ's south lay Nguyễn Nhạc, the Thái Đức emperor, who exercised authority south to the edges of Gia Định.[164] And finally, farther south still in the Gia Định stronghold he had wrested from Nguyễn Lữ in 1787 lay the armies of the Nguyễn survivor, Nguyễn Ánh. In the guise of an imperial loyalist, Ánh maintained fictive allegiance to the recently deceased Cảnh Hưng emperor through the continued use of that emperor's reign era to date his official documents.[165] There were at this juncture four political figures claiming to be (or being acknowledged as) emperor in a territory that up until 1778 had had only one.

The Qing army quickly advanced into this politically divided Đại Việt and on December 17 entered Thăng Long, where they reinstalled Lê Chiêu Thống as emperor of the Vietnamese territories. The Vietnamese ruler was, however, a virtual captive in his own palace, where he was kept under close supervision by the Qing military leader. He could not travel outside the capital without permission, nor could he issue decrees in his own name. The Qing insisted that Lê Chiêu Thống use the Qing reign name on all documents issued by his court, and this humiliation was extended by a similar Qing insistence on using Chinese coinage with their own emperor's reign name rather than permitting the Vietnamese ruler to issue a currency of his own.[166] This state of affairs did not last long.

After having named himself emperor in late November, Nguyễn Huệ quickly gathered an army of perhaps twenty thousand soldiers whom he marched toward the north. He issued a call to arms, invoking the historical memory of his predecessors who had similarly challenged large Chinese occupying forces:

> Under the Han, there were the Trưng queens. Under the Sung there were Đinh Tiên Hoàng and Lê Đại Hành. Under the Yuan, there was Trần Hưng Đạo. Under the Ming there was Lê Thái Tổ, the founder of the present dynasty. These heroes could not sit silently and watch the enemy indulge in violence and cruelty toward the people. They had to comply with the aspirations of the people and raise the banner of justice.[167]

Quang Trung was clearly placing himself in the ranks of these heroic figures—and suggesting that his attack on the Qing would be equally successful.

Taking advantage of the impending lunar New Year celebration, the Tây Sơn leader calculated his attack to coincide with the holiday. He reasoned correctly that the Chinese armies would be celebrating and would not be on guard against an attack from Tây Sơn forces, whom the Qing had seen retreat in the face of the numerically superior northern army. Quang Trung rallied his troops by promising them that their own holiday festivities would be delayed by only a few days and that seven days into the holiday they would be in Thăng Long to celebrate properly.[168] Thus, during the early days of the lunar New Year celebration (January–February 1789) Quang Trung mounted an attack that quickly destroyed the unprepared Qing army. Thousands of Qing soldiers were killed in the first days of the attack, and most of the rest fled in confusion, among them several of the leading Chinese generals. The Lê emperor had himself fled when word of the impending attack reached him, and he quickly made his way back to China. As their commander had promised, the Tây Sơn forces were back in Thăng Long in less than a week.

## QUANG TRUNG CONSOLIDATES HIS AUTHORITY

Having named himself emperor over the former Lê territories and driven out the occupying Qing army, Huệ was now in a position further to consolidate his political claims. He did so in several ways—restoring positive ties with the Chinese court, laying the foundations for a new political center in Nghệ An, and gaining the support and acknowledgment of influential northern scholar-officials.

*Gaining Recognition from the Qing*

On the one hand, Quang Trung's defeat of the Chinese had constituted yet another powerful claim to political legitimacy, for defense of the nation against the Chinese had a very strong resonance at both the popular and elite levels in terms of conferring political status. In his speech to the Tây Sơn army before launching the attack against the Qing, Quang Trung had invoked the line of heroic military figures who had preceded him in defeating Chinese armies. Such an act was perhaps the single most powerful source of political legitimation available to claimants to power in Đại Việt. On the other hand, and seemingly paradoxically, while defeating the Chinese was a powerful form of domestic legitimation, appeasing them in the aftermath of such a defeat and then receiving investiture from the Chinese court constituted an equally important form of political recognition. As had been the case since the earliest days of Vietnamese independence in the tenth century, good relations with the northern court were an absolute necessity to guard against the potential renewal of Chinese military ambitions.

After the initial Chinese retreat, Quang Trung was careful not to humiliate the Chinese army unnecessarily. He treated the captured Qing soldiers well and arranged for their speedy repatriation. He also began a lengthy correspondence with the Chinese (using the noted scholar Ngô Thì Nhậm as his scribe), in which he expressed a desire to restore harmony between the two nations and to begin normal diplomatic and economic interactions.[169] In exchange for his cooperation, Quang Trung requested Chinese recognition as the legitimate ruler of Đại Việt. The Qing emperor could have opted to defer the granting of this title and to attempt a second invasion in support of the Lê ruler. He chose instead to accede to the Tây Sơn emperor's request. The Qing court sent a delegation to their southern neighbor granting formal recognition of Nguyễn Huệ as the leader of "An Nam"—giving him the traditional Chinese title of An Nam Quốc Vương. The Qing later also recognized Quang Trung's son, Quang Toản, as his crown prince and successor.

This recognition was made with the understanding that the new Vietnamese ruler would subsequently pay a visit to the Chinese court. No Vietnamese emperor had ever made such a trip, and Quang Trung would be no exception. Instead, as noted previously, in 1790 he sent an embassy to the Qing court in which a look-alike traveled in his place. The Qing emperor was delighted by this visit, and the Tây Sơn entourage was well treated. This expedient reflected Quang Trung's efforts to keep the Chinese at arm's length, even as he sought to appease them. Not only did the emperor not travel to the Qing court, but he never met any of the Chinese emissaries who traveled to his kingdom. Instead, he sent representatives to meet them, claiming in numerous missives that political circumstances or poor traveling conditions on the route from Phú Xuân to Thăng Long made receiving them personally impossible.[170] Indeed, Quang Trung's continued residence in Phú Xuân was a convenient excuse for maintaining a physical distance from the Chinese, even as it enabled him to stay in touch with his territories in the central parts of Đại Việt.

*Building a New Capital: The Phượng Hoàng Trung Đô*

After defeating the Chinese, Quang Trung found himself emperor over a territory that stretched from the Chinese border south to, and even slightly beyond, the Hải Vân pass. This matched the greatest extent of Trịnh-Lê authority, which had occurred in 1775 at the farthest thrust of the Trịnh invasion. As Quang Trung developed his polity, his focus was no longer on the south—the Qui Nhơn center controlled by his brother—but on an entirely new and complex territory encompassing the former Lê capital of Thăng Long and the former Nguyễn capital at Phú Xuân. Although he had begun to settle at Phú Xuân, where he had rebuilt fortifications and created palaces for himself, Quang Trung decided it would be best to construct an entirely new capital, one more centrally located within this broad swath of territory now under his control. Recognizing the need to centralize his base, Quang Trung not surprisingly chose Nghệ An, situated roughly equidistant from these two centers, as the site of a grand new capital: the Imperial Phoenix Central Capital (Phượng Hoàng Trung Đô). This would be the central capital, relegating the former capitals of the Lê and Nguyễn to secondary status.

Nghệ An was not merely a location of geographical convenience; it also had a powerful spiritual pull for the Tây Sơn, for it was from here that the Tây Sơn ancestors had come in the seventeenth century. The Tây Sơn connection to Nghệ An was later described by the northern literatus Bùi Dương Lịch:

> The Tây Sơn communicated to the hamlet of Thái Lão [in the district of Hưng Nguyên] to erect a temple for the king's ancestors in order that

> worship could take place there, because according to the family registers, the hamlet of Thái Lão, in the district of Hưng Nguyên, had been the home area of his ancestors. The ancestors from the past had gone as soldiers to the south, and had been stationed at Quy Nhơn. In that year, Nguyễn Huệ had invaded the northern region, and had been victorious in battle, making a triumphal return to Nghệ An.[171]

For Quang Trung settling in Nghệ An thus represented a return to his ancestral home. A capital in Nghệ An would constitute a political as well as a spiritual center for the new regime. Quang Trung invested considerable effort in building up temples to his ancestors in this area, mimicking the traditional ancestral veneration practiced by the imperial house of the Lê, as well as the lesser seigneurial families.

Although Quang Trung's planned Imperial Phoenix Central Capital was never completed, the emperor had grandiose plans for his new political center. The citadel was to be built on a river outside of what is today the city of Vĩnh, with a commanding position surveying several rivers and the nearby mountains. It was designed on a massive scale, as indicated by the surviving remains of its outer walls, which are 20 meters in height and indicate a structure that would have been 300 meters wide and 450 meters long.[172] Because the city was not completed during his lifetime, Quang Trung continued to rule from Phú Xuân, but he clearly saw this as the eventual center of his reign and its future. On his deathbed in 1792 he is reported to have admonished his son Quang Toản that Nghệ An and not Phú Xuân should be the bedrock of his reign.[173]

### *Quang Trung and the Đàng Ngoài Scholars*

A third component of Quang Trung's process of political consolidation involved establishing his bona fides within the community of northern scholar-officials. For Quang Trung these scholars represented several things. First of all, their support or approbation would serve as an essential form of legitimation for the Tây Sơn leader. Legitimacy in the eyes of these scholars was critical because their stature in society could help convince the broader populations to follow the Tây Sơn. With their ties to specific rural areas, once scholars had been drawn to serve the Tây Sơn, the populations from their home districts might also support the new regime. Secondly, the Tây Sơn emperor needed these men as administrators for the newly captured territories and as ambassadors to China, particularly after defeating the Qing army. Finally, Quang Trung needed scholars for their knowledge of the north and its problems and populations. This was a territory largely unknown to the Tây Sơn leader, who had come from the distant southern realm. As a consequence of his need for the multifaceted assistance of these scholars, Nguyễn Huệ appears to have come under their considerable influence and to have deferred frequently to their knowledge and existing philosophical agendas.

Quang Trung recruited these officials in several ways, including issuing proclamations such as his 1789(?) Edict Seeking Worthy Men, which was aimed directly at the scholars living in his new realm.[174] The emperor also used much more direct (and more effective) approaches, such as using those who had already joined the new regime to recruit their friends and peers. The Tây Sơn emperor recognized that the easiest way to gain the support of northern intellectuals was to engage the assistance of a few key figures who could themselves serve as conduits to the others through their personal and professional relationships. This proved particularly effective because the elite scholars in the north formed an extremely close-knit community. Many of them were related by marriage, had studied together, or had become friends while taking the examinations or while serving in various postings.[175] This group of closely connected men included many of the most important northern scholars of their generation, and those whom the Tây Sơn emperor most hoped to draw into his service. If one of these scholars could be recruited to the rebel side, it considerably increased the likelihood that those connected to him might also be persuaded.

Of the core group of northern scholars, several were particularly important to Quang Trung's efforts in recruiting others. Trần Văn Kỷ (1740s?–1801) was the lynchpin for Quang Trung's recruitment efforts, and the support of nearly all the key northern literati can be traced either directly or indirectly to his efforts. Kỷ arranged introductions for Nguyễn Huệ with several noted scholars, including Nguyễn Thiếp, a renowned but reclusive scholar in Nghệ An, and later Ngô Thì Nhậm. Nhậm had connections to many important northern scholars because of his extensive service under the Trịnh and his prominent lineage, and he was able to recruit numerous prominent *tiến sĩ* to the Tây Sơn cause, including Phan Huy Ích, Ninh Tốn, Đoàn Nguyễn Tuấn, Nguyễn Nha, Trần Ba Lãm, and Vũ Huy Tấn. While Nhậm is often remembered for his service to the Tây Sơn as the man who drafted Quang Trung's edicts, his efforts in recruiting fellow scholars were also critically important to the new regime.

When popular appeals or personal contacts did not work, Quang

Trung was prepared to use force. For example, in the spring of 1788, after the Lê emperor had fled from Thăng Long, Nguyễn Huệ attempted to bring together the Lê court officials to assist him in conducting political affairs in the north. In this instance he gathered them and according to some sources forced them to sign a petition of loyalty.[176] They all did this, apparently more or less willingly, with two exceptions: the noted philosopher and compiler Bùi Huy Bích, who feigned illness and did not attend the session, and Nguyễn Huy Trạc (1733–1788), a 1769 *tiến sĩ* who killed himself by drinking poison.[177] From this episode it is clear that the pattern of forcing cooperation from reluctant Đàng Ngoài scholars was established fairly early by Quang Trung's regime. In this particular case, circumstances made it relatively easy to coerce cooperation inasmuch as the scholars were already resident in Thăng Long and had little means of escape. In many other cases, however, reluctant scholars had to be tracked down and brought to the Tây Sơn court by force. Those who on receiving the summons to the Tây Sơn court were unwilling to comply had two choices: suicide or flight. Only a small handful of men chose the former option, and they were subsequently honored for their decision in a nineteenth-century Nguyễn-dynasty chronicle, the *Đại Nam Nhất Thống Chí* (Records of the Unified Đại Nam).[178]

In response to edicts, personal appeals, or direct pressure, numerous Đàng Ngoài scholars elected to serve the new Tây Sơn government. Those who chose to join the new regime did so for a variety of reasons and with varying degrees of commitment. A few agreed to serve out of a genuine enthusiasm for the Tây Sơn project and the prospects it offered for a renewed political and social order. Others joined in the belief that their Confucian ideology required public service from those capable of providing it, even if they were unsure of the prospects for the new regime.[179] Yet others joined the new regime not on humanitarian or philosophical grounds, but on pragmatic ones, supporting what they perceived as the de facto political authority in order to continue their careers. The ultimate expression of this pragmatism is found in the case of Tuần Huyện Trang. After betraying the fleeing Trịnh *chúa* to the Tây Sơn troops in 1786, in defiance of his teacher who had entrusted the *chúa* to his care, Trang explained his actions by declaring, "I am not as much afraid of my teacher as I am of the rebels, and I do not love the *chúa* as much as I love myself."[180]

Most Đàng Ngoài scholars, however, decided not to serve the new regime, a decision motivated either by philosophical reasons of loyalty to the old regime or by more practical concerns. The majority of scholars who chose not to serve the Tây Sơn regime simply went into retreat, waiting for the situation to resolve itself, a common course of action in times of political turmoil. This led Quang Trung to lament (via the hand of Ngô Thì Nhậm), "Alas, when heaven and earth are in deadlock the virtuous and talented hide themselves."[181] While some scholars were able to go into retreat or retirement, others could not adopt such a simple expedient in the face of Quang Trung's tenacious pursuit of the more noted Đàng Ngoài literati. As one scholar of that era described the new Tây Sơn emperor's efforts, "[He] behaves toward scholars without differentiating between those of south or north, searching and inquiring everywhere in caves and forests, in grasses and thickets."[182] This assessment was probably not entirely metaphorical, reflecting instead the reality of Nguyễn Huệ's seeking to track down scholars who had taken to hiding themselves in caves and forests.

Ultimately, the scholars who joined the Tây Sơn court, whether enthusiastically or reluctantly, were of enormous importance to Quang Trung, providing him the credibility that he sought as well as giving him practical and philosophical assistance in governing his new realm. The influence of these scholars on Quang Trung's political agenda was considerable. Under their tutelage, and particularly that of Ngô Thì Nhậm, Quang Trung undertook a variety of projects, from restoring the civil service examinations to laying plans for a state-sponsored school system to orchestrating a large-scale project to translate the Confucian classics into the Vietnamese vernacular. It was through these scholars, and again primarily Nhậm, that Quang Trung expressed himself in edicts and correspondence with the Chinese court. The Đàng Ngoài literati, although unable to create fully functional institutional structures before Quang Trung's regime was overthrown, nonetheless shaped it in important ways that reflected their own objectives and long-term concerns.[183]

## CHINA AND QUANG TRUNG'S POLITICAL AMBITIONS

Having thus effectively worked to secure his political authority, including receiving formal Chinese recognition and gaining the assistance of talented Confucian scholars who helped rebuild the regime's bureaucratic apparatus and other institutions, Quang Trung would appear to have been in a position to rest from his labors. He did in fact remain in his capital at Phú Xuân for some time thereafter, but by 1791 he restlessly began to make plans to extract additional concessions from the seemingly cowed Chinese.[184] Among the concessions Quang Trung apparently hoped to receive from the Chinese was the hand of a Qing imperial princess in marriage.[185] As with his brother's earlier attempted marital connection to the Nguyễn and Nguyễn Huệ's own subsequent marriage to the Lê princess, such a request would have been a means by which to reinforce what was viewed as an important political connection. It must also be seen as yet another step toward legitimating this newcomer in the eyes of a suspicious Đàng Ngoài elite. Although the establishment of political connections through marriage was a long-understood principle, Quang Trung's request for a Chinese royal princess is without precedent in Vietnamese history. It is perhaps best read as an indication of the Tây Sơn emperor's conviction that he had sufficiently intimidated the Chinese that they might consider such a request.[186]

Bolder still was Quang Trung's plan to demand that the Chinese give back the two large southern Chinese provinces of Guangxi and Guangdong. The *Đại Nam Liệt Truyện* records that the impetus for this plan stemmed from a Chinese refusal to address a Vietnamese grievance about some border districts that they claimed had been seized by the Chinese. If the Chinese proved unwilling to turn over the two provinces, Quang Trung was apparently ready to take them by force.[187] The *Hoàng Lê Nhất Thống Chí* suggests that his message to the Qing requesting the provinces was merely an attempt to assess the Chinese response, not a heartfelt desire.[188] It appears, however, that the Tây Sơn emperor may have been driven by a less prosaic impulse, for he viewed this territory as having once belonged to the Vietnamese and saw its return as part of a restoration (rather than an expansion) of an ancient Vietnamese territory. As Alexander Woodside notes, "Quang-trung's determination to recover the primordial unity of the 'Hundred Yueh,' a legend which twenty centuries of imperial Chinese history had not obliterated, was so compelling, that at the time of his premature death in 1792, the Tay-son court was building giant war junks to transport Vietnamese war elephants to Canton, as the first step toward the necessary reconquest of Kwantung and Kwangsi."[189]

At some level a Vietnamese attack against the Chinese would appear suicidal given the relative size of the countries and the armies at their disposal. The underlying logic driving the emperor's intentions can perhaps be traced to his political situation within Đàng Ngoài. Quang Trung's credibility in the northern realm rested largely on his defense of the Vietnamese state against the 1788 invasion by the Chinese. It was this action, more than any other, that had solidified his stature in the eyes of northern scholars as well as within the general population. His victory over the Chinese had placed him squarely into the pantheon of Vietnamese national heroes—the Trưng sisters, Trần Hưng Đạo, and Lê Lợi—all of whom had defended the nation against its northern neighbor. He had invoked the feats of these heroes as he rallied his forces to attack the Qing, and his victory explicitly linked his accomplishments to theirs. Quang Trung's place on the national stage had been defined far more by his military feats than his political vision. It appears that after several years away from the battlefield, Quang Trung needed the excitement and potential rewards of another military confrontation. Indeed, the planned invasion of China demonstrates the degree to which military and political logic became linked in the mind of at least one Tây Sơn leader. Born as a military threat to existing political figures and structures, the Tây Sơn movement remained in many ways a militarized response to a situation that demanded more profound social and political solutions.

Quang Trung also appears to have become convinced that the Chinese were genuinely frightened of his armies after he routed their forces in 1789. A contemporary missionary letter described the situation:

> The Emperor of China appears to fear this new Attila, as he has sent to crown him the king of Tonkin by the hand of an Ambassador, it being only a few months later, and forgetting the honor and loss of more than 40 or 50,000 men whom the tyrant killed the previous year in a single battle, in which the Chinese were armed to the teeth with sabers and guns, and outnumbered them ten to one. It is true that this embassy is, in everyone's eyes, so unbelievable that one doubts with some justification that which the Emperor has done. The tyrant himself has not deigned to leave Cochinchina to have himself crowned at our capital, and he has contented himself with sending in his place a simple officer, who took the dress and name of his master and imposed himself on the Ambassador.[190]

According to the *Đại Nam Thực Lục*, moreover, the very intimate reception granted to Quang Trung's first embassy in 1790 further encouraged his convictions in this respect.[191] It was perhaps based on this interpretation of the situation that Quang Trung made the request for the Chinese to cede their two southern provinces. These grand plans never came to pass, however, for Quang Trung died in the late summer of 1792, just as his embassy was on its way to China to present these demands. When news of their emperor's death reached the Vietnamese envoys, they immediately turned back to Thăng Long. This marked the end of Quang Trung's bold plan, which was never revived under his successor.

Whatever the factors motivating the Tây Sơn ruler, the plans to challenge the Chinese indicate the ambitions driving Quang Trung to confirm his political stature both within Đại Việt and in the all-important relationship with the Chinese. He appears to have been largely successful in establishing his political position in both Vietnamese and Chinese eyes, and it was only his premature death at the age of forty in 1792 that cut short his aspirations of establishing his lineage as a new and long-term dynasty. Although Quang Trung's son and successor, Quang Toản, would rule for another decade (part of it under a regent), Tây Sơn political aspirations effectively died along with Quang Trung.

## CONCLUSION: THE TÂY SƠN LEADERS' LIMITED VISION

What then can we conclude about the aims and outlook of the Tây Sơn leadership over the last thirty years of the eighteenth century? The continual use of available political affiliations, to be retained until they had outlived their usefulness or simply to be accumulated as chance made them available, suggests that the Tây Sơn leaders were not innovators or revolutionaries, but political opportunists. They pragmatically made a wide variety of appeals in different ways and at different times, using the tools they found and the circumstances they encountered to gather support and to legitimate themselves and their movement. Despite some Vietnamese historians' attempts to impute grand designs to the Tây Sơn uprising, a closer look reveals no master strategy, much less any particular guiding philosophy.[192] The Tây Sơn leaders' pronouncements about certain objectives were calculated to advance their own interests and political authority, not to transform their kingdom or the lives of its inhabitants. The changes that did take place do not indicate a broad political or social vision on the part of any of the Tây Sơn brothers. The only possible exception is Quang Trung's articulation of some general policies after 1789, and even this was largely a result of the influence of Đàng Ngoài intellectuals.

The Tây Sơn case demonstrates the complex of sources of political authority and legitimacy that were available to claimants for power in the early modern period. Although there was some overlap, the strategies the Tây Sơn brothers used to legitimate themselves were clearly designed to appeal to different groups in society. Some strategies, such as seeking official titles, marrying into ruling families and restoring Confucian political structures, worked best at the elite level. Other appeals worked more at the popular level, including Tây Sơn efforts to link themselves to the supernatural and their concrete and symbolic acts of economic justice. Indeed, the hodgepodge of approaches is reflected in the fact that while Quang Trung was busy demonstrating his Confucian bona fides in the north, his brother in Qui Nhơn had no interest in Confucian niceties and as far as can be determined continued to derive his own legitimacy from his military successes, his links to the Chams, and his personal authority.

Finally, despite the grandeur of their political claims and the astonishing successes of their military campaigns, in many ways the Tây Sơn brothers remained remarkably parochial in their orientation and focus.[193] They could drive their armies to the very borders of the country or, as in the cases of Cambodia and the Lao principalities, indeed across those borders, but in the end they always returned to their bases, where they felt the most comfortable. That their most trusted political advisers and military strategists, with few exceptions, remained early supporters from their home region is yet another indication that the Tây Sơn leaders continued to look back to their origins even as their campaigns and ambitions expanded far beyond the Qui Nhơn–An Khê axis. Nhạc in particular stubbornly remained at his capital Chà Bàn, where he was vulnerable to repeated sieges.[194] Indeed, Nhạc's only grand departure from Chà Bàn was his extraordinary dash up to Thăng Long in the summer of 1786 to chase and retrieve his brother. Huệ, although demonstrating far greater mobility than Nhạc, also holed up at his new capital at Phú Xuân from 1786 until his death in 1792. While this great general led several military campaigns to the north, he preferred to delegate authority there to others, always more comfortable closer to his roots.

The nineteenth-century Nguyễn historians, not surprisingly, refused to recognize the Tây Sơn as having ever been legitimate rulers of the Vietnamese territories, rejecting them as usurpers who had taken political power that the Nguyễn viewed as their own. And yet, as has been argued in this chapter, in Việt Nam's long history there has always been a multiplicity of sources for demonstrating political legitimacy. Although the Tây Sơn were very much outsiders who came to power largely through military means, they were far from the first, or the last, to have done so, and indeed the eventual Nguyễn victory and claim to rule was itself the product of a protracted military campaign. In some respects, the Tây Sơn claims to power arguably rivaled those of their eventual successors, and in any case were a potent demonstration of the ways in which political contenders in Việt Nam could rise from obscurity to political prominence.

# 3

## The Peasants

### Life under Tây Sơn Authority

When buffalo and ox fight one another, flies and mosquitoes die unjustly.

—Vietnamese proverb

These barbarians come from the mountains of Cochinchina and know nothing about the arrangements for governance. They seek nothing but to pillage and desolate, without thinking about what follows. They have taken all of the silver in the kingdom . . . they have taken the cultivators from the fields to make them into soldiers; they have burned a large part of the villages and imposed on the people taxes and labor service. And what has this produced? All of the evils to which we have testified, and which continue still: Famine, pestilence, deaths of people and livestock, and all this without remedy.

—French missionary's letter, 1789[1]

As the Tây Sơn leaders worked to legitimize their political authority, they also began to exercise that authority over the populations being brought under their control. The Tây Sơn regimes' ability to control these populations was essential for dealing with the very immediate threats they confronted, from continuing warfare on several fronts to displaced populations to widespread disruptions of agricultural production. Tây Sơn authorities made frequent and heavy demands of the people living in the territories they controlled, demands necessitated by virtually ceaseless warfare and the destruction and costs that entailed. Foremost among the regimes' needs was manpower to support its military campaigns. Secondly, as the Tây Sơn leaders established their respective polities, they demanded labor service for the construction of new political centers and for a wide range of public works projects. Finally, the regime's leaders needed financial resources to pay the soldiers and for other government projects, and thus extracted tax payments from these populations, both in cash and in kind.

The consequences of these demands were enormous, for they often interrupted the critical rice-growing cycle of sowing seeds, transplanting seedlings, and then harvesting crops. Military conscription, which was reserved for men, drew many workers from their fields. Heavy corvée labor demands fell on both men and women. While such labor demands were often filled locally, allowing people to remain resident on their farms, the time involved in constructing new roads, building new ramparts, or repairing dikes or other aspects of the rural infrastructure obviously took away from time needed to cultivate crops. Warfare and the attendant movement of large numbers of troops across the countryside destroyed crops and frequently also dikes and paddy-field walls as soldiers moved through areas with underdeveloped or nonexistent roads. The alternative to conscription into armies or impressment into corvée labor was flight. With regard to agricultural productivity, of course, this had potentially the same consequence as actual military or labor service, namely, that fields were not being tended.

The relationship that developed between the Tây Sơn and the peasantry regularly pitted the demands of the rebel leaders against the needs of the peasantry. As had long been the case, particularly in times of turmoil, the relationship between Vietnamese rulers and those they ruled was a complex one, a struggle on the one side to gain control of human and natural resources and on the other to limit the state's ability to do so. It was a relationship further complicated by the vagaries of weather, warfare, and official malfeasance. In the beginning the Tây Sơn leaders merely hoped to expand their numbers to field an army against the Nguyễn regime and to gain the sympathy of those unwilling to serve as soldiers. Once the rebel force began to transform itself into a formal regime—beginning in 1775—its needs changed. Now it required more systematic control over the populations under its authority. To gain this control the Tây Sơn leaders repeatedly sought to count and categorize these populations, imposing order on a society that in many places had begun to slip beyond state control. Thereafter, the rebel leaders were able to exploit these populations for military and labor service as well as for contributions in cash and kind.

Although the pressures of constant military action during the Tây Sơn period intensified some of the tensions between rulers and those they ruled, it seems clear that the patterns of this relationship have been common at many times in Việt Nam's history. My purpose here is to use the Tây Sơn experience to reveal the specifics of this complex era, but also to suggest the kinds of dynamics that have plagued relations between rulers and their subjects throughout Vietnamese history. While many aspects of the relationship between the Tây Sơn leadership and the peasantry were distinctive or unique, the overall impact of the movement on the peasantry is part of a much older pattern. Whatever apparently unique elements the movement manifested, from the ground-level perspective of the Vietnamese peasant, the Tây Sơn era represented more of the same, or occasionally much of the same, only worse.

While peasants could and did physically resist the new regime in numerous ways, they could also use less direct means of resistance, including forms of psychological defiance. Since the Tây Sơn were just one among multiple contenders for political power in the late eighteenth century, the presence of numerous viable candidates for power and the shifting fortunes of the military campaigns meant that peasants could realistically hold out the hope that they might be rescued from their plight. Unfortunately for them, this hope was often shattered by the discovery that those eagerly anticipated as saviors were no better than the powers they had replaced. Ultimately, from the perspective of the peasantry, it appears there was often little to distinguish Tây Sơn rule from that of either the Trịnh or the Nguyễn.

The complex and frequently hostile relationship that existed between Vietnamese populations and the Tây Sơn leaders bears little resemblance to the idealized view of the Tây Sơn often found in the writings of modern Vietnamese historians. Frequent references to an undifferentiated "Tây Sơn movement" (*phong trào Tây Sơn*) in this context are even more problematic. This chapter disaggregates the overly broad category—"Tây Sơn"—and suggests that it masked deep divisions. I argue that the many and brutal military campaigns of the Tây Sơn uprising were far less about peasant desires or objectives than they were about the political ambitions of its leaders. Peasants during the Tây Sơn period were fodder for armies, bodies for corvée labor, and sources of supplies and revenues. These men and women may have had aspirations for a better life, reflected in their optimistic support for the early manifestation of the uprising, but these aspirations soon gave way to a more depressing reality, and most available evidence suggests that few peasants saw any measurable improvement in their lives as a result of Tây Sơn actions.

When I refer to peasants in this chapter, I am speaking primarily of people whose livelihood is centered on agricultural production on a small (family or extended-family) scale; they represented the vast majority of the population living in the Vietnamese territories in the eighteenth century. For convenience, this category also includes people connected to the rural economy centered on this agricultural production. It does not, however, include people whose vocation was linked to the commercial sector. Rural merchants as well as coastal merchants with larger-scale operations, while connected to the rhythms of the agricultural sector, were also more immediately affected by extralocal or extraregional factors. It is clear that there are multiple economic strata within the category of "peasant"—as exemplified by the Tây Sơn leaders themselves—but unfortunately the limited data rarely permit us to make such distinctions.

## CONTROLLING POPULATIONS

Each time the Tây Sơn leaders established a new political regime—in 1775 in Đàng Trong and in 1788 in Đàng Ngoài—they sought to assert control over populations in the territories under their political authority. These attempts reflected immediate military and fiscal needs, but they were also a response to population displacement and chaos caused by military conflict and social turmoil. Strategies to gain control over populations began with carrying out censuses, which would give the new government some idea of the number and distribution of people in these territories. Once populations had been counted, both Tây Sơn regimes instituted systems to classify populations based on age or economic status to calculate specific military, corvée, and economic obligations. Finally, in Đàng Ngoài, Quang Trung developed a unique system of identification cards that enabled the state to keep track of individuals as they moved about outside their villages. By these methods, most of which had been employed by earlier rulers, Tây Sơn leaders attempted to gain control over populations that had been dislocated, only briefly in Đàng Trong, where this had been a consequence of the Tây Sơn uprising itself, but for more than a quarter of a century in Đàng Ngoài, where popular uprisings, floods, and famines had driven tens of thousands from their homes.

*The Census*

The major device employed by the Tây Sơn leaders to gain control of their populations was the census (*sổ hộ khẩu*). The information collected in this fashion was essential for levying taxes, for determining corvée labor responsibilities, and more generally for gaining a sense of the demographics of the realm. As Phan Huy Chú observed in the early nineteenth century, "In order to profit from the three realms [heaven, earth, people], one must know how many are ready to work for the country so that there are no concerns about having an insufficient number [of people]."[2] Well aware of the importance of such information, Vietnamese rulers had carried out population counts since at least the middle of the eleventh century in the early independence period. Although there were attempts to regularize these enumerations, the intervals between them and their effectiveness varied over the centuries, reflecting political and social circumstances and the relative strength of any given ruler.[3]

In Đàng Ngoài, the Trịnh-Lê rulers had conducted periodic, if sometimes unsystematic, enumerations of their populations, but the last relatively precise survey of this kind had been carried out in 1658.[4] Events of the eighteenth century, including the disruptions of a half-century of popular unrest and the consequences of years of famine and widespread death, would have rendered extremely inaccurate any surviving population registers still held by village leaders or the central authorities. Consequently, in 1773, after the last major popular uprising had been suppressed, the Trịnh court attempted to revise and update the census figures. The project proved a complete failure, as it met widespread and sustained resistance, which eventually forced the regime to halt the effort.[5] In Đàng Trong, where the Nguyễn court had similarly conducted periodic censuses for tax and conscription purposes, the record-keeping system was in considerably better condition. There had been a systematic Nguyễn population survey in 1769, part of the regime's efforts to increase tax revenues and, as we have seen, one of the major sources of popular discontent. Having been thus updated only two years before the Tây Sơn uprising broke out, Nguyễn population records would have been up to date when the rebellion began.[6]

Although it is unclear when the first Tây Sơn census took place, Nguyễn Nhạc's announcement in 1775 that one in five villagers would be subject to conscription suggests that the Tây Sơn leader had gained access to the existing Nguyễn administrative records. The *Đại Nam Thực Lục* further reports that in the following year Nhạc was forcing people into his armies based on registered names (*hào*) in the villages around Qui Nhơn, similarly indicating that he controlled at least some population registers.[7] It is not until 1784, however, that we have the first report of a census being carried out by Nhạc's regime. The French bishop Pigneau de Béhaine, writing in March 1785, indicated that when he left Cochinchina in August 1784, the Tây Sơn were carrying out a precise enumeration of their populations and that a large number of people were fleeing their villages to avoid being counted.[8] The following year Nhạc ordered another, less comprehensive census. This count specifically targeted Vietnamese Christians. In response to concerns about the political loyalties of Christians in his territories, Nhạc had ordered that they be registered so that he could either tax them or force them to renounce their religion.[9] While this enumeration would have encompassed only a fraction of the population of Đàng Trong, its target, Vietnamese Christians, represented a particularly vulnerable population that could quite readily be exploited for financial or labor resources.

Following their 1786 invasion of the northern territories, the Tây Sơn extended their use of such methods to this region as well. At some point in 1787 or 1788, the Tây Sơn began to register populations in upper Đàng Trong, the former Nguyễn territories, recaptured from the Trịnh in 1786. Then, once Nguyễn Huệ had assumed imperial authority from the Lê in late 1788, this effort was formally expanded into Đàng Ngoài. The Tây Sơn leader hoped to restore order and stability in Đàng Ngoài by turning migrant populations into sedentary ones, and in so doing restoring the long-disrupted agricultural economy. With this objective in mind, in the fourth month of the year *kỷ dậu* (April–May 1789), Quang Trung "repaired the legal status registers" of the population as the prelude to a larger population count.[10] Early the following year he issued a decree that read in part, "In all of the provinces from the Linh Gianh River northward, an effort should be made within the prefectures and districts to record the number of villagers according to their ranks."[11] In the same year, he issued another decree concerning taxation, population classification, and village expenditures, in which the onus for maintaining current population records was placed on the villages. Villages were expected to continue to pay taxes based on existing registries, with assessments being reduced only if the village chief formally certified that inhabitants had died.[12]

Perhaps around the same time Quang Trung issued an edict—though it is not dated—directly addressing the agricultural crisis. In it he described the problems that had developed with vagabondage during the years of turmoil, which in turn had led to declining crop output and growing concerns about hunger. The emperor estimated that perhaps only 40–50 percent of the recorded population was still in place and that a similar percentage of farmland was currently under cultivation.[13] The edict called for village and hamlet chiefs to carry out surveys of people and land and to record these figures in village registers, which were then to be submitted to Tây Sơn officials for examination. Ultimately, the edict required all people who had left their homes and abandoned their farms to return to their villages and to resume their agricultural activities.[14] The purpose of this policy was clearly twofold: to restore agricultural productivity to support the northern populations and to return people to their villages where they could be counted and thus controlled more effectively by the state. Although from a peasant point of view this increasing degree of state control might have been seen as a drawback, it is possible (though the data are very limited) that the more immediate effect of the edict was to improve social stability and to enable the resumption of agricultural work.

In 1792, shortly before his death, Quang Trung ordered an even more systematic census, suggesting that previous efforts had been either unsuccessful or insufficiently thorough. Bùi Dương Lịch described the problems of the population registers as they existed at that time:

> The village registers had been set up in the year *nhâm dần* [1722] during the old Lê times, and by now sixty or seventy years had passed, in which time the numbers of inhabitants had increased in some places and decreased in others. Thus there were wide divergences and taxes and corvée labor did not reflect [the actual situation]. In the year *quý tị* [1773] there was an order to record [the registers] again, but the people were stubborn and unyielding, and the officials accepted bribes, and they were unable to complete [the project] and after that they had to follow the old registers. In the current period, the Tây Sơn sent down an order that the people in the communes in every place should open the registers of the hamlets and villages.[15]

At the behest of the Tây Sơn ruler, a census was conducted and was described by a missionary as having been carried out with the strictest of rigor, tallying every citizen between the ages of nine and seventy. The census figures were then to be used for assessing both military and tax obligations.[16]

The final Tây Sơn census for which we have evidence took place in 1801 under Quang Trung's son and successor, Nguyễn Quang Toản. This enumeration may have been part of a wider restructuring of the Tây Sơn regime then being undertaken. This effort had begun in 1800 with a change in the ruler's reign name from Cảnh Thịnh to Bảo Hưng, a change designed to rejuvenate a regime faltering under Nguyễn attacks and in imminent danger of losing its capital at Phú Xuân. This was also a period of growing popular unrest against the Tây Sơn in their northern provinces, in which increasing numbers of small-scale revolts were being reported, rebellions spurred by expectations regarding the imminent arrival of Nguyễn forces. Whether the new census was part of the ritual renewal of the Tây Sơn state is uncertain. What is clear is that it was designed not so much to gain a population count as to establish which men were away from their villages. Based on this census, any individual not registered in the village records was assumed to be part of the emergent resistance movements.[17]

Despite the inherent risks, villages sought to foil the state's efforts to get an accurate population count. Villagers and village leaders understood very well that it was in their best interests to register the lowest possible population count for their particular village to protect themselves against state demands. Because a village had a collective obligation to meet tax and conscription demands of the state, its residents had a common interest in deceiving the central authorities. Consequently, many northern villages sought to reduce their military and tax obligations by underreporting population figures.[18] In the midst of the 1801 census a French missionary reported that those villages that were able to underreport their populations would be in the best position to survive the demands of the state. From his description it is clear that this process was not simply a matter of fiddling with the population figures, but of substantially underreporting the population. His village, for example, with a true population of approximately three hundred, reported only about 10 percent of that figure.[19] Clearly, if a village could get away with such extreme miscounting, its residents would be in a much better position vis-à-vis the state. The Tây Sơn regime was no doubt aware of these deceptions, and so took precautions to prevent them, but in most such cases the state would have been largely powerless to enforce accurate counts, which of necessity required local cooperation.

*Population Classification*

As the peasants were being counted under the Tây Sơn governments, they were also being classified, continuing another practice developed by earlier dynasties. The Lê and Trịnh regimes, for example, used a classification scheme in which categories were created that established a hierarchy of commoners within villages. This system had been introduced by Emperor Lê Thánh Tông in 1470, its details spelled out in his Hồng Đức legal code. According to the code, villagers reaching the age of eighteen would be enrolled in the village registers and classified for tax and labor purposes. Failure to register one's name was punishable by impressment into military service. The categories into which enrolled villagers were divided consisted of the following:

*tráng hạng*—young men and adults subject to military service
*quân hạng*—young men and adults subject to military reserve service
*dân hạng*—the general population
*lão hạng*—the aged (50–60 years of age)
*cố hạng*—landless wage laborers
*cùng hạng*—the indigent[20]

The Nguyễn had similarly categorized their own populations, though they had created two additional categories: *tàng tật* (the infirm) and *đào* (vagabonds).[21] These categories would be applied within particular regions or villages, with emphasis on the first two classifications, in which fixed numbers of younger men would be marked either for active or reserve military duty. The classification of particular individuals would vary, depending on the local circumstances in a given village as well as its location.[22] In theory, moreover, the Nguyễn regulations stipulated that there be regular updates of these records, on a modest scale every three years and in a more comprehensive fashion every six years.[23]

The Tây Sơn regimes also classified people based upon their age, clearly drawing on the earlier Nguyễn and Trịnh designations. There are indications that the Thái Đức emperor used such a system, for the nineteenth-century Nguyễn histories speak of Tây Sơn population records in his realm using at least the categories of *lão hạng* and *lão nhiêu*, the latter another age-based category.[24] This suggests that he was continuing to use the older village records that he had captured and the Nguyễn classification system that these records used. There is, unfortunately, no other information on Thái Đức's use of this mechanism, and at best it can be surmised that he continued to use the existing Nguyễn system in an essentially unaltered form.

We have considerably more detail concerning Quang Trung's implementation of this schema in his northern realm. In that region populations were classified in the following manner:

*vị cập*—those 9–17 years of age
*tráng hạng*—those 18–55 years of age
*lão hạng*—those 56–60 years of age
*lão nhiêu* —those 61 and up[25]

Several elements of this classification arrangement constituted a clear departure from Trịnh and Nguyễn methods. Most obviously, the new system was a streamlined one that reduced the number of categories to four. Secondly, this simplified system eliminated classifications based on landlessness and other manifestations of poverty, focusing strictly on age. It is also noteworthy that in the Tây Sơn scheme a new category had been added for those under the age of eighteen. In the earlier classification schemes, people only entered the rolls on reaching their eighteenth year. Now an effort was made to bring people onto the records at age nine. This may have been an attempt to prevent people from escaping the control of the state, by making them appear on the records much earlier. But it was also clearly motivated by an attempt to expand the number of people whom the new government could call on for military and labor service. Thus, virtually everyone between the ages of nine and fifty-five was potentially subject to military service, which would require active service from between one out of three and one out of seven eligible villagers.[26] It seems clear that the Tây Sơn considered the young as an important resource, and we shall see that they were periodically deployed as soldiers and in corvée labor projects.[27]

*Identity Cards*

Once the populations had been counted and classified, the Tây Sơn regimes sought to control their movements and to tie them more firmly to their homes. A preliminary step toward such measures in Đàng Ngoài was reported by a French missionary in 1788. He noted that all travelers were required to have an identity card if they wished to travel around the country. Moreover, each village was required to construct two or three offices in which passersby would have to register, thus constituting a means by which to regulate internal movement as well as to gather population figures.[28] This system, which is not reported in any other sources, appears not to have been widely established.

Soon after Nguyễn Huệ ascended the throne as Emperor Quang Trung, and in conjunction with one of the censuses he ordered, he instituted a much more systematic and rigorous attempt to impose these controls. Like the earlier system, this new one involved the use of personal identity cards developed by the Tây Sơn emperor as a way to monitor and control peoples' movements and readily to identify the villages to which they belonged. These documents became known colloquially as trust cards (*tín bài*) for the slogan they bore: *thiên hạ đại tín* (great trust of the empire). A later source provides a useful description of the cards and the way in which the system functioned:

> Each person would have a placard, on which would be engraved "The Great Trust of the Empire" and an official seal. On the four edges [it] made known their surname, given name and antecedents, and contained an imprint of their left thumb.... When they went out the people always had to carry it, and if they should happen to be questioned they had to take it out and present it. This was called "the trust card." And if one did not have the card then... the people were permitted to look and know it. This could then be reported and [the person without the card] would be taken and placed into the army.[29]

This system of identity cards was an innovation on the part of the Tây Sơn: it appears to have no precedent in Vietnamese history. It was part of a systematic attempt to impose direct state control over individuals rather than the more conventional exercise of state authority, which took place largely at the village level. The new regime insisted that all people register with the state and carry their registration card, and decreed that failure to possess such a card and present it on demand would lead to immediate impressment into the Tây Sơn armies.

The *Hoàng Lê Nhật Thống Chí* suggests that these cards were part of the preparation for Quang Trung's planned invasion of China.[30] Another account, however, the *Tây Sơn Thuật Lược* (Summary Record of the Tây Sơn), describes the trust-card policy as having been designed by Ngô Thì Nhậm, the prominent scholar and adviser to Quang Trung. If true, this suggests that the policy was more likely a population control device rather than a way to enhance conscription of soldiers.[31] While there are no indications of Nhậm's having had any military ambitions, he was greatly concerned about vagabond populations, something about which he had memorialized to the Trịnh ruler already in the 1770s. Such a system would have helped achieve his desire to bring populations under control. If the identity-card system was indeed Nhậm's invention, it is possible that he was inspired by the *Zhouli*, a preimperial Chinese text, which describes systems of identification documents to control population movement.[32]

Whatever their origin, or original purpose, it is clear that such identification cards could be used for a variety of purposes, even as their most notable effect appears to have been intimidation of the northern populations. Regardless of their purpose, the identity cards were extremely unpopular among the people and were carried only with great reluctance. As one account described it, only fear led the people to consent to carrying the cards: "The people feared the power and the severity of Huệ and they hung the identity cards around their necks."[33] A French missionary reported that the system had the effect of discouraging people from leaving their own villages for fear of being questioned about their identity cards and possibly forced into military service.[34] The *Hoàng Lê Nhất Thống Chí* described the opposite reaction: people leaving their villages and fleeing into the hills to avoid having to wear and produce the cards on demand.[35] Yet another witness described the populations as so resenting the identity cards that they rose up numerous times in rebellion, only to be crushed by powerful Tây Sơn forces.[36] This hostility is not difficult to understand, for the system, at least in theory, greatly expanded the influence and reach of the new state, rendering the people much more vulnerable to its authority and less easily able to dissimulate before its officials. The continued popular hostility toward the system of trust cards eventually led the Tây Sơn regime to reconsider it, and shortly after Quang Trung's death in 1792 the trust-card system was abolished by the new emperor, Cảnh Thịnh, who also halted the rounding up of vagabonds.[37]

## EXTRACTING SERVICE: SOLDIERS AND CORVÉE LABOR UNDER THE TÂY SƠN

### *Military Service*

Once people had been counted, classified, and registered, they could be tapped by the regime for a variety of tasks and resources. The most critical need was in the area of military service, for the Tây Sơn leaders were fundamentally concerned with the mobilization and deployment of armies. Although these men were merely the latest in a long line of Vietnamese rulers who had called on the populations to serve in their armies, the military demands they made were particularly onerous. There was always an enemy confronting the Tây Sơn, who were initially engaged in large-scale military campaigns against the Nguyễn from 1773 to 1778 and then again from 1782 to 1785, conflicts that resumed again in the early 1790s. In addition, there was the brief but large-scale Tây Sơn campaign to drive out the Qing in 1788–1789. When they were not being challenged by the Nguyễn or Qing, the Tây Sơn sought out conflict: with the Trịnh in 1786; then the major invasions of Laos in 1790 and 1791; and finally in 1792, when Quang Trung contemplated attacking China in an effort to retrieve the two "lost" provinces of Quảng Đông (Guangdong) and Quảng Tây (Guangxi) and then planned a major offensive against the Nguyễn. There were, in addition, periodic episodes of open warfare within the Tây Sơn camp, including most dramatically the brief war between Nguyễn Nhạc and Nguyễn Huệ in 1787, but also Nguyễn Huệ's attacks against Nguyễn Hữu Chỉnh in 1787 and Võ Văn Nhậm in 1788, followed by conflicts of the late 1790s that pitted the Tây Sơn court at Phú Xuân against renegade generals at Qui Nhơn.

Under the Nguyễn rulers there had been a decline in large-scale warfare in Đại Việt after 1672 once the wars with the Trịnh had come to an end. Consequently, life for those in the Đàng Trong armies of this period had not always been one of great hardship. European observers' accounts of the seventeenth-century Nguyễn army described it as being relatively well looked after and reported that soldiers were allowed to keep their families with them.[38] By the middle of the eighteenth century, however, the situation appears to have become more bleak. As Pierre Poivre noted in 1749, "These soldiers are malnourished and even more poorly paid. They languish in slavery until the caprice of the prince results in their elevation to a particular position."[39] Declining living standards for soldiers coincided with increasing military operations, particularly in the neighboring Khmer kingdom, but also periodically in upland areas. And yet, despite this deterioration in conditions for those serving in the Nguyễn military by the middle of the eighteenth century, there remained a qualitative difference between being forced into Tây Sơn armies and being forced into the pre-1771 Nguyễn military, as those compelled to serve in the Tây Sơn forces saw frequent and large-scale conflict.

During the Tây Sơn wars, not only the frequency of conflict, but also its scale boded ill for peasants forced to act as soldiers. As the armies grew in size so did the number of casualties and the corresponding impact that the wars had on the Vietnamese people, both soldiers and civilians. Fragmentary evidence suggests that several hundred thousand people were killed on the battlefields, and it is likely that tens of thousands more died as a result of wounds or illness. Scattered reports of casualties give some idea of the intensity of the conflict. There are accounts indicating that Tây Sơn forces had already killed 1,600 Nguyễn soldiers by early 1774.[40] The ensuing decade saw fierce, ongoing warfare between the Tây Sơn and Nguyễn armies, the intensity of which is revealed in a 1784 report which noted that there had been eighteen major battles over a six-month period, during which Nguyễn Nhạc lost "one-third" of his army.[41] Later as many as 30,000 Trịnh soldiers may have died in a single battle during Nguyễn Huệ's 1786 attack on Phú Xuân.[42] When Nhạc and Huệ fought a brief war early the following year, one missionary reported that Nhạc lost 40,000 troops.[43] In 1793 and 1794 the Tây Sơn were still fielding armies of as many as 50,000–60,000 troops, suggesting that large-scale confrontations continued to take place.[44] Then, in battles around Qui Nhơn in 1801, a European observer cited total casualties (dead and wounded) for Tây Sơn and Nguyễn forces as numbering more than 54,000.[45] These figures make clear the scale of the Tây Sơn wars and the corresponding need continually to find new recruits to fill large and regularly depleted forces.

Initially, the Tây Sơn armies were filled by volunteers, particularly as the movement confined itself to small-scale operations in the upland regions, seeking chiefly to increase its numbers. In this manner the Tây Sơn army had, by 1774, grown to more than 25,000 soldiers.[46] This was a considerable force, but it still faced a substantially larger Nguyễn military, and so in 1775 Nguyễn Nhạc, having named himself king, introduced a standardized troop quota for villages under his control. Each village was forced to send one out of every five men for military service.[47] From this point forward, the Tây Sơn ranks were no longer being filled by enthusiastic volunteers, but increasingly by reluctant conscripts. The formula used by the Tây Sơn leaders to recruit soldiers varied across time and place. While Nhạc required that one out of five men be subject to military service, Nguyễn Huệ in the north took one out of every three villagers.[48] The later Nguyễn records claim that the southern Tây Sơn regime established fixed guidelines for the number of soldiers drafted from each village at one in seven. This account suggested, however, that these guidelines were often suspended, with every villager being taken to serve as a soldier.[49] Lê Quý Đôn reported already in early 1776 that Nhạc had forced "all of the people of the prefecture of Quy Nhơn to serve as soldiers," suggesting that established guidelines were quickly set aside.[50] A later account similarly suggests that although Huệ did use village registers to recruit men for this army, rather than taking a percentage of the eligible men, in at least one instance he simply took every man between the ages of fifteen and sixty.[51]

Given the high risk of death or injury stemming from large-scale and protracted combat, combined with the harshness of life in the Tây Sơn armies, attrition rates were very high, often forcing the rebel leaders to round up troops indiscriminately. It is hardly surprising that many of those forced into the Tây Sơn armies deserted as quickly as was possible, fleeing lack of food, cruel treatment at the hands of their commanders, and the difficulty of lightning-fast forced marches. Numerous accounts (see below) describe the Tây Sơn leadership, particularly in upper Đàng Trong and Đàng Ngoài, as constantly having to recruit new men to replace the troops that had deserted, and frequently doing so in indiscriminate fashion.[52] Thus, when Nguyễn Huệ launched his 1787 war against Nhạc he quickly assembled an army to meet his needs: "[Huệ] returned here at the end of March or early April with around 50,000 men, or more precisely, 50,000 peasants or adventurers raised in haste, his former soldiers having nearly all abandoned him due to his cruelty, which left them to die of hunger."[53] One result of such recruitment strategies was the creation of ragtag forces whose subsequent high desertion rates would hardly be surprising. Even Nguyễn Huệ's recruitment of soldiers for his army to drive off the Qing was done in this ad hoc fashion, yielding a force evocatively described in a contemporary account:

> During that time [late 1788], the new Tyrant of Cochinchina became aware of the arrival of the Chinese and their exploits. As he was full of bravura, and passes here for another Alexander [the Great], he has added to his campaign all whom he has come across, men, children, the elderly, and his army has more the air of a hospital detachment than of fighters.[54]

Faced with routine resistance to serving in their armies and large numbers of troops fleeing the battlefields, Tây Sơn military leaders increasingly adopted coercive measures to keep their armies at full strength and regularly used brutality in their interactions with local populations

FIGURE 7. *Tây Sơn soldier, 1793. From a drawing made by William Alexander, a member of Lord McCartney's 1793 mission. Although stylized, the image gives some indication of the uniform and weaponry of Tây Sơn soldiers in and around the central Tây Sơn court. From John Barrow,* A Voyage to Cochinchina in the Years 1792 and 1793 *(London: T. Cadell and W. Davies, 1806; reprint, Kuala Lumpur: Oxford University Press, 1975).*

and officials. According to many accounts, the Tây Sơn were quick to force people into their armies and just as quick to punish those who refused to join them. In this respect the Tây Sơn were following practices established by the Nguyễn in the seventeenth century and possibly earlier. As Li Tana notes,

> The Nguyễn recruiting law was very strict. In approximately 1671 Vachet reported that "a man will lose his head if he is found trying to avoid being a soldier." He also added that if a recruiting officer accepted a substandard conscript, he too would lose his head. Judging from Da Shan's 1690s account, the process of military recruitment manifested itself in each village as little less than a disaster.[55]

The Tây Sơn innovation, if one can call it that, may have been to increase the level and scope of the brutality being exercised to intimidate populations into acceding to Tây Sơn demands.

Execution as a response to resistance was carried out during the earliest days of the uprising and remained a significant element of Tây Sơn military policy to the very end of the regime. Early in the course of the uprising, the same Spanish missionary who noted that the Tây Sơn were hailed as "virtuous and charitable thieves" also observed that "[t]hey set fire to the palace [of the provincial governor] to make themselves masters of the entire province, without encountering any resistance because they executed all who opposed them."[56] Indeed, the same source noted that it was fear of their leader, Nguyễn Nhạc, among other factors, that drove the early successes of the Tây Sơn troops. Such policies were sustained throughout the Tây Sơn era, and as late as 1801, a missionary letter reported that "even in the midst of all these troubles, the Tây Sơn are not losing their wits, and are carrying out another levy of soldiers; no one dares refuse, for those who do are summarily decapitated."[57] Thus, not only were people dying on the battlefields if they were unfortunate enough to find themselves pressed into service, but more than a few were dying for their efforts to resist conscription in the first place.[58]

While the Tây Sơn military leaders executed many who resisted their recruitment efforts, they practiced particular cruelty among those already in their armies—to harden them for battle, to intimidate them from attempting to flee, and probably to coerce cooperation from local populations. A 1788 missionary letter described the brutal control exercised by the Tây Sơn general Võ Văn Nhậm and his officers:

> The talent of these men was to kill a great many people to make them fearful and to obey promptly. They also killed many people for no reason. As they left and brought this large number of forced troops they made to redouble their cruelty. For an error or for bothering someone or any similar thing, or even for no particular offense [soldiers] would have their heads cut off. In the space of a half a league on the road, one could see 15 bodies killed in this manner.[59]

This description suggests an ongoing pattern of intimidation designed to force people into the Tây Sơn armies and to keep them there. At times such intimidation appears to have extended to acts of ritualized cannibalism. A letter, probably written around 1795, claimed that "[t]he rebels who occupy all of Tonkin and upper Cochinchina carry out vexations here and cruelties of the most extraordinary nature, to the point of making their soldiers drink human blood and to making them eat men who are still fully alive in order to accustom them to cruelty."[60] Reports of such conduct are found not only in the French missionary materials, but also in the nineteenth-century Nguyễn records. The *Đại Nam Thực Lục*, for instance, describes a 1776 encounter between Tây Sơn and Nguyễn forces in which a Nguyễn general was captured and, after refusing to compromise himself in the face of Tây Sơn threats, was killed, and then eaten.[61]

For all its threat, however, the use of execution and other forms of intimidation was not sufficient to maintain adequate troop strength within the Tây Sơn armies. Consequently, the Tây Sơn leaders also employed other strategies to retain and attract soldiers, including ones that relied on suasion rather than force. Most commonly, particularly in the final years of the regime, the Tây Sơn military leaders offered promotions to their soldiers, hoping, perhaps, that pride in rank might persuade troops to remain in their units. In 1797, a missionary reported of the situation in his district in Đàng Ngoài that "almost all of the men have died in the wars or other calamities that have been suffered in this country for 25 years, and the few men that remain are in the service of the Tyrant and *are almost all commanders or officers*, some in the service of the army, and others in the offices and the jurisdictions."[62] Similarly, a few years later, in 1801, a keen European military observer noted the peculiarly top-heavy structure of the Tây Sơn armies in Đàng Trong. Describing the rebel armies in the aftermath of an important Nguyễn victory, which had resulted in the capture of 13,700 Tây Sơn troops, he reported,

> There are more than 144 colonels, lieutenant-colonels, and majors in one large encampment at the palace to the right of the entrance. All are in chains. Moreover, there are 500 to 600 others who are more lightly chained. The captains, ensigns, sergeants and corporals number 3,500 to 4,000 and are all in the cangue.[63]

Although the ranks have been rendered here in European nomenclature, it seems clear that a disproportionate number of Tây Sơn forces held ranks above that of common soldier.[64]

Indications of this trend can be found in Vietnamese sources as well. A village register from a hamlet north of Phú Xuân in upper Đàng Trong, dated 1799, recorded that of 295 eligible males in the village, 122 of them carried either noble titles or officer-level military positions. It seems highly unlikely, under normal circumstances, that 41 percent of the men in a village would bear titles or such military ranks. Instead, this case suggests that titles and higher military ranks were at times liberally distributed to attract or retain supporters. Moreover, this dramatic expansion of the Tây Sơn officer corps was not lost on the general populations observing the military events of the late–Tây Sơn era. A mocking saying emerged in the last years of the Tây Sơn regime, commenting on the peculiar structure of the rebel armies:

> As for commanders-in-chief, we have 3,000;
> As for commanders we have 80,000;
> As for lieutenants and captains, they are too numerous to count.
> And as for corporals and sergeants, we need boats to transport
> them all.[65]

*Labor Service*

In addition to military service, the Tây Sơn regimes subjected Vietnamese populations to almost continuous demands for corvée labor. This was yet another onerous and time-consuming obligation that threatened peoples' livelihood and pulled them away from their fields. Like the Nguyễn and Trịnh rulers before them, and the Nguyễn dynasty after them, the Tây Sơn regimes relied on subject populations for labor service to carry out projects both grandiose and mundane.[66] In a period that saw as much warfare and destruction as the late eighteenth century, it was perhaps inevitable that enormous labor contributions would be required both to support these military campaigns and to build and rebuild infrastructure destroyed in the course of warfare. While some of the labor service demanded by the Tây Sơn regime can be said to have benefited local populations—repairing dikes, for example, or rebuilding damaged roads—many other projects were of little or no concrete benefit to those forced to participate in them.

The need for corvée labor manifested itself very early in the Tây Sơn movement, and it is likely that the particularly destructive Tây Sơn approach to warfare—putting to torch what might have been useful edifices—contributed to their insatiable corvée demands.[67] On seizing the provincial capital at Qui Nhơn in 1773, for example, rebel troops promptly burned down the governor-general's mansion. A short while later, "they burned the palace of the mandarin governor of Quang Ngai and built a new one."[68] Tây Sơn armies also caused widespread destruction in the important coastal cities of Đà Nẵng and Hội An, the latter of which was particularly devastated, and in cities farther north after their 1786 invasion of Đàng Ngoài.[69] Whether edifices were destroyed by torch or taken apart brick by brick, it was the general population that ultimately suffered from the need to reconstruct what had been destroyed.

More specifically, it was local populations that were called on to carry out these projects, and consequently the distribution of labor service was uneven. While there were numerous small-scale projects to reconstruct local buildings or roads, throughout the Tây Sơn era the heaviest labor burdens fell on populations living in close proximity to the regime's political centers. The first of these projects to construct a new political center began in 1775 when Nguyễn Nhạc started using local labor to reinforce fortifications and erect structures at Chà Bàn.[70] Although the remains of a Cham citadel already existed on the site, substantial work was required to fortify the walls and to construct living and working space within its grounds. The only detailed eyewitness description of Tây Sơn–controlled Chà Bàn dates from 1778 and tells of a city whose ramparts were still in a state of disrepair.[71] This suggests either that the work had not been completed—though the eyewitness (Charles Chapman) does not mention seeing any labor crews—or that work had been halted as forced labor had fled the scene, leaving the Tây Sơn ruler with insufficient numbers of workers to complete the project.

A similar pattern can be seen in the wake of the Tây Sơn northward advance in 1786. After his troops captured Phú Xuân from the Trịnh, Nguyễn Huệ rounded up local populations and forced them to work day and night to rebuild the fortifications of the city, which would serve as his own political center.[72] At the same time Huệ also began work to restore the Lũy Sầy ramparts north of Phú Xuân, which had formerly protected the Nguyễn against the Trịnh. This project, like that to rebuild the city's defense, required major labor contributions from local populations. The French missionary Jean La Bartette reported that the labor demands were so heavy that every segment of the population was forced to participate, with the only exemption being for nursing mothers.[73]

Four years later, in 1790, Nguyễn Huệ (now ruling as the Quang Trung emperor) began to recruit corvée labor for the preliminary construction of his new Imperial Phoenix Central Capital in Nghệ An. A contemporary account from 1791 described the hardships faced by those forced to labor on the project:

> The people and soldiers are overwhelmed, and they are continually occupied in the construction of a city that the rebels are erecting. Some are sent to search for wood in the forests, while others are digging in the ground for stones; [some] are baking bricks and tiles and others are working on the terraces and the ditches. . . . All of this is carried out at the expense of the people.[74]

A later Vietnamese chronicler added, "The officials of the region urged the people of all the districts to go to An Trường to fill in the lakes and ponds, and to cut down trees."[75] The popular response was to resist this project, and many people abandoned the undertaking and fled.[76] Thus, just as the Tây Sơn regime had repeatedly to enroll new soldiers as conscripts fled, the same was true of labor service.

While these large-scale projects to build new imperial centers were perhaps the most obvious sources of hardship for Vietnamese populations, they were also forced to provide labor for myriad other, more mundane projects. This was the case throughout the Tây Sơn realms, but it appears to have been particularly true in Đàng Ngoài, where Nguyễn Huệ and his lieutenants and successors made continual demands on their populations. This began with Huệ's exactions around Phú Xuân in 1786 and continued farther north in 1788, when the Tây Sơn general Võ Văn Nhậm reportedly put everyone to work repairing old citadel walls around Hà Nội, an action that alienated these populations and, as we have seen, contributed to his subsequent ouster by Nguyễn Huệ.[77] Then, as the war with the Nguyễn dragged on through the 1790s, Tây Sơn labor exactions—for projects ranging from the rebuilding of roads and bridges to the construction and repair of fortifications—only intensified. In 1794, there was another round of demands for labor services, described as exhausting the people living under Tây Sơn control.[78] Four years later, the situation had still not improved, and another missionary letter reported, "[T]he people are more troubled than ever before. They have to pay a double tribute this year, excavate canals for the transport of rice from Tonkin into upper Cochinchina, and make baskets to transport it over land in places where one cannot excavate."[79]

To meet their constant need for labor service, the Tây Sơn rulers greatly expanded the range of groups within society who were subject to such service. This included women and other formerly exempted (or less frequently used) groups in society including children, the elderly, and Buddhist monks. As was noted above, when Tây Sơn troops entered Thuận Hóa in 1786, they immediately put everyone to work, exempting only nursing mothers. There may have been a decline in the employment of women thereafter, but by the summer of 1792 a missionary in Đàng Ngoài reported that "there has recently come an order that in all the villages where there are insufficient men for public works, the women will be employed, and that unmarried women be sent to carry stones to construct fortifications."[80] Some villagers, at least in this instance, were able to deflect the force of this order by the expedient of tracking down the unmarried girls in the village and forcing them to marry. In this fashion the village could avoid having to bear the burden of providing supplies for the girls that would have been sent away on the construction project. Nonetheless, the incident suggests the difficulties and pressures being placed on local populations.

Such pressures also extended to those usually seen as too young or too old to be subjected to state labor demands. The classification scheme that enrolled village males by the age of nine was already an indication that the new regime was pushing back age limits for full participation in society and was ready to put children to use when necessary. As was noted above, in 1787 Nguyễn Huệ was conscripting fifteen-year-olds into his army.[81] It was not only military service, but other kinds of labor that were imposed on the young. A 1791 missionary letter reported that "[if] there remain any younger people [in the villages], it is because they have been exempted by paying very large contributions. What is more, there is an order these days to take all of the young men from around 12 to 15 years of age, to serve the children of the king."[82]

These children, and others as young as seven or eight, were being taken to create a special guard unit for one of Quang Trung's sons, who (aged six or seven) had just been appointed as the nominal head of the government in Đàng Ngoài.[83] There is also scattered evidence of the Tây Sơn regimes employing elderly men and women as laborers and of men as old as sixty being forced to serve as soldiers.[84] At other times older men may even have joined the Tây Sơn armies voluntarily. In one case a group of elderly men from the region of Thăng Long formed a "troop company of the aged" (*đội quân đầu bạc*) to help in the 1789 attack on the Chinese, an act for which Quang Trung personally rewarded them.[85]

Finally, the Tây Sơn leaders, who had little regard for institutional Buddhism, had no qualms about looking to Buddhist monasteries for labor. Most frequently, they forced the bonzes to leave their monasteries (many of which Tây Sơn troops had already ransacked or converted to other uses) to serve as porters or soldiers in the rebel armies.[86] The use of monks for such state-ordered labor was a highly unusual feature of the Tây Sơn era, for those living in monastic orders were traditionally exempt from labor service and taxation. The decision by the Tây Sơn leaders to tap what they saw as a convenient and unexploited source of labor once again suggests the high degree of pragmatism, rather than ideology, that was driving the movement. At the same time, the Tây Sơn attacks on Buddhist monastic centers and the dispersal of their residents as laborers may have had a secondary motive, namely, reducing the possibility of monasteries serving as sites of resistance, as there are some indications that this had been taking place.[87]

Although labor demands were frequent and onerous and extended to every group in society, they did occasionally have concrete benefits for the populations performing them. Projects to repair dikes, for example, were particularly important in Đàng Ngoài, where farming close to the Red River rendered earthen embankments critical to controlling its unpredictable course. Periodic dike breaks often caused destruction on an enormous scale, sometimes washing away thousands of homes. A description of a 1795 dike repair project in the province of Sơn Nam (the large alluvial region stretching along the southern banks of the Red River from Thăng Long to the coast) carried out under the supervision of a key Tây Sơn official, Phan Huy Ích, gives some indication of the significance of such work:

> I received the order to supervise the matter of building the dikes, and personally traveled to see and inspect all the places, and to communicate to all of the district officials [the need] to concentrate on the villages near the river and to force the people to assist by bringing bamboo wood in order to begin the work of setting them up, and [informing them of]

> the deadline by which it had to be completed, so they would not dawdle. After one month, the work was completed. The people were somewhat tired, but they had gained a common benefit, and they all recognized that this was advantageous.[88]

While Ích's description is clearly idealized, it is conceivable that the laborers did view their contributions in this manner. Indeed, it is likely that the workers understood the need for dike maintenance projects, which would have been left undone during years of turmoil. Dike repair projects such as this represented rare instances in which public labor would have been of direct benefit to the populations forced to perform it. The only other public works projects that might also have offered some incidental benefit would have been road reconstruction efforts, for these routes permitted transport of much-needed food supplies and commercial goods more generally. Most other projects, however—constructing ramparts, citadels, palaces, and offices—would have been of no immediate or apparent benefit to workers forced to labor on them.

## EXTRACTING RESOURCES: LOOTING, TAXATION, AND CORRUPTION

Military and labor service coerced out of a reluctant population represented only one aspect of Tây Sơn pressures on those living under their control. Although such services met various immediate needs, the rebel leaders and later rulers had an ongoing need for more tangible contributions as well. Consequently, throughout the Tây Sơn years, Vietnamese populations regularly found themselves forced to provide the regimes with material goods. These contributions occasionally took the form of cash payments, but more often they consisted of commodities ranging from produce to livestock to valuables. The forms of these extractions varied, reflecting the objectives or strength of those making them. Simple looting by armed forces, common during the early days of the uprising, remained a central component of Tây Sơn extractive strategies. Secondly, the more organized elements of the Tây Sơn regimes acquired goods in kind or cash by carrying out formal tax levies or using the military to force populations to make contributions. Finally, corrupt officials or local administrators associated with the Tây Sơn regimes would coerce resources or cash from local populations under their control. At some level for the average Vietnamese peasant, the particular mechanism by which goods were extracted was not relevant, for the final result was inevitably the same.

*Looting (the "Redistribution of Wealth")*

The seizure of goods and military supplies, either taken with the purpose of redistributing them or of retaining them for their armies, was a significant component of the pragmatic Tây Sơn leadership's approach to power. In one sense the uprising was initially driven and supported by such seizures, which contemporary observers called "charitable thievery," the nineteenth-century Nguyễn historians called "looting," and modern scholars have euphemistically described as a "redistribution of wealth." Evidence from the earliest days of the movement suggests that Tây Sơn armies were redistributing goods as a useful means of gaining popular support and increasing their ranks. While poorer peasants were no doubt beneficiaries of some of the early Tây Sơn acts of redistribution, as these armies grew larger their seizure of goods became more indiscriminate. The following description comes from 1774:

> Before they departed, the rebels devastated the entire region, without leaving a single chicken alive.... [T]hey seized the 82 bronze cannons given by the Dutch and the English to the Cochinchinese king for the defense of the capital of this province in which is found the port of Tourane; the rebels also took 45 elephants, numerous arms, the drums and flags, and an infinite number of other objects. Each mandarin left with more than 12 large boats filled with riches, which they took by sea to the province where they are based.[89]

As a result of such actions, the number of people who were victims rather than beneficiaries of Tây Sơn military campaigns increased dramatically. Consequently, the Spanish missionary who described this devastating Tây Sơn attack went on to observe that "as for the inhabitants, they rallied to the soldiers of the king, because the rebels had stolen all that they possessed, after having sacked the entire province; it was thus that the soldiers of the king had no difficulties in retaking the city and in setting their adversaries to flight."[90] This comment suggests that the political benefits of looting were transitory at best and that such actions often alienated populations rather than winning them to the rebel side.[91] Despite this, Tây Sơn armies appear to have continued their looting during military campaigns throughout the rest of the 1770s. When Charles Chapman visited coastal Cochinchina in 1778, he encountered starving villagers who had been plundered of their limited possessions by a Tây Sơn army that passed through in the midst of an ongoing famine.[92] Such looting continued during subsequent Tây Sơn attacks on Gia Định between 1782 and 1785.

The scale of looting carried out by Tây Sơn armies increased as the treasures of Đàng Ngoài came within range in 1786. Although Nguyễn Huệ sought to impose some discipline on his troops during the initial stages of the northern campaign, they nonetheless carried off much of the gold and silver found in the Trịnh palaces of Thăng Long, along with all of the arms and ammunition stored in the city. As one observer put it, "The Cochinchinese pillaged everything, gold, silver, canons, guns, furniture, elephants, horses; they left behind nothing but the shell of the [Trịnh] palaces."[93] On their retreat Tây Sơn forces continued their extensive looting, now turning their attention to villages in their path.[94] Several European missionaries who observed the Tây Sơn armies even suggested that their invasion of the north was carried out primarily as a looting expedition and show of force and was not intended as a sustained political effort.[95]

As was noted in the previous chapter, looting during the 1786 northern campaign caused some of the tensions that sprang up between Nguyễn Huệ and Nguyễn Nhạc. On the brothers' departure from Đàng Ngoài, Nhạc seized most or all of the loot taken from the northern capital for himself. In retaliation Huệ attacked his brother at Qui Nhơn in early 1787 but then also permitted (or possibly even sent) some of his troops back into northern territory for further plunder to make up for the booty he had lost to his brother.

> When the [Tây Sơn] had amassed enough supplies, both in terms of natural resources and in currency, they secretly brought them to their general depot in Xu Thanh. There extortion and violence continued on the part of the Tây Sơn and their troops until the middle of March, when these pillagers, for the most part at least, returned to Phú Xuân. [They did so] with an immense booty, which this time was all for Đức Ông [Nguyễn Huệ] to serve as ample compensation for the loss of that which the Tyrant Nhạc had seized in its entirety the previous year.[96]

As this letter makes clear, it was inevitably Vietnamese villages and their residents who felt the impact of the Tây Sơn armies as they scoured the countryside for booty, whether for themselves or their leaders.

With large-scale Tây Sơn attacks to the north taking place in 1787,

1788, and 1789, the regions of Nghệ An and Thanh Hóa, which lay between Phú Xuân and Thăng Long, were particularly hard hit. They regularly found themselves at the mercy of enormous armies that, despite periodic calls for restraint by their commanders, inevitably took their toll on local populations. A missionary letter from 1789 gives some sense of the impact of Tây Sơn armies in Đàng Ngoài:

> The enemy enters the homes, examines and takes that which pleases them. This is the state of the poor villagers, who are not in a condition to pay the tribute. The poor Tonkinese still have to sustain the insatiable cupidity of their enemy, and of the Tonkinese who are followers of the Cochinchinese.[97]

Other letters from this period described regular pillaging in which soldiers took even the most insignificant things.[98] A 1787 report speaks of Tây Sơn forces leaving the local missionaries with nothing except a few vases.[99] Another missionary reports seeing villages that had been burned (and presumably looted) by Tây Sơn armies three or four times in the period between 1786 and 1792.[100]

Although looting took place to satisfy the avarice of troops, generals, or political leaders, it was often prompted by more practical concerns. One consequence of the constant fighting during this period was the need to provide sufficient ammunition for the forces on all sides. To meet this need, armies frequently turned to the treasures of local communities, and most often their religious shrines. Soldiers would seize bronze bells, drums, and other artifacts, which could then be melted down to produce cannonballs for their artillery pieces.[101] During their early attacks on Nguyễn political centers, the Tây Sơn had also taken state ritual objects, including the nine bronze urns symbolizing the ancestors of the Nguyễn clan.[102] These items might be used to manufacture weapons and ammunition, but they also could be and were used to cast coins for the new regimes or even to help build and decorate their political centers.[103] Tây Sơn looting resulted in enormous numbers of valuable items being seized and melted down, though in some cases peasants took steps to protect locally prized items. When word of the seizure of pagoda artifacts spread in advance of Tây Sơn troop movements, many villages took the simple step of burying their artifacts until the threat had passed. Missionary letters described this means by which peasants sought to protect local treasures, but even more eloquent evidence is the steady stream of such artifacts being unearthed by contemporary archaeologists.[104]

*Taxation in Cash and Goods*

The Tây Sơn regimes' leaders also attempted to engage in more systematic extraction of revenues in the form of tax collection. This is a more complex undertaking, requiring an institutional infrastructure that the Tây Sơn were very slow to develop. Moreover, it is likely that during the uprising's early years loot and plunder served in substantial measure as a substitute for direct and systematic taxation. It is not until 1786 that we have the first evidence of the Tây Sơn attempting to collect taxes, and this in a region and under circumstances where such efforts would have been extremely difficult. The same social and political upheaval in Đàng Ngoài that had served to make the region vulnerable to attack by the Tây Sơn also rendered routine collection of taxes a near impossibility. It did not, however, prevent Nguyễn Huệ from beginning to extract revenue from the region, and particularly from Nghệ An. There were reports that by the summer of 1787 Nguyễn Huệ had already "levied exorbitant taxes in rice and silver."[105] Such taxes were unlikely to have been systematic, but rather to have been imposed by Tây Sơn officials in places where they had the ability to coerce payment.

Despite the difficulties and resistance the Tây Sơn regime faced in asserting its authority, once Nguyễn Huệ had taken the throne as Quang Trung in late 1788 and defeated the Chinese, he made attempts to begin the systematic levying and collection of taxes. In a 1790 decree, the new emperor spelled out the tax obligations that were to be imposed on villages according to the classifications of their inhabitants. The decree also addressed the taxes to be imposed on crops based on varying qualities of field lands and stipulated the manner in which taxes were to be collected and how taxes in kind were to be stored.[106] It is clear from this document that the Tây Sơn regime sought to reimpose order on the tax structures and to systematize what had become chaotic, particularly in the north, during the 1780s. It is unclear, however, to what degree regular tax collections were carried out prior to Quang Trung's death in 1792. There are isolated reports of heavy tax burdens, including in Nghệ An, from which region Nguyễn Thiếp wrote to Quang Trung to reprove him for the rising tax burden and forced contributions.[107] In any case, the system began to break down toward the end of the dynasty, as military and political crises became acute.

Even with the articulation of standardized tax obligations, the new regime continued to make irregular and additional demands to underwrite expensive state rituals. On the death of Quang Trung's first wife in the spring of 1791, the Tây Sơn emperor organized an elaborate funeral and period of mourning that followed and "incurred considerable expenses, which all fell on the impoverished people."[108] The following year, after Quang Trung's own death, equally lavish arrangements were made in the area around Phú Xuân to receive the formal Chinese recognition of the new Tây Sơn ruler, Cảnh Thịnh. These preparations were described by a European observer as "a scheme contrived to collect taxes from the people in the form of silver [and] animals."[109] Indeed, these preparations were not to receive the Chinese delegation itself, but merely for a formal procession of the investiture documents being transported to the Tây Sơn capital at Phú Xuân. Whatever the object of these ceremonies, the general population was once again forced to bear the financial burden. Demands such as these constituted an irregular form of taxation, imposing an additional layer of uncertainty on peasants already struggling with frequent and time-consuming military and labor service demands.

Even more common than tax obligations in cash were forced contributions of goods and products. This was a long-standing practice in Đại Việt, but particularly in Đàng Trong, where various localities were expected to pay some of their tax obligations in the form of local products, which ranged from beeswax to birds' nests to valuable woods.[110] The Tây Sơn continued this practice during their rule. In 1789, for instance, a missionary writing from northern Đàng Trong observed that "our Christians have been forced to make a contribution of ten thousand pieces of copper in order to cast cannons, and the Chinese living in Cochinchina are not exempt from this unjust exaction."[111] Reporting from the same region two years later, another missionary described the demands being placed on those living in his locality:

> In the single small district in Bố Chính, where I have been for the past 15 days [the people] have been ordered to build more than one hundred [small boats]: these poor men and all of our unfortunate Christians who have consecutively lost their harvests of the 10th and 5th months, and will perhaps also lose that of the following 10th month, have never before had to endure such an enormous burden: the number of planks that they must submit for this effort is two thousand five hundred. . . . Aside from these planks, everyone must submit all of their produce.[112]

It is clear from this description that particular regions were obliged to contribute locally available resources, and thus Bố Chính, a mountainous and heavily wooded area to the north of Phú Xuân, was called on to provide wood for boats. Also, as was described earlier, those forced to labor on Quang Trung's grand new capital in Nghệ An were expected to provide not only all the labor but also all the material and cash to accomplish the construction project. These descriptions also indicate the degree to which such exactions might be placed on particular groups within society, such as Christians, a topic that will be taken up in greater detail in the next chapter.

### *Corruption: Limits to Tây Sơn Institutional Authority*

The last form of resource extraction, and one of the most pervasive, was corruption by officials serving the Tây Sơn regimes. Corruption is a broad category, one that ranges from minor manipulation of state-mandated tax payments to outright extortion. Corruption stemming from a weak central authority is a long-running theme in Vietnamese history. It is to be found both in dynasties in decline and in newly established regimes still seeking to assert their authority and to restructure their administrations. The Tây Sơn regimes clearly suffered from numerous obstacles that prevented them from stemming the very corruption that had provoked their uprising in the first place. Massive social disorder and dislocation in all regions of the country made their task particularly difficult, but the lack of trained officials, the continued reliance on supporters with limited administrative skills, ongoing warfare, and the absence of a functioning judicial structure all compounded the problems faced by the regime. The result was continuing corruption, which in turn alienated the very populations the Tây Sơn leaders claimed to have been assisting and which continued to spark popular discontent and a desire for improvements.

The Tây Sơn regimes' failure to bring corruption under control may be attributed to the exigencies of ongoing warfare and the often limited bureaucratic skills of the rebel leaders and their close aides, both of which kept Tây Sơn administrative structures ad hoc in many places. As Charles Chapman observed of the Tây Sơn regime he encountered during his 1778 visit to Nhạc's court at Chà Bàn,

> Ignac [Nguyễn Nhạc] himself is allowed to have abilities, but these are ill-seconded by the Mandarines who govern under him. They are all low illiterate men chosen from amongst the inhabitants of his native village of Tyson who, as soon as they have got into power, have been remarkable

> only for their perfidy, cruelty and extortion, and if at a distance barely acknowledge a dependence on the hand that raised them.[113]

In short, the first Tây Sơn state was seen as being administered by officials who were uneducated, cruel, and corrupt and who paid little attention to directives coming from the center of power. This was, moreover, a pattern that would persist throughout the Tây Sơn years and that was not substantially different under the regime created by Nguyễn Huệ in Đàng Ngoài. A French missionary describing that regime in 1789 largely echoed Chapman's 1778 assessment of Nguyễn Nhạc's government: "These barbarians come from the mountains of Cochinchina and know nothing about the arrangements for governance."[114] Although there were places where administrative structures were more fully developed—including around Thăng Long under the reigns of Quang Trung and his successor—many other places were less fortunate in the nature of the officials serving them.

Systemic corruption in the Tây Sơn regimes was encouraged by the weaknesses of the regime's institutional structures and their leaders' inability to elaborate a judicial system, much less enforce one in an effective manner. There are indications that a new legal code had been written at some time in the period after Quang Trung came to power, but it was never formally introduced.[115] The absence of an enforceable judicial structure meant that official corruption would be that much more difficult to bring under control. The *Tây Sơn Thuật Lược* observed of Quang Trung's regime that "there was no establishment of written rules and regulations; matters regarding civil suits were all adjudicated orally before officials, and as for punishments the majority consisted of public caning."[116] Missionaries also reported in 1789 that the judicial system either no longer existed or was at best of a rudimentary nature, enforced by men of limited ability, many of whom could neither read nor write.[117] A decade later the situation was no better, as is reflected in another missionary's description of judicial structures that were extremely corrupt: "All of the mandarins look for ways to enrich themselves at the expense of the poor people. Justice is served in weights of gold, with the balance always tilted to the side of those who offer the most money."[118]

Particularly in the Đàng Ngoài region, there were numerous reports of malfeasance during the Tây Sơn years (1786–1802) and frequent comments both by Vietnamese and outside observers that local-level officials

FIGURE 8. *Tây Sơn official, 1793. From a drawing made by William Alexander, who accompanied Lord McCartney's mission during its visit to Emperor Cảnh Thịnh's court at Phú Xuân in 1793. Author's collection.*

were ill-trained and often venal. Some Tây Sơn administrative initiatives served only to exacerbate the situation, which was nowhere worse than in Nghệ An. In late 1789 Nguyễn Thiếp reported directly to Quang Trung regarding the problems with local officials serving in that province: "The more the number of officials increases, the more the people must bear mistreatment. Now the power is questionable and the work is inconsistent. The generals, the officers, and the mandarins continue to be without supervision."[119] These problems stemmed in part from the Tây Sơn decision to divide Nghệ An into twelve districts. Thiếp clearly saw a link between an enlarged bureaucratic structure and increasing oppression being suffered by the general populations. These problems were further compounded by Nghệ An's lying directly in the path of every large-scale Tây Sơn military campaign between 1786 and 1789. During that time Tây Sơn troops traveled through Nghệ An eight times, each time creating further difficulties for local populations.

Possibly in reaction to Thiếp's reports, or perhaps because of other information that was reaching it, Quang Trung's court ordered an extensive investigation into official corruption in that province. Bùi Dương Lịch described the Tây Sơn response to these problems, which began in June–July 1790:

> Before this, those at the highest levels had personally written an edict in vermillion characters secretly ordering all of the governors-general to restrain the disaster of corruption. All of the officials in the province ordered the three local bureau officials in the area to go out to interrogate the hamlet residents in order that all of the people in the hamlet might point out the offices that were corrupt. The officials secretly investigated, gathered petitions and requests, and then brought them back to the province [officials]. All of the provincial officials were sent down to the bureaus of the district officials to set up places to carry out investigations.[120]

From this report, it appears that the Tây Sơn government under Quang Trung was actively seeking to address the issue of corruption, especially in Nghệ An. The Tây Sơn response was no doubt spurred by Quang Trung's respect for Nguyễn Thiếp's advice, as well as Nghệ An's status as the future home of his central capital. It was an area in which a stable population would be essential.

Despite these investigations, the situation did not improve. Thiếp sent a second memorial to the emperor in 1791 in which, echoing language he used in his 1789 report, he wrote that the people were still suffering the double burdens of military service and forced requisitions for the Tây Sơn armies. Their miseries continued to be compounded by drought, which ruined their crops. Thiếp criticized the lack of any significant Tây Sơn response. The regime had yet to provide assistance for devastated peasants or to take steps to lower taxes. Thiếp urged the emperor to reduce forced contributions in proportion to the hardships that individuals were facing.[121] The situation in the province eventually became so difficult that the populations there rose up in rebellion against a particularly corrupt Tây Sơn governor in 1791.[122] This was a rare act of open popular defiance against Quang Trung's regime, for populations knew only too well the militarized state in which they lived. The rebellion suggests just how difficult the situation must have become for local residents. In 1797 reports still indicated that hardships continued because local Tây Sơn officials were concerned only with their own interests.[123]

## FORMS OF POPULAR RESISTANCE: LOOKING TO PROPHECIES, OMENS, AND SAVIORS

Although the Tây Sơn uprising's leaders initially portrayed their movement as a massive act of resistance against political and economic patterns that had developed in Đàng Trong, the movement's shift toward orthodox government, combined with the enormous and onerous demands it made of populations under its control, eventually provoked resistance against the Tây Sơn leaders themselves. The forms of this resistance varied greatly and displayed many levels of sophistication. Surviving documentation allows us only limited glimpses of overt physical resistance. I have already noted desertion from Tây Sơn armies and work crews, as well as the manipulation of tax and population registers, a few short-lived uprisings, and the burial of sacred items. There are also numerous reports of villages in Đàng Ngoài barricading themselves against all outside forces, asserting their traditional autonomy in the face of state efforts to extract revenues or other contributions.[124] These instances suggest that peasants attempted to resist Tây Sơn authority in numerous ways, even as the effectiveness of these methods varied considerably.

In addition to overt resistance, Vietnamese peasants (and elites) were also capable of what might be termed psychological defiance. Such defiance involved reference to prophecies and natural omens, but also included other forms of speculation or verbal resistance. These forms of defiance created an autonomous realm of thought that enabled the peasantry—and to a considerable degree elites as well—to gain some measure of control over the forces buffeting their lives and to come to terms with the difficulties of Tây Sơn rule. Efforts to use prophecies or omens to determine the course of future events frequently produced results open to numerous interpretations, with prophecies being particularly susceptible to multiple readings. But this is precisely the point: people tried to comprehend what was going on around them and regularly altered their readings of the signs to reflect changing circumstances. The existence of these signs, prophecies, and portents is not a means by which to understand the course of the Tây Sơn uprising, but a way to understand popular mentalités in a time of great uncertainty.

There is an inherent problem in trying to use signs and prophecies as evidence of the perspicacity of those who were interpreting them. After all, much of the documentation recording these prophecies postdates the events that were being predicted or anticipated. Clearly, it is the predictions that came true (or more accurately the proper interpretations of these predictions) that were recorded in the private and official chronicles. We do not hear about other interpretations, which must have existed alongside these, that did not come to pass. Despite this caveat, reports of these attempts to understand supernatural indications are important for showing how people in this period understood their world. Many of the sources describing these signs and prophecies date from the late–Tây Sơn period and the early years of the Nguyễn dynasty, making it likely that they were in circulation during the Tây Sơn period. Some of these prophecies were also recorded in contemporary missionary letters, further proof that such concepts were a central part of both popular and elite understandings of their world.

*Prophets and Prophecies*

As warfare swirled around them in the late eighteenth century, Vietnamese populations frequently sought to make sense of their times by looking for indications of what the future might hold. This practice was common to all levels of Vietnamese society during this era, and people of all strata often turned to individuals who might offer answers about what was to come. As one eighteenth-century European observer noted, "These imposters are to be found in great numbers in Tonkin; there is not a town or village in which one cannot find these Diviners and Mystics; their power extends from the lowliest of people up to the Monarch, where they control his principle undertakings."[125] Beyond the self-proclaimed seers, the so-called imposters, there were some individuals who were widely acclaimed for their skills of prophecy. In earlier centuries, the noted Đàng Ngoài scholar Nguyễn Bỉnh Khiêm (1491–1585) had gained a reputation as a seer, and his prognostications continued to draw popular attention well after his death. In the late eighteenth century, the renowned recluse-scholar Nguyễn Thiếp filled this role. As Bùi Dương Lịch noted of him, "People said that he knew all things before they happened."[126] It was this reputation that drew Nguyễn Huệ to consult Nguyễn Thiếp in late 1788 as he sought to determine the outcome of his impending battle with the invading Qing forces.[127]

Beyond consulting figures such as Thiếp, people during the Tây Sơn period took note of existing prophecies, trying to match the words of prophecies with events or figures of their time. Moreover, political figures in this period acted on prophecies, using them to justify their actions and encouraging popular belief in their own interpretations of these prophecies. As one missionary serving in Đàng Ngoài in the 1780s observed, "The pagans of this kingdom have prophecies that are called Sam Ki, as true and intelligible as those of Nostradamus. And these prophecies have announced, say the interpreters of the pagans, that the race of the Chua Trinh would be finished in this era."[128] This belief in omens and other indications of the future course of events closely linked Vietnamese popular and elite cultural worlds and extended to the rulers themselves. Prophecies could not easily be dismissed by political elites because they often had a powerful hold on the populace and thus the potential for swaying popular beliefs and actions.

A notable demonstration of the effect that prophecy could have on political elites occurred in the middle of the eighteenth century and anticipated the unrest that would culminate in the Tây Sơn upheavals. A prophecy that gained currency at the time was said to predict the demise of the Nguyễn polity: "After there have been eight generations, there will be a return to the central capital."[129] A more elaborated version declared, "When there are eight chiefs in Cochinchina, and not one more; when the mountains have been transformed into valleys; when the seaports are blocked up; when the natives of our houses have been dispersed; when new men appear, then this kingdom shall pass into other hands and be governed by strangers."[130] At that time Nguyễn Phúc Khoát did indeed represent the eighth generation of southern lords, and this prophecy, in wide circulation at the time, appeared to predict that his generation of leaders would be the last and that a return to the "central capital"—understood as the Lê-Trịnh capital of Thăng Long—would take place.

Intent on avoiding this outcome, in 1744 Khoát carried out a number of reforms at his court and ultimately declared his autonomy from the northern kingdom. In addition to changing official titles and court positions, the *chuá* also ordered the modification of regulations concerning clothing styles. Khoát ordered that people change their style of dress to emulate the attire once worn in Ming China. The rationale behind this was that by creating such a change in the physical appearance of his subjects, he would effectively be transforming Phú Xuân itself into a kind of "central capital." That a ruler would take such a prophecy seriously and respond directly to it suggests the power that such ideas held in Vietnamese society at this time.[131]

The French scholar Leopold Cadière, who chronicled the tale of Nguyễn Phúc Khoát's actions, concluded his study by hinting that this prophecy not only foreshadowed the eventual Tây Sơn uprising, but may also have encouraged its leaders:

> Who knows whether this revolt, which would (eventually) mark the rise of the Nguyễn Dynasty, did not have its deepest roots in the state of mind we have just seen; who knows if these rebels, at the very least, did not find some of their strength, or a confirmation of their claimed mission, in these confusing, but intense rumors, in these sounds of supernatural evils and of the general disruptions that troubled the court and the people these many years.[132]

Although Cadière's questions cannot be answered directly, it is likely that some elements of the Tây Sơn uprising can indeed be traced to the turmoil prompted by this episode. We have already seen that the origins of the uprising are widely traced to another long-standing local prophecy. Furthermore, we know that the prophecy that had so shaken the Nguyễn ruler remained in circulation well into the later years of the Tây Sơn movement. In a proclamation issued during his campaigns in Nghệ An in 1786, the Tây Sơn general Nguyễn Hữu Chỉnh declared that "everyone knows the throne of the *vua* [the Nguyễn ruler] will have [only] seven [generations]."[133] Chỉnh's reference to this phrase suggests that the population was aware of this prophecy and that despite the passage of more than a quarter century it was still part of the popular consciousness. Lê Quý Đôn reported that this prophecy's origins lay in Nghệ

An, suggesting that references to it in that region would have had a particular resonance.[134]

Even after 1786, prophecies continued to be a significant element of popular consciousness. In particular, Nguyễn Hữu Chỉnh, who had made reference to the prophecy regarding the fall of the Nguyễn in 1786, strategically deployed prophecies to advance his own political interests. Chỉnh is said to have derived confidence from an old saying: "The tiger himself advances from the western mountains, the dragon arrives from the eastern sea."[135] According to Chỉnh's interpretation of this phrase, the tiger from the western mountains (*tây sơn*) was an obvious reference to the Tây Sơn armies, while the dragon from the eastern sea (*đông hải*) was a reference to Chỉnh himself, for he was a native of the Đông Hải region. A 1787 missionary letter observed that such prophecies "gave great courage to Cong Chinh who here used the faith of the poor blind people who know nothing of the conduct of divine providence."[136] Popular beliefs regarding prophecies clearly shaped the mental landscape of the late eighteenth century, and political aspirants such as Chỉnh could either manipulate these beliefs or simply draw encouragement from them.

### *Reading Omens of Political Change*

Even more than prophecies, which were inherently ambiguous and vague with regard to the timing of their fulfillment, people looked to omens in the natural world around them. Such signs tended to be more immediate in their implications and could generally be understood as direct commentary on one or another ruling power. At the most obvious level, people interpreted continuing natural disasters—floods, famines, droughts, and storms—as indications that a ruler had lost the favor of heaven. Both official chronicles and unofficial histories recorded major and catastrophic climatalogical events, as well as unusual natural phenomena of all types. They also recorded the portents in the skies: solar and lunar eclipses, star positions, shooting stars, and a miscellany of events that defy ready categorization. It was out-of-the-ordinary occurrences—powerful storms, bright comets, unusually long eclipses (both lunar and solar)—that attracted the most attention and concern. Also, while heaven might inscribe its message across the skies, bodies of water and mountains were also surfaces on which such messages of warning or fate might be written. Such signs included rivers changing color, lake waters boiling over, harbors filling with stones, and mountaintops collapsing. All of these signs were available to be read by the people as indicators of good or ill, suggestions as to the future course of events, or judgment on one or another political or military faction.

The Tây Sơn period, with its often convulsive political upheavals, was, not surprisingly, one in which natural as well as supernatural indications of impending changes were frequently being observed and reported. Among the phenomena observed were ones later taken to have been indications of the supposedly inevitable Tây Sơn rise to power. Lê Quý Đôn reported such an instance, which he learned of during his investigations into the demise of the Nguyễn court in the early 1770s: "In the year *kỷ sửu* [1769], there was the *Chổi* star [a comet], and Nguyễn Quang Tiền spoke with people at that time, saying, 'In the province of Quảng-nam, in not more than five or six years, there will certainly be an uprising . . . and then the destiny of the Nguyễn house will be at an end.' "[137] Nguyễn Quang Tiền was an official at the Nguyễn court and appears to have been predicting the rise of the Tây Sơn by the mid-1770s.

Further portents of the rise of the Tây Sơn were also reported by near-contemporary chronicles. In 1771, in the twelfth month of the lunar year, on the Thạch Bi mountain in Phú Yên Province (in the central coast area), there was a sudden loud crash of thunder at which moment its prominently black stones instantly became white. From a distance, the mountain, which was now as white as lime, had the appearance of an upright stele. This phenomenon's significance was heightened by the fact that it was on this very spot that Emperor Lê Thánh Tông had placed an inscribed border marker at the culmination of his successful 1470 campaigns against the southern Cham empire. The plaque was to mark the newly established boundary between Vietnamese and Cham territories.[138] Although the compiler of the text did not offer an interpretation of this event, it was likely seen as suggesting renewed unrest in the Cham lands (where the Tây Sơn had their origins) and a reversal of power that would mark the eventual end of the Lê.[139]

While there were numerous signs relating to the rise and early years of the Tây Sơn, even more portents manifested themselves in the period leading up to the 1786 Tây Sơn attack on the Trịnh in Đàng Ngoài. These portents first appeared in 1782 in the wake of Trịnh Sâm's death and the coup that followed it. In late 1782 it was reported that sounds like gunfire could suddenly be heard resounding in the sky, a phenomenon that lasted for a quarter of an hour. Not long thereafter, in early 1783, it was said that the peaks of a northern mountain range suddenly collapsed.[140] Later that same year, a meteorite apparently landed in a lake in Thăng Long while the imperial examinations were being administered. This was reported to the ruler along with the ominous interpretation that the event marked the beginning of a thirty-year period in which "scholars would suffer bowing in shame."[141]

Perhaps the most portentous event of this period was the reported emergence in 1786 of a glistening creature or object from the waters of Hoàn Kiếm Lake in Thăng Long. This lake was popularly revered as the site where in the early fifteenth century a magical turtle had provided Lê Lợi with a sword with which to defeat the Ming army. It was to this same lake that he had returned the sword on the completion of his mission. The 1786 tale described a mysterious object or animal that flew toward the southern shore of the lake and then vanished. As this took place, the waters of the lake were suddenly roiling with waves, and the following day the lake's surface was covered with dead shrimp. Others reported seeing a similar phenomenon taking place at the palace compound of the *chúa* at about the same time.[142] The popular interpretation of this event was that the mysterious item seen departing the lake had been Lê Lợi's magical sword.[143] The implication was clearly that the sword, which had been used to help establish the Lê regime in the early fifteenth century, was now abandoning the Lê, suggesting their inevitable downfall.

The omens that manifested themselves in the Đàng Ngoài region in the early 1780s may have served as a kind of self-fulfilling prophecy, for they apparently encouraged the political and personal ambitions of Nguyễn Hữu Chỉnh. Chỉnh, as we have already seen, paid particular attention to prophecies and had used them to great effect in his climb to power. Two near-contemporary texts, the *Hoàng Lê Nhất Thống Chí* and the *Lịch Triều Tạp Ký*, describe a conversation that allegedly took place in Đàng Trong in early 1786 between Chỉnh and a nephew who was visiting from the north. This text reports that Chỉnh discussed the situation in the northern realms with his visitor, inquiring if there had been any recent occurrences of natural catastrophes or omens. In reply, his nephew detailed a long litany of such phenomena dating to 1782, the year that Trịnh Sâm had died and Chỉnh himself had been forced to flee in the turmoil that followed:

> On the 15th day of the 11th month of the year *nhâm dần* [1782], in the middle of the sky there was suddenly a loud sound that could be heard everywhere in the heavens and on earth; it lasted for more than two hours, and no one knew its source. . . .

> Furthermore, in the second month of the *quý mão* year [1783], the Hùng Sơn mountains suddenly lost more than 80 meters in height. In the sixth month of that year, the waters in the Thiên Đức River suddenly dried up for a day and a night.
>
> On the night of the first day of the tenth month in the year *giáp thìn* [1784], in the Thủy Quân Lake in the capital, there was a sound like thunder, and the waters of the lake boiled over, and on the following day all of the shrimp and fish in the lake were dead.
>
> In the palace of the *chúa*, there have been thousands of black ravens flying around day and night, cawing raucously. . . .
>
> Moreover, the walls of the citadel have for no apparent reason suddenly dropped more than 10 *trượng*.[144]

The accounts go on to suggest that this lengthy list of troubling omens gave added confidence to Chỉnh's plans to attack Đàng Ngoài later in the summer. Thus, we find omens serving not merely as signs of an inevitable change of power, but also as inspiration for those who might view them as an opportunity to act against those in power. After all, someone had to be the agent of heaven, bringing these omens to fulfillment. Chỉnh saw himself as such a man, just as Nhạc had earlier seen himself as the man to fulfill the prophecy that guided his movement in its early years.

### *Reading between the Lines*

A final method used by Vietnamese of this era to discern the future was the analysis of words and phrases. The literati, and possibly literate villagers, looked to individual words (Chinese characters), parsing them for hidden meanings or prophetic indications. Chinese characters lend themselves particularly well to a curious strain of analysis in which the characters are dissected into their component parts, and messages discerned therein.[145] Since these characters are often made up of smaller parts that themselves have distinct meanings, the smaller parts can be "read" separately and in a manner that suits the interpreter's objectives. Alternatively, messages could be hidden in seemingly innocent written or spoken lines. A good example of this practice comes from the early Tây Sơn era and was reported in the *Lịch Triều Tạp Ký*. The case in question describes a brief poem that was written as an oblique comment on the political situation of the period (1780): "*Tổ tư vân gian nguyệt, hoàng hoa nhật diệu hương*" (the earth will transmit and speak a dishonest oath [against] the imperial flower, which the sun makes beautifully fragrant). The characters for *tổ* and *tư* can be combined to form the character for brother-in-law, a reference to Hoàng Tổ Lý, a relative of the Trịnh lord, while the characters for *hoa* and *nhật* can form the character for *việp*, a reference to the noble title of the important Trịnh general Hoàng Ngũ Phúc. The character *diệu* (sheep) was a reference to the zodiacal year in which both men were born. The entire phrase was interpreted as suggesting that the two men were planning to act against the Trịnh ruler.[146]

Such forms of wordplay, acting either as predictions or as discreet political criticisms, continued and appear to have multiplied in the Tây Sơn period. In particular, there were numerous attempts to discern the fate of the Tây Sơn and other political leaders by using the characters that made up their reign names. Among the popular responses to Nguyễn Nhạc's declaring himself the Thái Đức emperor was an examination of those two characters for portents. The subsequent analysis concluded that Nhạc's reign would be over in fourteen years. "Knowledgeable people explained that the two characters for Thái Đức meant that 'Three people fight over the water, and in fourteen years they will be lost.'" The characters suggest this complicated prediction. Thái includes within it the characters for "three" and for "water," the latter term being a homophone for the word "country" (*nước*); Đức includes within it the characters for "fourteen" and for "lost." And indeed, as Bùi Dương Lịch, the scholar who recorded this analysis noted, the reign of Thái Đức lasted for fourteen years, from 1778 to 1793.[147]

Similar analyses were applied to the other major political figures of the late eighteenth century. One such dissection of the characters for the Lê emperor, Lê Chiêu Thông, was said to predict his inevitable and imminent demise as well:

> Filial people broke up the two characters of Chiếu and Thông [to mean]: "The sun covers the knife, which lies above the mouth and cuts the inferior family cord of the second elder brother." After this the *vua* fled over to the northern country, and Nguyễn Chỉnh was killed, and all was just as these words had spoken it.[148]

Although obscure, this interpretation was claimed to have predicted the future course of events. Like the previous example, the seeming accuracy of this prediction is reported only after the event, and so we cannot determine whether this process of word analysis had taken place before the emperor's ouster. It is likely, however, that such efforts to determine the future of the Lê were being undertaken at the time. Later the same technique was applied to the characters of the names for the two northern Tây Sơn rulers, Quang Trung and Cảnh Thịnh. The two rulers' names were analyzed and then dissected in popular verse, which produced the following result:

> The head of the father we take to serve as the feet of the son;
> In fourteen full years the final number will be reached.
> The father has a small head, and the son small feet;
> Reaching the year *nhâm tuất*, they will be no more.[149]

This poem described the fact that the characters for Quang and for Cảnh each has the character for "small" in it, Quang on top, Cảnh on the bottom. As this brief aphorism apparently predicted, after fourteen years of rule beginning in 1788, the final year of the Tây Sơn dynasty arrived in 1802—*nhâm tuất*.

Finally, while the results of such character dissection might be rendered in verse, other popular sayings could also use Chinese characters slyly to hint at the fates of various individuals. A brief ditty said to have been contemporary to the movement created rhymes for the major figures in the northern Tây Sơn polity to comment on their predicted (or perhaps hoped-for) fates:

> Inviting one another to carry the water for the boat,
> The Quang breaks, the Chỉnh is destroyed, and the
> Gánh immediately falls into the water.[150]

The *quang*, a holding frame for shoulder-borne water jars, referred to Quang Trung, and his own death. The *chỉnh*, or *chĩnh*, is a water vessel, and referred to Nguyễn Hữu Chỉnh, who had earlier been defeated by the Tây Sơn. And the *gánh*, a virtual homophone for the word *cảnh*, referred to the last Tây Sơn emperor, Cảnh Thịnh.

*Awaiting Salvation: Looking for Political Alternatives*

In addition to attempting to discern the course of future events, Vietnamese commoners and elites could also express resistance to their rulers by voicing a preference for political alternatives. Thus, for example, those living under Trịnh authority periodically voiced hopes that the Nguyễn might come to liberate them. Similarly, some of those living in Tây Sơn–held Đàng Ngoài anticipated salvation first by the Qing army that came to aid the ousted Lê emperor in 1788 and later by the Nguyễn when the Chinese expedition failed. Finally, those living under the

Nguyễn in the 1780s and 1790s and then into the early nineteenth century periodically expressed a desire to be rescued by the armies of the Tây Sơn. In times of hardship it is common for people to hope for new rulers, guided perhaps by the belief that any alternative would be preferable to their current oppressor. The distinctive feature of such a search for political alternatives in the Tây Sơn period lay in the fact that Vietnamese populations could actually look to a variety of genuine alternatives.

During the final three decades of the eighteenth century, peasants (and others) had a choice of several political forces to whom they might offer allegiance in exchange for relief from their suffering. The Nguyễn and the Tây Sơn (and to some degree the Trịnh and Lê) had thus to compete not only on the battlefields, but also in the arena of public opinion. While the Tây Sơn and Nguyễn political offerings might not have been all that different in absolute terms, from the peasant perspective the force that was not oppressing them at the moment could be looked to for salvation, however illusory that might prove to be. Indeed, it is highly probable that the positive reputation the Tây Sơn developed in the popular memory over the course of the nineteenth century was partially a result of their being the "not-Nguyễn." To a degree, the Tây Sơn regime came to represent an idealized era (however misremembered) preceding the heavy corvée demands and other difficulties that sparked the widespread peasant uprisings of the first half of the nineteenth century.

The notion of populations awaiting liberation developed early in the Tây Sơn period, beginning with the 1774 Trịnh invasion of Nguyễn territories. The Trịnh ruler and his commanders portrayed their action partly as a mission to rescue the people of Thuận Hóa and Quảng Nam. The people in these regions were depicted as suffering from corrupt officials, heavy taxation, and regular raids by upland populations. In short, the Trịnh invasion would constitute deliverance for people who had suffered "for more than one hundred years."[151] Lê Quý Đôn also recorded letters presented to him by several Đàng Trong scholars in which these men expressed their great joy at the arrival of the emperor's armies and at the long-awaited unification of the Vietnamese territories.[152] Although perhaps not broadly representative, the sentiments expressed in these letters reflected a sense among some that the arrival of the Trịnh would remedy the difficulties they had been experiencing.

Any enthusiasm for the arrival of the Trịnh soon gave way to disillusionment, and the people in Thuận Hóa found themselves chafing under the authority of their putative saviors and hoping to be rescued from them. By 1776, the *Đại Nam Thuực Lục* reported, Trịnh officials were already harassing the people of Thuận Hóa, who resented this and other hardships being imposed on them.[153] A missionary living in the Trịnh-controlled region reported a few years later, in 1779, that "Cochinchina [here a reference to the northern part of Đàng Trong then held by the Trịnh] is constantly hoping to see its king [the Nguyễn ruler] at the head of an army coming to deliver them from the harsh servitude of the Tonkinese."[154] The situation continued to deteriorate, becoming particularly difficult under the last Trịnh governor-general of Thuận Hóa. Phạm Ngô Cầu acted "cruelly, rudely and greedily, molesting the people and paralyzing the area into miserable poverty."[155] As one missionary reported in mid-1786, shortly before the Tây Sơn invasion of Đàng Ngoài, "All the peasants of these parts have developed an implacable hatred for all the Tonkinese without exception."[156] Indeed, the fact that the Trịnh official who visited the Tây Sơn camp in early 1786 invited Nguyễn Hữu Chỉnh to launch an attack reflects the degree of discontent being experienced by these populations.[157]

As hostility toward the Trịnh was developing among the populations they had "liberated" in upper Đàng Trong, their popularity in Đàng Ngoài was also rapidly diminishing. This was reflected in, among other things, popular expressions of support for political alternatives. Eventually this situation reached such a state that in 1779 a European missionary wrote regarding popular attitudes toward an uprising developing near Thăng Long, "Everyone supports the rebels and very few are for the king. One would like to see them victorious in the hopes of finding under a new administration the end to an infinite number of evils to which they have been subjected for a number of years."[158]

In the meantime, unrest was already stirring in the heart of the Tây Sơn camp. Although the Tây Sơn brothers had risen up in part to liberate the peoples of Đàng Trong from political hardship, as their uprising was transformed into a formal regime, it soon began to place heavy burdens on these populations. Writing in the *Phủ Biên Tạp Lục* in 1776, only three years after the Tây Sơn forces had brought their uprising into the populous lowland regions, Lê Quý Đôn observed that "the people in the region of Quảng-nam at that time had undergone much hardship. They were all awaiting the troops of the house of the king [i.e., the Lê/Trịnh] to go there to liberate and rescue them."[159] Two years later Charles Chapman similarly recorded popular discontent with the increasingly onerous governance of Nguyễn Nhạc. Based on his conversations with Vietnamese during a month's stay in Tây Sơn territory including a visit to Nhạc's capital at Vijaya, Chapman reported of the situation,

> [Nhạc's] government is held in the utmost detestation.... Many of his soldiers and almost all principal people I met with openly declared to me and to those with me how reluctantly they submit and expressed their wishes that the English would take them under their protection, assuring us that upon the least appearance of a force the whole country would fly to join them.[160]

This suggests that some people living under Tây Sơn authority were already starting to think about political alternatives. While there was little chance that the English would become involved in what Chapman considered an internal affair, the sentiments he described reflected a general hope that political alternatives might present themselves.

When the Tây Sơn forces finally invaded Trịnh-held parts of the former Nguyễn territories late in June of 1786, the people were ready to retaliate against their harsh rulers and to welcome the Tây Sơn as liberators. As the Trịnh troops fled Phú Xuân in the face of the rebel attack, some local people captured their former tormenters and turned them over to Tây Sơn forces, who in one instance took two hundred Trịnh soldiers and threw them into the ocean.[161] In other instances local people were reported to be killing the Trịnh forces themselves.[162] The enthusiastic popular response that the Tây Sơn invasion of upper Đàng Trong received probably reflected the sentiments of people who had felt themselves occupied by what they considered "foreign" troops for more than a decade and who had experienced considerable hardship during this time. To them, the Tây Sơn represented salvation. This is not to argue that the peoples of Phú Xuân and the region to its north necessarily saw a strong political or cultural affinity for the troops riding out of the hills of Tây Sơn, but rather that they welcomed them as "others" relative to their recent Trịnh overlords.

The initial acquiescence to Tây Sơn rule in Đàng Ngoài was largely a reaction to the previous difficulties of life under Trịnh control combined with the hardships caused by several years of famine. As a missionary noted, "The people were very tired of the tyrannical domination of [the *chúa*'s] family, and even more exhausted by the vexations of the soldiers who had made them suffer since the beginning of his reign."[163] Also, despite initial uncertainty about the impact of this invading army, the Tây Sơn troops had been enjoined by their commanders not to disturb the populations of the northern capital. The southern forces largely obeyed this injunction, a restraint that no doubt came as a relief to the peoples of Thăng Long. Finally, the northern populations probably responded to the Tây Sơn claims that they were restoring the power and authority of the Lê dynasty. This restoration in itself represented a form of political salvation in the popular imagination, even if that imperial family was but a shadow of its former self. One might say that the populations of Đàng Ngoài were rallying not to the Tây Sơn, or even to the restored Lê ruler, but rather to the idealized Lê dynasty of the fifteenth century, whose restoration was implicitly being promised by the Tây Sơn.

The initial Tây Sơn forbearance in the summer of 1786 changed substantially on their return trip, as we have seen. The widespread looting and mistreatment of local populations may already have indicated the end of the very brief period of Tây Sơn popularity in the north.[164] According to missionary letters, by 1788 the populations of the north were beginning to express an overt hatred for their new Tây Sơn overlords and a desire to be rescued from them.[165] Another witness reported a few years later that "there is nothing but taxes and corvées, which have thrown the dear people into a crisis, and which have given them the desire for deliverance."[166]

As a result of growing discontent with Tây Sơn rule, Vietnamese living in upper Đàng Trong and in Đàng Ngoài began to look to the south, and the burgeoning strength of the Nguyễn forces, for their deliverance. Because of the imposition of strict controls over the borders between Tây Sơn–controlled territories and Nguyễn-held areas, it was difficult for populations in the north to receive detailed information about events in the south. They relied on speculation fueled by bits of news that might travel by boats coming in a roundabout way via Macao. The information received was enough to make northern populations aware of the survival of the Nguyễn and of their growing strength. They had no information about the precise nature of Nguyễn rule in the Gia Định region, but they held out hope that the Nguyễn might represent a form of salvation, just as they had earlier placed their hopes in the largely unknown Tây Sơn. Indeed, it is likely that an idealization of life under Nguyễn rule was already beginning to take place in areas where the Nguyễn lords had once held sway and that it was this idealization, combined with the difficulties of life under the Tây Sơn, that fueled the backward-looking popular imagination.

The Nguyễn chronicles for 1791 record (though hardly without bias) that "the people of Thuận {Hóa} and Quảng {Nam} had hated the cruel policies of the Tây Sơn for a long time, {and} each day awaited the troops of the king. Thus every time they felt the blowing of the southern wind they all said, 'Our old lord is arriving.' "[167] The record for the following year also describes people in the Tây Sơn–held prefectures of Phú Yên and Khanh Thuận taking their wives and children and fleeing to Nguyễn-controlled regions farther to the south.[168] The *Tây Sơn Thuật Lược* similarly noted, "In the north, the peoples truly hated the Tây Sơn dynasty, and awaited the {arrival of} the *chúa*. From the time that Gia Định was pacified, every time that the winds blew, the people all said that this was the wind of Ông Chưng {Nguyễn Ánh}."[169] In the 1790s, the arrival of the Nguyễn thus continued to be expected, even as the hopes of those living under Tây Sơn control were constantly being raised and then dashed. A missionary letter of May 1792 referred to "[t]he king of Lower Cochinchina, whom all of Tonkin awaits with the utmost impatience."[170] Plausible rumors periodically reported the imminent arrival of the Nguyễn forces, as in 1794, when word spread that the Nguyễn would arrive shortly, after their destruction of the Tây Sơn navy at anchor in Qui Nhơn the previous year.[171] But somehow the arrival of the Nguyễn was always forestalled, either by the weather or by Nguyễn Ánh's cautious military strategy.

By the mid-1790s, northern populations began to speculate about when, not if, the Nguyễn might arrive on their shores. A missionary letter from August of 1794 reported on the sense of anticipation that had developed in Đàng Ngoài. "One continues to await the arrival of the legitimate seigneur of Cochinchina, but when will he come?" asked Pierre Eyot in a letter dated August 6, 1794.[172] A few weeks later, a missionary in lower Đàng Ngoài, Charles La Mothe, noted that the recovery of that kingdom by the dethroned king of Cochinchina was "that which everyone ardently hopes for and desires."[173] Moreover, the populations in Đàng Ngoài were not only speculating as to what they saw as the inevitable arrival of the Nguyễn ruler, but beginning to make plans to rise up in support of a Nguyễn advance. In 1794 a man in Thanh Hóa contacted Nguyễn Ánh and was told to recruit soldiers to plan an uprising against the Tây Sơn.[174] In 1797 a missionary reported that "{the Tây Sơn} must fear the Tonkinese, who do not support their yoke, do not aid them and turn against them. They have already risen up a number of times, but without success. . . . They await the king from Đông Nai as their liberator."[175]

As the northern populations began to hear more rumors about the impending arrival of the Nguyễn in 1800 and 1801, they intensified plans for challenging the Tây Sơn, whose authority became increasingly unbearable as that regime faced a desperate struggle against the Nguyễn. A missionary letter of 1801 summarized the situation of the Đàng Ngoài populations:

> As for the civilians, the greatest fermentation reigns among their spirits. All of the world, both Christian and pagan being crushed under the cruel servitude of the Tây Sơn Rebels, desires the arrival of the prince of Cochinchina with the greatest ardor; there is a confusion of noises of all types, so that one does not know what to believe, some are saying that there are some resistance groups being formed on all sides, ready to rise up against the Tây Sơn rebels at the first appearance of the legitimate prince.[176]

In one case, the leader of a planned rebellion against the Tây Sơn secretly traveled to the south, where he received documents from Nguyễn Ánh authorizing his uprising and designed to help him in recruiting followers. The uprising was crushed by the Tây Sơn government. The failure of such uprisings can probably be attributed to a combination of poor organization, small numbers (rarely more than a few hundred), and the highly militarized condition of the Tây Sơn state, which allowed for rapid mobilization to suppress such popular revolts. Nonetheless, the uprisings and the widespread popular sentiment reported by the European missionaries give some indication of the persistent and growing hostility developing toward the Tây Sơn regime.

Ironically, even as populations in Đàng Ngoài were increasingly expressing the hope that the Nguyễn would soon be delivering them from the Tây Sơn, people already living under the political control of these same Nguyễn forces in the far south were hoping to be rescued from them. No less a figure than Bishop Pigneau de Béhaine, Nguyễn Ánh's most ardent European supporter, described the emergence of this popular sentiment when he wrote already in 1791 of a situation that was increasingly becoming intolerable to Vietnamese living under Nguyễn control: "[Nguyễn Ánh] has burdened his people with taxation and with works projects, and at the present time the poor people are tormented by famine to the point that they desire the arrival of the Tây Sơn."[177] Two years later, in 1793, the situation for those living under Nguyễn authority does not appear to have improved. Another French missionary reported, regarding the interval since the bishop's comments, that "[t]hese last two years everyone has been taken for public works, and [people] are not occupied with anything else but searching for ways to stay alive, the misery having become extreme."[178] Clearly, the demands of the Nguyễn, like those of the Tây Sơn, were alienating the general population and fueling their desire to be rescued by another party.

The situation in the south remained unbearable for many into the mid-1790s, and even the Nguyễn records report that by 1795 large numbers of people were fleeing from the agricultural plantations (*trại đồn điền*) that had been established in Nguyễn-controlled territory.[179] A report in a missionary letter from the same year elaborated on the hardships confronting those living under the rule of Nguyễn Ánh and indicated that some continued to view the Tây Sơn as a preferable alternative to the Nguyễn:

> That which is most unfortunate for the prince [Nguyễn Ánh] is that he has alienated the hearts of his subjects for some time by this conduct, which is full of pride, and some acts of folly, such as wishing to build a magnificent temple to Confucius, and to rebuild his city of Saygon, etc. These projects are ordered at a time in which the people are already so overwhelmed by [demands for] labor and contributions for the war that they are revolting to the people, who desire to see the rebels take them, hoping that they will finally relieve them of all these vexations.[180]

That the Tây Sơn would continue to appear as a desirable political alternative in 1795 suggests the degree to which both sides faced severe difficulties in securing popular support. Juxtaposing this testimony from the Nguyễn-controlled regions with the hopes entertained by the northern populations for salvation at the hands of the Nguyễn indicates once again that hope lay not in concrete knowledge of the policies of a particular ruler. Rather, it derived from a belief that any ruler would constitute an improvement over the one currently in power.

In 1802 the long-awaited Nguyễn armies made their way into Đàng Ngoài, finally "rescuing" those populations from the Tây Sơn. The people of the northern region soon discovered that their hopes had been illusions. Even before capturing Thăng Long in July 1802, the Nguyễn forces had already begun to create difficulties for the populations of Đàng Ngoài. In their northern campaigns the Nguyễn reportedly forced the people to make contributions of horses, saddles, and ornate weapons. In some cases when villages could not procure the items demanded of them they were forced to contribute money. "This," the missionary Pierre-Jacques de la

Bissachère noted, "was the beginning of the discontents against the new Government."[181]

Antipathy toward the Nguyễn increased steadily during the early years of the new dynasty. Only a few years after his initial report, de la Bissachère wrote that "the prince [Ánh] is greatly hated by the people, particularly since he named himself Emperor, due to the exorbitant corvées that he imposes to construct fortresses and to build cities."[182] He concluded, "The Tonkinese appealed to the current king to assist them in destroying the Tây Sơn, but now that he has governed them for less than six years, they curse him daily because he has imposed corvées on them that are twice as onerous as those of the Tây Sơn; their hearts are disposed to revolt, but they are without the energy (to do so) and are lacking leaders capable of stirring them to action."[183] The anger of the northern populations was compounded by the fact that the Nguyễn had broken their promise to restore the Lê. As de la Bissachère observed in the early nineteenth century,

> The Tonkinese . . . waited impatiently for him [Ánh] to deliver them from the tyranny of the Tây Sơn rebels and to reestablish the former royal family on the throne, but these Tonkinese were cruelly deceived in their expectations, because no sooner had this prince conquered Tonkin, which had awaited him as its liberator, than he declared himself king and received the political investiture of the Chinese Emperor.[184]

Or, as Đặng Phương-Nghi observed in his study of eighteenth-century Việt Nam,

> Exhausted by the Trịnh, the people acclaimed the rise of the Tây-Sơn; it was not long, however, before they came to regard the power of the latter as an odious yoke, and prayed for the arrival of Nguyễn Anh; when Gia Long seated himself on the throne, they groaned again, and regarded the new ruler as a barbaric tyrant.[185]

Taken collectively, the available evidence suggests that life was not necessarily better or worse under any particular politico-military force during the Tây Sơn years. Each side placed great demands on those living under their authority to support rebuilding, fortification, resource extraction, and military designs. To the people, the other side, whichever it might be, seemed to offer the possibility of salvation. Thus, for instance, at the same time that southern populations hoped to be rescued *by* the Tây Sơn, those living in the north hope to be rescued *from* them. Indeed, it appears that the people were never entirely content. They always held the collective hope that the next ruler, or some alternative ruler, would be better and less demanding. As the events of the Tây Sơn period made clear, the expected salvation never came. Those who had been under Trịnh domination and were then rescued by the Tây Sơn soon hoped for the Nguyễn to rescue them. Those in the far south who had been liberated from the Tây Sơn by Nguyễn forces soon longed for the return of their former political masters. And those under the Trịnh, who were first liberated by the Tây Sơn and then again liberated by the Nguyễn, soon longed to throw off the yoke of the Nguyễn.

## CONCLUSION

In this chapter I have only touched the surface of the complex relationships that existed between the Vietnamese peasantry and the leadership of the Tây Sơn movement. The populations are too large, the terrain too varied, and the time period too long to allow for a definitive description of peasant life during the Tây Sơn years. What I have hoped to do, however, is to show that prevailing descriptions of the Tây Sơn regime are often far too benign. The facile description of the Tây Sơn uprising as a "peasant movement" masks the far more complicated relationship that existed between the leaders of this movement (themselves not peasants in the general sense of the word) and those whom they sought to bring into their armies and under their political authority. One cannot assume that the interests of the leaders of this movement were the same as those of the broad masses of the peasantry, and so interpretations that conflate the Tây Sơn brothers with the movement as a whole are extremely misleading.

There were notable instances of popular cooperation with and enthusiasm for the Tây Sơn movement and some of its objectives, but there are many more cases of local struggles against the demands of this new regime. It is also important to note that these acts of resistance or defiance should not be seen as representing any particular antipathy toward the Tây Sơn as such. Instead, these should be considered acts of resistance against any increased impositions by the powers of the state, whatever the sources or claims of that power. In other words, it did not so much matter that it was the Tây Sơn who were the ones making these claims on the population, but rather that any prevailing political party was doing so. That this was the case is demonstrated by the fact that the general populations in this period alternatively complained loudly about the Nguyễn, the Trịnh, and the Tây Sơn. Moreover, no sooner had the people been "delivered" from the cruelties of one regime than they began to decry the excesses of their new overlords and to hope for salvation from yet another one of the military-political forces of their time.

It is within this context that the glorification of the Tây Sơn that emerged in the nineteenth-century popular imagination must be understood.[186] This changed popular view of the Tây Sơn movement and regime was as much a product of antipathy toward the Nguyễn as an actual collective memory of the Tây Sơn. This nostalgia for a better time is, of course, a universal pattern. The point here is that we must be aware of such nostalgias and the ways in which they are created. The twentieth-century Vietnamese historians who came to rely heavily on oral and other folk traditions regarding the Tây Sơn are, I believe, seeing a great deal of this type of nostalgia. In many respects, the historical record shows the Tây Sơn to have been no better or worse than their predecessors or successors.

# 4 The Social Margins

## Christians, Pirates, and Others

> This is the year 1787 and I am still alive. But I have remained alive only thanks to the mercy of the Virtuous Lord of Heaven, because I live amidst the points of swords and knives, and surrounded by death.
>
> —Visente Liêm Ký, 1787[1]

Vietnamese lowland peasants were not the only group profoundly affected by events of the Tây Sơn era. The uprising and the regimes it eventually produced also had an important impact on groups living at the margins of eighteenth-century Vietnamese society. Among others, these groups included Vietnamese Christians; various ethnic and immigrant groups, most prominently migrants from China, but also members of groups living in the highlands, and sometimes across the borders in Siam, Cambodia, and the Lao principalities; bandits in their various guises, who emerged and disappeared in response to changing circumstances; and finally pirates, distinct from bandits not merely because of their location on the seas and rivers, but in this case because of their origins in China. Although their numbers were sometimes small, these groups had a significant effect on the course of the uprising, and on its successes and failures.

There are numerous ways to classify what I call the "social margins," and the groups I have chosen are ones that have emerged in the documentation and are notable for the roles they played in the Tây Sơn period. There are other groups, no doubt, whose traces have been erased by time. In some instances there is considerable overlap between members of these groups and the broader category of "peasants" addressed in the previous chapter. Many Christians, for instance, were lowland agriculturalists, and many peasants became bandits of necessity or by choice. The issue of marginality is a complex one, because the term has meaning only when viewed within a specifically defined context. Some groups' marginality—that of upland ethnic groups, bandits, pirates, and Christians—was evident throughout the entire Vietnamese territories. Other groups, such as the Chinese, the Chams, and the Khmers, for instance, were found in large numbers in the southern parts of Đàng Trong, where they often (at least collectively) constituted majority populations. Defining such groups as "marginal" is thus problematic within the narrower context of central and southern Đàng Trong, even as it has slightly more utility when viewed within the larger context of Đại Việt in its entirety. Clearly, the marginalization of such groups in the south was partially a product of political, demographic, and finally historiographical factors that developed over the course of the later nineteenth century in what was an increasingly ethnically Vietnamized south.

With such caveats in mind, there are, nonetheless, good reasons to study these groups in their own right. First, these are groups directly identified by eighteenth-century political actors, observers, and chroniclers as distinctly separate elements within Vietnamese society. Secondly, each of these groups was, as a group, profoundly affected by the events of the Tây Sơn period and in turn left its mark on the uprising and later regimes as well as on their adversaries. Finally, each of these groups can be classified as "marginal" in some way, even if this marginality varied throughout the Vietnamese realms and was sometimes ideological or cultural more than numerical or geographical. The Christians, for example, could sometimes be found at the centers of power, and their marginality emerges from their minority status, as well as the marginalization of their religious doctrines within state discourses regarding ritual practices, observances, and social conduct. Bandits and pirates were marginalized legally, and often geographically. Groups such as the Chinese were to a degree politically, and sometimes culturally, marginalized, though there were areas (such as around Sài Gòn, Hội An, and Hà Tiên) where they had a strong demographic presence and considerable political influence.

The heightened interaction between peoples at the margins of Vietnamese society and those at the society's center is not surprising during a time of conflict, for it is at such times that political elites turn to the margins for supporters. The history of Việt Nam is replete with both clashes and alliances between Vietnamese lowlanders and their highland counterparts. Clashes often stemmed from competition for resources and land and from efforts by lowland political powers to tap the wealth of upland regions. Alliances were frequently a by-product of the fact that many

Vietnamese popular movements and most anti-Chinese resistance efforts of the premodern and early modern eras began with a retreat into peripheral (often upland) regions, where adherents could gather strength, resources, and followers before launching attacks against lowland political centers.

This pattern of alternating conflict and cooperation dates to the early centuries of Chinese colonial domination, a period in which ethnic differentiation between lowland and upland communities was still far from fixed. This pattern continued into the postindependence period beginning in the second half of the tenth century, periodically linking the lowland Vietnamese populations with upland groups. From the anti-Mongol forces in the second half of the thirteenth century to Lê Lợi's fifteenth-century uprising against the Ming, Vietnamese military leaders were frequently and substantially supported by upland ethnic groups and their chieftains, living in areas to which the Vietnamese military commanders often retreated. Later, when the Mạc court was driven from Thăng Long in the late sixteenth century, it found refuge in the northern highlands of Cao Bằng and established links to local ethnic groups. Many eighteenth-century uprisings in Đàng Ngoài also prominently involved non-Vietnamese ethnic groups.[2] The Tây Sơn alliances with upland groups thus represented the continuation of a long tradition, even as the creation of such alliances was something quite new within the specific context of Đàng Trong, where uneasy coexistence between upland and lowland groups had been the norm under Nguyễn rule in the sixteenth through mid-eighteenth centuries.[3]

In addressing the issue of marginalized groups my aim is to bring these groups more fully into narratives of the Tây Sơn era, for existing accounts either ignore or misconstrue the nature of their participation. Some, like pirates and bandits, are almost entirely absent in histories of this period. The failure to include such groups is not surprising in accounts by modern nationalists who have depicted the Tây Sơn army as a coalition of virtuous, if downtrodden, members of Vietnamese society striving for the national good. These depictions have been consciously and unconsciously responding to Nguyễn historiography that explicitly labeled the Tây Sơn as "bandits." Although the three brothers from Tây Sơn were hardly "bandits," many who joined the movement or at least paralleled it could unambiguously be labeled as such. They preyed on the very society the Tây Sơn leaders were said to be aiding. To ignore the presence and contributions of these elements of the Tây Sơn uprising is grossly to misrepresent the complex dynamics of this era.

The relationship between the Tây Sơn and other groups such as Christians and non-Vietnamese ethnic populations, while not ignored, has been greatly oversimplified in existing historical accounts. These oversimplifications stem from a selective use of sources that reinforces a historiography holding up the Tây Sơn leaders as paragons of progressive social policy.[4] These accounts by Vietnamese researchers have depicted the Tây Sơn era as a high-water mark in the treatment of indigenous Christians. To support this claim, these historians have frequently singled out a handful of letters written by European missionaries praising the Tây Sơn regime for its religious tolerance and comparing it favorably with its predecessors.[5] While there were times when the Tây Sơn regime was sympathetic to the Christians living under its control, there were also numerous instances of Tây Sơn crackdowns against this religious minority. Similarly, existing interpretations of the dynamic that developed between the Tây Sơn leadership and non-Vietnamese groups are also greatly oversimplified.[6] The Tây Sơn movement did come to involve members of various non-Vietnamese ethnic groups, including highland groups, ethnic Chinese, and Chams. However, there was far from uniform support for the Tây Sơn among these communities. At times some within these groups did assist the Tây Sơn. Just as frequently, however, their members gave support to the Tây Sơn's rivals.

## CHRISTIANS AND CHRISTIANITY IN THE TÂY SƠN ERA

Vietnamese Christians formed a complex element of eighteenth-century Vietnamese society, and one whose role was very fluid. When I speak of Vietnamese Christians I am describing a group that was in some ways a fiction, for it included many whose status as Christians was nominal at best. That is, their adherence to the newly introduced faith was not exclusive, whatever the desires or assessments of the European missionaries, for Vietnamese tended to keep their options open and to view religion in often very material ways. Nonetheless, the category "Christian" has some utility, for it was used by elements of Vietnamese society, at both the state and popular levels.[7] It is also clear from the sources that there were some Vietnamese who genuinely attached themselves to the faith and responded to the exhortations of their European prelates. These people were willing to take considerable risks, or pay certain (often monetary) prices to be permitted to continue their religious practices. Furthermore, members of the Tây Sơn leadership deliberately cracked down on Christians (however identified) from time to time, not as a genuine social, much less theological, category, but as a group seen as affiliated with foreign missionaries, who were viewed, in a material sense, as potential or actual threats to the regime. Finally, at the local level, conflicts within villages and between individuals sometimes saw the label "Christian" invoked when doing so might serve particular interests.

*Christianity in Đai Việt before the Tây Sơn Era*

The first European missionary arrived in Đại Việt in 1533, but it was not until 1596 that the first formal mission was established there. Moreover, it was only after 1615, with the expulsion of the Jesuits from Japan and that order's turning its attention to other parts of East Asia, that Christianity began to gain a real foothold in the Vietnamese territories. The arrival in Đàng Ngoài of the noted French Jesuit Alexandre de Rhodes in 1627 marked a turning point in the expansion of Christianity in the Vietnamese territories. De Rhodes spent time in both Đàng Ngoài and Đàng Trong over the next eighteen years, before being expelled in 1645.[8] His expulsion did nothing to slow the growth of the religion, and others soon followed de Rhodes in establishing missions, schools, and churches, particularly in Đàng Ngoài, but in smaller numbers in the southern polity as well.

Christianity's entry to Đại Việt was a relatively easy one, at least at the theological level, for the existing Vietnamese religious structures—comprising a loose mixture of Buddhism, Daoism, Confucianism, and folk beliefs—were quite open and not inherently hostile to the introduction of new belief systems or forms of worship. The new religion made inroads at various levels of society, though it was perhaps most successful among people at the economic margins of Đàng Ngoài society. Despite a tolerant cultural atmosphere regarding the new religion, Christianity did face a number of obstacles, both theological and political. As preached by European missionaries, Christianity was at odds with existing religious practices, particularly those that accepted the possibility that there was no single divinity and that obeisance might be made to entities other than one elevated God. This tension manifested itself in concrete terms during the eighteenth century, when some missionaries, and later indigenous clerics, forbade devout Vietnamese Catholics from participating in ritual practices deemed pagan or idolatrous. Thus, when villages held their festivals and requested contributions or participation, more-devout

Christian members occasionally refused. Debates also raged within the missionary community in the late eighteenth century (though the issue had certainly been discussed earlier) about whether various traditional Vietnamese practices were to be considered civil or religious.[9] The most notable manifestation of this debate centered on the question of proper attitudes among Vietnamese Christians toward their ancestors. Since many missionaries considered offerings and prostrations before ancestral altars to be false worship, they discouraged or openly forbade Vietnamese Christians from performing these rituals. Consequently, Vietnamese Christians and the European missionaries who served them went through the same rites controversy that had created enormous problems for the Catholic mission in China in the seventeenth and early eighteenth centuries.

While the social and philosophical implications of Christianity constituted one element of challenge to Vietnamese rulers, those who were responsible for introducing this religion to Đại Việt constituted another. Suspicion of the European missionaries at times manifested itself in outright attempts to capture and expel them, while during other periods an uneasy tolerance prevailed at the Vietnamese courts. During the Nguyễn-Trịnh civil war of the mid-seventeenth century, missionaries were able to portray themselves as conduits for advanced weapons technologies by exaggerating their own roles in and influence over the weapons trade and by threatening that their expulsion would bring an end to the flow of weapons. The rulers, while concerned about the social and spiritual impact of the foreign religion, were more concerned, for the time being, with maintaining the technological advantage they believed these missionaries could offer. The missionaries, and particularly the French, were thus able to use their apparent trade connections as leverage to stay in Đại Việt even as their situation remained a tenuous one.

As the Trịnh-Nguyễn wars ground to a standstill in the early 1670s, circumstances for European missionaries became more perilous, particularly in Đàng Ngoài. Although the religion was proscribed in both Trịnh and Nguyễn territories and rulers in both regions prohibited European missionaries from entering their countries, it was the northern rulers who pursued the more aggressive course. The Trịnh ruler first banned the religion in a 1664 edict and then reiterated this proscription in 1669. Sometime later the apparent French involvement in a plot against the Siamese ruler in 1685—news of which eventually reached the Vietnamese rulers—renewed suspicions of the missionaries and contributed to further efforts to crack down on the "Portuguese religion." These efforts continued into the eighteenth century, during which Trịnh rulers regularly issued edicts proscribing Christianity.[10]

Despite these repeated interdictions, themselves evidence of the ineffectual nature of Trịnh efforts to halt the spread of Christianity, there appears to have been a de facto expansion of religious freedom in Đàng Ngoài from the mid-1720s into the early 1770s.[11] With the death of Chúa Trịnh Dinh in 1767, the situation once again became uncertain, but his successor Trịnh Sâm initially continued the policy of tolerance. In 1771, the new *chúa* even released two European missionaries who had been captured several years earlier. This proved to be the high point of tolerance during Sâm's reign, for two years later another crackdown led to the arrest and subsequent execution of a Spanish Dominican and a Vietnamese preacher.[12] The response of the Christian community to the executions, including veneration of the two bodies, provoked an edict by Sâm demanding the eradication of Christianity within two months.[13]

Even this sequence of events did not drive the practice of Christianity underground, and in some cases practice of the faith moved from the margins to the mainstream of society. Some members of the northern ruling family itself were alleged to be Christians, including a sister of Trịnh Sâm and one of his brothers-in-law.[14] The leader of the 1774 Trịnh invasion of Đàng Trong, the eunuch Hoàng Ngũ Phúc, was also widely reputed to be a Christian and to be tolerant of the faith.[15] Indeed, one missionary reported in 1775 that a number of the major Trịnh figures associated with the invasion were Christians, a circumstance he hoped would bode well for Christians in the area.[16] Despite these promising indications, the very next year a missionary writing from the Red River Delta region opined that the religious situation there had become very bad and that it would be a major setback for Christianity in Đại Việt were the Trịnh forces to be successful in conquering the Nguyễn.[17] This skepticism was borne out a few years later, in 1779, when the Trịnh ruler issued another edict calling for the immediate capture and execution of all European missionaries.[18]

Meanwhile, in Đàng Trong Christianity was allowed to exist with relatively little official interference from the late seventeenth century into the middle of the eighteenth, despite periodic official prohibitions.[19] European missionaries, most notably Jesuits, could be found at the Nguyễn court itself during portions of the seventeenth and eighteenth centuries. The Nguyễn rulers were willing to overlook the Jesuits' religious affiliations because they wanted to employ their noted scientific talents.[20] These men served as doctors, mathematicians, interpreters, and astronomers at Phú Xuân, in much the same capacity as their earlier counterparts had at the Chinese court.[21] The Portuguese Jesuit João Loureiro, for instance, was in residence at the Nguyễn court from the 1740s until his departure in 1777 (with a two-year interlude from 1750 to 1752), and two other Jesuits, Johann Köffler and Xavier de Monteiro, were also at the court for some time in the 1750s.

There was a renewed crackdown on Christianity in 1750, instituted by the powerful Nguyễn ruler Nguyễn Phúc Khoát, a continuation of his efforts to stave off the prophecies predicting the demise of Nguyễn rule.[22] Yet even through this period of renewed persecution, the Nguyễn ruler allowed Köffler and Monteiro to remain at his court (though Köffler had gone by 1755) and Loureiro to return after just two years' absence. Clearly, the ruler remained ambivalent concerning Christianity, as he sought to separate the missionaries as European men of science from their mission work. The death of the long-reigning *chúa* in 1765 brought a further relaxation of Nguyễn official attitudes toward Christianity, culminating in a 1774 decree permitting free exercise of the religion and the granting of reprieves to those previously punished for their faith.[23] Coming on the cusp of the first major Tây Sơn attacks against the Nguyễn, it is not clear, however, whether officials had time to act on the terms of this decree before the Nguyễn were driven out of Phú Xuân.

In spite of frequent anti-Christian edicts and periodic crackdowns, the number of Vietnamese being baptized in the seventeenth and eighteenth centuries continued to grow. An estimate from the 1660s already placed the number of Christians in the north at 350,000, and while the figure is probably optimistic, it suggests the dynamism of the European mission work.[24] A more conservative accounting in 1754 found only 30,000 to 40,000 in the same region, reflecting perhaps a century of active state intervention against Christianity and possibly also a more narrow definition of an adherent.[25] Thirty years later, a 1784 count placed the number of adherents once again at between 350,000 and 400,000.[26] Estimates for Christians in the more lightly populated Đàng Trong at this same time were much lower, ranging between 10,000 and 15,000.[27] In both places, though particularly in Đàng Ngoài, Christians constituted a visible minority in a combined population that at the time was somewhere within the rather wide range of 5.5 to 10 million.[28]

### *Vietnamese Christians and the Tây Sơn: 1771 to 1786*

By the early 1770s, as the Tây Sơn brothers were beginning their climb from village obscurity to imperial titles, the situation of Christianity in both Nguyễn and Trịnh territories remained in some confusion, as formal state disapproval continued to compete with the appeal of the religion among both large groups of villagers and small groups of court elites. It is not surprising, consequently, that the religion continued to have a considerable influence within Vietnamese society, an influence that came to be heightened during the Tây Sơn era as tensions between the state apparatus and this group were magnified.

Although Christians as a group lay at the social margins, they were soon embroiled in the events of the Tây Sơn period, and there are some indications that they could be found at the very heart of the uprising. There are numerous anecdotes suggesting that the Tây Sơn brothers came from a family with Christian connections and may even themselves have been Christians.[29] One European priest wrote that their father was an apostate Christian and that Nguyễn Nhạc had been baptized as an infant. Another gave Nhạc's baptismal name as Paul and claimed that the Tây Sơn leader called himself "Paul Nhạc."[30] Tales of the Tây Sơn brothers' supposed Christian background gradually spread, and when the Tây Sơn leaders arrived in Thăng Long in 1786, a missionary reported that "the news has been spreading for some time that the two *Đức ông* [virtuous brothers] are Christians, and that there are a number of Christians among their mandarins as well as their soldiers."[31] Another letter, a year later, noted that the eldest Tây Sơn brother was commonly referred to as "that apostate Nhạc."[32] Finally, a Vietnamese Jesuit priest, Philiphê Bỉnh, reported not only that the brothers came from a Christian family, but that it was their parents' religious devotion that had driven them to rebellion:

> The two brothers Thái Đức and Quang Trung [using their future imperial titles] were brought up together, and their father was a Christian. He could not, however, instruct his sons [in that faith] because in the early evenings when the father and mother read the scriptures and sang songs and called them, they would flee and could not bear reading the scriptures and singing with their parents. When their mother and father tried to punish them, the brothers immediately took themselves away into the forests and became robbers.[33]

It is impossible to verify any of these accounts, which may well have reported contemporary rumors or reflected wishful thinking among members of the missionary community. Yet there is evidence that the Tây Sơn brothers' family included some Christians. A missionary passing near Qui Nhơn in 1778 met a woman whom he described as an aunt of the rebel leaders and reported that she was a devout Christian. She treated the missionaries who visited her with great hospitality and made a substantial monetary contribution to their mission.[34] We also know that the Tây Sơn brothers' ancestors had been transplanted to Qui Nhơn from the northern regions of Nghệ An in the 1650s during the Trịnh-Nguyễn wars, and it is conceivable that the family had been reached by Jesuit missionaries who had been active in Đàng Ngoài in the 1630s and 1640s.[35]

Even if the brothers did have some personal connection to Christianity, this had no discernible effect on their attitudes toward the religion or its practitioners. The Tây Sơn leaders' actions toward the faith varied considerably, and it is impossible to correlate any alleged Christian background on their part with a particular treatment of the religion. The unpredictable nature of Tây Sơn attitudes had manifested itself already during the very early days of the uprising. In some places churches were looted by Tây Sơn troops and by armies allied with them. A Spanish missionary writing in 1774 reported that a group of seventeen rebels showed up at his small rural church in mid-March and took everything of value they found, including candles and an altar cloth.[36] The following year, the French missionary Pierre-Jacques Halbout, living only six miles from Đà Nẵng, reported that sixty homes belonging to Christians in his small district had been burned by rebels.[37]

Even as some of their troops looted church compounds and put the homes of Christians to the torch, other elements of the Tây Sơn army demonstrated goodwill toward the faith and its European missionaries. A nineteenth-century account commented on the generally positive Tây Sơn treatment of Christians in this early period:

> With regard to matters of the faith, the situation was calm because the Tây Sơn troops were not concerned with matters of religion. Thái Đức's maternal aunt was a Christian and assisted in many ways to help the faith prosper. Perhaps [he] recalled that his own mother had also been a Christian. For these reasons, all of the missionaries, whether from West or East, were able to go everywhere and do anything without interference.[38]

Furthermore, the Spanish missionary who had earlier reported that all of his possessions had been looted by the rebels wrote that not long after this encounter he was visited by some Tây Sơn mandarins who promised him the protection of thirty armed troops, as well as the freedom to preach publicly and to erect churches. They also offered him "large quantities of silver," which he refused to accept.[39] In return for these promises and gifts, the Tây Sơn officials requested medications, and even tried to recruit his services as a doctor, an offer the missionary also declined. The effort to recruit the missionary indicates that Tây Sơn leaders were aware of the Europeans' skills, and helps to explain the good treatment sometimes offered to the missionaries.

The Tây Sơn army's unpredictable treatment of Christians during the uprising's early days was based on local circumstances and not dictated from the center. As the Tây Sơn leaders solidified and institutionalized their hold on power, however, they began to issue formal decrees regarding the religion. The first of which we know is a 1779 edict by Nguyễn Nhạc granting religious freedom to those living in his territories, a decree specifically aimed at Christians.[40] The impetus for this decree is not clear, though it was likely a calculated attempt by the Tây Sơn leader to win the assistance of the European missionaries. There are also indications that Nhạc was granting written permits to some missionaries authorizing their free movement and religious activities, at least in the immediate area around the Tây Sơn political center.[41] Possibly because of such gestures, Nhạc was able to recruit two Spanish Dominicans to serve for several years as mathematician and astronomer at his court at Qui Nhơn during the early 1780s.

Despite this edict of tolerance and the employment of missionaries at their court, elements of the Tây Sơn leadership, and Nhạc in particular, continued to harbor suspicions concerning the Christian community and its European sponsors. These suspicions increased through the early 1780s, amid evidence that the Nguyễn side was receiving assistance from a number of European missionaries, most notably Bishop Pigneau de Béhaine. The French missionary bishop had been a close confidant and indefatigable champion of the young Nguyễn Ánh since 1777, and his increasingly visible role raised suspicions among the Tây Sơn leaders about all Europeans then living in Đại Việt. The Tây Sơn leaders, unsurprisingly, assumed that Europeans, and missionaries in particular, might well have ties to the bishop.

Underlying this tension was a tendency among missionaries to regard the Tây Sơn as illegitimate rulers, a view that emerged during the uprising's earliest days. A Spanish missionary noted that he and his fellow missionaries were reluctant to endorse the Tây Sơn because they interpreted this movement as directed against a legitimate ruler:

> All of the missionaries were indebted for the good favors of the [Tây Sơn] mandarins, but as the movement was fashioned against the king . . . we

> affected in public a total indifference, declaring that we were not dealing with these questions, counseling our Christians to be obedient to their sovereign. We said to them that in good conscience they must not rally to the insurrection, in spite of some of the political goals that were motivating this uprising. We thought thus to instill in the Christians obedience to their king and to avoid all susceptibility of prejudice against the mission.[42]

The missionary effort to promote this biblically ordained notion of loyalty to established civic rulers was an ongoing source of tension between the Tây Sơn leaders and the Europeans.[43] Such attempts to avoid "prejudice against the mission" were, in any case, irretrievably damaged by Pigneau's ongoing actions on behalf of Nguyễn Ánh, which would later prove a source of immense hardship for the Europeans living under Tây Sơn authority.

The period of relaxed attitudes toward Christianity marked by the 1779 edict was short-lived, as a series of events brought about a formal crackdown on Christians living in territories under Tây Sơn authority. In 1780 Nhạc arrested Jean-Pierre-Joseph D'Arcet, the only French missionary then active in Tây Sơn territory, along with a large number of his Christian followers.[44] Although D'Arcet may have been seized because of his proselytizing in close proximity to Qui Nhơn (a project begun during the period of greater tolerance), there was some contemporary speculation that he had been captured because the Tây Sơn hoped to use him as an envoy to Europe.[45] Given the highly pragmatic outlook of the Tây Sơn leaders, the latter explanation is a highly plausible one, suggesting again that their actions toward Christians were guided much more by immediate political objectives than by larger ideological considerations.

If the Tây Sơn leaders were apprehensive about missionary activity near Qui Nhơn, they appear also to have been concerned about it much further afield. When the Tây Sơn army was campaigning in Cambodia in 1782, it seized a number of Spanish priests and took them back to Sài Gòn in cangues. Among these men was Ferdinand de Olmedilla. When Nguyễn Nhạc saw the priest he is reported to have cried out, "It is the Father Felon who promised us a shipment of copper, then went to his country and brought the copper to 'Ong Chung' [i.e., Nguyễn Ánh] for his engines of war [instead]. . . . Throw him immediately into the cangue."[46] This suggests that the Tây Sơn were continuing their (apparently unsuccessful) efforts to employ the missionaries in their contest with the Nguyễn. When Olmedilla sought to deflect Nhạc's wrath by displaying a permit Nhạc had earlier granted him to proselytize in Qui Nhơn, the Tây Sơn ruler declared that it was not valid beyond the immediate area of Qui Nhơn.[47] After dragging the Spaniard back to Sài Gòn, the Tây Sơn ruler ordered that Olmedilla be returned to the rebel capital. As he was being taken to Qui Nhơn by sea a storm blew up, and several of the ships accompanying him capsized. The Tây Sơn leader accused Olmedilla of having conjured up the storm and immediately ordered his execution.[48]

Even as Nhạc developed his hard-line position, his younger brother Huệ maintained a more moderate and pragmatic attitude toward Christians. The brothers' divergent viewpoints are illustrated in an anecdote concerning an episode that probably took place in 1783 or early 1784. As a French missionary recounted the tale,

> The young prince named Đức Êm [Nguyễn Huệ] passing through the place after having gone to visit the king, his brother, was astonished to see such a crowd . . . the great and small informing him what it was about. The mandarin made it known to him that it was the order of the King [Nhạc] to seize the Preachers and all of the Christians. The prince, unhappy with this, sent a request that they be released and that Father Emmanuel be sent to him. The judge responded that he could not, having received the order from the King to seize them. The prince then sent a second request that the Father be sent, and that he would take him under his own responsibility, but the mandarin still refused.
>
> The prince became furious, charging through the crowd and to the house of the judge, commanding his soldiers to make an appeal to all of the Mandarins and to take from them all of their goods and at the same time to take the missionaries from the cangue. These he then conducted to an audience with the King, where he presented them in great anger saying to him: "What is your majesty doing? We have war on all sides, we are uniting everyone in order to do this, and you are making to seize all of the Christians. If all the Christians turn against us, what will we do? How will we be able to resist them?" To all of this, the King did not know how to respond . . . and then with the coming of evening, he said: "I did not know anything of this; do as you wish." To which the Đức Êm boldly answered, "if it is entirely up to my own wishes, then I will command that they all be released." "Do it then," replied the king . . . [and] the prince ordered the release of all the Christians.[49]

This account suggests that there were divisions within the Tây Sơn leadership regarding the treatment of Christians, even as the brothers' views remained flexible.

While Nhạc apparently cracked down on Christians in 1783 or 1784, by the summer of 1785 there were reports that he had eased these restrictions and had given the European missionaries complete freedom to minister to their followers in the region around Qui Nhơn.[50] This too proved a short-lived period of tolerance, for in November 1785 Nhạc cracked down on Christianity by issuing a formal edict against the religion:

> We wish now to exterminate from our state a European religion that has become widespread. This is a sect that acknowledges neither father nor king; which gives unto men I do not know what sorts of poisons in order to make them follow it; which is without respect for our laws, without veneration for our tutelary spirits; which passes the nights in prayer and reading, and is without any sort of shame about finding gathered together men and women; idlers and loafers, they do not take any sort of actions in order to gain for themselves goods and inheritances; finally, they do not blush when they are punished. . . . For these reasons and others known to us, we order the destruction of all of their communal houses, [and] that an exact enumeration of all of those who are engaged in this religion be carried out. Those who are in the state of transporting weapons will be enrolled in our service.[51]

This decree summarizes the standard Vietnamese state arguments against Christianity, portraying the decision to ban the religion as stemming from its disruptive social impact. Christianity is viewed as challenging Confucian familial and political obligations, for it "acknowledges neither father nor king." Being at the heart of the Confucian-ordained submissions to superiors, deference to one's father and the ruler (another father figure) were fundamental to social order, and religions interpreted as challenging this were viewed as inherently seditious (whether or not its adherents in fact did reject the prevailing social order, and many did not). Inasmuch as Nhạc was not overtly Confucianist in his outlook, the rationale laid out in this edict may well have reflected the influence of his advisers.

Christians are also singled out in this decree because they are "without veneration for our tutelary deities." This was perhaps the most common and visible source of social tension found in regions where Christians lived. Their unwillingness to make expected contributions toward village rituals relating to tutelary spirits marked them as outsiders and as social, if not political, dissidents. Although some missionaries, particularly the Jesuits, had emphasized accommodation with local custom, others (primarily from the secular orders such as the Missions Étrangères de Paris; MEP) insisted that Vietnamese Christians were not to contribute money for ceremonies commemorating or venerating local tutelary genies. Consequently, many villages found themselves profoundly divided. In some instances non-Christian villagers took the matters to court, attempting to force Christian villagers to pay their share of the community expenses for these ceremonies.[52] In other instances, villages literally split apart, with one group moving en masse to another area to establish a new settlement.

For all its elaborated reasons for suppressing the religion, this decree was described by European missionaries as motivated primarily by a desire for vengeance. Nhạc was apparently upset at his failure to persuade European missionaries to procure copper for him from Europe, having of course already been deceived on this issue by Olmedilla, and he thus used the decree as a means by which to punish Christians collectively for the alleged misdeeds of the missionaries.[53] At the same time, however, the decree provided Nhạc with several practical benefits. D'Arcet, the French missionary active in Tây Sơn–controlled territory in the 1770s and 1780s, reported that the edict had ordered that all Christians be registered and that this registry be sent to the court, so that all those listed there might be "employed as slaves in the service of the king and his officers."[54] Nhạc provided a second option for Christians, allowing them to pay a "fine" calculated at ten "livres" of copper instead of having to renounce their faith.[55]

The collection of such fines (or taxes)—a practice earlier carried out by Trịnh provincial officials and also by Nguyễn leaders in the south—was helpful to the Tây Sơn leaders for a number of reasons. First, it enabled them to identify Christians more easily, for when money was collected in any systematic fashion, registers of local Christians had to be compiled. Secondly, the collection of money from Christians was a means of defusing potential local resentment toward Christianity, and thus reducing social tensions. By imposing this fine on Christians, governments could demonstrate that being a Christian was unacceptable, and thus discourage this or other forms of heterodoxy. Finally, of course, this was a useful way to collect additional revenue from a relatively defenseless group. While Tây Sơn officials were pleased to see public renunciations of the faith, they were not so insistent on it that they would not be equally happy to be paid off. This was very clear to the European missionaries who observed these policies being carried out. As one noted, "It is less against the enemies of the religion, than against the lovers of money that we must guard ourselves."[56] Another reported specifically of Nhạc's 1785 crackdowns that "it is very likely the Tyrant acts more out of avarice than out of hatred for our blessed religion."[57]

Christians were particularly vulnerable to such forms of "taxation" because as a religious minority subject to official persecution, they did not have the same recourse to state protection that other Vietnamese had. Indeed, their primary objective was to avoid the attention of the officialdom that frequently banned their religion. Consequently, Christians were regularly at the mercy of ruling powers, not merely the central authorities, but avaricious local officials and soldiers as well. Because the collection of state-ordered fines was frequently ad hoc and might be supplemented by additional demands from local officials, making the demanded payment might only temporarily resolve the problem and was no guarantee against future exactions. In addition, having paid off one official at one level of government did not prevent officials at higher levels from making similar demands.[58] Finally, since these arrangements were so often informal, if an official was transferred from his post, his successor would not necessarily be bound by the terms of the existing agreement and could demand further payments.[59]

Although many reportedly chose to pay the fines, large numbers of Christians were still forced into the Tây Sơn armies shortly after Nhạc's edict was issued. Consequently, it appears that the Tây Sơn armies marching north in 1786 contained a disproportionate number of Christians. As one European missionary in Đàng Ngoài reported that year, "A great many of these rebels are Christians, or at least they have been baptized: many of them went to offer confessions to Father Khiêm, the curé at the capital."[60] Another reported that, of the Cochinchinese troops temporarily stationed near his small village, a large number were Christians.[61] The presence of Christians in the Tây Sơn armies, perhaps in numbers disproportionate to their representation in the Đàng Trong population, is an indication of the prominence of this group. Many had probably been drafted into the rebel forces along with anyone else the Tây Sơn could lay their hands on. Others, as we have seen, had been singled out for service in the Tây Sơn army *because* they were Christians and as such vulnerable to state demands. Whatever the reasons, it is clear that Christians, although a small minority of the overall population, were a significant and visible element of Vietnamese society during the Tây Sơn period, and one that could not be ignored.

*Post-1785 Tây Sơn–Christian Relations in Đàng Trong*

Although Nhạc had alternately tolerated and attacked Christianity in the first half of the 1780s, the post-1785 period was marked by a growing and irreversible anti-Christian sentiment on the part of the eldest Tây Sơn brother. Nhạc's increasing antipathy was exacerbated chiefly by steadily rising European support for Nguyễn Ánh, most notably that supplied by Bishop Pigneau de Béhaine. It was at this time that the bishop was escorting Nguyễn Ánh's son to Europe in hopes of gaining French support for the Nguyễn cause. Although the treaty failed to provide the hoped-for assistance, the mere fact of this embassy had made clear the degree of European missionary involvement on behalf of the Nguyễn cause, an involvement of which the Tây Sơn leaders were only too aware. As a 1786 missionary letter, written from Tây Sơn–held territory, noted, "We fear only one thing. That is to have our heads chopped off, not out of hatred of our blessed religion, but out of hatred of Europeans who wish to reestablish the king of Cochinchina on his throne."[62] A French missionary writing from Đàng Ngoài reported in August of 1786 that everyone there knew of the mission that the bishop was carrying out for the Nguyễn.[63] With reports like this circulating, Nhạc gave orders that all the Christian men in his territory be enrolled in his armies and their churches destroyed. Once again, according to this account, Nguyễn Huệ stepped in to moderate his brother's demands, gaining an exemption from the military service in exchange for a small payment.[64] Nhạc's anxiety regarding the anticipated return of the mission to France was further heightened by Nguyễn Ánh's own return to southern Đàng Trong in 1787 after several years of exile in Siam.

Nhạc's antagonism toward Christians living in his territories continued to increase, and in 1789 he was reported to have ordered the village chiefs in his territories to carry out another census of Christians in their respective settlements. This was followed by another demand that Christians pay a fine of ten copper pieces for continuing their adherence to the religion.[65] When a Nguyễn fleet sailed into Thái Đức's harbor at Thi Nại in the summer of 1792 and captured or destroyed his entire navy, Nhạc's anger was further inflamed. According to some accounts, he swore vengeance for this act, vowing that if he were successful in achieving victory over the Nguyễn, he would see to the complete destruction of Christianity in his territory.[66] Nhạc was not to achieve his objective, for he died on December 13 of the following year, allegedly consumed by his anger. The European missionaries who reported his demise interpreted it as an act of divine retribution, and contrasted Nhạc's treatment of Christians with that of his brother: "What a difference between his [Nhạc's] death and that of his younger brother! The one [Huệ] who never did anything against the Christians died as King in the midst of his glory; and the one [Nhạc] who had persecuted them all of his life, and who had still sought their complete ruin, has died in the midst of ignominy, having lost the scepter and his Empire."[67]

After Nhạc's death in 1793, the situation for Christianity in the Tây Sơn–controlled territory in the south apparently improved, at least temporarily. In 1795 a missionary reported that the Tây Sơn "whether for political [reasons] or by being persuaded that the persecutors of our blessed religion usually come to a bad end, have shown themselves to be favorable to the religion."[68] In another letter, the same man cited a high-ranking Tây Sơn official in the area as praising Christianity and criticizing the earlier Nguyễn treatment of it.[69] It is possible that these sentiments reflected a rethinking of Nhạc's hostility toward Christians, with a view to wooing them to the Tây Sơn cause. There is, unfortunately, virtually no further evidence about the situation of Christians in the southern reaches of Tây Sơn–held territory after 1795.

### *Post-1785 Tây Sơn–Christian Relations in Đàng Ngoài*

The situation of Christians in the upper Đàng Trong and Đàng Ngoài regions in the period beginning in 1786 was, as in the more southern areas, subject to the vicissitudes of political factionalism and shifting military tides in the war with the Nguyễn, each of which profoundly affected the nature of attitudes and state actions vis-à-vis both Vietnamese Christians and European missionaries. It was Tây Sơn actions toward Christians in the north after 1786, and particularly after 1788, that have produced the standard interpretation of Tây Sơn religious policy as being favorable toward Christianity. There is some truth to this view, and the situation of Vietnamese Christians in the area north of Phú Xuân after 1788 was often positive, with considerable European missionary testimony to this fact. A closer examination reveals, however, that there were also periods of sometimes generalized and sometimes localized attacks on Christians, particularly from 1794 to 1795 and 1798 to 1800, and that the situation always remained precarious, constantly subject to changing political fortunes.

After the death of Trịnh Sâm in 1782, the official attitude toward Christianity in the north became less hostile, something noted in numerous missionary letters.[70] In 1784 one missionary even reported that he had been able to enter Thăng Long itself shortly after Easter.[71] This increasing tolerance may have been the by-product of expanding political chaos in the north, which allowed little time for pursuing policies directed against Christians. The arrival of Tây Sơn armies in 1786 does not appear to have altered the generally positive situation for Christians in Đàng Ngoài. When Nguyễn Hữu Chỉnh rose to political prominence in late 1786, he demonstrated a favorable attitude toward the religion and its adherents. Chỉnh had apparently become acquainted with some Christians while in the south with the Tây Sơn, and both his confidential secretary and personal physician were Christians.[72] Some people even claimed that he was himself a Christian, based on his open attacks on Buddhist sites and their ritual objects.[73] Whatever the source of his actions, Christians were generally left in peace during the roughly twelve months of Chỉnh's political preeminence in Đàng Ngoài.

The aftermath of Chỉnh's ouster in late 1787 saw a period of increasing political instability in Đàng Ngoài, which culminated in the Qing invasion and subsequent defeat of their army in early 1789. Christian communities and churches suffered considerably in this period, though indications are that this was not disproportionate to the sufferings of the population at large, and a general tolerance toward the faith seems to have continued.[74] After having stabilized his position on the throne, Emperor Quang Trung made it clear that he was well-disposed toward the Christians under his immediate control. That one of his highest-ranking mandarins was (reportedly) a Christian may have influenced the emperor's attitudes on the subject as well.[75] Missionaries reported that although there had been some discussion among Quang Trung's advisers about cracking down on Christians, most of the emperor's confidants had argued against this. They had pointed out that Christians were considerable in number, that they paid their taxes faithfully, and that they were not creating problems. Consequently, the advisers had concluded, there was no reason to go after Christians, and indeed, doing so would do more harm than good.[76] Quang Trung took this advice, which appears to have coincided with his own views on the matter, and the general religious tranquility continued as testified to by other letters written from Tonkin at this time.[77]

Like his predecessors and contemporaries (including his brother),

Quang Trung was prepared to make use of European missionaries for their scientific knowledge when it suited him. When his senior wife fell ill in 1791, he turned to the French MEP missionaries living in his territories, hoping that European medicine could save her. Reluctant to send one of their own into what they viewed as the proverbial lion's den, the French missionaries nonetheless decided to send the young François-Joseph Girard. Delays by Quang Trung's court officials prevented Girard from administering any medication, and the woman died. Despite this, the Tây Sơn emperor welcomed the European at his court in Phú Xuân and apparently further relaxed his stance toward Christianity.[78] Although the emperor was not ignorant about missionary support for the Nguyễn camp, this information does not appear to have concerned him as it did his elder brother. This attitude may in part be attributed to the fact that he continued to enjoy the protection of what amounted to a buffer zone between himself and the Nguyễn armies. In any case, as long as Quang Trung held out the hope that he could win the missionaries, the Christians, or both to his side, he continued his policy of tolerance.

Even as Quang Trung remained tolerant of Christians in his domain, he was not above drawing on them for resources, as his older brother had earlier in the 1780s. Most notably, Quang Trung, like Nhạc, decided to impose a special tax on Christians in his domains. In 1790 he issued a decree mandating payments from Christians in exchange for their being permitted to continue to practice their faith. He fixed the sum that Vietnamese Christian communities living north of Phú Xuân would have to pay at ten thousand units of copper cash. Those to the south, where fewer Christians lived, would have to pay five thousand. The sums being demanded were to be paid collectively, reflecting Quang Trung's awareness that the community was (at least in places) relatively cohesive and could be tapped for resources in this fashion.[79] This was not unlike earlier incidents in which local officials had kidnapped European missionaries or indigenous prelates and held them for ransom to be paid by the affected community, acts driven by a belief that European missionaries were wealthy and thus a useful target.[80]

A relaxed policy toward Christians continued in the northern Tây Sơn realm for some time even after Quang Trung's premature death in 1792. His successor, supported by a regent, maintained his father's policies for the next several years. Charles La Mothe wrote to Paris in June 1793 that there was much greater religious tolerance than had earlier existed under the Trịnh and Lê.[81] Pierre Eyot noted at the same time that "since Tonkin has been under the domination of the Cochinchinese, there is no talk of persecuting the religion."[82] Another missionary, writing in 1794, compared the religious situation in Tonkin favorably to that in his native France, then in the throes of the French Revolution. He wrote that the two situations of civil war were similar, but for the fact that "our rebels do not touch the religion at all and on the contrary, they have given more freedom than it has ever had before."[83] Others writing in that year made similar observations.[84]

The religious peace described in these letters, however, did not last. By 1793 there were already indications that elements of the Tây Sơn leadership were growing apprehensive of Europeans in their midst, suspecting them of being in contact with the Nguyễn forces and with Nguyễn agents active in the north. There were also rumors that the Nguyễn were directing missionaries into Tây Sơn–controlled regions under the guise of religious activities. Although these accusations were dismissed by a senior Tây Sơn official, the suspicions were clearly part of the general political atmosphere of the time.[85] A major Nguyễn offensive in 1794 further provoked some Tây Sơn leaders, for "the viceroy of upper Cochinchina [Bùi Đắc Tuyên, the regent of the young emperor] who saw some French officers at the head of the troops of his enemies and who was defeated by them is in a terrible rage against us [European missionaries] and our Christians, and has made great threats."[86] The sight of these Frenchmen in the ranks of the Nguyễn was to some Tây Sơn officials a clear and further indication that Europeans, and by extension the missionaries, were actively involved in supporting their bitter rival.

The religious calm, already precarious, was shattered with the publication of two edicts in February 1795.[87] One missionary reported the circumstances around the edicts and the motive behind it quite clearly:

> [F]our days ago there was an order from the king to bring together all of the first-rank bonzes of Tonquin in order to help the said king, through their prayers and their prestige, in opposing the progress that we [the missionaries] are supposed to have made against the spirit of the people in gaining their hearts for the king of Đồng nai.[88]

This comment makes clear that the anti-Christian sentiment developing at this time was directly linked to a fear that the Christians, whether missionaries or natives, were becoming Nguyễn partisans. The Vietnamese Jesuit Philiphê Bỉnh described the impetus for these decrees as being fear of losing the country to the Europeans, rather than any particular hostility toward Christianity.[89] While both edicts were in the name of the young Tây Sơn emperor, Cảnh Thịnh, the missionaries uniformly attributed them to the regent and his anger at the assistance that Europeans were providing to Nguyễn Ánh in the south combined with his implacable hatred of the faith.

According to another missionary, Bùi Đắc Tuyên gave a speech in 1795 in which he explicitly described his regime's views regarding missionary and European involvement on behalf of the Nguyễn cause. In it Tuyên noted the support being given by specific Europeans to the Nguyễn cause and urged missionaries to use their supposed influence to persuade their countrymen to shift allegiance to the Tây Sơn side:

> I have . . . said to our masters of the religion that if they deliver to me Mr. Olivier and his confederates of lower Cochinchina, I will leave them in peace, but that without this I will take them and destroy all of their churches in conformance with the edict. . . . The previous kings had always banned the Religion, but these (the present ones) on the contrary have allowed its observance without saying a word, and here we have Mr. Olivier presiding over all of the works in lower Cochinchina, inventing machines of war, and the masters of the Religion appealing to Europeans for help in making war on a king who is so benevolent and so tolerant towards them: the Christians are ingrates.[90]

The "Mr. Olivier" referred to in this speech was Olivier de Puynamel (1768–1799). Known in the Vietnamese chronicles as "Ông Tín," de Puynamel had gained a considerable reputation for his knowledge of military tactics and weaponry.[91] A French missionary, Charles-François Langlois, writing in 1795 noted that "the tyrants wish to take at least one or two Europeans to send them to Cochinchina to engage Mr. Olivier no longer to give aid to the King of Cochinchina or to Manila to request of the Viceroy to send [someone] to take this Mr. Olivier if this is in his power."[92] Another European cleric similarly reported in the summer of 1795 that Tuyên wanted to use some European missionaries to travel to Đồng Nai to persuade Olivier to halt his support for the Nguyễn and to make a similar appeal to other Europeans in the Nguyễn camp.[93]

The 1795 edicts also included calls to restore or revive local traditions, both Buddhist and Confucian, in an effort to extirpate the apparent contamination of Vietnamese society by Christianity. Thus, the edicts called for a restoration of adherence to Confucian precepts and a revitalization of the state's commitment to maintaining proper Confucian social structures.[94] As the decree noted, "[The missionaries] have secretly come into the country in order to poison and mislead the hearts of all the people in the land. They have directly transmitted lies in order to mislead the ranks of the people into going astray along this way of heterodoxy."[95] The edicts thus appear to have been part of a larger attempt to restore orthodoxy as a means to strengthen the Tây Sơn regime against its enemies. The heterodox principles being advocated by the European missionaries, and being adopted by Vietnamese Christians, constituted a fundamental challenge to the unity of the state and society and thus, in this view, needed to be eliminated.

The episode of the 1795 anti-Christian edicts revealed major schisms within the Tây Sơn leadership. The regent Bùi Đắc Tuyên had apparently manipulated his charge, the young Cảnh Thịnh emperor, into issuing the anti-Christian edicts, and may have done so partly as cover for a planned coup to replace Quang Trung's sons with the regent's own offspring. This plot was revealed, and a countercoup resulted in Tuyên's capture and summary execution. With the death of Tuyên, the edicts were revoked, though it is not clear whether because of their anti-Christian content or the fact that they had been manufactured by the now disgraced Tuyên. As one letter noted, "An edict was published that destroyed all that the viceroy had done during the three months in which he was in charge." The letter went on to note that the missionaries had been told that if the anti-Christian edict was found to be the work of Cảnh Thịnh and his counsel it would stand, but if, as was widely suspected, it was the work of Tuyên, it would be revoked.[96]

The divisions within the Tây Sơn leadership about how to treat Christians lasted until the regime's end. Some officials continued to insist on harsh treatment, while others advocated greater tolerance. In some instances, the advocates of tolerance were pragmatists who feared that cracking down on Christians would alienate another segment of an already disaffected population. Other officials were themselves Christians and sought to look out for their coreligionists. Missionary letters written during this period speak of some high-ranking Tây Sơn officials who were Christians and accordingly were sympathetic to the situation of the missionaries. Thus, for example, even in the midst of the 1795 crackdown on Christians, one missionary reported that in August of that year, only six months after the edicts were issued, he was called into the fortified compound of the first governor of the "province Royalle" to celebrate mass.[97] He reported that the mandarins were beginning to return churches and money that had been seized by these officials during the brief period of formal persecution.[98] Other missionaries reported similarly positive experiences and continued religious freedom over the course of 1797.[99]

Even as religious calm continued, the same issues that had previously contributed to anti-Christian actions persisted. The Nguyễn continued to gain strength in the south, repeatedly threatening to launch a decisive attack on the Tây Sơn court at Phú Xuân, and suspicion of the Europeans living in Tây Sơn territory inevitably increased. This suspicion was heightened particularly as the Nguyễn developed the ability to send secret missions to the north. A French missionary reported in early 1797 that "the spies of the King of Cochinchina, who are arrested from time to time, revive the suspicions that one has against us."[100] Under these circumstances, a renewed crackdown was all but inevitable, and occurred in the summer of the following year. A new anti-Christian edict was issued, reflecting Tây Sơn suspicion not merely of the missionaries, but of Christianized Vietnamese as well.[101] Apparently some Christians had joined in a 1798 anti–Tây Sơn uprising led by a "Magicien" who claimed for himself the title of king. While the missionary reporting this incident, Pierre Eyot, noted that evidence showed that Christians were not leading the movement, suspicion remained.[102]

The zenith of this persecution was reached in September 1798, when a Vietnamese Christian, Immanuel Triệu, was executed along with six thieves on the seventeenth of that month. This marked the first public execution of a Christian since the death of Ferdinand de Olmedilla, the Spanish Dominican, in 1782. Moreover, the crackdown on Christianity was accompanied by an order to make an inventory of all the existing churches and "houses of God." This order was directed to each parish (*chrétienté*) and was followed up by visits from mandarins who checked the mandated catalogues. Apparently this was to be the prelude to a campaign to destroy existing churches; but as was often the case, this drastic action could be forestalled by paying a bribe, an amount that was fixed in at least one region at five thousand strings of cash.[103]

After a few years, however, the pressure on Vietnamese Christians appears to have abated even as problems persisted. Pierre Eyot reported in April of 1800 that "the Christians are less troubled, it is true, than at the beginning of the persecution."[104] Yet in the very same year spies arrested near Phú Xuân declared that they had been sent by the Nguyễn to persuade the Europeans living under the Tây Sơn to remove themselves to Nguyễn territory. While their claim was eventually deemed to be false, suspicion of the Europeans was revived.[105] Still, the situation remained stable as the missionaries and Vietnamese Christians found themselves under less, not more, pressure, perhaps because of the increasing intensity of the Nguyễn threat. The Tây Sơn government was by then in a fight for its survival and could no longer be bothered with using its resources to track down the European missionaries or their adherents.[106]

In the summer of 1802, Nguyễn Ánh and his forces entered Thăng Long, finally triumphant over the Tây Sơn. A chaotic era had ended for Vietnamese society, and yet for Vietnamese Christians 1802 did not mark a turning point. Their lives remained marked by uncertainty. Although the new Nguyễn ruler had incurred debts to French missionaries in the course of his campaigns, his ascension to the imperial throne did not mark the triumph of religious freedom, but rather another chapter in the tensions between a quasi-Confucianized state and a heterodox faith.

## TÂY SƠN RELATIONS WITH NON-VIETNAMESE ETHNIC GROUPS

In chapter 2 I explored some of the ways in which the Tây Sơn leadership established linkages to various ethnic groups as a means of legitimizing their political claims. These linkages continued to be of considerable importance throughout the Tây Sơn years, not only for their symbolic but also for their substantive value. While the Tây Sơn armies marched down from the highlands in 1773 to capture Qui Nhơn, the upland regions remained a central part of their conflict with the Nguyễn throughout the next thirty years. Armies from both camps traversed the uplands in the course of their campaigns, and the upland regions served as important conduits for the movement of forces along and across borders with neighboring states. As a result, both sides sought to develop alliances with members of ethnic groups in these regions, even as they also contested for support from ethnic groups, such as the Chams, Chinese, and Khmers in lowland coastal areas.

The category "non-Vietnamese ethnic groups" is problematic, both because it defines groups in the negative and because it suggests a coherence within these groups that did not exist. Nonetheless, the category has some value in that contemporary sources do point to a sense of separateness between different self-identified or externally identified ethnic groups during the Tây Sơn period. I will use the terms conventionally applied to these groups, ones that frequently invoke identities more commonly associated with distinct national boundaries, which are largely products of nineteenth-century European colonial intervention.[107] Thus, while I speak of "Khmer" peoples and when I use the term "Chinese," I am not invoking contemporary national identities, but classifications (however translated) that reflected eighteenth- or nineteenth-century labels. The fundamental point I seek to make in this discussion is that participants in the events of this period and those who later recorded them recognized a sense of linguistic or cultural difference. While the specificities of these differences might have varied, and the ways in which people classified themselves might well have overlapped, I suggest that there was a recognized sense of difference that had a relevance for the political and military dynamics of this period. Still, it is useful to bear in mind Li Tana's observation that "a defining understanding of ethnicity in the context of the Water Frontier... is that all labels should be taken as tentative, fluid, even temporary."[108]

There were three important groups of lowland non-Vietnamese ethnic groups, also clearly identified as such in contemporary sources. The first of these was the ethnic Chinese, who were recognized by the Vietnamese court, and by later historians, as a distinct category, even though within that broad group there were internal subdivisions reflecting the particular communities, language groups, or regions in China from which they had originated.[109] Most obviously, ethnic Chinese were singled out by being enumerated as a separate category in population counts of the eighteenth and nineteenth centuries. The second group of lowland dwellers recognized as distinct from the Vietnamese settlers in the southern region was the Chams, who were distinguished by their cultural and religious practices as well as their political connections to surviving Cham principalities. Finally, and of somewhat lesser significance for the Tây Sơn conflicts, were the Khmers, who constituted an important group in the far south, in the Mekong Delta region, and inland toward the Cambodian border.

A fourth group of non-Vietnamese I address, though briefly, is the broad category of people living in the high plateaus of what is today south-central Việt Nam, sometimes classified as "highlanders" or "uplanders." This is a group whose distinctiveness comes from geographical location as much as from any concrete cultural or social differences. Both Vietnamese and European observers of this period referred to them generically as "barbarians" (*man* or *mọi*), a term reflecting a smug and shared sense of cultural superiority. Although this is a relatively undifferentiated category that encompasses an extremely wide range of peoples, languages, and cultural practices, there was a clear sense that this was a distinct category of people, separate from the lowland Vietnamese and distinguished by their economic pursuits, language, and dress. The surviving documentation rarely allows discussion of these groups beyond the broad "uplander" category, and consequently my own account of these peoples will be relatively undifferentiated, even as it must be clear that members of these groups recognized themselves as distinct from one another as much as from the lowland groups.

*The Ethnic Chinese in Đàng Trong*

The most prominent ethnic group embroiled in the Tây Sơn wars was the Chinese in Đàng Trong, who by the late eighteenth century numbered as many as thirty thousand.[110] The Chinese in Đại Việt were generally differentiated in contemporary Vietnamese historical chronicles by when they arrived in the Vietnamese realm. The *minh hương* (Ming exiles) were those who had arrived in the late seventeenth or early eighteenth century, many of them loyalists of the deposed Ming dynasty, while the *thanh nhân* (Qing people) were subjects of the Qing dynasty, most of whom had come in the middle to latter part of the eighteenth century.[111]

The Ming loyalists, many of whom were soldiers, fled the last redoubts of their dynasty in the southern parts of China and made their way by sea along the Vietnamese coast, arriving in Đà Nẵng in 1679. The Nguyễn rulers granted them formal permission to settle in the coastal areas of Đàng Trong, and soon thereafter settlements were established in various parts of the Nguyễn realm.[112] The Nguyễn decision to permit this heavily armed party to settle in their territory stemmed in large part from the fact that the Chinese refugees were seen as potentially useful for settling areas that were still lightly populated and in many cases only loosely controlled by the court at Phú Xuân. Many of these immigrants established themselves in and around the trading center at Hội An, while others moved farther south into the sparsely settled Biên Hòa and Mỹ Thọ areas of the Mekong Delta; a few organized a community in the remote fishing port of Hà Tiên, which lay in an area of contested space in the Việt-Khmer border region.

A second group of ethnic Chinese, the so-called *thanh nhân*, began to migrate to Vietnamese territory slightly later, and for different reasons. This latter group came to Đại Việt as part of the growing coastal trade between south China and Đàng Trong, a trade rapidly expanded in the late seventeenth and early eighteenth centuries in part because of the easing of Qing restrictions on their subjects' participation in overseas trade.[113] Many of these later arrivals settled in Hội An, but they also spread into other communities along the central coastal area. Unlike the earlier group of Chinese settlers, whose members had begun to assimilate to their new home and were integrating themselves into Vietnamese society, the more recent arrivals remained closely connected to their south China roots through regular commercial activities and ongoing contacts with clans and secret societies.

While time of relocation was an important distinguishing characteristic of Chinese in Đại Việt, there was another, potentially more significant source of distinction, namely, their place of origin within the larger Chinese empire. This distinction, perhaps more than time of relocation, would have been what differentiated ethnic Chinese living in Đại Việt among themselves. Chinese immigrants to the Vietnamese territories came primarily from coastal China, but within that area had origins in numerous provinces, speaking distinct languages and bringing with them their particular social and historical backgrounds. Within Đại Việt these peoples tended to group themselves by place of origin, which was of course directly linked to a shared spoken language.[114] Thus, Chinese people living in Đại Việt clearly recognized differences within and between their communities, differences reflecting varying places of origin and historical migration experiences.

Because of these multiple forms of differentiation within the Chinese populations of Đại Việt, it is clearly a considerable simplification to refer to "ethnic Chinese" in the collective form as I do here. My decision to use this collective form is largely a matter of expedience, though it is legitimated to some degree by the common engagement of its members in the commercial world with connections to the larger coastal trading arena. It also stems from the fact that sources rarely differentiate fully distinct members of the larger category. Nonetheless, I recognize that beneath the surface of the crude descriptor "ethnic Chinese" lay wide and frequently tangible differences. This should be borne in mind throughout the following discussion, though I continue to believe that the generic term has some utility that reflects a sense of difference of which people in eighteenth-century Đàng Trong were quite aware.

### *The Tây Sơn and Ethnic Chinese Communities*

Although establishing the precise motivations of ethnic Chinese merchants' support for the Tây Sơn uprising is virtually impossible, we do know that members of this group supplied both money and manpower to the Tây Sơn movement in its early years.[115] The chief motivation may have been economic—a hope for better trading opportunities and lighter taxation on imported goods—but it is possible that there were also political considerations. One missionary writer claimed that "in the province of Cham [Quảng Nam] the rebels made an agreement with the Chinese, promising that if they gave their support in this enterprise, to liberate their populations from the tyranny that they suffered to that time and to name one of their mandarins as the King of Cochinchina."[116] It is extremely unlikely that the Tây Sơn actually contemplated such a concession, but they may have used the promise as yet another recruiting tactic. Whatever their motivation, Chinese merchants established important connections with the Tây Sơn leaders, and Chinese soldiers played an instrumental, and possibly dominant, role in the first four years of the movement.

Their primary contribution was in the form of manpower, with Chinese troops dramatically increasing the size of the military force being fielded by the Tây Sơn. The number of Chinese soldiers fighting for the Tây Sơn was such that in 1775 a European observer reported that a majority of the rebel army's troops were ethnic Chinese.[117] The ethnic Chinese armies were headed by the rebels' two most prominent early Chinese supporters, the Hội An merchants Tập Đình and Lý Tài. When they joined the Tây Sơn in 1773, each man brought with him an army composed entirely of Chinese soldiers.[118] Tập Đình's army called itself the Trung Nghĩa (Loyal and Righteous) Army, while that of Lý Tài came to be known as the Hòa Nghĩa (Peaceful and Righteous) Army. It is possible that these armies had been mobilized by the two merchants using either secret-society or merchant-guild connections. By the late seventeenth century, secret societies had emerged as significant commercial and political forces in south China. Engelbert claims that such groupings, organized along linguistic lines, were already emerging in Hội An at about this same time.[119] In the middle of the eighteenth century, organizations of this type had already established themselves in parts of Southeast Asia, and so it would not be surprising to find such "brotherhoods" of ethnic Chinese appearing in Đại Việt a few decades later.[120] We know, moreover, that the ethnic Chinese who settled in Đại Việt and other parts of Southeast Asia often did so in family or clan groups, structures central to secret-society organizations. There is, unfortunately, little evidence about the nature of these armies, or their composition, so possible connections to secret societies or other preexisting organizations must remain speculative. Although we do not know much about their structure or composition, it is clear that these armies were arguably the most powerful component of the Tây Sơn force during the first two years of the uprising.

Even as some ethnic Chinese stepped forward to assist the Tây Sơn in the early days of the movement, others provided support to competing forces. Toward the end of 1775, for example, a Chinese merchant by the surname of Tất bankrolled an uprising led by two members of the Nguyễn royal family, Tôn-thất Quyền and Tôn-thất Xuân, who raised troops in Quảng Nam and soon seized the two prefectures of Thăng Hoa and Điện Bàn. This competing military faction soon attracted the attention of the Tây Sơn, and Nguyễn Nhạc spent two months in battle with these armies before finally getting the upper hand when Quyền and Xuân's troops ran out of supplies.[121] At virtually the same time, another ethnic Chinese, Đỗ Thanh Nhân, joined the fleeing Nguyễn *chúa* and headed to Gia Định, where he quickly recruited an army of more than three thousand to fight for the Nguyễn. Nhân named his force the Đông Sơn (Eastern Mountain) Army as a direct challenge to the Western Mountain rebels of the Tây Sơn.[122] The Đông Sơn force remained an autonomous army under Nhân's direct control, but it was critical to the Nguyễn survival during the late 1770s. Cases such as these make clear that assumptions about uniform support for the Tây Sơn among the coastal ethnic Chinese merchant class are misplaced. Such divisions within a community that was far from uniform in its composition is hardly unexpected. Indeed, particularly during the early years of the movement, even those merchants who sought political or economic change would not necessarily have viewed the Tây Sơn as the only possible agents of that change.

Meanwhile, also in 1775, Nguyễn Nhạc's recently established alliances with Tập Đình and Lý Tài were already starting to crumble. A major reason for this seems to have been that the ethnic Chinese armies were particularly ruthless, frequently alienating the very populations the Tây Sơn were seeking to recruit. According to some accounts, the armies of Tập Đình and Lý Tài were responsible for harassing the populations and for molesting girls and women.[123] In a 1775 letter the missionary Pierre-Jacques Halbout noted that "the rebels . . . are for the most part Chinese, and they have committed a thousand abominations, such as eating human flesh, saying that this is tastier than other meats."[124] A Spanish missionary letter of the same period described the Chinese armies as committing worse atrocities than the Tây Sơn and their rivals combined.[125] In fact, during the early days of the Tây Sơn alliance with the Trịnh, the northern commander sent a message to Nguyễn Nhạc specifically requesting that he find a means to capture and kill the "wicked" Tập Đình and Lý Tài, suggesting that word of their excesses had reached the Trịnh.[126] It is not clear whether it was their misdeeds or perhaps their political or military ambitions that alienated Nhạc from his Chinese commanders, but at some point in 1775, Nhạc and Lý Tài plotted together to kill Tập Đình. When word of this reached the Chinese commander, he fled to south China, where he was later killed in the course of another uprising.[127] A short time later Lý Tài himself, perhaps seeing better opportunities with the Nguyễn or uncertain of his relationship with Nhạc, went south to join his erstwhile enemy. With his strong army, he became kingmaker at Đồng Nai for several years, before he was himself killed in 1777 during factional fighting with another pro-Nguyễn army.[128]

Even as the relationship that the Tây Sơn leaders had developed with Chinese merchants such as Tập Đình and Lý Tài collapsed, other tensions with the Chinese community also began to develop. It is likely that these strains were partly a function of the rural-urban tension manifested early in the movement. The rebel armies attacked cities, where most of the Chinese were to be found, because they perceived them as centers of political and economic power that had contributed to the problems of the countryside. Cities were also targeted for the riches they represented, riches that served to appease the rebel armies and their rural supporters, even as looting of cities alienated urban populations from these same armies.[129]

Tây Sơn armies, moreover, did not merely loot urban centers, but also appear to have specifically directed attacks against ethnic Chinese populations living in them. Tây Sơn forces were reported to have carried out massacres of ethnic Chinese living in the central coastal port cities of Đà Nẵng and Hội An in the mid-1770s, with a Spanish missionary reporting that "a number of Chinese were run through with swords; a number of others, in flight, were drowned in the river which ran near the city."[130] In 1782, when the Tây Sơn forces entered Cambodia, "they went out to search for the Chinese who had fled from Cochinchina [and] they exterminated them without any other reason than for having embraced the party of the king."[131] That same year, in the late spring, Tây Sơn relations with Chinese communities living in Đàng Trong reached their nadir when the rebel forces massacred a large percentage of the Chinese population in Sài Gòn.

According to numerous reports, Tây Sơn forces pillaged and burned the shops and vessels of Chinese merchants and then killed Chinese living in the city, with estimates of the dead ranging from four thousand to twenty thousand.[132] The *Đại Nam Thực Lục* recorded the event as follows: "[Nhạc] immediately ordered the capture of the more than ten thousand Chinese in Gia-định, regardless of whether they were soldiers, civilians or business people. They were then all killed and their corpses thrown into the river. For more than one month no one dared to eat shrimp or to drink water taken from that river."[133] To this observation Trịnh Hoài Đức added, in his *Gia Định Thành Thông Chí*, "All the mercantile goods such as muslin, silks, tea, medicines, perfumes, and paper were seized from the homes of the Chinese and were thrown out into the streets, and no one dared to pick them up."[134]

There is considerable debate over the Tây Sơn rationale for carrying out this gruesome attack and the symbolic looting that followed it. Vietnamese sources from the nineteenth century (including the *Đại Nam Thực Lục*) report that one of Nhạc's chief lieutenants had been killed by Lý Tài's ethnic Chinese Hòa Nghĩa troops and that the massacre of the ethnic Chinese constituted an act of revenge for this killing.[135] It is possible that the attack was also driven by financial reasons, an effort to destroy the commercial monopoly that the Chinese had developed in that city.[136] The idea that the attack might have been commercially motivated is supported by another source, which noted that not only ethnic Chinese, but Portuguese traders as well, were killed and had their goods looted.[137] The looting of the possessions of the Chinese homes and vessels tends to support this interpretation. It is also likely, as Nguyễn Thế Anh and Choi Byung Wook have each very convincingly argued, that Tây Sơn antipathy toward the Chinese community had already been heightened by the support it was providing to the Nguyễn.[138] Tây Sơn actions were driven by a combination of these factors, with revenge offering a convenient pretext for the attack. Whatever the rationale, the massacre is an event rarely discussed by Vietnamese nationalist or Marxist historians in their accounts of the Tây Sơn movement, for it complicates their portrayal of the Tây Sơn as virtuous leaders of an ethnically harmonious movement.[139]

Despite the difficulties in the Tây Sơn relations with ethnic Chinese reflected in the 1782 massacre, the Tây Sơn did not become irrevocably hostile toward this community, nor did implacable hatred of the Tây Sơn emerge among all Chinese. One year after the massacre in Sài Gòn, Chinese merchant ships were once again arriving to trade in its ports.[140] Moreover, Chinese soldiers were still to be found in the ranks of the Tây

Sơn as late as 1790, and, as we shall see, the Tây Sơn remained on friendly terms with Chinese coastal pirates, who were a cornerstone of their military strategy to the very last days of their reign.[141] This indicates that the Tây Sơn leaders did not continue to pursue a consistent anti-Chinese policy and underscores the notion that their actions ultimately represented opportunistic responses to circumstances rather than thoughtful implementation of any particular political or social agenda. Indeed, Thomas Engelbert, in a detailed study of the ethnic Chinese in Vietnam, plausibly suggests that the Tây Sơn attacked anyone whom they perceived as an enemy and that the Sài Gòn massacre did not represent a specifically new anti-Chinese direction to their movement.[142]

This attack nonetheless reflected the general difficulty the Tây Sơn leaders faced in recruiting support from the Chinese community in Đàng Trong. Although the rebel armies had initially been able to draw on the support of ethnic Chinese communities living in the south-central and central coastal areas, they were unable to translate this into a broader and enduring pro–Tây Sơn ethnic Chinese coalition that extended to the populations farther to the south. Tây Sơn armies made repeated efforts to establish firm political control over this region where the Nguyễn rulers had set up their court in exile after being forced out of Phú Xuân in 1774. In subsequent fighting, as we have seen, this southern region changed hands repeatedly between 1776 and 1787, with the Tây Sơn never able firmly to establish their own authority for any extended period. The Nguyễn, although driven from the area numerous times, repeatedly succeeded in recapturing the economically and strategically valuable Gia Định region. They were, moreover, able to organize local forces in that area—including prominent members of the Chinese community—with greater effectiveness than the Tây Sơn.

There are several reasons why the Nguyễn were consistently able to draw the support of the Chinese community even as the Tây Sơn struggled to do so. First, the Nguyễn leaders had arrived in the Gia Định region nearly eighteen months before the first Tây Sơn armies arrived there and took the opportunity to publicize their plight and their claims to power. They were able effectively to argue their legitimacy and demonstrate an authority that resonated with local populations. Another reason for the inability of the Tây Sơn to solidify their control in this region is suggested in a memorial allegedly submitted to the Thái Đức emperor by his teacher and adviser, Trương Văn Hiến:

> Gia Định is far from Phú Xuân, and the people there have not felt oppression because of the disturbances of Trương Phúc Loan. Therefore they do not have the same hatred for the Nguyễn that the people of the center do. Thus when our troops go in to attack the troops of the Nguyễn, the people of the South will view it as a dispute between competing powers, and not as an attempt at liberating them. Thus, whichever side is stronger they will follow at first. Then, whoever wins or loses, they will surrender themselves indifferently. It is for this reason that our troops are able to take Gia Định, but then lose it again. If we wish to retain that territory for a long time, then we must do what is necessary to seize the hearts of the people, and chiefly those of the scholars.[143]

As the author of this memorial plausibly suggests, the Tây Sơn leaders had not fully appreciated that the situation in this region, and its experiences under the Nguyễn, had been quite different from those in the south-central area around Qui Nhơn. Moreover, it highlights the relative outsider status of the Tây Sơn in the far south, for while the Nguyễn had come from even further afield, they represented a political authority with an established credibility in the region.

The Nguyễn success in establishing good relations with ethnic Chinese in the Gia Định area probably also stemmed from historical circumstances. The Nguyễn family's connection to these communities dated back more than a century, and it is likely that at some level, acknowledgment of the Nguyễn aid to the Ming refugees may have contributed to support for the anti–Tây Sơn cause. The 1782 Tây Sơn massacre of Chinese in Gia Định, in part designed as punishment for existing Chinese support for the Nguyễn, only served to drive the Chinese further into the Nguyễn camp.[144] Finally, after permanently retaking Gia Định in 1788, Nguyễn Ánh took steps to integrate the ethnic Chinese into his political and military structures, further solidifying his support within that community.[145] Thus, although the Tây Sơn appear to have derived early assistance from coastal merchants and their followers, it was the Nguyễn who were able to establish more enduring connections to this vitally important community.

### *The Tây Sơn and the Chams*

While the Chinese were the most prominent ethnic group to become involved in the Tây Sơn uprising, other non-Vietnamese ethnic groups such as Chams and uplanders also played prominent roles. As was argued in chapter 2, the Tây Sơn leaders relied on the Cham community early in their uprising, both for military support and for the more abstract support of signs and symbols. Tây Sơn reliance on the Chams reflected the proximity of the uprising's home to the territory of the former Cham rulers. Moreover, by inducing the Cham princess Thị Hỏa to join their movement, the Tây Sơn leaders were able to bring a sizeable number of Chams into their army. For the Chams the Tây Sơn may have represented an opportunity to restore some of their former political strength, while for the Tây Sơn the Chams and their semiautonomous political centers constituted an alternative site of political power to be drawn upon in their struggle with the Nguyễn. Nguyễn Nhạc's decision to use the ancient Cham capital of Vijaya as his own political center clearly reflected this logic.

The appropriation of Vijaya as his political capital, as well as Nhạc's seizure of the Cham imperial regalia at some point in the mid-1780s, both suggest that the Tây Sơn leader was more inclined to use the Chams than to serve their interests. Despite this, the Cham prince whose regalia was seized by the rebel leader became an important political ally of the Tây Sơn. He joined the uprising sometime in the mid-1780s and served the Tây Sơn cause for nearly a decade, until his death in 1794. Known to the later Nguyễn historians as Chưởng Cơ Tá, the Cham prince was recognized by the Nguyễn as a centrally important figure in the Qui Nhơn region, and they made repeated efforts to win him over to their side. The *Đại Nam Nhất Thống Chí* described these efforts in the period shortly after Nguyễn Ánh's return to Gia Định: "In the year *mậu thân* [1788], the Great Ancestral High Emperor [i.e., the future Gia Long] retook Gia Định and many times summoned [the Cham leader Tá], but Tá was frightened because of his crimes and did not dare to come out. Our troops went forth to attack that territory many times but were defeated."[146] Tá's defiance probably reflected continuing Tây Sơn military strength in the late 1780s and early 1790s, though the Nguyễn efforts to woo Cham supporters revealed their own determination to undermine Tây Sơn alliances.

As Nhạc's territorial control slowly eroded in the face of growing Nguyễn strength and their expanding territorial control, the Tây Sơn leader's hold over the Chams crumbled as well. Already by 1790, there are indications that important Cham political figures were beginning to throw their support behind the Nguyễn. When in 1793 the Nguyễn retook Bình Thuận, the coastal province south of Nha Trang, a Cham leader led his troops to join the Nguyễn in attacking the Tây Sơn, in exchange

FIGURE 9. *Cham tower at Chà Bàn. Standing on a mound in the center of the first Tây Sơn political center, this is one of countless Cham towers found in the south-central coastal area where the Tây Sơn uprising began. Author's photo.*

for which the Nguyễn recognized his authority over the local Cham populations.[147] A 1793 missionary letter commenting on the situation in the south also reported that Cham troops had changed their allegiance to the Nguyễn and were rising up against the Tây Sơn.[148] Eventually, the Cham prince Tá himself succumbed to this changing dynamic, and was betrayed by a tribal leader in 1794, as the *Đại Nam Nhất Thống Chí* describes:

> Then in the year 1794 the *tù trưởng* [tribal chief] of Thuận Thành, Nguyễn Văn Hào showed the route for our troops to follow in order to capture [Tá]. Tá was killed. The title of King of Thuận Thành was immediately abolished, and Hào was named as the *chưởng cơ lĩnh chánh* [primary leading captain] of the *trấn* of Thuận Thành; Nguyễn Văn Chấn was also appointed as *chưởng cơ* [captain] to serve as his assistant, and they were ordered to gather together the peoples and every year to submit taxes; and they would be attached to the Bình Thuận military camp.[149]

As this account suggests, the Tây Sơn were involved in a competition with their Nguyễn adversaries for the loyalties of the Cham community. It also illustrates the conflicting loyalties evident in the larger Cham community. Although the Nguyễn records describe Hào as a "tribal chief," other indications are that he, like Nguyễn Văn Chấn, was a Cham (their Cham names are rendered in the Nguyễn records as Thôn ba hú and Bô kha đáo). Both were joined in aiding the Nguyễn by several other Chams, all of whom were rewarded for their assistance by the granting of titles and military responsibilities.[150]

### *The Tây Sơn and the Khmers*

Another prominent southern ethnic community involved in the Tây Sơn wars was that of the Khmers. The Gia Định region that was so heavily contested during the wars, particularly in the 1770s and early 1780s, had once been an extension of the Khmer Empire and had only come under nominal Nguyễn control in the early eighteenth century. Despite the expansion of Nguyễn political authority in the area, there remained a sizeable Khmer population that extended through the Mekong Delta region and toward the remaining territory of the Khmer kingdom itself. Both the Khmer peoples living in Vietnamese-controlled territory and the Khmer kingdom had become increasingly involved in Vietnamese affairs over the course of the eighteenth century. This involvement increased during the Tây Sơn era. During the 1770s and early 1780s, both Nguyễn and Tây Sơn armies entered Khmer territory, becoming involved in political transitions on the throne at Oudong. Furthermore, Khmer peoples on each side of the border were recruited, sometimes by force, into the armies of both camps. As the Khmer scholar Khin Sok observed in a history of seventeenth- through nineteenth-century Cambodia, "During ten years—from 1783 to 1794—Cambodia was a field of battle between the Siamese and the Vietnamese; the Khmer people, conscripted by force by the two camps, continued to suffer massacres, destruction and desolation."[151]

The Tây Sơn had had ambitions of seizing Khmer territory since at least 1778, when Nguyễn Nhạc confided his long-term military ambitions to Charles Chapman during the Englishman's visit to the Tây Sơn capital. The Tây Sơn invasion of Cambodia in 1782 thus represented an attempt to fulfill this objective. While the rebel army was not able (or chose not) to hold any Khmer territory in the aftermath of this invasion, it did accept the surrender of a number of Cambodian troops, who were probably brought into the ranks of the Tây Sơn force.[152] It is also likely that the Tây Sơn seized Khmer civilians to further augment their army, since people would have been far more valuable to the Tây Sơn leaders than the relatively distant Khmer territory. Soon after their retreat from Cambodia, the brothers received additional Khmer assistance from one of the claimants to the Khmer throne. Recorded in the Vietnamese annals as Tèn, this prince was forced to flee the Cambodian capital at Oudong, eventually making his way to Gia Định, where he was given refuge by the Tây Sơn governor.[153]

Throughout the rest of the 1780s, Khmer soldiers and communities continued to take sides in the ongoing Tây Sơn contest with the Nguyễn. Nguyễn Ánh's return from Bangkok in 1787, however, substantially changed the dynamics of Khmer involvement. Nguyễn Lữ was forced to flee to Qui Nhơn as the Nguyễn force advanced on Sài Gòn, and this marked the end of any substantial Tây Sơn presence in the far southern regions. Despite this, a few Khmers did continue to assist the remaining Tây Sơn military in the Mekong region. In early 1788, a Khmer named Ốc Nha Long joined the Tây Sơn, bringing a small number of boats with him. He fought the Nguyễn at Cần Thơ but was defeated. The *Đại Nam Thực Lục* describes another Khmer in the Mekong region, Ốc Nha Ốc, who allied himself with the Tây Sơn in the same year. He was assigned to defend the strategic regions of Trà Vinh and Mân Thít, which lay at the mouths of the Mekong.[154] After the death of his Tây Sơn patron, however, Ốc Nha Ốc was forced to flee further inland to Cần Thơ, where he was eventually captured and killed by the Nguyễn.[155] The death of Ốc marked the end of Tây Sơn connections with the ethnic Khmers in the Gia Định region. Thereafter, it was the Nguyễn who maneuvered to create alliances with the Khmers resident in the area—or at least to ensure that they would not create problems for their newly established political base in Gia Định.[156]

*The Tây Sơn and Upland Populations*

Indigenous populations living in the highland regions also became embroiled in the Tây Sơn wars. These groups had long been in contact with the lowland Vietnamese, through both regular trade and occasional warfare. The frequency of this contact appears to have increased over the course of the seventeenth and eighteenth centuries.[157] Nguyễn Nhạc, through his early days as a betel-nut trader, had developed extensive contacts with various ethnic groups in the highland regions to the west of Tây Sơn. When the Tây Sơn brothers established their first base on the An Khê plateau, these existing contacts proved useful in attracting followers and gaining access to resources. With this region as a base, the early Tây Sơn uprising came to rely heavily on groups living in the highland regions.

It was not merely proximity that appears to have stirred support for the Tây Sơn mission among these groups, but also their shared antipathy toward the Nguyễn. As was noted in chapter 1, the increasing tax burden being shifted onto upland peoples was a significant factor contributing to this hostility toward the Nguyễn regime. This tension led to growing numbers of uprisings and attacks against lowland communities beginning in the 1750s. When the Tây Sơn launched their campaign against the Nguyễn, upland groups constituted natural allies of the rebel armies, contributing not least their experience in attacking Nguyễn positions. Upland groups, such as the Bahnar, were a significant element of the Tây Sơn armies throughout the 1770s, a position they did not relinquish even as the Tây Sơn brothers launched their attacks into Đàng Ngoài in 1786. Commenting on the ethnically diverse force that constituted the rebel army as it entered the northern region in that year, a Frenchman reported that it included "Muong, Man-di, and other barbarians from Cao-mien [Cambodia], Cambien, Siame, etc."[158] This observation highlights the extremely heterogeneous nature of the Tây Sơn force and the continuing presence of upland peoples, who had over time been joined by soldiers from across the Vietnamese borders.

As with the ethnic Chinese, the Tây Sơn could not take the support of upland populations for granted. Instead, they were, almost from the outset, forced to compete with the Nguyễn and even other autonomous armies for the assistance of these groups. Although the rebel armies were successful in recruiting members of upland groups to their side during the early years of their uprising, such recruitment faced challenges as other autonomous armed forces emerged among these populations. Most notable among such groups was the army recruited by Châu Văn Tiếp. Like Nhạc, Tiếp had been a merchant with upland connections, and according to the *Đại Nam Liệt Truyện* had even been acquainted with Nhạc before his uprising.[159] Tiếp and his four older brothers used these connections to recruit an army among highland populations in the interior of Phú Yên Province in the early years of the Tây Sơn conflicts. This army grew to more than one thousand soldiers. As Choi points out, the force Tiếp created effectively functioned as an independent army through much of the 1770s. While it generally supported the Nguyễn cause, at times it sided with the Tây Sơn for strategic reasons, particularly before 1776, when the Tây Sơn still claimed to be fighting on behalf of the Nguyễn.[160] The existence of Tiếp's army of uplanders underscores the fact that although there might have been considerable potential for Tây Sơn recruitment among these groups because of their inherent hostility to Nguyễn encroachments against their autonomy, this hostility did not by any means guarantee their support for the Tây Sơn.

## VAGABONDS, BANDITS, AND PIRATES IN THE TÂY SƠN UPRISING

> We are infested with a plague of bandits and pirates who pillage and ravage everything. The canton where I am, at the entrance to Cambodia, is infested with them.
>
> —Pierre-Marie Le Labousse[161]

Just as Vietnamese Christians and various non-Vietnamese ethnic groups came to play a significant role in the Tây Sơn years, so too did other groups at the social margins, none more dramatically than vagabonds, bandits, and pirates. Although most accounts of the Tây Sơn ignore the presence and role of such elements, a closer examination of the historical record and in particular the testimony of European observers suggests that these socially marginalized groups played significant roles in the Tây Sơn armies. While the Tây Sơn leaders themselves had political aspirations that transcended mere banditry, their movement was often and dramatically enlarged by the participation of bandit groups. The Tây Sơn appear to have accepted, and at times even welcomed, the involvement of such outlaw elements, for they were almost always in need of additional soldiers. Although affiliating themselves with bandits could jeopardize their relationship with the peasantry, there were many instances in which Tây Sơn leaders viewed the advantages of such connections as outweighing their potential costs.

*Vagabondage and Banditry in Late-Eighteenth-Century Đại Việt*

The widespread banditry in the latter decades of the eighteenth century was directly related to the phenomenon of "vagabondage"—the movement of peoples away from their farms and homes. Large numbers of Vietnamese were on the move throughout this period, creating unrest and uncertainty. The impact of famine and the state's inability to respond adequately to such crises contributed enormously to the dramatic problems of rural vagabondage, which helped fuel large-scale peasant uprisings in Đàng Ngoài from the 1720s into the 1760s. Although these uprisings were largely contained by the late 1760s, the problem of vagabondage was not so easily resolved. A 1780 survey of the northern region by the respected court official Ngô Thì Sĩ still reported large-scale problems. He reported that of ninety-seven hundred Red River Delta villages, more than a thousand had been abandoned or could no longer pay their taxes. In Thanh Hóa more than 20 percent of villages were in this condition; in Nghệ An it was 16 percent.[162] Enormous famines and floods in the early and mid-1780s only further accelerated this problem.

People on the move are antithetical to the interests of an agrarian state. Such states want populations to remain in their villages, where they can be counted, taxed, subjected to state labor projects, and kept under surveillance. Once people leave their villages, they become unproductive and at the same time constitute a ready source of man- (and sometimes woman-) power for groups, such as bandits, operating on the margins. Thus vagabondage and banditry fueled one another, creating a cycle that became increasingly difficult for the state to break. As Michael Adas has observed,

> Though many bandits were professional criminals, some of whom inherited their way of life from their fathers as one would a trade, others became brigands to escape the hardships of peasant life. . . . In Java and Burma, as in China and Vietnam, the growth of banditry beyond its normal endemic proportions was one of the key signs of dynastic decline. Peasant refugees from drought, famine, and excessive taxation often joined established bandit gangs.[163]

Similarly, Masaya Shiraishi has pointed out that "official chronicles often describe in the same passage the twin phenomena of the movement of people away from their native villages, and of the rampancy of banditry. This movement of peoples was an outcome of the general poverty of rural society, and at the same time it provided a reservoir for banditry."[164] Although Shiraishi's study focused on a post–Tây Sơn incident, the parallels to the late eighteenth century are clear. If anything, the situation of population movement and dispersal was even more acute in the earlier period.

As Shiraishi noted, outlaws and bandits had always been a feature of the precolonial landscape in Đại Việt, and, not surprisingly, such groups proliferated in regions where government control was weakest, including, he pointed out, the region of the south-central coast, where the Tây Sơn emerged.[165] Banditry was a complex phenomenon for rural populations. It clearly constituted a heavy burden for populations being preyed on, even as it represented an avenue for economic survival to those carrying out the attacks. Consequently, Shiraishi argued, "The relations of villagers (and more especially of village notables) with bandits, thieves, and vagabonds were ambivalent, just as their relations with the state were ambivalent. In some cases villagers rejected and fought the bandits, but in others they tried to negotiate and coexist with them. In either case, their aim was the same: to protect themselves and survive in a turbulent society."[166] For the common person then, the Tây Sơn uprising, and the disorder to which it contributed, might have constituted either great opportunity or grave peril. Those who viewed it as opportunity were often living on the edge of subsistence and saw the shift to banditry as a relatively easy one in a period when official order was irregular at best. For those not tempted by such opportunities, however, the rise of banditry meant a corresponding increase in their own vulnerability. As one European missionary succinctly observed in 1786, "Two thirds of the inhabitants of the kingdom have become bandits, and the other third is in great distress."[167]

Banditry was already a major concern in the early Tây Sơn years, with attacks in the early 1770s severely reducing the ability of villagers and farmers to carry out their daily tasks. In some areas of central Đàng Trong in the 1770s, bandit attacks, some brazenly carried out in broad daylight, had become so frequent that peasants were forced to abandon their cultivated fields.[168] Writing in 1775, the French missionary Jean Labartette noted that there were large numbers of bandits in the region where he lived and that "each band has ordinarily between thirty and forty men, among whom there is not a single one not ready to murder or kill the others."[169] Local communities would sometimes come together in mutual defense against such bandit groups, which were rampant not only in Đàng Trong, but especially in Đàng Ngoài.[170] A European missionary described the dynamics of such an episode directed against a northern Christian village in 1785:

> On the 8th of March, two of his servants were seized along with four Christians in another part of his district, by a group of bandits who had burned the church, his residence and eight other houses, and when the residents of this place managed to seize two of these malefactors, their companions in brigandry returned two days later, numbering around four hundred men, determined to rescue these prisoners; they pillaged and sacked the village, and took away the rice, the furniture, the clothing, the animals, the domestic fowl, and generally everything that these poor people possessed.[171]

This incident makes clear the devastation that bandits could wreak on vulnerable villages and the untenable situation in which villagers often found themselves. Fighting back, as this case shows, might only exacerbate the problem.

*Bandits and the State in the Tây Sơn Era*

The rise of banditry constituted an ongoing dilemma for political authorities, who were forced to find effective means to combat the corrosive consequences of this phenomenon with often limited resources. At times the state did act to eradicate particular bandits, depending on circumstances and their crimes.[172] At other times, and indeed probably far more frequently, the state chose to co-opt bandits or rebels instead of suppressing them. This option was simpler, cheaper, and ultimately more effective in curbing, if not eliminating, the problem. The easiest means of co-opting outlaws or rebels was simply to enroll them in the state's armed forces. The idea of enrolling bandits in official armies has a long history and probably existed in any region where banditry was widespread. As Elizabeth Perry has pointed out for the Chinese case, "Government cooptation of bandit chiefs was frequent in traditional China. 'Pacification,' complete with official position, was such a common government tactic that more than a few bandit leaders saw their outlaw career as a quick means of attaining bureaucratic rank."[173]

One need only look at the relationship that developed between the Trịnh and the Tây Sơn to see how this dynamic between state and bandits functioned in Đại Việt. When the Trịnh first attacked Đàng Trong in 1774, they did so on the pretext of suppressing the Tây Sơn rebels, and referred to the eldest Tây Sơn brother as "that crazy Biện Nhạc."[174] When circumstances changed, however, and the Trịnh forces became bogged down in the south, their leading generals took a different view of the situation. The Trịnh commanders decided that rather than attempting to sustain a campaign that had encountered so many difficulties, it would be prudent to reach an accommodation with the rebel armies. Consequently, as we saw in chapter 2, Trịnh officials reached a compromise with the Tây Sơn leaders, agreeing to enroll them into the ranks of the northern army, naming Nguyễn Nhạc first a general and later a provincial governor and grand duke. By this simple expedient the Tây Sơn had been transformed from Đàng Trong rebels into Trịnh soldiers. As this case so clearly revealed, the lines between rebel, bandit, and official were often quite thin, dictated more by circumstance than by policy.

As the example of the Trịnh–Tây Sơn interaction suggests, the practice of co-opting bandits was not unknown, and probably not uncommon in Đại Việt. In 1783, a few years after the Trịnh had turned the Tây Sơn from rebels into imperial soldiers, a missionary in Trịnh territory reported that "in the province where I am and in which there are a great number of Christians, we have been given [as the new governor] a chief of thieves, who keeps in his pay a group of five hundred brigands taken from the dregs of the society, and solely occupied with pillaging and stealing."[175] In another instance, a missionary noted that a bandit chief had approached a provincial governor requesting an official order to seize a local European missionary. While the order was not forthcoming, the incident suggests the close relationship that existed between the government official and the bandit leader.[176] Indeed, the same account, speaking in more general terms, noted that "there reigns here an unbridled cupidity that produces and sustains without cease an infinite multitude of brigands, emboldened by the assurance of impunity and often [guided] by the example of those who call themselves here mandarins."[177] The phenomenon was described again in 1786 during the course of the Tây Sơn attack into Đàng Ngoài: "An adventurer, formerly a Chief of Thieves, whom the Chúa had elevated to a grand Mandarinate, and to which he had attached one of his brothers as a joint commander of his troop of bandits, metamorphosed all of a sudden into a defender of the nation."[178] This type of metamorphosis from bandit to "defender of the nation" was a frequent occurrence in the Tây Sơn period, highlighting the long-standing, ambivalent relationship that existed between the state, the village, and rural banditry.

Like the Trịnh, the Tây Sơn leaders' attitudes toward bandits were guided chiefly by expedience. During the early days of the uprising, its leaders regularly drew support from or established alliances with bandit groups operating in the highland regions. It was perhaps such alliances that later prompted one European observer to refer to Nhạc as "the king of brigands."[179] Bandit groups would have been particularly useful to the Tây Sơn in their early campaigns to seize goods from local economic elites including wealthy and unpopular landlords, who would have been the traditional targets of these bandits in many instances. One account suggests that at the outset of his rebellion Nhạc brought together twenty-three or twenty-four bandits to help serve as the core of his movement, while another gives the names of two bandit leaders—Nhưng Húy and Tứ Linh—who joined about the same time.[180] A folk tradition records that the noted Tây Sơn general Võ Văn Dũng had been a notorious bandit chieftain forced into a life of crime by the cruel administration of Trương Phúc Loan before his recruitment by Nguyễn Huệ.[181] This degree of bandit involvement in the early years of the uprising and the actions carried out by the Tây Sơn forces led European observers to report that they had difficulty distinguishing between Tây Sơn forces and bandits then active in Đàng Trong. Vietnamese rural populations appear to have had similar difficulties. It was reported that the Tây Sơn troops had to "announce that they were not bandits," suggesting that their appearance or actions, or both, were often difficult to distinguish from those of known bandit groups.[182] Later accounts of ongoing looting by Tây Sơn troops suggest that distinctions between the proclaimed "righteous troops" of the Tây Sơn and their bandit counterparts remained blurred.

Once the Tây Sơn armies moved into Đàng Ngoài, connections with bandits were established in that region as well. With their mobility and unofficial status, bandits and other such elements of Đàng Ngoài society were more likely than peasant agriculturalists to join the Tây Sơn armies willingly. The Tây Sơn campaigns represented an opportunity for personal gain, making bandits ideal candidates for joining the Tây Sơn armies. Moreover, since the Tây Sơn leaders, with the exception of Nguyễn Hữu Chỉnh, had no experience of or substantial information about the northern region, it would be logical for them to enroll outlaw elements with their knowledge of local terrain and conditions. Even Chỉnh recruited bandits into his army in large numbers. As one missionary reported of his military force, "For one Cochinchinese, one could count sometimes twenty or thirty of such Tonkinese brigands who, not content with their compensation, still lived up to their names, spreading terror among the peoples to extort large sums of money."[183] Such alliances with bandits would have been particularly useful for the Tây Sơn leaders as they entered Đàng Ngoài, allowing them to connect to the region in a way that might otherwise have been difficult.

The Tây Sơn leaders' general lack of information about the north, and indeed their naïveté about bandit issues there, is revealed in a brief account in the *Hoàng Lê Nhất Thống Chí*. According to this tale, Nguyễn Nhạc met a group of people along the road who lamented to him that they had just lost all their possessions to a band of Nghệ An robbers commanded by the notorious Chưởng Tiến. Nhạc questioned the men about the robbers' whereabouts, then sent his troops into the woods after them. No sooner had the Tây Sơn soldiers been lured into the woods than they were ambushed by the robbers, who took out their swords and announced themselves to be followers of Chưởng Tiến. They pounced on the Tây Sơn troops, killing several and forcing the rest to flee. Nhạc was greatly intimidated, and thereafter his troops were too frightened to sleep in the people's homes, choosing rather to sleep outside in the rice paddies.[184] Given such an experience, it would not be surprising to see the Tây Sơn seeking alliances with bandit leaders rather than attempting to challenge them on their own terrain.

Although the Tây Sơn leaders formally enrolled bandits in their forces, established alliances with bandit groups, and even employed local hooligans as officials, the rebel leaders were well aware that encouraging bandits risked alienating large segments of the rural populations. At times, seeking to gain the support of populations frequently terrorized by bandit attacks, the Tây Sơn took steps to suppress rather than facilitate banditry. In 1776, for example, Nguyễn Nhạc sent a message to his Trịnh superiors in which he announced that one of his intentions was to eliminate bandits then operating in the Quảng Ngãi region: "[B]ands of robbers in that region are turning into flocks. The people in those three prefectures are all being harassed. As soon as I heard this news, I provisionally brought my troops there in order to capture those robbers, because I wished for the people to be at peace."[185] Of course it is difficult to determine whether the Tây Sơn leader actually followed through on this initiative or whether instead this message reflected his sense of what he thought the Trịnh wished to hear. As a military representative of the Trịnh, he would almost certainly be expected to maintain the peace, including carrying out attacks to suppress banditry. From what we know of the dynamic between keepers of the peace and bandits, it is very likely that Nhạc's answer to the bandit problem was simply to integrate them into his own armies.

Ten years later, as the Tây Sơn troops marched north in 1786, their leaders again took steps to suppress banditry and brigandage to burnish their reputations as protectors of the political order. The Tây Sơn leaders cracked down on banditry, including the use of summary justice and executions of bandits (or those merely accused of being bandits) as well as others found harassing local populations. The official seals carried by the Tây Sơn commanders reflected the nobility of their mission: *phụng thiên phạt tội* (obey heaven and punish criminals).[186] While the "criminals" in the seal probably referred most immediately to the Trịnh lords, it would be logical to think that the notion might well have been extended to other elements in society. Once Nguyễn Huệ came to power as Emperor Quang Trung, the urgency of restoring order rather than facilitating banditry became even greater, something reflected in his 1789 decree calling on people to return to their villages and to resume cultivating their lands. In a further effort to restore stability, Quang Trung also called for each canton (*tổng*) to contribute one night watchman to patrol the villages to keep bandits and thieves at bay.[187]

The surviving evidence, however, reveals that bandits were frequently able to escape the rudimentary judicial institutions the Tây Sơn were able to establish. Many of that regime's officials appear, in any case, to have viewed bandits more as a source of potential revenue than as a social scourge. Some reached accommodations with bandits, allowing them to operate unchecked in exchange for sharing their loot with local officials.[188] Others did take steps to seize bandits, not as a systematic attempt to curb their excesses, but rather as a means of extorting payoffs in exchange for their release. As one missionary noted in the late 1790s,

> All of the mandarins look for ways to enrich themselves at the expense of the poor people. Justice is sold based on the weight of gold, with the scales always favoring the side that offers the most cash. The country is full of bandits, thieves and rogues, and when the mandarins are able to seize them they are always released for a cash payment, unlike the poor people who are punished, and the wealthy who do not fear either being robbed or being killed.[189]

This approach was not unlike that frequently applied to Christians, who, as we have seen, were often seized and then released in exchange for payments of various amounts to the official in question.

### *Tây Sơn Relations with Chinese Pirates*

The Tây Sơn regime of Quang Trung also developed significant alliances with Chinese pirates who operated in the coastal waters of the South China Sea. These pirates, who were active from the central Vietnamese coast through the Gulf of Tonkin and north as far as Zhejiang, became a central feature of Tây Sơn naval strategy and indeed of the regime's economy between 1786 and 1802.[190] Dian Murray's fine study, *Pirates of the South China Coast, 1790–1810*, describes in considerable detail the manner in which Quang Trung's government integrated numerous pirate groups into the ranks of its military, and my own discussion of this issue draws extensively on Murray's work, and to a lesser extent that of Robert Antony.[191]

The protected coastal region surrounding the Gulf of Tonkin and stretching from Canton and Macao south along the Vietnamese coast was ideal for piracy. Most significant, this was a region that saw high volumes of commercial shipping—both indigenous vessels and growing numbers of European trading ships—with every imaginable sort of cargo. Secondly, the geography of this region was well suited to piracy. The shallow seas were relatively calm, protected from the deeper waters that lay beyond the continental shelf. There were also countless small bays and islands that could serve as hiding places for those seeking to avoid contact with authorities and to which quick retreat could be made. Indeed, these islands were sometimes labeled "iles de Pirates" in late-eighteenth- and early-nineteenth-century European maps. After 1760, when the Qing court mandated that all European trade be funneled through the single port at Canton, these two elements were brought together as an intensely concentrated corridor of commercial activity came to intersect with prime conditions for piracy.[192] Thus, by the time Tây Sơn troops arrived in Đàng Ngoài in 1786, piracy was already well established in the Gulf of Tonkin region. Chinese pirates were taking advantage of the protection offered by Vietnamese coastal regions south of the Chinese border and were using Jiang-ping in An Quang Province, just inside the Vietnamese border, as their center of operations. Situated on a shallow river and virtually cut off from the interior by difficult terrain, Jiang-ping was an ideal retreat.[193]

This coastal region, with its maritime populations, was well suited to producing people ready to turn to piracy. There was already a large community of people who either lived or made their living on boats, meaning that the transition to piracy—either as a career or merely a temporary way to supplement one's income—was a simple one. Economic pressures in this region were considerable, and many people, including fishermen, lived on the edge of survival. As Murray points out, "Unable to discharge their financial obligations, fishermen were often compelled to supplement their incomes through sideline activities such as small-scale trade. Yet even then the result was a livelihood so miserable that, for many, a successful piratical foray was the sole hope for a better life."[194] Or, as Quang Trung rendered it in the first of several proclamations designed to lure pirates into his camp,

> All of the people of the ten ranks are this year hiding in places by the edges of the sea, gathering together their bands, and taking the job of looting in order to make a living. They do this because they have gotten into this position unwillingly, or because they were hungry or cold and forced into it, or because oppression drove them away, and only then did they arrive at the point where they relied on this place of waves and wind and had no means of escape.[195]

Although the Tây Sơn emperor suggested that resorting to piracy was a choice of last resort, it seems clear that for some, and perhaps many, the decision to engage in piracy was based on pragmatism rather than desperation. The choice was, in any case, neither irrevocable nor exclusive. Fishermen could and did make the transition between fishing and piracy in the same way that some of their inland counterparts could shift between farming and banditry.

The Tây Sơn recruited pirates in a variety of ways, both indirect and direct. Indirect recruitment took the form of issuing and then circulating edicts calling on these men to join the Tây Sơn cause. The edicts the Tây Sơn leaders issued, crafted by Ngô Thì Nhậm, were replete with rhetorical flourishes designed to assuage the consciences of the Confucian officials taking part in these recruitment efforts. Thus, the first of these edicts began,

> I have heard it said that the great wind does not blow throughout the morning, and the great rain does not last throughout the entire day. The road of heaven is like this. Therefore people who were good as children cannot be cruel throughout their entire lives. In ages past there were people who first acted as thieves, and later became noted generals, and this was in fact because they dared to mend their errors were brave, and performed virtuous deeds. They thoroughly understood things of ritual, and understood that some ways must be abandoned and some followed, and they knew how to choose those things which must be done. Thus their names and ages were placed into the history books and their labors recorded in the ledgers of public service.[196]

The Tây Sơn were clearly seeking to cajole pirates into serving their regime, using Confucian rhetoric that sought to excuse their criminal activities and suggesting that their service might constitute both an opportunity to turn over a new leaf and a chance to make a name for themselves.

The ongoing Tây Sơn interest in recruiting pirates is reflected in the fact that two subsequent edicts were issued in an effort to win over more such men.[197] Like the first appeal, these later edicts portrayed the option of joining the Tây Sơn as turning one's back on a life of crime and piracy while moving toward noble government service. It would be a distortion to suggest, however, that joining the Tây Sơn constituted a renunciation of their former employment. While the scholar who wrote these edicts on behalf of the Tây Sơn ruler perhaps wished to believe that the Tây Sơn were seeking to convert these "misguided" pirates, the reality was very different. The pirates were being recruited precisely because of their background, their ability to provide the Vietnamese regime with booty, and their fighting skills.

More effective than the circulation of edicts was the direct recruitment of pirates through the personal efforts of those who had already joined the Tây Sơn. The lynchpin of these personal recruiting efforts was Chen Tianbao, whom the Tây Sơn allegedly captured in 1783.[198] He was named a *tổng binh* (brigade commander), and a companion, Liang Gui-xing, was given the title of Hiệp Đức Hầu (Total Virtuousness Marquis). According to Murray, the two men fought in the 1786 Tây Sơn advance to the north that captured Phú Xuân and Thăng Long. Thereafter, as she writes, they became a central pillar of the northern Tây Sơn regime's military structure, especially after 1788. Having given Chen the title of *đức hầu*, the Tây Sơn also granted him the authority to recruit additional pirates to the rebel cause and to grant these new recruits military positions of their own.[199] Chen apparently did so with great enthusiasm, and brought large numbers of pirates to serve the Tây Sơn, men who found such service to be a convenient means of gaining protection from Chinese crackdowns while taking part in organized raids on behalf of the Vietnamese.[200] Chinese pirates were subsequently involved in all of the major Tây Sơn military campaigns of the 1790s, serving the rebel government until its final days.

The military ranks and lofty political titles were particularly useful recruiting devices, for they bestowed both prestige and legitimacy. As Murray notes, "The association with the Tay-son gave pirate leaders other means of incorporating outsiders into their organizations. The ability to confer status through the granting of titles that were recognized by the government was an important recruiting tool."[201] Men who were once simply pirates of no rank or status were now being recognized as commanders, generals, military governors, and marquis, while a few were even named as kings. A pirate leader by the name of Mo Guanfu was given the title of Đông Hải Vương (King of the Eastern Seas), while another, Wushi Er, was named the Bình Ba Vương (King Who Pacifies the Waves) in 1797.[202] Just as in the mid-1770s the Tây Sơn leaders had drawn strength and status from the titles and formal positions granted them by the Trịnh, so too the Chinese pirates gained stature from titles given them by the Tây Sơn. This legitimation was important for the pirates vis-à-vis one another and the Chinese regime, but it was also useful to the Tây Sơn leaders, for it provided a gloss of propriety to their relationship with these outlaws.

The pirate navies serving the Tây Sơn were substantial, with Mo Guanfu at one point commanding more than one thousand men and another pirate leader, Zheng Qi, leading a force of more than two hundred vessels.[203] Navies of this size were immensely useful to the Tây Sơn and served a variety of crucial functions for Quang Trung's regime. In the first place, the pirates enabled him dramatically to expand his regime's naval strength, giving it additional capacity to patrol the coastal waters from the Chinese border as far south as Qui Nhơn.[204] Equally important, by interdicting sea traffic of virtually every type moving to, from, and along coastal areas of Đại Việt, including fellow Chinese merchants, Nguyễn agents, missionaries coming from Macao, and European vessels of all nationalities, pirate ships provided a valuable layer of security for the Tây Sơn regime. The pirates could not entirely halt the movement of vessels in and out of Tây Sơn–controlled areas, but they could substantially restrict their passage.

Pirate patrols served to curtail the movement of Nguyễn spies into Tây Sơn–held territories while simultaneously preventing northerners from traveling south to join the Nguyễn. They further helped the Tây Sơn by hindering the movement of supplies from Chinese ports to Gia Định, where they might be used to support the Nguyễn military efforts. These patrols also impeded the movement of Europeans—including both missionaries and commercial agents—in and out of the country.[205] Restricting the movement of these men would have been particularly advantageous both because of the actual presence of French advisers in the Nguyễn ranks, a presence the Tây Sơn did not wish to see expanded, and because of the perceived threat that European missionaries posed as potential conduits of information to the Nguyễn side. Substantial efforts were made to block the movement of these men, either south toward Gia Định or north toward Macao, where information might also be passed to Nguyễn representatives. These efforts had important repercussions within Đại Việt too, for the pirates, who patrolled down the coast as far as Qui Nhơn, made it difficult for contact to take place between different regions.[206] This served Tây Sơn purposes, particularly with regard to the movement of people or information between territories under their control and those held by the Nguyễn.[207]

Valuable for their ability to limit the movement of peoples, the pirates were also financially useful to the Tây Sơn regime. In exchange for providing safe havens for pirates in the hidden bays of the Gulf of Tonkin, the Tây Sơn were to receive a certain percentage of the booty captured by their ships. Given the riches that were passing through these waters, this operation was of considerable benefit to both sides. Every spring and summer the pirate vessels would head out for a season of looting, then in the fall would return to their safe havens.[208] Murray reports that the pirates would (at least in theory) turn over their booty to the Tây Sơn, who would turn around and sell it in Việt Nam and then give 20–40 percent of the profits back to the pirates.[209] On occasion pirates would seize entire vessels, which in at least one case were taken to Phú Xuân, where they were put into service in the Tây Sơn navy.[210] Sometimes the Tây Sơn leaders gave specific instructions to their pirate allies, requesting, for instance, raiding campaigns into Guangdong and other Chinese coastal provinces. In other cases, the Tây Sơn regime supplied vessels to the pirates and encouraged those in charge of these ships to recruit more men into their ranks.[211]

While the Tây Sơn–sponsored pirates sometimes merely seized goods or ransomed ships, at other times they seized passengers, both Vietnamese and European. One Frenchman, recorded only as "Savard," was captured by a pirate vessel with a mixed Chinese and Vietnamese crew; he spent the next several years alternately held captive on an island and forced to work on a pirate vessel.[212] At other times, and perhaps depending on the degree of resistance they encountered, pirates might massacre the crews of ships they encountered. A French missionary described a Chinese pirate attack by more than a dozen ships on a small English vessel, resulting in the capture and subsequent murder of the eight English sailors. The same expedition also captured two Portuguese men on a nearby island, whom a small group of Vietnamese Christians attempted to rescue. The rescue failed, as the pirate leader refused to surrender the two men, preferring to take them to the Tây Sơn capital at Phú Xuân, no doubt in hopes of a reward for their capture.[213]

Just as the coastal pirates eagerly allied with the Tây Sơn because the alliance provided them immunity from capture by Chinese troops, the same Tây Sơn involvement made the Qing government reluctant to pursue pirates for fear of alienating the new Vietnamese regime.[214] Despite this reluctance, the Chinese government was greatly disturbed that the Tây Sơn regime was harboring pirates, and made periodic attempts to deal with the problem. In May of 1797 a missionary wrote that the Chinese had sent one hundred ships in an attempt to suppress the Tây Sơn–sponsored coastal pirates but that the pirates had easily escaped, heading inland on various rivers in the northern part of Đại Việt.[215] Two months later the same missionary offered a fuller description of the sequence of events that revealed both the futility of the Chinese attempts to suppress the pirates and the Tây Sơn role in hindering the Chinese efforts:

> Your Chinese came with a flotilla in order to seize the pirates, but I believe that they were not able to take a very large number of their vessels. The Tonkinese mandarins helped them escape and then deceived the Chinese with flattering words, without however, allowing them to enter the grand river that leads to the Royal city; after having waited some

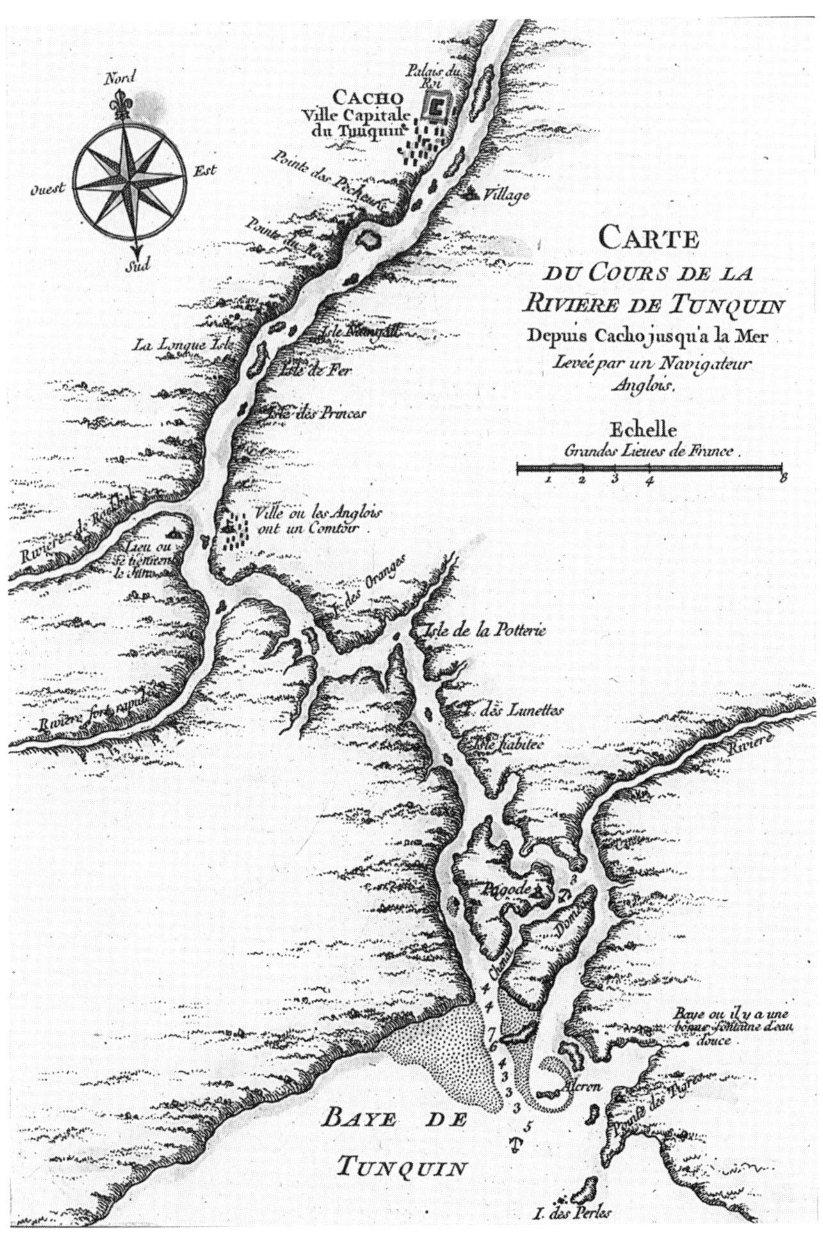


FIGURE 10. *Red River from its mouth to Thăng Long, 1771. Map by Nicholas Bellin tracing the Red River from the Gulf of Tonkin to the northern capital of Thăng Long, labeled on the map as Cacho. Chinese pirates could flee up the river to avoid capture by Qing authorities. Author's collection.*

> time to see if [the Tây Sơn] would deliver the pirates to them, [the Chinese] retreated. As for the pirates, they then advanced along the coast to Phú Xuân in concert because the king had summoned them.[216]

While the Vietnamese were clearly not intimidated by the threat of Chinese naval action, they valued the good relationship they had developed with the Qing court and wanted to present an appearance of cooperation. Consequently, the Tây Sơn government responded to Chinese concerns and made a few gestures to demonstrate their goodwill by cracking down on the pirates. These apparent attempts by the Vietnamese to suppress pirate activity were largely for show and did little to interfere with the operations of their allies. After such a "crackdown," the pirates would be free to operate as before. The Chinese were not able to bring the pirate situation under control until well after the Tây Sơn regime had been driven from power.[217]

In 1792, after the death of Quang Trung (known to the pirates as "the big boss of Yueh Nan"), Tây Sơn political prospects began to look less promising, and yet the Chinese pirates continued to serve them in many capacities. In 1794 Chen was named a military governor (*đố đốc*), giving him, in theory, even greater authority. A few years later, in 1797, the pirate adjuncts to the Tây Sơn military were organized in even more systematic fashion, under the overall command of Chen. The main pirate leaders were all given the title Ô Tàu Tổng Binh (General of the Black Vessels), each reporting directly to Chen.[218] Indeed, the title *tổng binh* appears to have been the primary designation for the pirate chiefs who agreed to ally themselves with the Tây Sơn, while their underlings were designated as *thiện tầu* (ship's master).[219]

The advantages of service as mercenaries for the Tây Sơn cause, perhaps enhanced by the newly elaborated nomenclature and structure, meant that Chinese pirates continued to serve the Tây Sơn regime into its final years. Pirate vessels took part in several naval campaigns against the southern forces in 1797, ranging as far south as Qui Nhơn. In 1798 pirates engaged Nguyễn forces in Khanh Hóa, and then in 1799 they served in the defense of Qui Nhơn against a particularly determined Nguyễn attack. The Tây Sơn defeat there, despite pirate support, "combined with the earlier setback at Khanh Hoa, considerably weakened the power of the pirates and led to numerous defections."[220] Yet even in the face of this defeat, and despite a large number of subsequent defections, pirates continued to fight on behalf of the Tây Sơn to the very end of the regime in 1802. Numerous pirate vessels were involved in the 1800 Tây Sơn counterattack and subsequent siege of Qui Nhơn, and they continued to be involved in defense of the Tây Sơn state even as the Nguyễn moved inexorably up the coast toward Thăng Long. In 1802, even though Chen had surrendered to Chinese authorities a year earlier, two hundred more pirate ships were committed to the Tây Sơn coastal defense, an effort that ultimately proved unsuccessful.[221]

## CONCLUSION

It is clear that throughout the Tây Sơn period groups at the margins of Vietnamese society came to play important roles, whether as supporters of the rebellion, as its adversaries, or as people caught up in a tumult that excluded no one. These groups included Christians, non-Vietnamese ethnic groups, bandits, pirates, and mercenaries. Some elements, such as the ethnic Chinese pirates, were absolutely indispensable components of the Tây Sơn regime's military might. Modern historians' interpretations of the Tây Sơn movement as a nationalist crusade peopled by noble peasants fighting for national unity or in defense of the nation against outsiders greatly misstate the realities of this period. The Tây Sơn routinely employed or made alliances with bandits, thieves, vagabonds, and pirates in a pragmatic attempt to bolster their armed forces. Indeed, it would have been surprising to find them not taking advantage of the opportunities presented by such social groups. These relationships of course cut both ways, benefiting not only the Tây Sơn but also those with whom they created alliances. The complex nature of such relationships is neatly encapsulated in a sobriquet that was applied to the Tây Sơn emperor, Quang Trung, in this period—"rebel protector of pirates."[222] In other words, the rebel leader connected himself to the Chinese pirates as their protector, just as these same pirates were, through their control of the seas, protecting the Tây Sơn leader and his regime.

While twentieth-century Vietnamese historians have often been highly critical of the nineteenth-century Nguyễn and other historical records for referring to the Tây Sơn as "bandits" (*giặc*), the older accounts were quite accurate in characterizing elements of the movement, if not the movement's leaders themselves, in this manner.[223] To conclude that bandits and pirates played significant roles in the Tây Sơn uprising is not to discredit its leaders, as was the intention of the Nguyễn historians.

Rather, it is more honestly to depict the complex composition of the uprising, which reflected the heterogeneity of late-eighteenth-century Vietnamese society. The Tây Sơn, like their Nguyễn rivals, were above all pragmatists who thought not in terms of social background in recruiting for their armies, but rather in terms of sheer numbers, and experience. A thief or pirate was, to the Tây Sơn recruiter, not a criminal to be suppressed, but a person with some fighting experience, probably carrying his own arms, and ready to challenge authority. These were useful traits in times such as these, and it was for these reasons that such men (and probably a few women) were brought into the movement. Ultimately, the Tây Sơn armies were quintessentially Southeast Asian in their complex composition, a characteristic they shared with their Nguyễn rivals, whose forces Alexander Woodside has described as being "based upon the shifting brigand populations of the Gulf of Siam and the South China Sea."[224]

# Conclusion

## Looking Back and Looking Ahead

The dynamics of the Tây Sơn era were immensely complex, reflecting the geography, historical experience, and particularist interests of contending political and social forces. The interactions between rebel leaders and the various and frequently contending segments of eighteenth-century Vietnamese society do not lend themselves to easy explanations or to the simplified interpretations often applied to the Tây Sơn. This movement profoundly affected the lives of all people living in the Vietnamese territories and indeed well beyond their boundaries. It revealed many of the schisms that had been developing over several centuries between both various socioeconomic groups and the separate geopolitical entities that had emerged in the aftermath of the Mạc usurpation of the Lê throne in the early sixteenth century. The Tây Sơn uprising as well as the political and military resistance to it both by the northern Lê/Trịnh and the southern Nguyễn forces divided Vietnamese society further, shaping some of the political and social contours of the nineteenth century.

Given the complex social interactions that were central to this era, it is extremely difficult to apply a simple label to the series of events set in motion by the Tây Sơn uprising. It has often been called a peasant rebellion, but this is a term whose accuracy is belied by the substantial evidence that its leaders were not peasants and that a large number of its early supporters were not themselves small-scale agriculturalists. Moreover, as I have argued, it was Vietnamese peasants who suffered most immediately at the hands of the regime eventually established by the Tây Sơn brothers. Categorizing this event as a popular movement is equally problematic, for although its origins lay in a collective military endeavor, what had been a movement (of debatable popularity) quickly became a regime and then several regimes. By 1775, Nguyễn Nhạc already saw himself as a ruler rather than simply the leader of a "righteous uprising," and from this point it makes considerably less sense to speak of the Tây Sơn leaders and their armies as a "movement." In short, the events of the Tây Sơn era defy easy classification. The political structures mobilized or utilized by the Tây Sơn leaders were continually evolving, as were their objectives. What is clear is that the uprising's origins lay in economic frustrations compounded by official corruption and that its accomplishments were driven by a combination of vulnerable political regimes and the considerable political and military skills of the Tây Sơn brothers and those who advised them.

Ultimately, the deaths of the two most capable brothers, Nguyễn Huệ and Nguyễn Nhạc, doomed the Tây Sơn regimes. The momentum that had carried the brothers to a series of military triumphs disappeared as their respective regimes could not resolve the troubles facing them. The dislocations of warfare, compounded in the northern region by crop failures and official corruption, required time and patience that neither Huệ nor Nhạc had. Moreover, neither regime had become sufficiently institutionalized nor widely enough accepted to cope with the transitions that followed the deaths of the primary Tây Sơn leaders. In each case a young crown prince followed in the footsteps of his father and found himself at the mercy of a regency that provoked struggles within his courts. That both regimes survived the deaths of Huệ and Nhạc by nearly a decade is testament to the formidable military force that the Tây Sơn had assembled, which permitted little active internal resistance. It may also be ascribed, in part, to the cautious monsoon-dictated military strategy pursued by their rival, Nguyễn Ánh, whose forces made only slow, albeit generally steady, progress in establishing control over incrementally larger sections of the southern Vietnamese coast.[1]

When the armies of Nguyễn Ánh finally entered Thăng Long in the summer of 1802, it was the culmination of a struggle that had lasted for the better part of a quarter century and had left considerable physical and psychological wounds across the spectrum of Vietnamese society. In the aftermath of the Nguyễn victory, the surviving Tây Sơn leaders were rounded up, and some, including Emperor Bảo Hưng and all members of his immediate family as well as the noted female general Bùi Thị Xuân, were pulled apart limb from limb. Others, such as the officials Ngô Thì Nhậm and Phan Huy Ích, were publicly flogged, a beating that caused Nhậm's death within a year. Not content with punishing the living, Nguyễn Ánh ordered the exhumation of the remains of his long-time rivals Huệ and Nhạc. He then directed that their bones be ground into a powder and ordered his soldiers to urinate on them.[2] In this manner, Nguyễn Ánh sought to ensure that the period of Vietnamese history that has subsequently been labeled the "Tây Sơn era" was definitively over. The final triumph of the Nguyễn over their long-term foe was supposed to mark a new chapter in Vietnamese history, the commencement of a new dynasty (although one whose forebears had already ruled part of the country in their own right), and an ongoing effort to pull together the disparate geographical threads that constituted the newly joined Vietnamese realms.

And yet, while ostensibly unifying the country under a single leadership, the Nguyễn triumph did little to resolve the conflicts that had been stirred up by the Tây Sơn wars. The peasant discontents that provoked the Tây Sơn uprising, and that were then exacerbated by it, were not adequately addressed by the new regime. If anything, peasant grievances to which the French missionary de la Bissachère testified in the early nineteenth century multiplied throughout the early decades of Nguyễn rule. The year 1802, in which the Nguyễn seized political authority from the Tây Sơn, must be recognized as constituting a somewhat arbitrary point of disjuncture from the perspective of the Vietnamese peasantry, for whom the transition of regimes proved to be meaningless. There was a decline in warfare certainly, but the heavy labor and military demands long imposed by the Tây Sơn regimes were continued and perhaps even accelerated under the rule of their Nguyễn successors. The Nguyễn, moreover, were able to tax more effectively than their predecessors—an ability that, from the peasant perspective, constituted an absolute increase in tax demands.[3] The peasants complained loudly about these further exactions from their putative saviors, and the hundreds of peasant and other uprisings that challenged Gia Long—some featuring thousands of participants—suggest that in some respects this regime was considerably weaker than that of its Tây Sơn predecessors.[4]

Furthermore, it was not only peasants who were upset with the new regime, for it faced resistance from other quarters as well. Tây Sơn loyalists continued to find ways to stir up unrest, despite the relentless Nguyễn efforts to remove all traces of Tây Sơn rule. The new court's efforts in this direction continued to confront reminders of the Tây Sơn, both material and psychological. Although the Nguyễn could tear down some of the structures that had been erected by the Tây Sơn, they could not put an end to the use of Tây Sơn–minted coinage. These coins, bearing the names of the three Tây Sơn emperors, represented a constant reminder of that dynasty well after it had been overthrown. Nguyễn efforts to halt the use of these coins were limited and ineffectual, reflected in the fact that as late as 1839 edicts were still being issued against their continued circulation.[5] At the psychological level, the Nguyễn were also confronted with strong memories of that regime, even if these were romanticized with the passing of time. As was noted in chapter 3, there were already strong indications that although many peasants were unhappy with the difficulties of life under Tây Sơn rule, these same peasants were equally displeased with Nguyễn authority, and at least some compared Tây Sơn governance favorably to that of the Nguyễn. That the Tây Sơn and memories of that regime continued to haunt the Nguyễn is perhaps best revealed in their continued pursuit of surviving members of the Tây Sơn royal family into the 1830s. When two remaining sons and a grandson of the Thái Đức emperor were finally tracked down, they were summarily executed.[6]

But it wasn't only the relics of the Tây Sơn and their memory that troubled the Nguyễn regime. Even stronger challenges emerged from those who continued to evince loyalty to the Lê, a loyalty quite a few literati and others had retained through the years of Tây Sơn rule.[7] Many of these loyalist scholars had expected the Nguyễn to restore the Lê, believing the long-stated Nguyễn claim to be fighting on behalf of that dynasty. When the Nguyễn took power in their own name after ousting the Tây Sơn in 1802, those who had placed their hopes in the Nguyễn felt betrayed. Some rose up in rebellion periodically over the first several decades of the nineteenth century, and a number of uprisings could be identified as either originating among, or having the support of, Lê loyalists. Other scholars simply remained in retirement, having resolved not to serve the Tây Sơn, and then being equally unwilling to support the new Nguyễn regime. These men were further aggrieved by the fact that Thăng Long had lost its status as a political capital and had been relegated to secondary rank as the Nguyễn elevated Phú Xuân as the new imperial center.[8] Meanwhile, Gia Định (Sài Gòn), a relatively new political and economic center, which had come into its own during the Nguyễn wars against the Tây Sơn, was growing in influence in ways that challenged the primacy of the other two cities. The political tensions between these multiple power centers contributed, at least in part, to defining the emergent regionalisms of the later nineteenth and twentieth centuries.

Facing these multiple sources of resistance, the Nguyễn dynasts never entirely succeeded in their project to build a unified and stable kingdom. Their legitimacy was tenuous at the outset, and even a long-term project to build an elaborate façade of Confucian orthodoxy through examinations, government structures, and all manner of written histories and genealogies went only so far. The Nguyễn found themselves, moreover, masters of a territory that had never been ruled as a unified kingdom. Although the Trịnh had crossed the Gianh River boundary that had divided Đàng Ngoài from Đàng Trong in 1774 and the Tây Sơn had then dispatched the Trịnh in 1786, neither of these actions effectively integrated the Vietnamese territories. Indeed, the Tây Sơn conquests of the northern regions eventually produced a further set of divisions reflecting both political expedients and historical realities. Thus, the Nguyễn inherited a still highly divided territory, a situation the new regime sought to address through the expedient of effectively ruling the country as three different regions. The Nguyễn dynasts themselves controlled only the center directly; warlords governed in the northern and southern reaches of Việt Nam. This was hardly a formula for political or territorial integration, and the division continued to pose many difficulties for the new regime through the reign of the first Nguyễn emperor, Gia Long (r. 1802–1820), and more than a decade into the rule of his son and successor, Minh Mạng (r. 1820–1841).[9]

The post–Tây Sơn battles also took place in the realm of historiography, in which contested interpretations of the uprising and the regimes that it created developed over the course of the nineteenth century. The Nguyễn sought to depict the Tây Sơn as rebels and as bandits who had never had any political legitimacy, even as they confronted the awkward reality that more than a few of the officials who came to serve their regime had previously been loyal to the Tây Sơn. Moreover, while the Nguyễn could dictate the ways in which their official histories were written, they could not control the unofficial histories, those being privately recorded by scholars. With the decline of the dynasty, and the onset of French colonialism, reinterpretations of the Tây Sơn era continued, with greater credit being given to Quang Trung at least for his efforts to create an integrated state and for having repelled the Chinese invasion of 1789. Thus, the Nguyễn continued to be haunted by the Tây Sơn regimes at several levels. Although the Nguyễn depicted themselves as the direct heirs of the Lê and refused to recognize even a Tây Sơn interregnum, they could not escape the fact that the Tây Sơn had ousted the Lê and ruled much of the country for more than a decade, leaving marks impossible to eradicate.

Whatever its concrete accomplishments and whatever the legacies its failures bestowed on its successors, the Tây Sơn uprising captured the imagination of subsequent generations—both scholars and peasants—with each seeing a certain heroism in the powerful armies of the era. Time, and the notorious failures of the Nguyễn, helped burnish the image of the Tây Sơn that emerged after their demise. I have tried in this work, however, to view the Tây Sơn from the perspective of the eighteenth century, and not from that of the nineteenth, twentieth, or twenty-first. In doing so, I have tried to move away from the overly critical historiographies of the Nguyễn and also away from the hagiographies of the uprising's leaders and the glorification of noble peasants that became dominant themes in much of later-twentieth-century scholarship. This has enabled me, I hope, to detail the great difficulties endured by most segments of late-eighteenth-century Vietnamese society, while exploring the dynamics that existed between those who led the Tây Sơn uprising and those confronted by the three decades of turmoil that it unleashed.

# NOTES

**INTRODUCTION**

1. This account, in varying versions, is found in several sources: *Đại Nam Chính Biên Liệt Truyện* (Principal Record of the Biographies of Đại Nam), 2:493 (hereafter cited as *ĐNLT*). Slightly more detail can be found in Ngô Gia Văn Phái, *Hoàng Lê Nhất Thống Chí* (Unification Records of the Imperial Lê), 1:92 (hereafter cited as *HLNTC*); *Đại Việt Sử Ký Tục Biên* (A Continuation of the Historical Records of Đại Việt), 359 (hereafter cited as *ĐVSKTB*).

2. P. Lorenzo Pérez, "La Révolte et la guerre des Tayson d'après les Franciscains Espagnols de Cochinchine," 74. The Tây Sơn became popularly known as the "hissing armies" because of this tactic. The detail concerning red kerchiefs is found in Lê Quý Đôn, *Phủ Biên Tạp Lục* (Chronicles of the Prefectural Borders), 76 (hereafter cited as *PBTL*).

3. *PBTL*, 312.

4. Philippe Sérard to Pierre-Antoine Blandin, August 1787, Archives des Missions Étrangères de Paris, vol. 691, 1044 (hereafter cited as MEP).

5. Pierre-Yves Manguin, *Les Nguyễn, Macau et le Portugal: Aspects politiques et commerciaux d'une relation privilégiée en Mer de Chine 1773–1802*, 100.

6. Jean-François Le Roy to Blandin, 3 July 1789, MEP 692, 112; Charles La Mothe to Blandin, 20 January 1790, MEP 692, 158.

7. Li Tana, "An Alternative Vietnam? The Nguyen Kingdom in the Seventeenth and Eighteenth Centuries," 119.

8. Alexander Woodside, *Vietnam and the Chinese Model: A Comparative Study of Vietnamese and Chinese Government in the First Half of the Nineteenth Century*, 4.

9. Woodside later wrote a brief, unpublished pamphlet entitled "The Tay-son Revolution in Southeast Asian History." This work offers some keen insights into the larger patterns of the Tây Sơn period and later portrayals of the uprising, though its unpublished nature has kept its academic influence very limited.

10. David Marr, *Vietnamese Anticolonialism, 1885–1925*.

11. David Marr, *Vietnamese Tradition on Trial, 1920–1945*.

12. Li Tana, *Nguyễn Cochinchina: Southern Vietnam in the Seventeenth and Eighteenth Centuries.*

13. Ibid., 147.

14. Charles Maybon, *Histoire moderne du pays d'Annam (1592–1820).*

15. Lê Thành Khôi, *Le Viêt-Nam: Histoire et civilisation*, 296–322.

16. Philippe Langlet, *L'ancienne Historiographie d'état au Vietnam*, tome 1, *Raisons d'être, conditions d'élaboration et caractères au siècle des Nguyễn*.

17. Yang Baoyun, *Contribution à l'histoire de la principauté des Nguyên au Vietnam méridional*.

18. For a detailed description of the lengths to which the Nguyễn went in this regard see the account in Quách Tấn and Quách Giao, *Nhà Tây Sơn* (The Tây Sơn Dynasty), 234–249. On the other hand, it should be noted that the Nguyễn did not indiscriminately destroy all Tây Sơn documentation. In 1802 Nguyễn Ánh specifically ordered his troops not to burn collections of Tây Sơn public records, but to gather them to determine if they contained crucially important information. See *Đại Nam Thực Lục* (Veritable Records of Đại Nam), 497 (hereafter cited as *ĐNTL*).

19. Marr, *Vietnamese Anticolonialism*, 23, note 1.

20. Such characterizations are found in the biographies of the brothers contained in the official Nguyễn biographical compilation; *ĐNLT*, 2:491–492.

21. Langlet, *L'ancienne Historiographie*, 15.

22. Nola Cooke, "The Myth of the Restoration: Dang-Trong Influences in the Spiritual Life of the Early Nguyen Dynasty (1802–47)," 271ff.

23. See, for example, Nguyễn Bá Huấn, *Tây Sơn Văn Thần Liệt Truyện* (Biographies of Tây Sơn Officials) and "Cân Quắc Anh Hùng Truyện" (Tales of a Female Hero), 172–194. The latter is an account of the noted Tây Sơn female general Bùi Thị Xuân. Both of these texts were written in the second half of the nineteenth century.

24. See, for example, such *dã sử* (private histories) as Ngô Cao Lãng, *Lịch Triều Tạp Ký* (Miscellaneous Records of Past Dynasties) (hereafter cited as *LTTK*); and Bùi Dương Lịch, *Lê Quý Dật Sử* (Unusual Tales of the Late Lê) (hereafter cited as *LQDS*).

25. See, e.g., Thiện Đình's 1905 introduction to Đặng Xuân Bảng, *Việt Sử Cương Mục Tiết Yếu* (The Essential Mirror and Commentary on the History of the Việt), 9; Trần Trọng Kim, *Việt Nam Sử Lược* (A Summary History of Việt Nam), 2:127–128.

26. See Trần Trọng Kim, *Việt Nam Sử Lược*, 2:129; Phan Bội Châu, *Việt Nam Vong Quốc Sử* (History of the Loss of the Vietnamese Nation), 23.

27. Đào Duy Anh, *Việt Nam Văn Hóa Sử Cương* (An Outline History of Vietnamese Culture), 321.

28. Văn Tân, *Cách Mạng Tây Sơn* (The Tây Sơn Revolution); Trần Huy Liệu, "Đánh Gia Cuộc Cách Mạng Tây-Sơn và Vai Trò Lịch Sử cuả Nguyễn Huệ" (Evaluating the Tây Sơn Revolution and the Historical Role of Nguyễn Huệ).

29. See, e.g., Trần Thị Vinh, "Tìm Hiểu về Tổ Chức Nhà Nước Thời Tây Sơn" (Inquiry into the Establishment of the State in the Tây Sơn Period).

30. Nguyễn Lương Bích, *Quang Trung-Nguyễn Huệ*; also Nguyễn Duy Hinh, "Những Suy Nghĩ Về Nhà Tây Sơn" (Some Thoughts about the Tây Sơn Dynasty).

31. Trương Bưu Lâm, *Resistance, Rebellion, Revolution: Popular Movements in Vietnamese History*, 14.

32. Michael Adas, "From Avoidance to Confrontation: Peasant Protest in Precolonial and Colonial Southeast Asia," 98–99.

### CHAPTER 1: THE TÂY SƠN ERA AND THE LONG EIGHTEENTH CENTURY IN ĐẠI VIỆT

1. Because of its location above the Linh Gianh River, this territory was also sometimes colloquially known as Bắc Hà, literally "north of the river." For some discussion of the origins and use of the terms "Đàng Ngoài" and "Đàng Trong," see Keith Taylor, "Surface Orientations in Vietnamese History," 958–959.

2. John Whitmore, "*Chung-Hsing* and *Cheng-T'ung* in Texts of and on Sixteenth-Century Vietnam," 117–130; Lê Thành Khôi, *Histoire du Viet Nam*, 246–247.

3. *ĐNTL*, 26.

4. The complexities of Nguyễn Hoàng's departure for the south and its depiction in Vietnamese historiography are detailed in Keith Taylor's illuminating "Nguyen Hoang and the Beginning of Vietnam's Southward Expansion"; see also *ĐNTL*, 27–28.

5. Li, *Nguyễn Cochinchina*, 22.

6. Taylor, "Nguyễn Hoàng," 45, 64. Nola Cooke has challenged Taylor's argument, suggesting that the Nguyễn continued, well into the seventeenth century, to contemplate a return to the north; see Nola Cooke, "Regionalism and the Nature of Nguyen Rule in Seventeenth-Century Dang Trong."

7. This declaration was softened by the claim that tax revenues could not be submitted because weather conditions had resulted in poor crop yields. However, this justification appears to have been no more than a means by which to defer a potential Trịnh attack. *ĐNTL*, 41.

8. Lê Thành Khôi, *Histoire du Viet Nam*, 255–256.

9. Brief details of the brothers' family background can be found in Quách Tân and Quách Giao, *Nhà Tây Sơn*, 17. See also *Minh Đô Sử* (The Minh Đô History), 5:74a–b.

10. *Minh Đô Sử*, 5:74a; *ĐNLT*, 2:491; Li, *Nguyễn Cochinchina*, 28.

11. Quách Tân and Quách Giao (*Nhà Tây Sơn*, 20–23) give the father's name as Nguyễn Phi Phúc. Regarding the forced resettlement of the family see *Khâm Định Việt Sử Thông Giám Cương Mục* (The Imperially Ordered Mirror and Commentary on the History of the Việt), 2:719–720 (hereafter cited as *CM*).

12. Li, *Nguyễn Cochinchina*, 12–17; idem, "An Alternative Vietnam?" 120; Cooke, "Regionalism and the Nature of Nguyen Rule," 122ff.

13. See Taylor, "Surface Orientations," 949–978.

14. A description of these attempts can be found in John Whitmore, "Literati Culture in Dai Viet, 1480–1830," 234–238.

15. Victor Lieberman, *Strange Parallels: Southeast Asia in Global Context, c. 800–1830*, 401.

16. Đặng Phương-Nghi, *Les Institutions publiques du Viêt-Nam au XVIIIe siècle*, 106ff.; Nguyên Thanh-Nhã, *Tableau economique du Viet Nam aux XVIIe et XVIII siècles*, 28–35. More detailed descriptions can be found in Phan Huy Chú, *Lịch Triều Hiến Chương Loại Chí* (Monographs of the Institutions of the Dynasties), 3:74–81 (hereafter cited as *LTHCLC*).

17. Lê Thành Khôi, *Histoire du Viet Nam*, 303–309.

18. Li, *Nguyễn Cochinchina*, 37–41.

19. Over the course of the eighteenth century a more elaborated bureaucratic structure was slowly created, though this remained of relatively limited importance in defining the state's political course.

20. Li, *Nguyễn Cochinchina*, 134–135.

21. *ĐNTL*, 174.

22. *ĐNTL*, 115; *PBTL*, 64.

23. On changing titles and nomenclature, see *PBTL*, 67–68. A thorough discussion of the impulse toward autonomy is also found in Maurice Durand, "Tây Sơn," typescript, 11–24.

24. Li, *Nguyễn Cochinchina*, 47; *PBTL*, 67.

25. The Trịnh decision to retain the Lê as figureheads has been attributed to Nguyễn Bỉnh Khiêm, the Hải Dương literatus who served as an informal adviser to various political figures in the sixteenth century. See Trần Thiều, "Giữ Chùa Thờ Bụt mà An Oản: Vì Sao Họ Trịnh Không Dứt Nghiệp Nhà Lê?" (Retain the Buddhist Temple and Altar and Protect Its Offerings: Why Did the Trịnh Clan Not Dispense with the Lê House?), 38–39.

26. *Liệt Truyện Dã Sử* (Unofficial Biographical Histories), 106b.

27. See, for example, the *nôm* proclamation by Lê Duy Mật recalling the contributions of the Lê and detailing the sins of the Trịnh: "Tài Liệu Tham Khảo: Hịch của Lê Duy Mật kể tội họ Trịnh" (Research Documents: The Edict of Lê Duy Mật Telling of the Crimes of the Trịnh), 58–59.

28. *CM*, 2:501.

29. Cited in Nguyễn Văn Hoàn, "Phong Trào Khởi Nghĩa Nông Dân và Văn Học Việt Nam Thế Kỷ XVIII và Nửa Đầu Thế Kỷ XIX" (Righteous Uprising Peasant Movements and Vietnamese Literature of the Eighteenth and First Half of the Nineteenth Centuries), 26.

30. Maybon, *Histoire modern*, 181.

31. For details on Khoát's rule see *PBTL*, 66–70.

32. For a good description of the rule of Trịnh Doanh see Lê Thành Khôi, *Histoire du Viet Nam*, 307–309. For a brief survey of Trịnh Sâm's accomplishments, see *LTHCLC*, 1:178.

33. As will become clear in chapter 4, the notion of "conversion" is a complicated one, and in the Vietnamese context rarely meant a renunciation

of existing "religious" practices, but rather a supplementing of those practices with new ones.

34. Nguyên Thanh-Nhã, *Tableau economique*, 146–147.

35. Alexander Woodside, "Central Vietnam's Trading World in the Eighteenth Century as Seen in Lê Quý Đôn's 'Frontier Chronicles,'" 166.

36. *PBTL*, 234–236.

37. Nguyễn Tài Thư, ed., *Lịch Sử Tư Tưởng Việt Nam* (History of Vietnamese Thought), 1:414.

38. Phan Đại Doãn, ed., *Một Số Vấn Đề Về Nho Giáo Việt Nam* (Some Matters regarding Vietnamese Confucianism), 65; see also Marr, *Vietnamese Anticolonialism*, 52–53. By the eighteenth century, increasing numbers of advanced degree holders did come from the immediate areas around Thăng Long, so they were not entirely disassociated with that city. On the other hand, even those living on the perimeter of the capital would have had very real roots within rural, village society.

39. This view is set forth in the *Kinh Thư* (Book of History), cited in Nguyễn Tài Thư, *Lịch Sử Tư Tưởng*, 461; on Nhậm, e.g., see ibid., 461–462.

40. Hoàng Xuân Hãn, *La Sơn Phu Tử* (The Master of La Sơn), 141–142.

41. This vernacular script was derived from Chinese characters, combining characters or subcomponents of Chinese characters to represent the meaning and Vietnamese pronunciation of that word.

42. A brief overview of eighteenth-century cultural issues can be found in Lê Thành Khôi, *Histoire du Viet Nam*, 286ff.

43. Ngô Thế Lân, a Nguyễn official, specifically commented on the consequences of these dramatic demographic and territorial changes in the Nguyễn realms in a 1770 memorial to the court. See *ĐNTL*, 175.

44. Ibid., 163–164.

45. Ibid., 171ff.

46. Khin Sok, *Le Cambodge entre le Siam et le Viêtnam (de 1775 à 1860)*, 37; also Lieberman, *Strange Parallels*, 422–423. For more on Taksin's ambitious military ventures, see David Wyatt, *Thailand: A Short History*, 140–145.

47. *ĐNTL*, 176–177.

48. See, e.g., Yang, *Contribution à l'histoire*, 179–181; Loan's excesses are also detailed in *PBTL*, 336–337.

49. *ĐNTL*, 170; *ĐVSKTB*, 359, 375; *PBTL*, 336.

50. *PBTL*, 71; *ĐNTL*, 173.

51. *PBTL*, 232.

52. Li, *Nguyễn Cochinchina*, 97.

53. Ibid., 83. See also *ĐNTL*, 158, which details Nguyễn Phúc Khoát's grand construction projects. The same source (165) lists the tariffs that were imposed on the merchant vessels of various foreign countries in 1755.

54. Nguyên Thanh-Nhã in *Tableau economique* (167ff.) describes the import of Chinese and Japanese copper and the entire Vietnamese monetary

system in the eighteenth century; *PBTL*, 220–221; Li, *Nguyễn Cochinchina*, 94.

55. Lê Thành Khôi, *Histoire du Vietnam*, 311; Lê Quý Đôn reports on the copper problem as well in *PBTL* (221ff.).

56. *PBTL*, 220.

57. The text of the memorial can be found in *ĐNTL* (175). For an extended discussion of this issue see Li, *Nguyễn Cochinchina*, 94–98.

58. Li, *Nguyễn Cochinchina*, 144–146.

59. *ĐNTL*, 173.

60. Pérez ("La Révolte," 83) reports that sometimes more than a thousand boats of rice per month were coming from the far south to the central region.

61. Li, *Nguyễn Cochinchina*, 146; *PBTL* (240–241) enumerates the various transport boats available, making clear that Qui Nhơn had by far the largest number.

62. *ĐNTL*, 173.

63. Ibid., 172–173.

64. *PBTL*, 204.

65. Manguin, *Les Nguyễn, Macau et le Portugal*, 163; John Barrow also noted that this tax "created a general discontent among the people." *A Voyage to Cochinchina in the Years 1792 and 1793*, 250. Li (*Nguyễn Cochinchina*, 49–53) has pointed out that the head tax had long served as the primary source of revenue for the Nguyễn rulers, so it may be that Loan was simply increasing the head tax rates.

66. Nguyên Thanh-Nhã, *Tableau economique*, 36–38.

67. Li, *Nguyễn Cochinchina*, 57–58.

68. Nguyên Thanh-Nhã, *Tableau economique*, 36.

69. Li, *Nguyễn Cochinchina*, 147–148, for a description of the additional pressures placed on the Qui Nhơn region. See also Woodside, "The Tay-son Revolution," 2.

70. *PBTL*, 337.

71. Ibid., 162.

72. Văn Tân, *Nguyễn Huệ: Con Người và Sự Nghiệp* (Nguyễn Huệ: His Life and Works), 58–59.

73. Li, *Nguyễn Cochinchina*, 137–138.

74. *ĐNTL* (170) describes the efforts of Trương Phúc Loan to increase tax extractions in those areas.

75. Li, *Nguyễn Cochinchina*, 136.

76. Ibid., 138.

77. *ĐNLT*, 1:202.

78. Ibid., 202.

79. *ĐNTL*, 173; Phan Khoang, *Việt Sử: Xứ Đàng Trong, 1558–1777* (Vietnamese History: The Region of Đàng Trong, 1558–1777), 250–251.

80. *ĐNLT*, 2:202; *ĐNTL*, 170.

81. As early as 1776 Lê Quý Đôn (*PBTL*, 70–71) was already ascribing the difficulties that the south was facing, and the Tây Sơn uprising in particular, to the policies and actions of Loan. See also *ĐVSKTB* (375) in which the commander of the Trịnh invasion offers a scathing indictment of Loan's crimes.

82. *ĐNTL*, 173.

83. This sequence of events is described in great detail in *HLNTC* (1:29–58) and will be taken up in chapter 2.

84. *HLNTC*, 1:91; *ĐVSKTB*, 358. *Nam Sử* (History of the South; 34b) more explicitly suggests that Nhạc had gambled away these revenues.

85. Durand, "Tây Sơn," 28.

86. Although the 1771 date is difficult to ascertain, it is reported (as the year *tân mão*) in *ĐNLT*, 2:492. Many other nineteenth-century histories start their account of the Tây Sơn in 1773, when the rebel armies attacked Qui Nhơn.

87. The Nguyễn records themselves describe the inaccessibility of this area as a reason for their failure to suppress the Tây Sơn movement in its earlier years. *ĐNTL*, 177.

88. Taylor ("Surface Orientations," 964) comments on An Khê's pivotal location at the intersection of numerous transport and trade routes. A detailed examination of the crucial role played by this upland region is in Vũ Minh Giang, "Tây Sơn Thượng Đạo, Căn Cư Đầu Tiên Của Cuộc Khởi Nghĩa" (The Tây Sơn Upper Region, the First Foundation for the Righteous Uprising), 22–32. See also Li, *Nguyễn Cochinchina*, 123.

89. Lê Thành Khôi, *Histoire du Vietnam*, 313.

90. For accounts of this event see *ĐNLT*, 2:493; *HLNTC*, 1:92, and *ĐVSKTB*, 359.

91. Pérez, "La Révolte," 74.

92. Ibid., 74.

93. *ĐNLT*, 2:492.

94. On the complaints of the Chinese merchant community, see Trương Bửu Lâm, *Resistance, Rebellion, Revolution*, 11. In chapter 4 I will take up an extended examination of the complex role played by ethnic Chinese in the Tây Sơn period.

95. *PBTL*, 71; *ĐVSKTB*, 359; *ĐNTL*, 177–178.

96. *ĐNLT*, 2:492.

97. Pérez, "La Révolte," 74.

98. *PBTL*, 71; see also *ĐNLT*, 2:493.

99. *ĐNTL*, 205.

100. Ibid., 214.

101. Jean Labartette to Jean-Jacques Descourvières, 1 August 1786, MEP 746, 181.

102. Hoa Bằng, *Quang Trung Anh Hùng Dân Tộc, 1788–1792* (Quang Trung a National Hero, 1788–1792), 151–159.

103. The sequence of events is detailed in *HLNTC*, 2:194ff.

104. Văn Tân, *Cách Mạng Tây Sơn*, 157. There is some dispute about who served as a double for the emperor. *Đại Việt Quốc Thư* (National Documents of Đại Việt), 356–357, notes that the double may simply have been a person from Nghệ An who resembled the ruler.

105. For detailed discussion of Sino-Vietnamese relations in this period see Hoa Bằng, *Quang Trung*, esp. pp. 208–260; also Trương Bưu Lâm, "Intervention versus Tribute in Sino-Vietnamese Relations, 1788–1790," 165–179.

106. A useful overview of Quang Trung's domestic policies during the 1789–1792 period can be found in Hoa Bằng, *Quang Trung*, 267ff.

107. An account of Pigneau and young Prince Cảnh's journey to France and its aftermath can be found in Georges Taboulet, *La Geste française en Indochine*, 1:163–279.

108. Joseph Buttinger, *The Smaller Dragon*, 239.

109. Pigneau to Denis Boiret, 18 July 1792, MEP 746, 395.

110. Several missionary letters talk about Tây Sơn efforts to recruit "Ông Tin" (M. Olivier). Langlois to Boiret, 20 July 1795, MEP 692, 652.

111. See Lavoué to Boiret and Descourvières, 13 May 1795, MEP 746, 465.

112. Durand, "Tây Sơn," 212.

113. *Nguyễn Thị Tây Sơn Ký* (Records of the Nguyễn Tây Sơn Clan), A. 3138, 38a.

114. Pierre Eyot to Claude-François Letondal, 19 June 1801, MEP 701, 450.

115. This crackdown and its causes and consequences will be taken up in chapter 4.

116. Durand, "Tây Sơn," 210–216, in particular this last page, which describes the key role played by the Diên Khánh citadel.

117. Tạ Chí Đại Trường, *Lịch Sử Nội Chiến ở Việt Nam từ 1771 đến 1802* (History of the Civil War in Việt Nam from 1771 to 1802), 282; *ĐNTL*, 317ff.

118. Dian Murray, *Pirates of the South China Coast, 1790–1810*, 39.

119. For further information see Nguyễn Đình Hòe, "Note sur les cendres des Tây Sơn dans la prison du Kham Đường."

#### CHAPTER 2: THE LEADERS

1. Trần Huy Liệu, "Đánh Gia Cuộc Cách Mạng Tây Sơn"; Văn Tân, *Cách Mạng Tây Sơn*.

2. Many popular movements in Siam, Burma, Cambodia, the East Indies, the Philippines, and China in the eighteenth and nineteenth centuries were largely inspired by recognizable religious ideologies, including Buddhism, Islam, and Christianity. These include the White Lotus, the Boxers, and the Taiping in China; in Southeast Asia one finds popular uprisings in

Burma and Siam stirred by Buddhism, in Java by Islam, and in the Philippines by Christianity.

3. Hue-tam Ho Tai, *Millenarianism and Peasant Politics in Vietnam*, 5.

4. Nguyễn Khắc Đạm, "Tại Sao Các Cuộc Khởi Nghĩa Nông Dân ở Việt-Nam Ít Có Màu Sắc Tôn Giáo?" (Why Do Righteous Peasant Uprisings in Việt Nam Seldom Have Religious Elements?).

5. Barrow, *Voyage to Cochinchina*, 251. The references to the "merchant," the "general" and the "priest" are to the Tây Sơn brothers, Nhạc, Huệ, and Lữ, respectively.

6. Keith Taylor, "Authority and Legitimacy in 11th Century Vietnam."

7. O. W. Wolters, "Le Van Huu's Treatment of Ly Thanh Ton's Reign (1127–1137)," 208–209, 215.

8. Ralph Smith, "The Cycle of Confucianization in Vietnam," 1–5.

9. See Whitmore, "*Chung-hsing* and *Cheng-t'ung*," 116–136. This article also constitutes an important study of the ways in which orthodoxy of succession was addressed in the context of Vietnamese historiography.

10. For more on this see, for example, Cooke, "Regionalism and the Nature of Nguyễn Rule," 122–161; also, Li, "An Alternative Vietnam?" 112–113.

11. Regarding the problems with the civil service examinations, see *LQDS*, 33; also *LTHCLC*, 3:18.

12. *ĐNLT*, 2:512.

13. Michael Adas, *Prophets of Rebellion: Millenarian Movements against the European Colonial Order*, 112.

14. Regarding the Vietnamese case see the useful discussion by Ngô Vĩnh Long, *Before the Revolution*, ix–xi.

15. Alexander Woodside, "Conceptions of Change and of Human Responsibility for Change in Late Traditional Vietnam," 106.

16. Nguyễn Tài Thư, *Lịch Sử Tư Tưởng*, 1:419.

17. Ibid., 418.

18. Ngô Đức Thọ, *Nghiên Cứu Chữ Huý Việt Nam Qua Các Triều Đại* (Research into Tabooed Characters in Việt Nam throughout the Dynasties), 108.

19. Pérez, "La Révolte," 74.

20. Pierre-Marie Le Labousse (?), 20 June 1793, MEP 746, 405–406.

21. Barrow, *Voyage to Cochinchina*, 251.

22. Pigneau to MEP directors, 5 June 1776. *Nouvelles lettres édifiantes des missions de la Chine et des Indes orientale*, 6:293.

23. *ĐNTL*, 186.

24. Charles Chapman (Chapman's narrative of his mission to Vietnam) in Alistair Lamb, *Mandarin Road to Old Hue*, 94–95. This is obviously a paraphrase in which the reference to "God" is almost certainly Chapman's interpretation (in line with long-standing Western missionary parlance) of "heaven" in the more traditional Vietnamese understanding of the word.

25. Pérez, "La Révolte," 93.

26. *ĐVSKTB*, 467.

27. *ĐNLT*, 2:507.

28. It was almost certainly known to Nguyễn Huệ that the monsoonal winds favored a seaborne expedition at this time of the year.

29. Nguyễn Lộc, *Văn Học Tây Sơn* (Tây Sơn Literature), 92.

30. For further discussion of Nhậm's role in drafting this edict, see Alexander Woodside, "Classical Primordialism and the Historical Agendas of Vietnamese Confucianism," 120.

31. Nguyễn Cẩm Thúy and Nguyễn Phạm Hùng, *Văn Thơ Nôm Thời Tây Sơn* (Nôm Literature of the Tây Sơn Period), 265. "Hội Thuận ứng thế đừng được chớ..." This edict was probably written for them by the Trịnh defector Nguyễn Hữu Chỉnh.

32. Ibid., 268. "*Chúng điêu tàn mong cờ nghĩa về đầu.*"

33. Nguyễn Lộc, *Văn Học Tây Sơn*, 92.

34. Anonymous to ?, 31 August 1802, MEP, 701, 485.

35. *ĐNLT*, 2:491. The "north" in this prophecy is ambiguous, and could have been interpreted to refer to the Nguyễn capital at Phú Xuân or even the Lê capital of Thăng Long.

36. The role of prophecy will be addressed in greater detail in chapter 3.

37. *Chiao Chou Wai Yu Chi*, as cited in the *Shui Ching Chu*, 37, 7a. Quoted in Keith Taylor, *The Birth of Vietnam*, 25.

38. Li, *Nguyễn Cochinchina*, 150.

39. *Những Mẩu Chuyện về Tây Sơn* (Some Tales about the Tây Sơn), 9–10; also Lê Xuân Lít, "Lòng Dân Đối Với Cuộc Khởi Nghĩa Tây Sơn" (The Hearts of the People with Respect to the Tây Sơn Righteous Uprising), 289–290. Yet another variant features Nguyễn Huệ instead of his brother, and this time he finds in the chicken not a sword handle but a golden seal.

40. Viet Chung, "Recent Findings on the Tay Son Insurgency," 38.

41. Lê Xuân Lít, "Lòng Dân," 290–291.

42. Quách Tấn, "Di-tích và Truyền-Thuyết về Nhà Tây-Sơn" (Vestiges and Traditions concerning the Tây Sơn), 175. The dragon knife is symbolic of a king. The idea of a magical creature presenting such a blade is reminiscent of the tortoise that presented the sword to Lê Lợi for his fifteenth-century anti-Chinese campaigns. Once again Nguyễn Huệ is clearly being viewed as part of a long lineage of Vietnamese heroes who have come to the aid of their country.

43. *ĐNLT*, 2:491; *Minh Đô Sử*, 5:74b.

44. Quách Tấn, "Di-tích," 172. The idea of the apparently magical appearance of words of divine instruction is not unique to the Tây Sơn. This tale bears some resemblance to one told about the earlier Lê Lợi rebellion against the Ming in the early fifteenth century. That account reports that the Vietnamese rebel leader's close adviser, Nguyễn Trãi, wrote the phrase "Lê Lợi will become king and Nguyễn Trãi his minister" in grease on a tree. Over

time, as insects and other animals came to eat away the grease, the phrase appeared, as if by magic, on the bark of the tree. While the particulars are not entirely the same, the notion of a prophetic phrase magically appearing certainly links the two tales. Lê Thành Khôi, *Histoire du Viet Nam*, 207.

45. This tale, with small variations, is found in a variety of sources, though many are undated, making it difficult to establish its origins. See, for example, *Bản Quốc Ký Sự* (Records of the Affairs of Our Country), 103a; *Dã Sử* (Unofficial History), 106b; *Minh Đô Sử*, 5:75b; the *Lê Ký Chronicle*, cited in Nguyễn Phương, *Việt Nam Thời Bành Trướng: Tây Sơn* (Việt Nam in a Time of Expansion: Tây Sơn), 32.

46. This tale is found (unsourced) in *Những Mẩu Chuyện về Tây Sơn*, 31–32.

47. For more on these and other elements of the Vietnamese worldview see Neil Jamieson, *Understanding Vietnam*, 1–41; also Pierre Huard and Maurice Durand, *Connaissance du Việt Nam*, 83–90.

48. Woodside, "Conceptions of Change," 113.

49. Nola Cooke, "Nineteenth-Century Vietnamese Confucianization in Historical Perspective," 284.

50. For the Japanese case, for example, see Stephen Vlastos, *Peasant Protests and Uprisings in Tokugawa Japan*.

51. James Scott, *The Moral Economy of the Peasant*, 8ff.

52. "Hịch Của Lê Duy Mật," 58–59.

53. Woodside, "Conceptions of Change," 112.

54. Ralph Smith, *Viet-Nam and the West*, 14.

55. Cited in Nguyễn Tài Thư, *Lịch Sử Tư Tưởng*, 1:420.

56. See, for example, Trần Văn Quý, "Một Số Tư Liệu Thời Tây Sơn Mới Phát Hiện" (Some Recently Discovered Documents from the Tây Sơn Period); also *Lệnh Chí* (An Imperial Command).

57. Nguyễn Lương Bích, *Quang Trung-Nguyễn Huệ*, 20.

58. Nguyễn Cẩm Thúy and Nguyễn Phạm Hùng, *Văn Thơ Nôm*, 268 (Chỉnh), 170 (Ích).

59. It is not clear how widely this new designation was used. While some sources do note this change in name, few contemporary sources call this region anything other than Nghệ An.

60. *HLNTC*, 2:100, 115.

61. See his various edicts, in Nguyễn Cẩm Thúy and Nguyễn Phạm Hùng, *Văn Thơ Nôm*, 306–327.

62. *LQDS*, 72.

63. Cited in O. W. Wolters, *Two Essays on Đại-Việt in the Fourteenth Century*, 53, note 136.

64. Ibid., 9. For further commentary on Vietnamese notions of "virtue" see Lucian Pye, *Asian Power and Politics*, 239.

65. References of this type can be found from 1784 through 1792. See, e.g., Langenois to Jean-Jacques Descourvières, 30 June 1784, MEP 800,

1776; "Journal de la Procure de Macao en 1784," MEP 306, 929; "Journal de ce qui s'est passé de plus remarquable dans la mission du Tong-king, depuis le mois de julliet 1786 jusqu'à mois de julliet 1787," MEP 691, 899–900; Jean Labartette to Denis Boiret, 22 March 1787, in *Nouvelles lettres*, 6:2; de Gortyne to Pierre-Antoine Blandin, 21 December 1792, MEP 692, 405.

66. Jean-François Le Roy to Claude-François Letondal, 6 December 1786, MEP 700, 1308.

67. Veang Thiounn, *Preah Réach Pongsavadar Krong Kampuchéa Thipadei* (The Royal Chronicle of the Country of Grand Kampuchea), cited in Khin Sok, *Le Cambodge*, 39.

68. Ủy Ban Khoa Học Xã Hội, *Lịch Sử Việt Nam* (History of Việt Nam), 2:337.

69. Pérez, "La Révolte," 74.

70. *ĐNLT*, 2:492.

71. See, e.g., John K. Whitmore, *Vietnam, Hồ Quý Lý, and the Ming (1371–1421)*, 84; *Minh Đô Sử*, 6:3a; see also 7:53a, describing the same procedure.

72. "Journal de ce qui s'est passé de plus remarquable dans la mission du Tong-king, depuis le mois de mai 1785 jusqu'à mois de juin 1786," MEP 691, 668, describes the wealthy barricading themselves in their homes during a time of famine to avoid food requests.

73. Trương Bưu Lâm, *Resistance, Rebellion, Revolution*, 5.

74. Philippe Sérard to Blandin, 31 July 1786, in Leopold Cadière, "Documents relatifs a l'époque de Gia-Long," 10.

75. *LQDS*, 69.

76. Pérez, "La Révolte," 75. The cangue is a portable version of the stocks.

77. Li, *Nguyễn Cochinchina*, 147, note 32; *ĐNLT*, 2:493.

78. For more on Tây Sơn coinage see Đỗ Văn Ninh, "Tiền Cổ Thời Tây Sơn" (Ancient Money from the Tây Sơn Period).

79. Nguyễn Duy Hinh, "Những Suy Nghĩ Về Nhà Tây Sơn," 23.

80. Đỗ Văn Ninh, "Tiền Cổ," 107.

81. *ĐVSKTB*, 417.

82. Ibid., 467; see also *Biểu Sách Văn Sao Tập* (Copies of Collected Writings), 1b; Hoa Bằng, *Quang Trung*, 312.

83. *Đại Việt Quốc Thư*, 94.

84. Nguyễn Cẩm Thúy and Nguyễn Phạm Hùng, *Văn Thơ Nôm*, 100.

85. *ĐNTL*, 390.

86. On the death of the previous Nguyễn *chúa* it had been assumed that his second son, Chương Võ, would succeed him. Instead, possibly because of Trương Phúc Loan's interference, the *chúa*'s sixteenth son, Định Vương, succeeded him. This choice also left out another possible candidate, the *chúa*'s ninth son, Hiếu, whose claims were strengthened when Chương Võ died shortly after his father. When Nhạc rose up, he put his support behind Prince

Dương, who was Prince Hiều's son and designated heir. Lamb, *Mandarin Road*, 88–89, note 2.

87. *ĐNLT*, 2:492; Nhạc also cites Loan's corruption and evil as the impetus for his actions in a letter he sends to the Trịnh in 1776 (*ĐVSKTB*, 417); Loan is similarly blamed by contemporary Nguyễn supporters; see, e.g., Hoàng Quang's epic poem "Hoài Nam Khúc" (Lament for the South) in Nguyễn Cẩm Thúy and Nguyễn Phạm Hùng, *Văn Thơ Nôm*, 345–346.

88. Trương Bưu Lâm, *Resistance, Rebellion, Revolution*, 11.

89. *ĐNLT*, 2:491.

90. The Nguyễn records note that it was Hiến who had urged Nhạc to see himself as fulfillment of the prophecy regarding "an uprising in the west," so it would not be surprising to see Hiến involved in plotting strategy concerning political slogans or objectives for the early movement.

91. *ĐNLT*, 2:492; *Minh Đô Sử*, 5:76a.

92. The Tây Sơn are also referred to in this manner in "Hoài Nam Khúc"; see Nguyễn Cẩm Thúy and Nguyễn Phạm Hùng, *Văn Thơ Nôm*, 350.

93. Cited in Văn Tân, *Nguyễn Huệ*, 62–63.

94. There is some dispute on this point: Quách Tấn and Quách Giao argue that the brothers had changed their name well before the uprising (*Nhà Tây Sơn*, 21) while the *Minh Đô Sử* claims that Nhạc deliberately changed it at the outset of his rebellion (5:75a).

95. For some discussion of this see Văn Tân, *Cách Mạng Tây Sơn*, 34; for an example see *Đại Nam Nhất Thống Chí* (Unification Records of Đại Nam), 5:115 (hereafter cited as *ĐNNTC*).

96. Phan Trần Chúc, *Vua Quang Trung Nguyễn Huệ (Lịch Sử)* (A History of the King Quang Trung Nguyễn Huệ), 10.

97. Interestingly, this perfectly mirrored Trương Phúc Loan's own actions, for Loan had married *his* daughter to the young *chúa* whom he had manipulated onto the throne.

98. For a detailed description of the importance of kinship ties in the Nguyễn polity, see Cooke, "Regionalism and the Nature of Nguyễn Rule."

99. Li, *Nguyễn Cochinchina*, 120.

100. *ĐNLT*, 2:495.

101. Ibid., 496 (presumably to either request).

102. *HLNTC*, 1:148; Pérez, "La Révolte," 85, cites a Spanish missionary who reported that "Duong did not wish to take as a wife the one who was proposed for him but being a prudent man, and in order to avoid great trouble, he kept her for six months in his house, without making a communal life with her, not allowing her to his bed or table."

103. *Minh Đô Sử*, 5:75a; see also Ngô Đức Thọ, *Nghiên Cứu Chữ Huý*, 108. This apparently marked the only time in Vietnamese history that a character was tabooed out of antipathy for an individual, rather than to protect the sanctity of royal names.

104. *ĐVSKTB*, 365.

105. Ibid., 379.

106. *Bình Nam Thực Lục* (Veritable Records of the Pacified South), 12–17 (hereafter cited as *BNTL* [qn]). The *Bình Nam Thực Lục* is a detailed, near-contemporary Trịnh account of their military expedition into the south. It was ordered compiled by Trịnh Sâm and was printed in woodblock form in the later 1770s or early 1780s.

107. *ĐVSKTB*, 417.

108. Biện was a reference to Nhạc's minor position as a tax collector (*biện lại*) for the Nguyễn. See, for example, a letter by the Trịnh general to the Nguyễn, recorded in *PBTL*, 312.

109. Described in *ĐVSKTB*, 396; see also *Bình Nam Thực Lục* (Veritable Records of the Pacified South), 39a–49a (hereafter cited as *BNTL*).

110. Chapman, in Lamb, *Mandarin Road*, 95.

111. Nguyễn Ngọc Huy and Tạ Văn Tài, *The Lê Code: Law in Traditional Vietnam*, 1:217.

112. *ĐVSKTB*, 393; *BNTL*, 41a, 42a.

113. *ĐVSKTB*, 395–396. Among the Trịnh emissaries involved in these exchanges was Nguyễn Hữu Chỉnh, who would later defect to the Tây Sơn camp in the aftermath of political upheavals in Đàng Ngoài in 1782.

114. For a much more detailed discussion of the relationship and communications between the Tây Sơn and the Trịnh, see the *BNTL* and also *ĐVSKTB*, 360ff.

115. I thank Nola Cooke for pointing out that this had been Nguyễn Hoàng's former title. The use of terms such as "duke," drawn from attempts at rendering European parallels, is clearly problematic. However, the longstanding practice of using such translations, as well as a lack of good alternatives, suggests that the best translation, however imperfect, may be the conventional one.

116. Vũ Minh Giang, "Tây Sơn Trượng Đạo," 28.

117. Li, *Nguyễn Cochinchina*, 149.

118. Contemporary Vietnamese historiography makes much of early Tây Sơn connections to upland peoples, drawing heavily from collected folk tales. See, for example, Nguyễn Dương Bình, "Vài Suy Nghĩ Về Phong Trào Nông Dân Tây Sơn với Các Dân Tộc Ít Người Và Căn Cứ Địa Miền Núi" (Some Thoughts about the Tây Sơn Peasant Movement with the Minority Peoples and Their Base in the Mountain Regions), 142–146. Written evidence is, however, very slight regarding these connections, and so it is difficult to make more definitive statements regarding the relationship the Tây Sơn leaders developed with these groups.

119. See, e.g., "Hoài Nam Khúc," in Nguyễn Cẩm Thúy and Nguyễn Phạm Hùng, *Văn Học Tây Sơn*, 348; Pérez, "La Révolte," 76.

120. *ĐNNTC*, 3:143. *Chưởng cơ* here appears to be used as a generic political title; it is sometimes translated by the military term "captain." The date for this transfer is unclear, but was probably sometime in the early 1780s.

121. Jean-Pierre-Joseph D'Arcet to Descourvières, 20 September 1785, MEP 801, 80–81. Written from Nha Trang.

122. See, for example, *Nguyễn Thị Tây Sơn Ký*, 4b, 60a; for a detailed essay on this site see Phan Huy Lê, "Di Tích Thành Hoàng Đế" (Vestiges of an Imperial Citadel); also *Chiêm Thành Khảo* (Research on Champa).

123. *Nguyễn Thị Tây Sơn Ký*, 4b–5a.

124. Li, *Nguyễn Cochinchina*, 153.

125. Pérez, "La Révolte," 80.

126. *Nguyễn Thị Tây Sơn Ký*, 4b.

127. Ibid., 4b–5a.

128. *BNTL* [qn], 18; *ĐVSKTB*, 417.

129. The reference to Nhạc as the "Heavenly King" is found in *HLNTC*, 1:93; also in *Nguyễn Thị Tây Sơn Ký*, 5a. The *ĐVSKTB* (416–421) describes the Trịnh displeasure at the Tây Sơn actions, and yet also reports that the northern regime continued to grant decrees and titles to the Tây Sơn leader.

130. Li, *Nguyễn Cochinchina*, 150–151.

131. *Nguyễn Thị Tây Sơn Ký*, 5a; see also *ĐNTL*, 186. Both accounts ominously report that the golden seal was cracked in the first two castings, and only properly accomplished in the third.

132. According to *CM* (2:810), he only named himself *vương* at this time and did not actually take the title of *hoàng đế* (emperor) until 1787, after his return from Thăng Long. This assessment seems unlikely, as the use of a different reign year implies the imperial title.

133. Although the Nguyễn *chuá*s had effectively declared their autonomy from the north in 1744, they continued to use the Lê reign titles in their documentation and calendars.

134. On the continued Nguyễn use of Lê reign titles see, for instance, Cooke, "Regionalism and the Nature of Nguyen Rule," 161, note 201.

135. Chapman, in Lamb, *Mandarin Road*, 100.

136. Ibid., 98.

137. Ibid., 97–98.

138. *Nguyễn Thị Tây Sơn Kí* (Records of the Tây Sơn of the Nguyễn Clan), 9 (emphasis added) (hereafter cited as *Nguyễn Thị Tây Sơn Ký* [qn]). Note that Nhạc simply transformed his earlier title of *minh đức chúa công* to *minh đức vương*.

139. "Journal de la Procure de Macao en 1784," MEP 306, 928–929. This incident is detailed in chapter 4.

140. Chapman, in Lamb, *Mandarin Road*, 100.

141. A description of the circumstances that brought Chỉnh to the Tây Sơn camp can be found in *HLNTC*, 1:55–61, 91ff. For an extended biography of Chỉnh, see Phan Trần Chúc, *Bằng Quận Công Nguyễn Hữu Chỉnh* (The Bằng Duke: Nguyễn Hữu Chỉnh).

142. *HLNTC*, 1:100; *LTTK*, 547–548.

143. *HLNTC*, 1:103. Labartette to Blandin (23 June 1786, MEP 746, 176) mentions that these rituals were still in progress when the Tây Sơn troops arrived.

144. Labartette to Letondal, 1 August 1786, MEP 801, 127.

145. The former view is widespread among post-1954 northern historians, including Nguyễn Khắc Viện, *Vietnam: A Long History*, 107; and Huỳnh Công Bá, *Lịch Sử Việt Nam* (History of Việt Nam), 221. The latter view is represented by Nguyễn Phương, *Việt Nam Thời Bành Trướng*, 156–157, 401.

146. The *ĐNTL* (215) notes that Chỉnh had originally gone over to the Tây Sơn side with the intention of using the southern forces to route the renegade soldiers in the north who had precipitated his removal from office; see also *HLNTC*, 1:94. European missionaries reported the same view. Journal de ce qui s'est passé dans la mission du Tong-king, depuis le mois de juin 1784 jusqu'à mois de mai 1785, MEP 691, 522.

147. *HLNTC*, 1:106–109.

148. "Diệt Trịnh, Phú Lê." This was not the first time a banner with this slogan had been raised in the north. During his long-running campaigns in the 1730s–1760s Lê Duy Mật had used the identical slogan.

149. *Sử Ký Đại Nam Việt Quốc Triều* (Historical Records of the Great Southern Việt National Court), 37–38.

150. Le Roy to Letondal, 6 December 1786, MEP 700, 1307. Other sources that describe this ruse include *Cao Bằng Thực Lục* (Veritable Records of Cao Bằng); Philiphê Bỉnh, "Truyện Anam Đàng Trao" (Tales of the Inner Regions of Annam), 658–659.

151. See, e.g., Nguyễn Thu, *Lê Quý Ký Sự* (A Record of Events of the Late Lê), 39; *HLNTC*, 1:133; *ĐVSKTB*, 468.

152. Some sources credit Nguyễn Hữu Chỉnh with having suggested this request to Nguyễn Huệ. See, e.g., *HLNTC*, 1:133. The *ĐVSKTB* (468) indicates that Chỉnh had urged the Lê emperor to offer the princess without a prior request from Huệ; Nguyễn Thu, *Lê Quý Kỷ Sự* (39) claims that Huệ ordered Chỉnh to make the request on his behalf.

153. *ĐNLT*, 2:506; *HLNTC*, 1:147.

154. *HLNTC*, 1:159–160.

155. See Hoàng Xuân Hãn, *La Sơn Phu Tử*, 121, 122, 125.

156. *LQDS*, 78.

157. Doussain to ?, 8 July 1787, MEP 746, 205; more details can be found in *ĐNLT*, 2:510.

158. *ĐVSKTB*, 469.

159. Some French missionary accounts suggest that it was Ngọc Hân who pressured Huệ to go north on his 1787 campaign against Chỉnh. See "Journal de ce qui s'est passé de plus remarquable dans la mission du Tongking, depuis le mois de juillet 1786 jusqu'à mois de juillet 1787," MEP 691, 899.

160. *ĐNLT*, 2:511. This source suggests that Huệ had already been suspicious of Nhậm, even as he had dispatched him to the north.

161. Huệ is alleged to have said to Nhậm shortly before executing him, "Nothing much needs to be said at this point; you have talents that surpass my own and thus you are not a person whom I can use." *CM*, 2:834.

162. The Qing commander claimed to have five hundred thousand soldiers in his army (*HLNTC*, 2:162). The figure of thirty-six thousand comes from a European missionary. Boisserand to Blandin, 14 March 1789, MEP 746, 237. Quách Tấn and Quách Giao (*Nhà Tây Sơn*, 122) and *ĐNLT* (2:515) give a figure of two hundred thousand. Charles La Mothe, in a letter to Blandin, estimates the Chinese force at three hundred thousand (La Mothe to Blandin, July 1789, MEP 692, 135).

163. Ngô Thì Nhậm, *Tuyển Tập Thơ Văn Ngô Thì Nhậm* (Collected Writings of Ngô Thì Nhậm), 2:103–104.

164. Though in his edict on ascending the throne, Nguyễn Huệ describes his brother's territory as restricted to the single prefecture (*phủ*) of Qui Nhơn. See ibid.

165. Nguyễn Ánh's insistence on continuing to use the Cảnh Hưng reign name was so effective that he is referred to by some contemporary European observers by their attempted transliteration of that reign era—"Caung Shung." See, e.g., Barrow, *Voyage to Cochinchina*, 256ff.

166. *ĐVSKTB*, 481.

167. Quoted from Truong Buu Lam, *Patterns of Vietnamese Response to Foreign Intervention, 1858–1900*, 63–64.

168. *HLNTC*, 2:192.

169. Quang Trung's correspondence with the Chinese can be found in *Đại Việt Quốc Thư*, 67 passim.

170. Ibid., 67–68, 78–79, 83.

171. *LQDS*, 91.

172. Chu Trọng Huyến, "Phượng Hoàng Trung Đô" (The Imperial Phoenix Central Capital), 148.

173. *Việt Sử Chính Biên Tiết Yếu* (Primary Summary History of the Việt), 38.

174. Ibid., 123.

175. For example, Ngô Thì Nhậm was Phan Huy Ích's brother-in-law and had studied with Lê Quý Đôn. Nguyễn Du was Đoàn Nguyễn Tuấn's (1750–?) brother-in-law. Ninh Tốn (1743–?), another noted northern scholar, had received either poems of praise or personal written introductions for his literary works from Phạm Nguyễn Du, Phan Huy Ích, Ngô Thì Nhậm, Vũ Huy Tân (1749–1800), Đoàn Nguyễn Tuấn, Nguyễn Thế Lịch (1748–1817), and Vũ Huy Đĩnh (1730–1789). With the exception of Vũ Huy Tân, each of these men had attained the rank of *tiến sĩ*. Hoàng Lê, ed., *Thơ Văn Ninh Tốn* (The Poetry of Ninh Tốn), 17.

176. *CM* (2:835) specifically mentions Huệ's forcing the Lê officials to

sign a petition requesting that he ascend the throne. The *ĐVSKTB* (479) notes that Huệ summoned the old court officials, but does not speak of the forced petition. One source claims that when Bích refused to sign, Huệ was upset but had someone else sign for him. Trúc Khê, *Bùi Huy Bích: Danh Nhân Truyện Ký* (Bùi Huy Bích: Recorded Tales of a Famous Man), 55–56.

177. Hoa Bằng, *Quang Trung*, 140; see also Ngô Đức Thọ, ed., *Các Nhà Khoa Bảng Việt Nam, 1075–1919* (The Enrolled Men of Việt Nam, 1075–1919), 730.

178. *ĐNNTC*, 4:135.

179. Ngô Trọng Khuê, a noted Lê official, used this phrase in a letter to Quang Trung describing the attitude of many officials of the former dynasty. Ibid., 41.

180. *HLNTC*, 1:119; see also *ĐVSKTB*, 466.

181. Ngô Thì Nhậm, *Tuyển Tập Thơ Văn*, 124.

182. Ngọc Liễn, "Từ Mấy Văn Bản Viết Đời Tây Sơn Mới Phát Hiện" (Recently Discovered Texts from the Tây Sơn Period), 41.

183. For more discussion of this relationship and the influence of these scholars see George Dutton, "Reassessing Confucianism in the Tây Sơn Regime (1788–1802)."

184. Among other sources, the *ĐNTL* (258) reports, though hardly without prejudice, that the Chinese emperor was ashamed because he had been defeated by the Vietnamese.

185. *Tây Sơn Thuật Lược* (A Summary Record of the Tây Sơn), 16; *ĐNLT*, 2:528.

186. The immediate impetus for Huệ's request is depicted in the *Tây Sơn Thuật Lược* (16) as having been the death of one of his principal wives in 1791.

187. *Nam Sử* (History of the South), 60a; Gire to his family, 11 January 1796 (MEP 746, 542) touches on the plan indirectly, noting that Quang Trung "could easily have become master of China"; [anonymous] to Pigneau, 7 July 1792 (MEP 313, 983), notes of Quang Trung that "he contemplates nothing less than making war on the Chinese."

188. *HLNTC*, 2:220.

189. Woodside, "The Tay-son Revolution," 5–6.

190. La Mothe to Blandin, 20 January 1790, MEP 692, 158.

191. *ĐNTL*, 258; details of this mission can be found in Truong Buu Lam, "Intervention versus Tribute," 165–179.

192. For some examples of this see Phan Ngọc Liên and Nghiêm Đình Vỳ, "Về Một Đặc Điểm Nổi Bật Của Phong Trào Nông Dân Tây Sơn"; Nguyễn Duy Hinh, "Suy Nghĩ," 20–27; Nguyễn Danh Phiệt, "Nhà Tây Sơn Với Sự Nghiệp Dựng Nước" (The Tây Sơn Court and the Task of Reestablishing the Nation).

193. Keith Taylor appears to point to this provincial attitude in his comment on the "surface orientation" of the Bình Định region and its im-

pact on the vision of the Tây Sơn brothers. Taylor, "Surface Orientations," 965.

194. Labartette to Letondal, 11 June 1788, MEP 801, 178.

CHAPTER 3: THE PEASANTS

1. Le Roy to Blandin, June 1789, MEP 692, 112.
2. *LTHCLC*, 3:47.
3. Ibid., 48ff.
4. Đặng Phương-Nghi, *Les Institutions publiques*, 112.
5. *LTHCLC*, 3:52–53; also *LQDS*, 106.
6. *ĐNTL*, 172–173.
7. *ĐNTL*, 186.
8. Letter by Pigneau, 20 March 1785, *Nouvelles lettres*, 6:419.
9. This topic will be taken up at greater length in chapter 4.
10. *LQDS*, 90.
11. Ibid., 95.
12. *Lệnh Chí*, 3.
13. Ngô Thì Nhậm, *Tuyển Tập Thơ Văn*, 2:119.
14. Ibid., 119.
15. *LQDS*, 106.
16. Philippe Sérard to Chaumont, 6 May 1792, MEP 692, 495.
17. Pierre Eyot to Letondal, 19 June 1801, MEP 701, 450.
18. It is inherently difficult, of course, to determine the extent and scope of such evasions, but the relatively limited strength of Vietnamese regimes at the local level would suggest that such activity was a common occurrence. The strong popular opposition to the earlier 1773 census in Đàng Ngoài and the 1784 count in Đàng Trong, for instance, suggests that state attempts to exert controls of this nature would be met with resistance.
19. Eyot to Chaumont and Blandin, 15 December 1801, MEP 693, 547.
20. Đặng Phương-Nghi, *Les Institutions publiques*, 112–113; see also Stephen B. Young, "The Law of Property and Elite Prerogatives during Vietnam's Lê Dynasty, 1428–1788," 8.
21. *ĐNTL*, 49; also Phan Khoang, *Việt Sử*, 482.
22. An elaboration of the ways in which these classification schemes operated in the north prior to the nineteenth century can be found in *LTHCLC*, 3:48–53.
23. Phan Khoang, *Việt Sử* (481–488), details the Nguyễn system of classification, military service, and taxation.
24. *ĐNTL*, 247.
25. *Nguyễn Thị Tây Sơn Ký* [qn], 70.
26. Members of families involved in political administration of their local areas were exempt from military service obligations.
27. Although the systematic exploitation of those below the age of

eighteen appears to have been a Tây Sơn innovation, there are some indications that other sides in the fighting also used young troops, though perhaps not as frequently. See, e.g., *LQDS* (66) describing Trịnh forces looking like "young buffalo boys."

28. M. Jean-André Doussain to Blandin, 16 June 1788, in Cadière, "Documents relatifs," 19–20.

29. *Nam Sử*, 59b. Similar descriptions can be found in other sources as well. See, e.g., *HLNTC*, 2:218; Đào Nguyên Phổ, *Tây Sơn Thủy Mạc Khảo* (Preliminary Research into the Tây Sơn), 30–31.

30. *HLNTC*, 2:218.

31. *Tây Sơn Thuật Lược*, 12.

32. *Le Tcheou–Li Ou rites des Tcheou*, 222. This was a very influential text among Đàng Ngoài scholars in the late eighteenth and early nineteenth centuries; see Woodside, "Classical Primordialism," 133, 135.

33. *Tây Sơn Thuật Lược*, 16; Durand, "Tây Sơn" (201) also discusses the unpopularity of the identity cards.

34. Guérard to ?, 14 May 1792, *Nouvelles lettres*, 6:138.

35. *HLNTC*, 2:219.

36. Sérard to Chaumont, 6 May 1792, MEP 692, 495.

37. See, for example, *Nguyễn Thị Tây Sơn Ký*, 38a; or *ĐNLT*, 2:531. A missionary letter from the summer of 1793, however, still speaks of people being registered on village rolls and then given identity cards. Le Roy to Blandin, 12 July 1793, MEP 692, 482.

38. Li, *Nguyễn Cochinchina*, 38–39.

39. L. Malleret, "Voyage de Pierre Poivre en Cochinchine," 89.

40. Pérez, "La Révolte," 78.

41. Jean-Pierre-Joseph D'Arcet to ?, 30 May 1784, MEP 801, 20; D'Arcet to Descourvières, 20 September 1785, MEP 801, 80.

42. Durand, "Tây Sơn," 9. See also Đỗ Bang, "Tình Hình Đấu Tranh Giai Cấp Ở Thuận Hóa Thế Kỷ XVIII" (The Situation of the Class Struggle in Thuận Hóa in the Eighteenth Century), 43.

43. Jean-André Doussain to ?, 8 July 1787, MEP 746, 205. It is not entirely clear what percentage of these were dead or wounded and what percentage had merely fled the ranks of Nhạc's armies.

44. Le Labousse to Boiret, 13 May 1795, *Nouvelles lettres*, 7:283; see also *ĐNTL*, 307.

45. Barisy letter in Cadière, "Documents relatifs," 43.

46. Pérez, "La Révolte," 78.

47. *Nguyễn Thị Tây Sơn Ký*, 5a; the later *ĐNTL* reported the figure at one in seven. *ĐNTL*, 521.

48. *HLNTC*, 2:218.

49. *ĐNTL*, 521.

50. *PBTL*, 77.

51. Longer to Boiret, 3 May 1787, *Nouvelles lettres*, 7:6.

52. The Nguyễn forces suffered from the problem of desertion as well. See *ĐNTL*, 246.

53. "Journal de ce qui s'est passé de plus remarquable dans la mission du Tong-king, depuis le mois de juillet 1786 jusqu'à mois de juillet 1787," MEP 690, 899.

54. Le Roy to Blandin, 3 July 1789, MEP 692, 112.

55. Li, *Nguyễn Cochinchina*, 39.

56. Pérez, "La Révolte," 70.

57. Eyot to Boiret, 21 June 1801, MEP 693, 497.

58. Although frequently used as a form of punishment or coercion in recruitment, the execution of soldiers was not always used for those purposes. On occasion, it was used instead to inspire popular support for the Tây Sơn, as was the case during the 1786 campaign into Đàng Ngoài, during which Tây Sơn leaders executed members of their own troops for even minor offenses against civilians. See Le Roy to Letondal, 6 December 1786, MEP 700, 1307; see also Gerard to Blandin, 31 July 1786, MEP 691, 749.

59. Louis-François Le Breton to MEP Directors, July 1788, MEP 692, 12(8).

60. Charles-François Langlois to ?, 1795, MEP 692, 359.

61. *ĐNTL*, 186. That such an incident is not implausible is suggested by other accounts of later-nineteenth and even twentieth-century episodes of Vietnamese soldiers ritually eating parts (usually internal organs) of their enemies.

62. Sérard to Letondal, 26 July 1797, MEP 701, 253 (emphasis added). The Nguyễn used such incentives as well; at one point in 1788, Nguyễn officers were sent on campaigns with thousands of blank promotion certificates that could be used for field promotions. *ĐNTL*, 234.

63. Barisy to Marquini and Letondal, 16 July 1801, MEP 801, 964.

64. Bùi Thị Tân, "Nhân Dân Làng Dã Lê Thượng với Phong Trào Tây Sơn" (The People of Upper Dã Lê Village and the Tây Sơn Movement).

65. Phạm Văn Đang, *Văn Học Tây Sơn* (Tây Sơn Literature), 27–28.

66. The imposition of labor service was of course something endured by populations regardless of who their overlords happened to be. The Nguyễn made heavy labor demands of the populations under their control in constructing their new citadel at Gia Định, and the Trịnh had earlier "recruited" populations of Thuận Hóa to labor in gold mines in the mid-1770s. See *ĐNTL*, 186, 257.

67. The destruction of government structures may, of course, have been carried out for political or symbolic reasons rather than merely as random acts of destruction. For those asked to rebuild such structures, the reasons for their initial destruction would, however, have been irrelevant.

68. Pérez, "La Révolte," 76. The Tây Sơn were hardly unique in this particular practice. The new Nguyễn regime in the nineteenth century also destroyed numerous structures associated with their predecessors, and then

promptly rebuilt them using corvée labor. See Huỳnh Sanh Thông, "Folk History in Vietnam," 73–74.

69. Chapman, in Lamb, *Mandarin Road*, 103, 105. *ĐNNTC* (2:271) reports a Trịnh palace in Thanh Hóa that was completely destroyed by the Tây Sơn.

70. *LQDS*, 35.

71. Chapman, in Lamb, *Mandarin Road*, 96.

72. "Extrait d'une lettre de Mgr. L'Eveque de Veren coadjuteur de Mgr. l'Eveque d'Adran en date de 23 juillet, 1788," MEP 306, 1008.

73. Jean Labartette to Blandin, 23 June 1786, MEP 746, 177; Labartette to Boiret, 15 July 1786, *Nouvelles lettres*, 6:491; also Đặng Xuân Bảng, *Việt Sử Cương Mục*, 608.

74. Sérard to MEP Directors, 26 April 1791, *Nouvelles lettres*, 7:98.

75. *LQDS*, 90.

76. Ibid., 90.

77. *ĐNTL*, 232; *ĐVSKTB*, 479.

78. Sérard to Letondal, 20 September 1794, MEP 701, 69.

79. De Gortyne to Letondal, 31 March 1798, MEP 701, 287.

80. Guérard to ?, 14 May 1792, *Nouvelles lettres*, 7:142–143.

81. Longer to Boiret, 3 May 1787, *Nouvelles lettres*, 7:6.

82. Pierre Gire to Letondal, 13 July 1791, MEP 801, 375.

83. Sérard to de Chaumont, 6 May 1792, MEP 692, 495; La Mothe to Blandin, 28 May 1790, MEP 692, 216.

84. Letter from Longer to Blandin, 26 July 1786, and 3 May 1787, in Cadière, "Documents relatifs," 17; Longer to Boiret, 3 May 1787, *Nouvelles lettres*, 7:6.

85. Nguyễn Vinh Phúc, "Nhân Dân Hà Nội và Tây Sơn" (The People of Hà Nội and the Tây Sơn), 53.

86. Labartette to Blandin, 23 June 1786, MEP 746, 177–178; La Mothe to Blandin, 8 July 1787, MEP 691, 1015; Le Roy to Blandin, 3 July 1789, *Nouvelles lettres*, 7:48–49.

87. Alexander Woodside, "Buddhism, the Vietnamese Court and China in the 1800s," 15.

88. Introduction to his poem, "Recording the Work of the Spring, Obeying the Order to Supervise the Work of Constructing Dikes in the Trấn of Sơn Nam," in Phan Huy Ích, *Thơ Văn Phan Huy Ích, Dụ Am Ngâm Lục* (The Poetry of Phan Huy Ích, Recorded Recitations of Dụ Am), 147–148.

89. Pérez, "La Révolte," 80–81.

90. Ibid., 80.

91. The Tây Sơn armies hardly had a monopoly on looting during this period, for large-scale warfare always brings with it such problems. The Nguyễn armies were equally guilty of regular looting in the southern reaches of Đàng Trong, where they were active from the 1770s through the 1790s.

According to the *Đại Nam Thực Lục Tiền Biên* (Preliminary Compilation of the Veritable Records of Đại Nam; 233, 234, 287, 293, 300), Nguyễn Ánh regularly issued decrees in an effort to halt looting and harassment of local populations (decrees concerning looting were issued in 1788, 1792, and 1793), their repetition suggesting their relative inefficacy.

92. Chapman, in Lamb, *Mandarin Road*, 90.

93. Le Roy to Blandin, 6 December 1786, Cadière "Documents relatifs," 7.

94. Le Roy to Letondal, 6 December 1786, MEP 700, 1308; La Mothe to Blandin, 8 July 1787, MEP 691, 1012–1013; *Sử Ký Đại Nam Việt Quốc Triều*, 39.

95. Labartette to Blandin, 23 June 1786. MEP 746, 178; Le Roy to Blandin, 6 December 1786, Cadière, "Documents relatifs," 8.

96. "Journal de ce qui s'est passé de plus remarquable dans la mission du Tong-king," [July 1787], MEP 691, 900.

97. Eyot to Grinne, 5 July 1789, MEP 692, 123. For other accounts of Tây Sơn looting see, e.g., Le Breton to MEP Directors, July 1788, MEP 692, 12(7); "Journal de ce qui s'est passé de plus remarquable dans la mission du Tong-king," MEP 691, 898.

98. Le Breton to MEP Directors, July 1788, MEP 692, 12(7).

99. Le Roy to Descourvières, 28 June 1787, MEP 691, 708.

100. De Gortyne to de Dolicha, 2 November 1792, MEP 692, 381.

101. Labartette to Boiret, 15 July 1786, *Nouvelles lettres*, 6:491.

102. Pérez, "La Révolte," 80–81.

103. *LQDS*, 90–91.

104. See, e.g., Le Roy to ?, 26 July 1787, MEP 691, 827–828. Ironically, the small number of temple bells that were produced during the Tây Sơn period itself had then to be hidden against the subsequent Nguyễn campaigns to eradicate vestiges of their predecessors. See Phạm Thúy Hằng and Trần Thu Hương, "Phát Hiện Quả Chuông Cảnh Thịnh ở Chùa Phương Trì Đại Phùng" (The Discovery of a Cảnh Thịnh–era Bell at the Phương Trì Pagoda in the Village of Đại Phùng), 223.

105. Gerard to Blandin, 20 August 1787, MEP 691, 795.

106. *Lệnh Chí*. See also Hoa Bằng, *Quang Trung*, 283–286.

107. Hoàng Xuân Hãn, *La Sơn Phu Tử*, 141.

108. Sérard to Letondal, 30 April 1791, MEP 700, 1443.

109. Sérard to Letondal, 9 June 1793, MEP 700, 1513.

110. Lê Quý Đôn describes this in great detail in his *Phủ Biên Tạp Lục* (Chronicles of the Prefectural Borders), 203–241.

111. Jean-André Doussain to Letondal, 23 July 1790, MEP 801, 330.

112. Sérard to Letondal, 17 July 1791, MEP 700, 1468.

113. Chapman, in Lamb, *Mandarin Road*, 101.

114. Le Roy to Blandin, June 1789, MEP 692, 112.

115. Phan Huy Lê, "Có Một Bộ Luật Đời Tây Sơn" (There Was a Tây

Sơn Legal Code), 182–190. This legal code apparently survived into the 1960s, only to be inadvertently used as cigarette paper by a member of the family that had preserved it.

116. *Tây Sơn Thuật Lược*, 17.

117. Le Roy to Blandin, 3 July 1789, MEP 692, 112; Le Roy to Blandin, 12 July 1793, MEP 692, 487; Le Roy to Blandin, June 1789, MEP 692, 112.

118. Le Pavec to his parents, 3 July 1799, MEP 693, 211.

119. Hoàng Xuân Hãn, *La Sơn Phu Tử*, 142.

120. *LQDS*, 99.

121. Hoàng Xuân Hãn, *La Sơn Phu Tử*, 145.

122. *LQDS*, 104–106.

123. Le Pavec to his parents, 7 April 1797, *Nouvelles lettres*, 7:383–384.

124. Sérard to Blandin, 3 December 1786, MEP 691, 756; Sérard to Blandin, 20 August 1787, MEP 691, 793; Gerard to Blandin, 12 July 1789 (MEP 692, 137), describes the anarchy and tax resistance that sprang up in the wake of the Tây Sơn invasion.

125. A. Richard, *Histoire naturelle, civile et politique du Tonquin*, 225.

126. *LQDS*, 44.

127. Hoàng Xuân Hãn, *La Sơn Phu Tử*, 130–131.

128. Le Roy to ?, 26 July 1787, MEP 691, 829. *Sấm ký* is the Vietnamese term for "prophecy."

129. L. Cadière, "Le Changement de costume sous Vo-Vuong, ou une crise religieuse a Hué au XVIII siècle," 418.

130. Ibid., 418.

131. For a description of this episode, see *PBTL*, 334.

132. Cadière, "Le Changement," 424.

133. Nguyễn Cẩm Thúy and Nguyễn Phạm Hùng, *Văn Thơ Nôm*, 266. This suggested that the eighth generation would see the collapse of the ruling house.

134. *PBTL*, 334.

135. *LQDS*, 66.

136. Le Roy to ?, 26 July 1787, MEP 691, 829.

137. *PBTL*, 261.

138. *ĐVSKTB*, 346.

139. This account is also reported in the late-nineteenth-century *ĐNNTC*, 3:68.

140. Both occurrences are reported in *LQDS*, 53.

141. Ibid., 55.

142. Phạm Đình Hổ and Nguyễn Án, *Tang Thương Ngẫu Lục* (The Vicissitudes of This Life), 22–23.

143. Ibid., 129.

144. *LTTK*, 546; see also *HLNTC*, 1:99–100. A *trượng* is approximately four meters.

145. Maurice Durand and Nguyen Tran Huan, *An Introduction to Vietnamese Literature*, 73.

146. *LTTK*, 465.

147. *LQDS*, 36.

148. Ibid., 76.

149. Phạm Văn Đang, *Văn Học Tây Sơn*, 21–22.

150. Ibid., 27. Indeed, the Chinese public continues to use the multiple homophones found in their language to make political statements. During the 1980s and 1990s, people would throw and break small bottles in public spaces as a subtle form of political protest, for the words for "small bottle" are homophones for (Deng) "Xiaoping" the Chinese political leader at the time.

151. *PBTL*, 72–73.

152. Ibid., 313ff.

153. *ĐNTL*, 187.

154. Sérard to Jean Steiner, 3 May 1779, MEP 700, 935.

155. *ĐNLT*, 2:504.

156. Labartette to Blandin, 23 June 1786, MEP 745, 176; see also Longer to Blandin, 26 July 1786, with a postscript dated 3 May 1787 in Cadière, "Documents relatifs," 16.

157. *HLNTC*, 1:100; *LTTK*, 547–548.

158. Sérard to ?, 12 May 1779, MEP 700, 937.

159. *PBTL*, 78.

160. Chapman, in Lamb, *Mandarin Road*, 102.

161. Doussain to Blandin, 25 July 1788, in Cadière, "Documents relatifs," 18.

162. *ĐNLT*, 2:504.

163. Sérard to Blandin, 31 July 1786, in Cadière, "Documents relatifs," 11.

164. See, e.g., *Sử Ký Đại Nam Việt Quốc Triều* (39), which described indiscriminate looting and burning by Tây Sơn troops, and noted that the two provinces hardest hit were those of Thanh Hóa and Nghệ An.

165. "Extrait d'une lettre de Mgr. L'Eveque de Veren coadjuteur de Mgr. l'Eveque d'Adran en date de 23 juillet 1788," MEP 306, 1007.

166. Sérard to Descourvières, 2 May 1791, MEP 692, 279.

167. *ĐNTL*, 282. The blowing wind would have indicated a shift in the monsoon patterns that would allow the Nguyễn to advance north toward Tây Sơn–held territories.

168. Ibid., 283.

169. *Tây Sơn Thuật Lược*, 18.

170. Sérard to Letondal, 4 May 1792, MEP 700, 1488.

171. Sérard to Letondal, 20 September 1794, MEP 701, 68.

172. Eyot to Blandin, 6 August 1794, MEP 692, 563.

173. La Mothe to Blandin, 25 August 1794, MEP 692, 567.

174. *ĐNTL*, 306.

175. Le Labousse to ?, 24 April 1800, MEP 746, 875.

176. Eyot to Marchini, 23 June 1801, MEP 701, 453. Similar sentiments are found in Le Pavec to Letondal, [no date given] 1801, MEP 701, 472; and Gerard to Letondal, [no date given] 1801, MEP 701, 468–469.

177. Pigneau to ?, 14 September 1791, MEP 801, 417.

178. Pierre Lavoué to Blandin, 1 August 1793, MEP 746, 432.

179. *ĐNTL*, 332.

180. Lavoué to ?, 27 April 1795, MEP 801, 573.

181. Charles B. Maybon, *La Relation sur le Tonkin et Cochinchine de Mr. de La Bissachère*, 115.

182. Ibid., 127.

183. Ibid., 156.

184. Ibid., 126.

185. Đặng Phương-Nghi, *Les Institutions publiques*, 133.

186. See Nguyễn Bá Huấn, *Tây Sơn Văn Thần Liệt Truyện* and "Cân Quấc Anh Hùng Truyện," both of which were written in the nineteenth century to glorify the Tây Sơn. People also began to establish shrines to the Tây Sơn brothers, an act that the Nguyễn rulers had explicitly to ban. See Quách Tấn and Quách Giao, *Nhà Tây Sơn*, 250–251.

### CHAPTER 4: THE SOCIAL MARGINS

1. Visente Liêm Ký to ?, 18 July 1787, MEP 691, 1036.

2. The uprisings of Lê Duy Mật, Nguyễn Hữu Cầu, and Hoàng Công Chất, for example, all saw close alliances between rebel leaders and upland groups. See Lê Thành Khôi, *Histoire du Vietnam*, 306–308.

3. For some discussion of this relationship, see Phan Khoang, *Việt Sử*, 510–518; also Li, *Nguyễn Cochinchina*, 119–138.

4. E.g., Trương Hữu Quýnh, ed., *Đại Cương Lịch Sử Việt Nam* (A Broad Outline of Vietnamese History), 1:416; Văn Tân, *Cách Mạng Tây Sơn*, 214–215; *Lich Sử Việt Nam*, 338–339.

5. See, e.g., Hoa Bằng, *Quang Trung*, 292; Quách Tấn and Quách Giao, *Nhà Tây Sơn*, 148; Văn Tân, *Cách Mạng Tây Sơn*, 167, 214.

6. See note 4.

7. Vietnamese officials describing Christianity used various terms including *đạo hoa Lang* (the way of the Portuguese), *đạo thiên chúa* (the way of the lord of heaven), and *đạo cơ đồ* (the way of the cross).

8. For a brief description of Christianity in this early period, and especially de Rhodes' role, see Peter Phan, *Mission and Catechesis: Alexandre de Rhodes and Inculturation in Seventeenth-Century Vietnam*, 8–13.

9. Alain Forest, *Les Missionaires français au Tonkin et au Siam, XVIIe–XVIII siècles*, livre 2, *Histoires du Tonkin*, 173ff.

10. These repeated proscriptions—in 1712, 1721, 1750, 1754, 1761, 1765, and 1776—testify to the tenacity of some of the faith's adherents and

to the determination of European missionaries. See ibid., livre 3, *Organiser une église convertir les infidèles*, 331.

11. Ibid., 2:216.

12. Bertrand Reydellet to MEP Directors, 11 July 1774, MEP 700, 866.

13. Forest, *Les Missionaires français*, 2:217.

14. Ibid., 216–217.

15. Labartette to Boiret, 21 July 1775, *Nouvelles lettres*, 6:286–287.

16. Labartette to ?, 28 June 1775, MEP 800, 1471,

17. Reydellet to Steiner, 19 June 1776, MEP 700, 903.

18. Labartette to ?, 17 July 1779, MEP 745, 811.

19. Trương Vĩnh Ký, *Cours d'histoire Annamite*, 194; Phan Khoang, *Việt Sử*, 588–590.

20. Lamb, *Mandarin Road*, 63.

21. A useful summary of major European missionaries at Vietnamese courts is found in Phan Khoang, *Việt Sử*, 589–590; see also Forest, *Les Missionaires français* (3:287ff.), which includes a list of missionaries' names and the orders to which they belonged.

22. Cadière, "Le Changement," 417–424.

23. The text of this decree can be found in Cadière, "Documents relatifs," 3.

24. Cited in Forest, *Les Missionaires français*, 2:126.

25. Meyere to Lacere, 9 June 1754, MEP 700, 221–222. There was, at times, considerable debate among the missionaries about how committed many of the Vietnamese Christians actually were, and so different estimates may have reflected such considerations.

26. La Mothe to Deson, 15 June 1784, MEP 700, 1208.

27. See, e.g., Longer, 14 June 1783, *Nouvelles lettres*, 6:341.

28. Li Tana in *Nguyễn Cochinchina* (171) estimates a population of 5.6 million in the north for the year 1750. At the higher end are estimates noted in Forest (*Les Missionaires français*, 2:56), which vary between 6 and 10 million for the early part of the eighteenth century. Anthony Reid also gives an estimate for the north and center of approximately 7 million in 1800, though this later date comes after thirty years of warfare. Anthony Reid, *Southeast Asia in the Age of Commerce*, 14.

29. Jacinto da Fonçeca e Sylva, "Description chorographique du royaume de Cochinchine," in Manguin, *Les Nguyễn, Macau et le Portugal*, 160.

30. Faulet to ?, 6 July 1778, MEP 746, 1576.

31. Le Roy to Letondal, 6 December 1786, MEP 700, 1308.

32. Sérard to Blandin, August 1787, MEP 691, 1044.

33. Bỉnh, "Truyện Anam Đàng Trao," 657.

34. Jacques Liot to ?, 1 May 1778, *Nouvelles lettres*, 6:307; see also *Sử Ký Đại Nam Việt Quốc Triều*, 11.

35. Phan, *Mission and Catechesis*, 57.

36. Pérez, "La Révolte," 79.

37. Letter by Halbout cited in a letter by Labartette to Boiret, 21 July 1775, MEP 745, 751.

38. *Sử Ký Đại Nam Việt Quốc Triều*, 11.

39. Pérez, "La Révolte," 79.

40. Labartette to Descourvières, 27 July 1780, MEP 800, 1672. The text of this decree is found in MEP 800, 1691.

41. Langenois to Descourvières, 30 June 1784, MEP 800, 1775.

42. Ibid., 80.

43. For a discussion of (mostly Tonkin-based) missionary attitudes regarding whom to view as the "legitimate" ruler, see Forest, *Les Missionaires français*, 2:247–250.

44. "Precis des nouvelles et de l'etat actuel des missions Etrangers," [1782], MEP 306, 781.

45. Descourvières to ?, 16 January 1782, MEP 313, 622.

46. Pérez, "La Révolte," 91.

47. Langenois to Descourvières, 30 June 1784, MEP 800, 1775.

48. Details of this episode can be found in Pérez, "La Révolte," 90–91; see also copy of a letter by Pigneau to Descourvières, written from Bangkok, 5 October 1783, MEP 800, 1784–1785.

49. "Journal de la Procure de Macao en 1784," MEP 306, 928–929 (paragraph division added for clarity).

50. Le Roy to Alary, 4 July 1785, MEP 691, 585.

51. The decree is dated the ninth year of Nhạc's reign, the fourth day of the tenth month; the full text in French can be found in MEP 691, 1035.

52. See, e.g., Louis-François Le Breton to Blandin, 24 June 1786, *Nouvelles lettres*, 6:460–461.

53. Ibid., 694.

54. Reported in an undated and anonymous letter, probably of 1787, MEP 691, 1051.

55. Longer to Dufresse, 1 May 1786, MEP 801, 116. The practice of making payments in exchange for certain civil liberties did not originate with the Tây Sơn. Vietnamese traditional civil law, like that of China, for example, contained schedules of payments whereby punishments could be redeemed for fixed sums of cash. For examples in the Vietnamese legal tradition, see Nguyễn Ngọc Huy and Tạ Văn Tài, *The Lê Code*, 1:115, 116.

56. "Extrait du journal rédigé par Mgr. l'evêque de Ceram, vicaire apostolique du Tong-king occidental, depuis le mois de juin 1784 jusqu'au mois de mai 1785," *Nouvelles lettres*, 6:384.

57. Longer to Dufresse, 1 May 1786, MEP 801, 116.

58. See, for example, "Relation de la persécution excitée dans la Tongking et une partie de la Cochinchine, au mois d'août 1798, rédigée d'après les lettres écrites par les missionaries de ces deux missions en décembre 1798

et juin 1799," *Nouvelles lettres* (8:11ff.), which describes the various layers of officials who could demand payments from Christians.

59. Langlois to Chaumont, 8 June 1799 (MEP 693, 192), describes just such a situation.

60. Le Roy to Blandin, 6 December 1786, in Cadière, "Documents relatifs," 7.

61. Le Roy to ?, 26 July 1787, MEP 691, 825.

62. Longer to Dufresse, 1 May 1786, MEP 801, 117.

63. Longer to Letondal, 9 August 1786, MEP 801, 131.

64. Gerard to Blandin, 31 July 1786, MEP 691, 744bis. This episode sounds a great deal like that mentioned in the 1784 account, and it is possible that they are the same, though the two-year time difference makes it equally possible that separate incidents are being reported.

65. Le Labousse to ?, 13 October 1790, MEP 746, 296.

66. See, e.g., *Sử Ký Đại Nam Việt Quốc Triều*, 71.

67. Le Labousse to Boiret, 13 May 1795, MEP 746, 473.

68. Lavoué to Alary, Chaumont, and Blandin, 1795? (received in London, 6 August 1796), MEP 746, 525–526.

69. Ibid., 526.

70. Le Breton to Frizier, 24 July 1782, MEP 700, 1107–1108; Sérard to ?, 1782, MEP 700, 1126.

71. "Extrait du journal rédigé par Mgr. l'evêque de Ceram, vicaire apostolique du Tong-king occidental, depuis le mois de juin 1784 jusqu'au mois de mai 1785," *Nouvelles lettres*, 6:389.

72. "Journal de ce qui s'est passé de plus remarquable dans la mission du Tong-king, depuis le mois de juillet 1786 jusqu'à mois de juillet 1787," MEP 691, 904.

73. Le Roy cites reports that Chỉnh was reputed to be a Christian (Le Roy to Alary, 10 July 1787, MEP 691, 705), but then in another letter asserts that he was not (Le Roy to ?, 27 July 1787, MEP 691, 828).

74. See Le Breton letter, July 1788, MEP 692, 12(7). Attacks on Christians were also seen in early 1789; see Le Roy to Blandin, 3 July 1789, MEP 692, 114.

75. Girard to Boiret, 25 November 1792, *Nouvelles lettres*, 7:154.

76. Le Roy to Letondal, 13 June 1790, MEP 700, 1403.

77. Eyot to Blandin, 24 May 1790, MEP 692, 208.

78. *Sử Ký Đại Nam Việt Quốc Triều*, 56. He also developed plans to send Girard as an envoy to European traders either in Macao or in Manila to urge them to trade in Tây Sơn–controlled territories.

79. Longer to ?, 14 April 1790, *Nouvelles lettres*, 7:94.

80. See, e.g., Le Labousse to Boiret, 20 June 1792, MEP 746, 371; Pocard? to ?, 30 May 1789, MEP 746, 242.

81. La Mothe to Boiret, 19 June 1793, MEP 692, 450.

82. Eyot to Blandin, 19 June 1793, MEP 692, 444.

83. Sérard to Blandin, 5 June 1793/28 May 1794, MEP 692, 517.

84. De Gortyne to Boiret, 22 April 1794, MEP 692, 540; Eyot to Blandin, 6 August 1794, MEP 692, 560.

85. See, for example, Le Roy to Blandin, 12 July 1793, MEP 692, 478.

86. La Mothe to Blandin, 25 August 1794, MEP 692, 569–570.

87. La Mothe in a letter of 31 March 1795, MEP 692, 625.

88. Pierre-Jacques Lemonnier de la Bissachère to Letondal, late February 1795, MEP 701, 84.

89. Bỉnh, "Truyện Anam Đàng Trao," 1:305.

90. La Mothe to Letondal, 31 March 1795, MEP 692, 626.

91. Nguyễn Triệu, "Ông Tín (1768–1799)." Among other things, he is noted for having suggested to the Nguyễn that they use hot air balloons to drop explosives and incendiary devices on a Tây Sơn citadel in the early 1790s.

92. Langlois to Boiret, 20 July 1795, MEP 692, 652.

93. Le Roy to Blandin, 3 August 1795, MEP 692, 663.

94. This edict can be found in MEP 701, 98–99.

95. *Cảnh Tịnh Triều Công Văn* (Public Documents of the Cảnh Tịnh Court).

96. Le Pavec to his parents, 5 July 1795, MEP 692, 638.

97. De la Bissachère to Letondal, 20 August 1795, MEP 701, 132; see also de la Bissachère to Blandin, 25 August 1795, MEP 692, 690–691.

98. Le Pavec to ?, 22 September 1795, MEP 701, 148–149.

99. De Gortyne to Blandin, 29 January 1797, MEP 692, 773; Eyot to Letondal, 25 March 1797, MEP 701, 202; Sérard to Boiret, 29 March 1797, MEP 692, 802; La Mothe to Boiret, 30 June 1797, MEP 692, 859; Guerard to Blandin, 17 July 1797, MEP 692, 856; Eyot to Blandin, 15 August 1797, MEP 692, 890.

100. De Gortyne to Blandin, 29 January 1797, MEP 692, 773.

101. [Author unknown, possibly de Gortyne], 3 June 1799, MEP 701, 345–352.

102. Eyot to Letondal, 10 April 1798, MEP 701, 290.

103. Eyot to Letondal, 3 June 1799, MEP 693, 142.

104. Eyot to Letondal, 28 April 1798, MEP 701, 379.

105. De Gortyne to Letondal, 8 July 1800, MEP 701, 386.

106. See, for example, de la Bissachère to Letondal, 6 May 1801, MEP 701, 416.

107. For a thoughtful and illuminating discussion of the question of ethnic identity in this era see Li Tana, "The Water Frontier: An Introduction," 5–8.

108. Ibid., 7.

109. A good discussion of these terms and the particular Chinese groups they described is found in Choi Byung Wook, *Southern Vietnam under the Reign of Minh Mang*, 38–41.

110. Studies of the history of ethnic Chinese in Việt Nam are surpris-

ingly still quite limited. Useful reference may be made to the following: Li, *Nguyễn Cochinchina*; Chen Chingho, *Historical Notes on Hoi An*; Thomas Engelbert, *Die Chinesische Minderheit im Süden Vietnams (Hoa) als Paradigma der kolonialen und nationalistischen Nationalitätenpolitik*, of which pp. 110–117 directly speak of ethnic Chinese in the Tây Sơn period; Nguyễn Thế Anh, "L'Immigration chinoise et la colonisation du Delta du Mékong"; Yang, *Contribution à l'histoire*, 165–174. Nola Cooke and Li Tana's *Water Frontier* includes several studies of the Chinese in Việt Nam as well.

111. Li, "The Water Frontier" (6), points out that these terms, like others for the ethnic Chinese, were also fluid and might be used differently at different times.

112. *ĐNTL*, 91. Engelbert notes that there may already have been small Chinese settlements in place by the mid-1640s, having resulted from existing trade routes and structures. *Die chinesische Minderheit*, 88.

113. Nguyễn Thế Anh, "L'Immigration chinoise," 154.

114. Yang (*Contribution à l'histoire*, 199) gives a map of Chinese settlements in Đàng Trong in 1770, showing, for example, that the large majority of ethnic Chinese were concentrated by place of origin, with Fujianese settled in the Hội An–Đà Nẵng region and Cantonese settled in the southern Gia Định–Hà Tiên area.

115. See Nguyên Thanh-Nhã, *Tableau economique*, 148–149, 183–186.

116. Pérez, "La Révolte," 68.

117. Labartette to Boiret, 28 June 1775, MEP 800, 1471.

118. The idea of individuals being placed in charge of "private" armies was not atypical for this period. The Nguyễn armies also comprised a coalition of semiautonomous armies led by prominent military figures, rather than a single, integrated force.

119. Engelbert, *Die chinesische Minderheit*, 83.

120. See, for instance, Mary Somers Heidhues, "Chinese Organizations in West Borneo and Bangka: *Kongsi* and *Hui*."

121. *ĐNLT*, 2:496–497.

122. A biography of Đỗ Thanh Nhân can be found ibid., 468–470. Nhân eventually came to clash with Nguyễn Ánh, and the Nguyễn ruler killed him in 1781 in an attempt to take over the Đông Sơn force.

123. Phạm Văn Đang, *Văn Học Tây Sơn*, 22.

124. Halbout to MEP Director, July 1775, cited in Labartette to Boiret, 21 July 1775, *Nouvelles lettres*, 6:288.

125. Pérez, "La Révolte," 85.

126. *ĐVSKTB*, 393.

127. *ĐNTL*, 184.

128. *ĐNTL*, 189. A detailed discussion of the roles of Lý Tài and Tập Đình in the Tây Sơn forces during the early years of the uprising can be found in Choi, *Southern Vietnam*, 36–37.

129. Pérez, "La Révolte," 80.

130. Ibid., 80. Though the city is not named explicitly, the context suggests Tourane (Đà Nẵng). See also letter by F. Castuera in Pérez, "La Révolte," 91.

131. Ibid., 91.

132. Pérez ("La Révolte," 87) put the number of dead at four thousand, while Barrow's rather inexact account of this period cites the larger figure of twenty thousand (Barrow, *Voyage to Cochinchina*, 250).

133. *ĐNTL*, 212; the massacre is mentioned in numerous other accounts—for example, *ĐNLT*, 2:498; *Nguyễn Thị Tây Sơn Kí*, 7a.

134. Trịnh Hoài Đức, *Gia Định Thành Thống Chí* (Records of Gia Định), 38.

135. *ĐNTL*, 211; see also *Nguyễn Thị Tây Sơn Kí*, 11a; *Sử Ký Đại Nam Việt Quốc Triều*, 25–26; *LTTK*, 491.

136. Lê Thành Khôi, *Histoire du Vietnam*, 314.

137. Halbout to Macao, 13 July 1782, MEP 800, 1728.

138. Nguyễn Thế Anh, "L'Immigration chinoise," 161; Choi, *Southern Vietnam*, 36–37.

139. A sampling of texts that omits this significant event in the Tây Sơn period includes Văn Tân, *Cách Mạng Tây Sơn*; Đào Duy Anh, *Lich Sử Việt Nam*; and Trương Hữu Quýnh, *Đại Cương Lịch Sử Việt Nam*.

140. Andre Tôn to ?, 1 July 1784, *Nouvelles lettres*, 6:438; see also Engelbert, *Die chinesische Minderheit*, 114–115.

141. La Mothe to Blandin, 20 January 1790, MEP 692, 158.

142. Engelbert, *Die chinesische Minderheit*, 113.

143. Quách Tấn and Quách Giao, *Nhà Tây Sơn*, 106.

144. Choi, *Southern Vietnam*, 35–37.

145. Nguyễn Thế Anh, "L'Immigration chinoise," 161.

146. *ĐNNTC*, 3:143.

147. Bửu Cầm, "Một Đoạn Lịch Sử Chiêm-Thành" (An Article on the History of Champa).

148. Le Labousse to ?, 1793, MEP 746, 453.

149. *ĐNNTC*, 3:143–144.

150. Their names are given and this episode is described in Tạ Chí Đại Trường, *Lịch Sử Nội Chiến*, 239.

151. Sok, *Le Cambodge*, 51.

152. Liot to Descourvières, 25 July 1782, MEP 800, 1742.

153. Sok, *Le Cambodge*, 51.

154. *ĐNTL*, 237.

155. *ĐNTL*, 243.

156. For a brief discussion of the Nguyễn treatment of Khmers in this period and into the early nineteenth century, see Choi, *Southern Vietnam*, 33–35.

157. Not all of these groups were native to the highland regions. Li argues that some had moved into these more remote regions in response

to pressure from Vietnamese migrants moving south in the course of the Nguyễn geographic and demographic expansion (Li, *Nguyễn Cochinchina*, 34–35). Phan Khoang in *Việt Sử* (511) cites Chams as being among those who moved into the upland regions.

158. Letter from Le Roy to Blandin, 6 December 1786, in Cadière, "Documents relatifs," 8. A 1790 letter similarly noted that the Tây Sơn forces included "Indians, Chinese, Siamese, and Portuguese." La Mothe to Blandin, 20 January 1790, MEP 692, 158.

159. *ĐNLT*, 2:108.

160. Choi, *Southern Vietnam*, 26–27.

161. Le Labousse to Boiret, 20 June 1792, MEP 746, 371.

162. Cited in Trương Hữu Quýnh, *Đại Cương Lịch Sử*, 410–411.

163. Adas, "From Avoidance to Confrontation," 108–109.

164. Masaya Shiraishi, "State, Villagers, and Vagabonds: Vietnamese Rural Society and the Phan Bá Vành Rebellion," 352.

165. Ibid.

166. Ibid., 361.

167. La Mothe to Blandin, 3 December 1786, *Nouvelles lettres*, 6:473.

168. Pérez, "La Révolte," 72.

169. Labartette to ? 21 July 1775, MEP 800, 1474.

170. Le Roy to Letondal, 6 December 1786, MEP 700, 1309.

171. "Extrait du journal rédigé par Mgr. l'evêque de Ceram, vicaire apostolique du Tonking occidental, depuis le mois de juin 1784 jusqu'au mois de mai 1785," *Nouvelles lettres*, 6:392–393.

172. See ibid. (6:393–395) for the case of a notorious bandit chief in Đàng Ngoài.

173. Elizabeth J. Perry, *Rebels and Revolutionaries in North China, 1845–1945*, 72. See also George Dutton, "The Fat Sheep with the Precious Wool: Bandit Kidnapping of Foreigners in 1920s China," 9.

174. This reference to Nhạc is found in a letter to the Nguyễn sent by the leading Trịnh general. It is recorded in the *PBTL*, 312.

175. Sérard to ?, June 1783, *Nouvelles lettres*, 6:337.

176. "Extrait du journal rédigé par Mgr. l'evêque de Ceram, vicaire apostolique du Tonking occidental, depuis le mois de juin 1784 jusqu'au mois de mai 1785," *Nouvelles lettres*, 6:385.

177. Ibid., 384.

178. "Journal de ce qui s'est passé de plus remarquable dans la mission du Tong-king, depuis le mois de juillet 1786 jusqu'à mois de juillet 1787," MEP 690, 901.

179. Halbout to ?, 30 July 1782, MEP 800, 1743.

180. Pérez, "La Révolte," 68; Tạ Chí Đại Trường, *Lịch Sử Nội Chiến*, 55.

181. *Những Mẩu Chuyện*, 35–37.

182. Pérez, "La Révolte," 74.

183. Eveque de Ceram, "Journal de ce qui s'est passé," MEP 690, 900.

184. *HLNTC*, 1:148–149.

185. *ĐVSKTB*, 418.

186. *LQDS*, 69.

187. *Tây Sơn Thuật Lược*, 14–15.

188. Le Pavec to his parents, 7 April 1797, *Nouvelles lettres*, 7:383–384.

189. Le Pavec to his parents, 3 July 1799, MEP 693, 211.

190. Robert Antony, *Like Froth Floating on the Sea: The World of Pirates and Seafarers in Late Imperial South China*, 41.

191. Murray, *Pirates of the South China Coast*.

192. Jonathan Spence, *In Search of Modern China*, 121.

193. Murray, *Pirates*, 18–19. The territorial divisions in this border region were particularly murky, and some border officials had official capacities in both Vietnamese and Chinese administrative structures. See, e.g., de Gortyne to Boiret, 21 October 1792, MEP 692, 375.

194. Murray, *Pirates*, 17.

195. Nguyễn Lộc, *Văn Học Tây Sơn*, 99.

196. Ibid.

197. See Ngô Thì Nhậm, "A Second Edict Summoning Pirates," in *Hàn Các Anh Hoa* (Beautiful Flowers in the Writing Brush Pavilion), trans. Trần Lê Hữu, 17ff.

198. Murray, *Pirates*, 35. She claims that Chen was fishing in the area around Hà Nội at this time. If true, it is difficult to determine how the Tây Sơn, still restricted to the territory south of Phú Xuân, would have been able to seize him in that year, unless he had somehow drifted far to the south.

199. Ibid., 36.

200. *LQDS*, 52.

201. Murray, *Pirates*, 51.

202. Antony, *Like Froth Floating*, 39, 41; also Murray, *Pirates*, 54.

203. Antony, *Like Froth Floating*, 39.

204. This was particularly crucial after 1792, when the major part of the Tây Sơn fleet was burned at anchor in Thi Nại by an attacking Nguyễn force.

205. See, e.g., Sérard to Blandin (1 March 1792, MEP 692, 365) commenting on the fact that the pirates made communication up and down the coast nearly impossible.

206. *LQDS*, 105.

207. Many missionaries commented on the great difficult in exchanging information with their confederates in the south. See, inter alia, Sérard to Boiret, 6 June 1793, MEP 692, 426bis.

208. Antony, *Like Froth Floating*, 39.

209. Murray, *Pirates*, 41.

210. Sérard to Letondal, 23 July 1790, MEP 700, 1415.

211. Murray, *Pirates*, 41.

212. Bissachere, 20 December 1798, MEP 693, 85–86.

213. Sérard to Letondal, 30 March 1797, MEP 701, 211–214.

214. *Nguyễn Thị Tây Sơn Ký*, 36a; see also *Nam Sử*, 59a; *ĐNLT*, 2:528.

215. Sérard to Letondal, 14 May 1797, MEP 701, 228.

216. Sérard to Letondal, 26 July 1797, MEP 701, 255.

217. It was only in 1810 that the majority of the Chinese pirates were eliminated, and even then the effort required joint action by the Chinese, the Portuguese at Macao, and the new Nguyễn regime. See Manguin, *Le Nguyễn*, 104.

218. Murray, *Pirates*, 39.

219. *Nguyễn Thị Tây Sơn Ký* [qn], 45; see also *LQDS*, 105.

220. Murray, *Pirates*, 39.

221. Ibid., 39–40, 47–48.

222. Manguin, *Le Nguyễn*, 100.

223. See, e.g., Văn Tân, "Quốc Sử Quán Triều Nguyễn Đối Với Khởi Nghĩa Tây Sơn" (The Nguyễn Dynasty History Board and the Tây Sơn Righteous Uprising); Duy Minh, "Vài Ý Kiến Về Cuốn *Tây Sơn Thủy Mạt Khảo* Của Đào Nguyên Phổ" (Some Opinions about the Volume *Tây Sơn Thủy Mạt Khảo* of Đào Nguyên Phổ). The criticism of this term is also implicit in the deliberate use of quotation marks around it in some modern *quốc ngữ* translations of Nguyễn-dynasty texts. An elaborated explanation of this usage is found in *LTTK*, 486, note 7.

224. Woodside, *Vietnam and the Chinese Model*, 17.

## CONCLUSION: LOOKING BACK AND LOOKING AHEAD

1. A brief summary analysis of factors contributing to the Nguyễn success and the ultimate Tây Sơn failure can be found in Lê Thành Khôi, *Histoire du Vietnam*, 340–341.

2. Trần Trọng Kim, *Việt Nam Sử Lược*, 2:170.

3. Lê Thành Khôi in *Histoire du Vietnam* (377ff.) includes some discussion of the tax and other obligations demanded of the Nguyễn courts and Vietnamese peasant responses. Trần Trọng Kim in *Việt Nam Sử Lược* (173ff.) offers a more detailed discussion of labor and tax issues, but from the perspective of the state.

4. Woodside, *Vietnam and the Chinese Model*, 135; Lê Thành Khôi, *Histoire du Vietnam*, 382. For a detailed description of one such uprising against Minh Mạng and involving a cross-section of anti-Nguyễn forces, see Shiraishi, "State, Villagers, and Vagabonds," 345–400.

5. *Việt Nam Những Sự Kiện Lịch Sử (Từ Khởi Thủy đến 1858)* (Vietnam: Historical Events [from Its Origins to 1858]), 433.

6. Quách Tấn and Quách Giao, *Nhà Tây Sơn*, 194–195.

7. Trần Trọng Kim, *Việt Nam Sử Lược*, 202.

8. Woodside, *Vietnam and the Chinese Model*, 133. Woodside does note that the Nguyễn made various concessions to the northerners and that Thăng Long retained considerable prominence, even as it was no longer the imperial center.

9. Alexander Woodside has argued that although there were concerns about regionalisms, these declined over time from 1802 into the 1840s (ibid., 135). While it is true that the dissolution of the southern and northern special administrative zones in 1831 and the strong role of Minh Mạng substantially improved the situation, significant regionalisms still existed, and in any case were a crucially important element of the immediate post–Tây Sơn decades.

# BIBLIOGRAPHY

## VIETNAMESE PRIMARY SOURCES


*Bản Quốc Ký Sự* 本國記事 (Records of the Affairs of Our Country). Ms. A. 989. Viện Hán Nôm, Hà Nội.

*Biểu Sách Văn Sao Tập* 表冊文抄集 (Copies of Collected Writings). Ms. A. 2905. Viện Hán Nôm, Hà Nội.

Bỉnh, Philiphê. "Truyện Anam Đàng Trao" (Tales of the Inner Region of Annam). Ms. 2, Borgiana Tonchinese. Biblioteca Apostolica Vaticana.

(*BNTL*) *Bình Nam Thực Lục* 平南實錄 (Veritable Records of the Pacified South). Ms. VHv. 185. Viện Hán Nôm, Hà Nội.

(*BNTL*[qn]) *Bình Nam Thực Lục* (Veritable Records of the Pacified South). DC. 79. Tms. (photocopy). Bình Định Provincial Library, Qui Nhơn.

*Cảnh Tịnh Triều Công Văn* 景盛朝公文 (Public Documents of the Cảnh Tịnh Court). Ms. Vht. 45. Viện Hán Nôm, Hà Nội.

*Cao Bằng Thực Lục* 高平實錄 (Veritable Records of Cao Bằng). Ms. A. 129. Viện Hán Nôm, Hà Nội.

*Cao Bằng Thực Lục* (Veritable Records of Cao Bằng). DC. 92. Tms. (photocopy). Bình Định Provincial Library, Qui Nhơn.

*Chiêm Thành Khảo* 占城考 (Research on Champa). Ms. A. 970. Viện Hán Nôm, Hà Nội.

(*CM*) *Khâm Định Việt Sử Thông Giám Cương Mục* (The Imperially Ordered Mirror and Commentary on the History of the Việt). 2 vols. Translated by Hoa Bằng, Phạm Trọng Điềm, and Trần Văn Giáp. Hà Nội: Nhà Xuất Bản Giáo Dục, 1998.

*Dã Sử* 野史 (Unofficial History). Ms. VHb. 263. Viện Hán Nôm, Hà Nội.

*Đại Nam Thực Lục Tiền Biên* 大南寔錄前編 (The Preliminary Compilation of the Veritable Records of Đại Nam). 5 vols. Tokyo: Keio Institute of Linguistic Studies, 1961.

*Đại Việt Quốc Thư* (National Documents of the Great Việt). Translated by Hoàng Văn Hòe. Sài Gòn: Bộ Giáo Dục Xuất Bản, 1967.

Đặng Xuân Bảng. *Việt Sử Cương Mục Tiết Yếu* 越史綱目節要 (The Essential Mirror and Commentary on the History of the Việt). Hà Nội: Nhà Xuất Bản Khoa Học Xã Hội, 2000.

Đào Nguyên Phổ. *Tây Sơn Thủy Mạt Khảo* (Preliminary Research into the Tây Sơn). DC. 156. Tms. (photocopy). Bình Định Provincial Library, Qui Nhơn.

(*ĐNLT*) *Đại Nam Chính Biên Liệt Truyện* (Principal Record of the Biographies of Đại Nam). 4 vols. Translated by Đỗ Mộng Khương et al. Huế: Nhà Xuất Bản Thuận Hóa, 1993.

(*ĐNNTC*) *Đại Nam Nhất Thống Chí* (Unification Records of Đại Nam). Translated by Phạm Trọng Điềm. Edited by Đào Duy Anh. Huế: Nhà Xuất Bản Thuận Hóa, 1996.

(*ĐNTL*) *Đại Nam Thực Lục* (Veritable Records of Đại Nam). Translated by Nguyễn Ngọc Tỉnh. Hà Nội: Nhà Xuất Bản Khoa Học Xã Hội, 2001.

(*ĐVSKTB*) *Đại Việt Sử Ký Tục Biên* (A Continuation of the Historical Records of Đại Việt). Translated by Ngô Thế Long and Nguyễn Kim Hưng. Edited by Nguyễn Đổng Chi. Hà Nội: Nhà Xuất Bản Khoa Học Xã Hội, 1991.

(*HLNTC*) Ngô Gia Văn Phái. *Hoàng Lê Nhất Thống Chí* (Unification Records of the Imperial Lê). Translated by Nguyễn Đức Vân and Kiều Thu Hoạch. Thành Phố Hồ Chí Minh: Nhà Xuất Bản Văn Học, 1998.

*Hoàng Triều Sự Tích* 皇朝事跡 (Tales of the Affairs of the Imperial Court). Ms. A. 1086. Viện Hán Nôm, Hà Nội.

*Khâm Định Việt Sử Thông Giám Cương Mục* 欽定越史通鑑綱目 (The Imperially Ordered Mirror and Commentary on the History of the Việt) (1881). R. 524. Việt Nam National Library, Hà Nội.

Lê Quý Đôn. *Phủ Biên Tạp Lục* 撫邊雜綠 (Chronicles of the Prefectural Borders). Sài Gòn: Phủ Quốc Vũ Khanh Đặc Trách Văn Hóa Xuất Bản, 1972.

*Lệnh Chí* (An Imperial Command). Ms. VHc. 120. Viện Hán Nôm, Hà Nội.

*Liệt Truyện Dã Sử* 列傳野史 (Unofficial Biographical Histories). Ms. VHb. 263. Viện Hán Nôm, Hà Nội.

(*LQDS*) Bùi Dương Lịch. *Lê Quý Dật Sử* (Unusual Tales of the Late Lê). Translated by Phạm Văn Thắm. Hà Nội: Nhà Xuất Bản Khoa Học Xã Hội, 1987.

(*LTHCLC*) Phan Huy Chú. *Lịch Triều Hiến Chương Loại Chí* (Monographs of the Institutions of the Dynasties). Hà Nội: Nhà Xuất Bản Sử Học, 1961.

(*LTTK*) Ngô Cao Lãng. *Lịch Triều Tạp Ký* (Miscellaneous Records of Past Dynasties). Translated by Hoa Bằng and Hoàng Văn Lâu. Hà Nội: Nhà Xuất Bản Khoa Học Xã Hội, 1995.

*Minh Đô Sử* 明都史 (The Minh Đô History). Ms. Hv. 285. Viện Sử Học, Hà Nội.

*Nam Sử* 南史 (History of the South). Ms. VHv. 2743. Viện Hán Nôm, Hà Nội.

Ngô Gia Văn Phái. *Hoàng Lê Nhất Thống Chí* 皇黎一統志 (Unification Records of the Imperial Lê). Collection Romans et Contes du Viet Nam écrits en Han, vol. 5. Paris-Taipei: École Française d'Extrême-Orient and Student Book Company, 1986.

Ngô Thì Nhậm. *Hàn Các Anh Hoa* 翰閣英化 (Beautiful Flowers in the Writing Brush Pavilion). Ms. Hv. 95a. History Faculty, Hà Nội National University.

———. *Hàn Các Anh Hoa* (Beautiful Flowers in the Writing Brush Pavilion). Ms. VT. 17. Translated by Trần Lê Hữu. History Faculty, Hà Nội National University.

———. *Tuyển Tập Thơ Văn Ngô Thì Nhậm* (Collected Writings of Ngô Thì Nhậm). Vol. 2. Translated by Mai Quốc Liên et al. Edited by Ngọc Hy. Hà Nội: Nhà Xuất Bản Khoa Học Xã Hội, 1978.

Nguyễn Cẩm Thúy and Nguyễn Phạm Hùng. *Văn Thơ Nôm Thời Tây Sơn* (Nôm Literature from the Tây Sơn Period). Hà Nội: Nhà Xuất Bản Khoa Học Xã Hội, 1997.

*Nguyễn Thị Tây Sơn Ký* 阮氏西山記 (Record of the Tây Sơn of the Nguyễn Clan). Ms. A. 3138. Viện Hán Nôm, Hà Nội.

*Nguyễn Thị Tây Sơn Ký* [qn] (Record of the Tây Sơn of the Nguyễn Clan). DC. 112. Tms. (photocopy). Bình Định Provincial Library, Qui Nhơn.

Nguyễn Thu. *Lê Quý Ký Sự* (A Record of Events of the Late Lê). Translated by Hoa Bằng. Hà Nội: Nhà Xuất Bản Khoa Học Xã Hội, 1974.

(*PBTL*) Lê Qúy Đôn. *Phủ Biên Tạp Lục* (Chronicles of the Prefectural Borders). Translated by Đỗ Mộng Khương et al. Hà Nội: Nhà Xuất Bản Khoa Học Xã Hội, 1977.

Phạm Đình Hổ. *Vũ Trung Tùy Bút* (Random Notes from Amid the Rains). Translated by Nguyễn Hữu Tiến. Thành Phố Hồ Chí Minh: Nhà Xuất Bản Văn Nghệ Thành Phố Hồ Chí Minh, 1998.

——— and Nguyễn Án. *Tang Thương Ngẫu Lục* (The Viscissitudes of this Life). Translated by Trúc Khê and Ngô Văn Triện. Hà Nội: Nhà Xuất Bản Văn Học, 1972.

Phan Bội Châu. *Việt Nam Vong Quốc Sử* 越南亡國史 (History of the Loss of the Vietnamese Nation). Translated by Nguyễn Quang Tô. 1905. Reprint, Houston, Tex.: Xuân Thu, n.d.

Phan Huy Chú. *Lịch Triều Hiến Chương Loại Chí* 歷朝憲章類誌 (Monographs of the Institutions of the Dynasties). Sài Gòn: Bộ Văn Hóa Giái Dục và Thanh Niên Xuất Bản, 1973.

Phan Huy Ích. *Thơ Văn Phan Huy Ích, Dụ Am Ngâm Lục* (The Poetry of Phan Huy Ích, Recorded Recitations of Dụ Am). Hà Nội: Nhà Xuất Bản Khoa Học Xã Hội, 1978.

*Sử Ký Đại Nam Việt Quốc Triều* (Historical Records of the Great Southern Việt National Court). Sài Gòn: Nhóm Nghiên Cứu Sử Địa Việt Nam Xuất Bản, 1973.

*Tây Sơn Thuật Lược* 西山述略 (A Summary Record of the Tây Sơn). Translated by Tạ Quang Phát. Phủ Quốc: Phủ Quốc Vũ Khanh Đặc Trách Văn Hóa Xuất Bản, 1971.

Trịnh Hoài Đức. *Gia Định Thành Thống Chí* 嘉定城通志 (Records of Gia Định). Thành Phố Hồ Chí Minh: Nhà Xuất Bản Giáo Dục, 1998.

*Việt Sử Chính Biên Tiết Yếu* (Primary Summary History of the Việt). DC. 115. Tms. (photocopy). Bình Định Provincial Library, Qui Nhơn.

**VIETNAMESE SECONDARY SOURCES**

Bùi Thị Tân. "Nhân Dân Làng Dã Lê Thượng với Phong Trào Tây Sơn" (The People of Upper Dã Lê Village and the Tây Sơn Movement). *Nghiên Cứu Lịch Sử* 269 (July–August 1993): 67–70.

Bửu Cầm. "Một Đoạn Lịch Sử Chiêm-Thành" (An Article on the History of Champa). *Văn Hóa Nguyệt San* 36 (November 1958): 1247.

Chu Trọng Huyến. "Phượng Hoàng Trung Đô" (The Imperial Phoenix Central Capital). In *Gop Phần Tìm Hiểu Phong Trào Nông Dân Tây Sơn Nguyễn Huệ* (Contributions to Understanding the Tây Sơn Peasant Movement and Nguyễn Huệ), by the Sở Văn Hóa Thông Tin Nghĩa Bình, 147–160. Qui Nhơn: Sở Văn Hóa Thông Tin Nghĩa Bình, 1983.

Đào Duy Anh. *Lịch Sử Việt Nam* (History of Việt Nam). Thành Phố Hồ Chí Minh: Nhà Xuất Bản Văn Hóa Thông Tin, 2002.

———. *Việt Nam Văn Hóa Sử Cương* (An Outline History of Vietnamese Culture). Huế, 1938. Reprint, Houston, Tex.: Xuân Thu, n.d.

Đỗ Bang. "Tình Hình Đấu Tranh Giai Cấp Ở Thuận Hóa Thế Kỷ XVIII" (The Situation of the Class Struggle in Thuận Hóa in the Eighteenth Century). *Nghiên Cứu Lịch Sử* 216 (January–February 1984): 38–47.

Đỗ Văn Ninh. "Tiền Cổ Thời Tây Sơn" (Ancient Money from the Tây Sơn Period). *Nghiên Cứu Lịch Sử* 183 (November–December 1978): 96–112.

Duy Minh. "Vài Ý Kiến Về Cuốn *Tây Sơn Thủy Mạt Khảo* Của Đào Nguyên Phổ" (Some Opinions about the volume *Tây Sơn Thủy Mạt Khảo* of Đào Nguyên Phổ). *Nghiên Cứu Lịch Sử* 83 (February 1966): 46.

Hoa Bằng. *Quang Trung Anh Hùng Dân Tộc, 1788–1792* (Quang Trung a National Hero, 1788–1792). Hà Nội: Tri Tân and Đôn Dương, 1944. Reprint, Hà Nội: Nhà Xuất Bản Văn Hóa Thông Tin, 1998.

———. *Quốc Văn Đời Tây Sơn* (National Literature of the Tây Sơn Period). Sài Gòn: Vĩnh Bảo, 1950.

Hoàng Lê, ed. *Thơ Văn Ninh Tốn* (The Poetry of Ninh Tốn). Hà Nội: Nhà Xuất Bản Khoa Học Xã Hội, 1984.

Hoàng Thúc-Trâm. *Quốc Văn Đời Tây-Sơn* (National Literature of the Tây Sơn Period). Sài Gòn: Vĩnh Bảo, 1950.

Hoàng Xuân Hãn. *La Sơn Phu Tử* (The Master of La Sơn). Paris: Minh Tân, 1952.

Huỳnh Công Bá. *Lịch Sử Việt Nam* (History of Việt Nam). Huế: Nhà Xuất Bản Thuận Hóa, 2004.

Lại Nguyên Ân, ed. *Từ Điển Văn Học Việt Nam* (Literary Dictionary of Việt Nam). Hà Nội: Nhà Xuất Bản Giáo Dục, 1997.

Lê Thước and Trương Chính. "Tìm Hiểu Dòng Văn Học Tiến Bộ Thời Tây Sơn" (Seeking to Understand the Flow of Progressive Literature in the Tây Sơn Era). *Tạp Chí Văn Học* 6 (1971): 64–80.

Lê Xuân Lít. "Lòng Dân Đối Với Cuộc Khởi Nghĩa Tây Sơn" (The Hearts of the People with Respect to the Tây Sơn Righteous Uprising). In *Gop*

*Phần Tìm Hiểu Phong Trào Nông Dân Tây Sơn Nguyễn Huệ* (Contributions to Understanding the Tây Sơn Peasant Movement and Nguyễn Huệ), by the Sở Văn Hóa Thông Tin Nghĩa Bình, 288–303. Qui Nhơn: Sở Văn Hóa Thông Tin Nghĩa Bình, 1983.

Ngô Đức Thọ, ed. *Các Nhà Khoa Bảng Việt Nam, 1075–1919* (The Enrolled Men of Việt Nam, 1075–1919). Hà Nội: Nhà Xuất Bản Văn Học, 1993.

———. *Nghiên Cứu Chữ Huý Việt Nam Qua Các Triều Đại* (Research into Tabooed Characters in Việt Nam throughout the Dynasties). Hà Nội: Nhà Xuất Bản Văn Hóa, 1997.

Ngọc Liễn. "Từ Mấy Văn Bản Viết Đời Tây Sơn Mới Phát Hiện" (Recently Discovered Texts from the Tây Sơn Period). *Nghiên Cứu Lịch Sử* 162 (May–June 1975): 40–44.

Nguyễn Bá Huân. "Cân Quắc Anh Hùng Truyện" (Tales of a Female Hero). In *Tư Liệu về Tây Sơn-Nguyễn Huệ Trên đất Nghĩa Bình* (Documents concerning the Tây Sơn and Nguyễn Huệ in the Nghĩa Bình Region), edited by Phan Huy Lê et al., 172–194. Qui Nhòn: Sở Văn Hóa Và Thông Tin Nghĩa Bình, 1988.

———. *Tây Sơn Văn Thần Liệt Truyện* (Biographies of Tây Sơn Officials). Qui Nhơn: Ty Văn Hóa Và Thông Tin Nghĩa Bình, 1979.

Nguyễn Danh Phiệt. "Một Vài Suy Nghĩ về Phong Trào Tây Sơn Với Sử Nghiệp Thống Nhất Đất Nước Hồi Thế Kỷ XVIII" (Some Thoughts about the Tây Sơn Movement with Respect to the Matter of the Unification of the Country in the Eighteenth Century). *Nghiên Cứu Lịch Sử* 193 (November–December 1978): 57–75.

———. "Nhà Tây Sơn Với Sự Nghiệp Dựng Nước" (The Tây Sơn Court and the Task of Reestablishing the Nation). *Nghiên Cứu Lịch Sử* 244 (January–February 1989): 28–33, 41.

Nguyễn Dương Bình. "Vài Suy Nghĩ Về Phong Trào Nông Dân Tây Sơn với Các Dân Tộc Ít Người Và Căn Cứ Địa Miền Núi" (Some Thoughts about the Tây Sơn Peasant Movement with the Minority Peoples and Their Base in the Mountain Regions). In *Tây Sơn Nguyễn Huệ (Ký Yếu Hội Nghị Nghiên Cứu Phong Trào Nông Dân Tây Sơn, Qui Nhơn 2/25–2/28, 1978)* (Tây Sơn Nguyễn Huệ [Essential Notes of a Research Conference on the Tây Sơn Peasant Movement]), by the Ty Văn Hóa và Thông Tín Nghĩa Bình, 142–146. Qui Nhơn: Ty Văn Hóa và Thông Tin Nghĩa Bình, 1978.

Nguyễn Duy Hinh. "Những Suy Nghĩ Về Nhà Tây Sơn" (Some Thoughts about the Tây Sơn Dynasty). *Nghiên Cứu Lịch Sử* 244 (January–February 1989): 20–27.

Nguyễn Khắc Đạm. "Tại Sao Các Cuộc Khởi Nghĩa Nông Dân ở Việt-Nam Ít Có Màu Sắc Tôn Giáo?" (Why Do Righteous Peasant Uprisings in Việt Nam Seldom Have Religious Elements?). *Nghiên Cứu Lịch Sử* 81 (December 1965): 8–10.

Nguyễn Lộc. *Văn Học Tây Sơn* (Tây Sơn Literature). Qui Nhơn: Sở Văn Hóa Và Thông Tin Nghĩa Bình, 1986.

Nguyễn Lương Bích. *Quang Trung-Nguyễn Huệ*. Hà Nội: Nhà Xuất Bản Quân Đội Nhân Dân, 1989.

Nguyễn Phương. *Việt Nam Thời Bành Trướng: Tây Sơn* (Việt Nam in a Time of Expansion: Tây Sơn). Saigon: Khai Trí, 1967.

Nguyễn Q. Thắng and Nguyễn Bá Thế. *Từ Điển Nhân Vật Lịch Sử Việt Nam* (Dictionary of Historical Personages of Việt Nam). TP Hồ Chí Minh: Nhà Xuất Bản Văn Hóa, 1993.

Nguyễn Tài Thư, ed. *Lịch Sử Tư Tưởng Việt Nam, Tập 1* (A History of Vietnamese Thought, Volume 1). Hà Nội: Nhà Xuất Bản Khoa Học Xã Hội, 1993.

———. "Ngô Thì Nhậm: Nhà Tư Tưởng Lại Lạc Của Thời Kỳ Biến Loạn Xã Hội" (Ngô Thì Nhậm: An Outstanding Thinker in a Period of Social Upheaval). In *Lịch Sử Tư Tưởng Việt Nam, Tập 1* (A History of Vietnamese Thought, Volume 1), edited by Nguyễn Tài Thư, 460–484. Hà Nội: Nhà Xuất Bản Khoa Học Xã Hội, 1993.

Nguyễn Triệu. "Ông Tín (1768–1799)." *Tri Tân* (November 1941): 11.

Nguyễn Văn Hoàn. "Phong Trào Khởi Nghĩa Nông Dân và Văn Học Việt Nam Thế Kỷ XVIII và Nử Đầu Thế Ký XIX" (Righteous Uprising Peasant Movements and Vietnamese Literature of the Eighteenth and First Half of the Nineteenth Centuries). *Tạp Chí Văn Học* 4 (1973): 19–38.

Nguyễn Vinh Phúc. "Nhân Dân Hà Nội Và Tây Sơn" (The People of Hà Nội and the Tây Sơn). *Nghiên Cứu Lịch Sử* 244 (January–February 1989): 53–56, 82.

*Những Mẩu Chuyện về Tây Sơn* (Some Tales about the Tây Sơn). Qui Nhơn: Ty Văn Hóa Và Thông Tin Nghĩa Bình, 1979.

Phạm Thúy Hằng and Trần Thu Hương. "Phát Hiện Quả Chuông Cảnh Thịnh ở Chùa Phương Trì Đại Phùng" (The Discovery of a Cảnh Thịnh–era Bell at the Phương Trì Pagoda in the Village of Đại Phùng). In *Những Phát Hiện Mới Về Khảo Cổ Học Năm 1985* (New Archaeological Discoveries, 1985), edited by Viện Khảo Cổ Học, 222–223. Hà Nội: Viện Khảo Cổ Học, 1985.

Phạm Văn Đang. *Văn Học Tây Sơn* (Tây Sơn Literature). Sài Gòn: Lửa Thiên, 1973.

Phạm Văn Sơn. *Việt Sử Tân Biên: Từ Tây Sơn đến Nguyễn Sơ* (The New Annals of Vietnamese History: From the Tây Sơn to the Early Nguyễn). Sài Gòn: Nhà Sách Khai-Trí, 1961.

Phan Đại Doãn, ed. *Một Số Vấn Đề Về Nho Giáo Việt Nam* (Some Matters regarding Vietnamese Confucianism). Hà Nội: Nhà Xuất Bản Chính Trị Quốc Gia, 1998.

Phan Huy Lê. "Bàn Thêm Mấy Về Phong Trào Nông Dân Tây Sơn" (Some Further Discussions about the Tây Sơn Peasant Movement). Parts 1 and

2. *Nghiên Cứu Lịch Sử* 49 (April 1963): 2–26, 47; 50 (May 1963): 36–42, 61.

Phan Huy Lê. "Có Một Bộ Luật Đời Tây Sơn" (There Was a Tây Sơn Legal Code). In *Góp Phần Tìm Hiểu Phong Trào Nông Dân Tây Sơn Nguyễn Huệ* (Contributions to Understanding the Tây Sơn Peasant Movement of Nguyễn Huệ), by the Sở Văn Hóa Thông Tin Nghĩa Bình, 182–190. Sở Văn Hóa Thông Tin Nghĩa Bình, 1983.

———. "Di Tích Thành Hoàng Đế" (Vestiges of an Imperial Citadel). In *Tìm Về Cội Nguồn* (Search for Origins), edited by Phan Huy Lê, 103–123. Hà Nội: Nhà Xuất Bản Thế Giới, 1998.

———. *Quang Trung Nguyễn Huệ: Con Người và Sự Nghiệp* (Quang Trung Nguyễn Huệ: The Person and His Accomplishments). Qui Nhơn: Sở Văn Hóa và Thông Tin Nghĩa Bình Xuất Bản, 1986.

——— et al. *Tư Liệu Về Tây Sơn–Nguyễn Huệ* (Documents Concerning Tây Sơn–Nguyễn Huệ). 3 vols. Qui Nhơn: Sở Văn Hóa và Thông Tin Nghĩa Bình Xuất Bản, 1988.

Phan Khoang. *Việt Sử: Xứ Đàng Trong, 1558–1777* (Vietnamese History: The Region of Đàng Trong, 1558–1777). Sài Gòn: Nhà Sách Khai Trí, 1967.

Phan Ngọc Liên and Nghiêm Đình Vỳ. "Về Một Đặc Điểm Nổi Bật Của Phong Trào Nông Dân Tây Sơn" (About Some Particular Characteristics of the Tây Sơn Peasant Movement). *Nghiên Cứu Lịch Sử* 216 (January–February 1984): 33–37.

Phan Trần Chúc. *Bằng Quận Công Nguyễn Hữu Chỉnh* (The Bằng Duke: Nguyễn Hữu Chỉnh). Hà Nội: Nhà Xuất Bản Văn Hóa Thông Tin, 2001.

———. *Vua Quang Trung Nguyễn Huệ (Lịch Sử)* (A History of the King Quang Trung Nguyễn Huệ). Sài Gòn: Chí Ký Xuất Bản, 1957.

Quách Tấn. "Di-tích và Truyền-Thuyết về Nhà Tây-Sơn" (Vestiges and Traditions concerning the Tây Sơn). *Sử Địa* 9 (September–October 1968): 17–32, 170–176.

——— and Quách Giao. *Nhà Tây Sơn* (The Tây Sơn Dynasty). Qui Nhơn: Sở Văn Hóa và Thông Tin Nghĩa Bình, 1988.

Tạ Chí Đại Trường. *Lịch Sử Nội Chiến ở Việt Nam Từ 1771 đến 1802* (History of the Civil War in Việt Nam from 1771 to 1802). Sài Gòn: Văn Sử Học, 1973.

"Tài Liệu Tham Khảo: Hịch của Lê Duy Mật Kể Tội Họ Trịnh" (Research Documents: The Edict of Lê Duy Mật Telling of the Crimes of the Trịnh). *Nghiên Cứu Lịch Sử* 108 (March 1968): 58–59.

*Tây Sơn Nguyễn Huệ (Ký Yếu Hội Nghị Nghiên Cứu Phong Trào Nông Dân Tây Sơn, Qui Nhơn 2/25–2/28, 1978)* (Tây Sơn Nguyễn Huệ [Essential Notes of a Research Conference on the Tây Sơn Peasant Movement]). Qui Nhơn: Ty Văn Hóa và Thông Tín Nghĩa Bình, 1978.

Trần Huy Liệu. "Đánh Gia Cuộc Cách Mạng Tây-Sơn và Vai Trò Lịch Sử cuả

Nguyễn Huệ" (Evaluating the Tây Sơn Revolution and the Historical Role of Nguyễn Huệ). *Văn Sử Địa* 14 (February 1956): 30–44.

Trần Nghĩa and François Gros, eds. *Di Sản Hán Nôm Việt Nam Thư Mục Đề Yếu* (A Catalogue of the Hán Nôm Heritage of Việt Nam). 3 vols. Hà Nội: Nhà Xuất Bản Khoa Học Xã Hội, 1993.

Trần Thị Vinh. "Tìm Hiểu về Tổ Chức Nhà Nước Thời Tây Sơn" (Inquiry into the Establishment of the State in the Tây Sơn Period). *Nghiên Cứu Lịch Sử* 244 (January–February 1989): 42–47.

Trần Thiều. "Giữ Chùa Thờ Bụt mà An Oản: Vì Sao Họ Trịnh Không Dứt Nghiệp Nhà Lê?" (Retain the Buddhist Temple and Altar and Protect Its Offerings: Why Did the Trịnh Clan Not Dispense with the Lê House?). *Xưa Và Nay* 53, no. 7 (1998): 38–39.

Trần Trọng Kim. *Việt Nam Sử Lược* (A Summary History of Việt Nam). Hà Nội, 1928. Reprint, Los Alamitos, Calif.: Xuân Thu Xuất Bản, 1990.

Trần Văn Quý. "Một Số Tư Liệu Thời Tây Sơn Mới Phát Hiện" (Some Recently Discovered Documents from the Tây Sơn Period). *Nghiên Cứu Lịch Sử* 197 (March–April 1981): 84–86, 93.

Trúc Khê. *Bùi Huy Bích: Danh Nhân Truyện Ký* (Bùi Huy Bích: Recorded Tales of a Famous Man). Hà Nội: Nhà Xuất Bản Hà Nội, 1998.

Trương Hữu Quýnh, ed. *Đại Cương Lịch Sử Việt Nam* (A Broad Outline of Vietnamese History). 3 vols. Hà Nội: Nhà Xuất Bản Giáo Dục, 2001.

Ủy Ban Khoa Học Xã Hội. *Lịch Sử Việt Nam* (History of Viet Nam). 2 vols. Hà Nội: Nhà Xuất Bản Khoa Học Xã Hội, 1976.

Văn Tân. *Cách Mạng Tây Sơn* (The Tây Sơn Revolution). Hà Nội: Nhà Xuất Bản Văn Sử Địa, 1957.

———. *Ngô Thì Nhậm: Con Người và Sự Nghiệp* (Ngô Thì Nhậm: His Life and Works). Hà Tây: Ty Văn Hóa-Thông Tin, 1974.

———. *Nguyễn Huệ: Con Người và Sự Nghiệp* (Nguyễn Huệ: His Life and Works). Hà Nội: Nhà Xuất Bản Khoa Học, 1967.

———. "Quốc Sử Quán Triều Nguyễn Đối Với Khởi Nghĩa Tây Sơn" (The Nguyễn Dynasty History Board and the Tây Sơn Righteous Uprising). *Nghiên Cứu Lịch Sử* 65 (August 1964): 14–21.

*Việt Nam Những Sự Kiện Lịch Sử (Từ Khởi Thủy đến 1858)* (Vietnam: Historical Events [from its Origins to 1858]). Hà Nội: Nhà Xuất Bản Giáo Dục, 2001.

Vũ Đức Phúc. "Từ Ngô Thì Nhậm Đến Trào Lưu Văn Học Tây Sơn" (From Ngô Thì Nhậm to the Currents of Tây Sơn Literature). *Tạp Chí Văn Học* 4 (1973): 2–18.

Vũ Minh Giang. "Tây Sơn Trượng Đạo, Căn Cứ Đầu Tiên Của Cuộc Khởi Nghĩa" (The Tây Sơn Upper Region, the First Foundation for the Righteous Uprising). In *Góp Phần Tìm Hiểu Phong Trào Nông Dân Tây Sơn Nguyễn Huệ* (Contributions to Understanding the Tây Sơn Peasant Movement and Nguyễn Huệ), by the Sở Văn Hóa Thông Tin Nghĩa Bình, 22–32. Qui Nhơn: Sở Văn Hóa Thông Tin Nghĩa Bình, 1983.

**WESTERN-LANGUAGE SOURCES**

Adas, Michael. "From Avoidance to Confrontation: Peasant Protest in Precolonial and Colonial Southeast Asia." In *Colonialism and Culture*, edited by Nicholas Dirks, 89–126. Ann Arbor: University of Michigan Press, 1992.

———. *Prophets of Rebellion: Millenarian Movements against the European Colonial Order*. Chapel Hill: University of North Carolina Press, 1979.

Antony, Robert. *Like Froth Floating on the Sea: The World of Pirates and Seafarers in Late Imperial South China*. China Research Monograph, no. 56. Berkeley: Institute of East Asian Studies, University of California, 2003.

Barrow, John. *A Voyage to Cochinchina in the Years 1792 and 1793*. 1806. Reprint, Kuala Lumpur: Oxford University Press, 1975.

Bissachère, M. de La. *Etat actuel du Tonkin et de la Cochinchine et des royaumes de Camboge, Laos et Lac-Tho*. 2 vols. 1812. Reprint, Westmead, England: Gregg International, 1971.

Buttinger, Joseph. *The Smaller Dragon*. New York: Praeger, 1957.

Cadière, Léopold. "Le Changement de costume sous Vo-Vuong, ou une crise religieuse a Hué au XVIII siècle." *Bulletin des amis de vieux Hué* 4 (October–December 1915): 417–424.

———. *Croyances et pratiques religieuses des Viêtnamiens*. Tome 3. Hanoi: École Française d'Extrême-Orient, 1944. Reprint, Paris: École Française d'Extrême-Orient, 1992.

———. "Documents relatifs a l'époque de Gia-Long." *Bulletin de l'École Française d'Extrême-Orient* 12 (1912): 1–79.

———. "Quelques figures de la cour de Vo-Vuong." *Bulletin des amis de vieux Hué* 5 (October–December 1918): 253–271.

Chen Chingho. *Historical Notes on Hoi An*. Monograph Series 4. Carbondale: Center for Vietnamese Studies, Southern Illinois University, 1973.

Chesneaux, Jean. *Contribution à l'histoire de la nation Vietnamienne*. Paris: Editions Sociales, 1955.

Choi Byung Wook. *Southern Vietnam under the Reign of Minh Mạng (1820–1841): Central Policies and Local Response*. Ithaca, N.Y.: Southeast Asia Program Publication, [Cornell University], 2004.

Cooke, Nola. "The Myth of the Restoration: Dang-Trong Influences in the Spiritual Life of the Early Nguyen Dynasty (1802–47)." In *The Last Stand of Asian Autonomies: Responses to Modernity in Diverse States of Southeast Asia and Korea, 1750–1900*, edited by Anthony Reid, 265–296. London: Macmillan, 1997.

———. "Nineteenth-Century Vietnamese Confucianization in Historical Perspective: Evidence from the Palace Examinations (1463–1883)." *Journal of Southeast Asian Studies* 25, no. 2 (September 1994): 270–312.

———. "Regionalism and the Nature of Nguyen Rule in Seventeenth-Century Dang Trong (Cochinchina)." *Journal of Southeast Asian Studies* 29, no. 1 (March 1998): 122–161.

———, and Li Tana, eds. *Water Frontier: Commerce and the Chinese in the Lower Mekong Region, 1750–1880*. Lanham, Md.: Rowman and Littlefield, 2004.

Đặng Phương-Nghi. *Les Institutions publiques du Viêt-Nam au XVIIIe siècle*. Paris: École Française d'Extrême-Orient, 1969.

Durand, Maurice. "Tây Sơn." Typescript. Manuscripts Division, Yale University Library, New Haven, Conn.

———, and Nguyen Tran Huan. *An Introduction to Vietnamese Literature*. Translated by David Hawke. New York: Columbia University Press, 1985.

Dutton, George. "The Fat Sheep with the Precious Wool: Bandit Kidnapping of Foreigners in 1920s China." Manuscript, 1992.

———. "Reassessing Confucianism in the Tây Sơn Regime (1788–1802)." *Southeast Asia Research* 13, no. 2 (July 2005): 157–183.

Engelbert, Thomas. *Die Chinesische Minderheit im Süden Vietnams (Hoa) als Paradigma der kolonialen und nationalistischen Nationalitätenpolitik*. Frankfurt: Peter Lang, 2002.

Forest, Alain. *Les Missionaires français au Tonkin et au Siam, XVIIe–XVIII siècles*. Livre 2: *Histoires du Tonkin*. Paris: L'Harmattan, 1998.

Heidhues, Mary Somers. "Chinese Organizations in West Borneo and Bangka: *Kongsi* and *Hui*." In *"Secret Societies" Reconsidered: Perspectives on the Social History of Modern South China and Southeast Asia*, edited by David Ownby and Mary Somers Heidhues, 68–88. Armonk, N.Y.: M. E. Sharp, 1993.

Huard, Pierre, and Maurice Durand. *Connaissance du Việt Nam*. Paris: École Française d'Extrême-Orient, 1954.

Huỳnh Sanh Thông. "Folk History in Vietnam." *Vietnam Forum* 5 (1985): 66–80.

Ileto, Rey. "Religion and Anti-Colonial Movements." In *The Cambridge History of Southeast Asia*. Vol. 2, part 1: *From c. 1800 to the 1930s*, edited by Nicholas Tarling, 195–245. Cambridge: Cambridge University Press, 1999.

Jamieson, Neil. *Understanding Vietnam*. Berkeley: University of California Press, 1993.

Kelley, Liam. *Beyond the Bronze Pillars: Envoy Poetry and the Sino-Vietnamese Relationship*. Honolulu: University of Hawai'i Press, 2005.

Lamb, Alistair. *Mandarin Road to Old Hue*. London: Archon Books, 1970.

Langlet, Philippe. *L'ancienne historiographie d'état au Vietnam*. Tome 1: *Raisons d'être, conditions d'élaboration et caractères au siècle des Nguyễn*. Paris: École Française d'Extrême-Orient, 1990.

*Le Tcheou-Li Ou Rites des Tcheou*. Translated by Édouard Biot. Paris: L'Imprimerie Nationale, 1851. Reprint, Taipei: Ch'eng Wen, 1969.

Lê Thành Khôi. *Histoire du Viet Nam, des origines à 1858*. Paris: Sudestasie, 1992.

———. *Le Vietnam: Histoire et civilisation*. Paris: Editions de Minuit, 1955.

Li Tana. "An Alternative Vietnam? The Nguyen Kingdom in the Seventeenth and Eighteenth Centuries." *Journal of Southeast Asian Studies* 29, no. 1 (March 1998): 111–121.

———. *Nguyễn Cochinchina: Southern Vietnam in the Seventeenth and Eighteenth Centuries*. Ithaca, N.Y.: Cornell University Southeast Asia Program, 1998.

———. "The Water Frontier: An Introduction." In *Water Frontier: Commerce and the Chinese in the Lower Mekong Region, 1750–1880*, edited by Nola Cooke and Li Tana, 1–17. Lanham, Md.: Rowman and Littlefield, 2004.

Lieberman, Victor. *Strange Parallels: Southeast Asia in Global Context, c. 800–1830*. Cambridge: Cambridge University Press, 2003.

Malleret, L. "Voyage de Pierre Poivre en Cochinchine." *Bulletin de l'École de Française d'Extrême-Orient* 92 (1974).

Manguin, Pierre-Yves. *Les Nguyễn, Macau et le Portugal: Aspects politiques et commerciaux d'une relation privilégiée en Mer de Chine 1773–1802*. Paris: École Française d'Extrême-Orient, 1984.

Marr, David. *Vietnamese Anticolonialism: 1885–1925*. Berkeley: University of California Press, 1971.

———. *Vietnamese Tradition on Trial, 1920–1945*. Berkeley: University of California Press, 1981.

Maybon, Charles. *Histoire modern du pays d'Annam, 1592–1802*. Paris: Plon-Nourrit et Cie, 1919.

———. *La Relation sur le Tonkin et Cochinchine de Mr. de La Bissachère*. Paris: E. Champion, 1920.

McLeod, Mark W. *The Vietnamese Response to French Intervention, 1862–1874*. New York: Praeger, 1991.

(MEP) Archives des Missions Étrangères de Paris. Paris, France.

Murray, Dian. *Pirates of the South China Coast, 1790–1810*. Stanford, Calif.: Stanford University Press, 1987.

Ngaosyvathn, Mayoury, and Pheuiphanh Ngaosyvathn. *Paths to Conflagration: Fifty Years of Diplomacy and Warfare in Laos, Thailand, and Vietnam, 1778–1828*. Ithaca, N.Y.: Cornell University Southeast Asia Program, 1998.

Ngô Vĩnh Long. *Before the Revolution*. New York: Columbia University Press, 1991.

Nguyễn Đình Hòe. "Note sur les cendres des Tây Sơn dans la prison du Kham Đường." *Bulletin des amis de vieux Hué* 2 (April–June 1914): 145–146.

Nguyễn Khắc Viện. *Vietnam: A Long History*. Hanoi: Foreign Languages Publishing House, 1987.

Nguyễn Ngọc Huy and Tạ Văn Tài. *The Lê Code: Law in Traditional Vietnam*. 3 vols. Athens, Oh.; and London: Ohio University Press, 1987.

Nguyên Thanh-Nhã. *Tableau economique du Vietnam aux XVIIe et XVIIIe siècles*. Paris: Éditions Cujas, 1970.

Nguyễn Thế Anh. "L'Immigration chinoise et la colonisation du Delta du Mékong. *Vietnam Review* 1 (Autumn–Winter 1996): 154–177.

*Nouvelles lettres édifiantes des missions de la Chine et des Indes orientales*. Vols. 6–8. Paris: Chez Ad. Le Clere, 1821–1825.

Pérez, P. Lorenzo. "La Révolte et la guerre des Tayson d'après les Franciscains Espagnols de Cochinchine." Translated by M. Villa. *Bulletin de la Société des Etudes Indochinoises* 12, no. 3–4 (1940): 65–106.

Perry, Elizabeth J. *Rebels and Revolutionaries in North China, 1845–1945*. Stanford, Calif.: Stanford University Press, 1980.

Phan, Peter. *Mission and Catechesis: Alexandre de Rhodes and Inculturation in Seventeenth-Century Vietnam*. Maryknoll, N.Y.: Orbis Books, 1998.

Pye, Lucian. *Asian Power and Politics: The Cultural Dimensions of Authority*. Cambridge, Mass.: Belknap Press, 1985.

Reid, Anthony. *Southeast Asia in the Age of Commerce*. Volume 1: *The Lands below the Winds*. New Haven, Conn.: Yale University Press, 1988.

Richard, A. *Histoire naturelle, civile et politique du Tonquin*. Paris: Chez Moutard, 1778.

Scott, James. *Domination and the Arts of Resistance*. New Haven, Conn.: Yale University Press, 1990.

———. *The Moral Economy of the Peasant*. New Haven, Conn.: Yale University Press, 1976.

Shiraishi, Masaya. "State, Villagers, and Vagabonds: Vietnamese Rural Society and the Phan Bá Vành Rebellion." In *History and Peasant Consciousness in Southeast Asia*, edited by Andrew Turton and Shigeharu Tanabe, 345–400. Osaka: National Museum of Ethnology, 1984.

Smith, Ralph. "The Cycle of Confucianization in Vietnam." In *Aspects of Vietnamese History*, edited by Walter F. Vella, 1–27. Honolulu: University Press of Hawai'i, 1973.

———. *Viet-Nam and the West*. London: Heinemann, 1968.

Sok, Khin. *Le Cambodge entre le Siam et le Viêtnam (de 1775 à 1860)*. Paris: École Française d'Extrême-Orient, 1991.

Spence, Jonathan. *In Search of Modern China*. New York: W. W. Norton, 1990.

Staunton, Sir George. *An Authentic Account of an Embassy from the King of Great Britain to the Emperor of China*. London: C. Nicol, 1797.

Taboulet, Georges. *La Geste française en Indochine: Histoire par les textes de la France en Indochine des origines à 1914*. 2 vols. Paris: Librarie d'Amerique et d'Orient, 1955–1956.

Tai, Hue-tam Ho. *Millenarianism and Peasant Politics in Vietnam*. Cambridge: Harvard University Press, 1983.

Tanabe, Shigeharu. "Ideological Practice in Peasant Rebellion: Siam at the Turn of the Twentieth Century." In *History and Peasant Consciousness in Southeast Asia*, edited by Andrew Turton and Shigeharu Tanabe, 75–110. Osaka: National Museum of Ethnology, 1984.

Taylor, Keith. "Authority and Legitimacy in 11th Century Vietnam." In *Southeast Asia in the 9th to 14th Centuries*, edited by David G. Marr and A. C. Milner, 139–176. Singapore: Institute of Southeast Asian Studies, 1986.

———. *The Birth of Vietnam*. Berkeley and Los Angeles: University of California Press, 1983.

———. "Nguyen Hoang and the Beginning of Vietnam's Southward Expansion." In *Southeast Asia in the Early Modern Era: Trade, Power and Belief*, edited by Anthony Reid, 42–65. Ithaca, N.Y.; and London: Cornell University Press, 1993.

———. "Surface Orientations in Vietnam: Beyond Histories of Nation and Region." *Journal of Asian Studies* 4 (1998): 949–978.

Thongchai Winachakul. *Siam Mapped*. Honolulu: University of Hawai'i Press, 1994.

Trương Bưu Lâm. "Intervention versus Tribute in Sino-Vietnamese Relations, 1788–1790." In *The Chinese World Order*, edited by John K. Fairbank, 165–179. Cambridge: Harvard University Press, 1968.

———. *Patterns of Vietnamese Response to Foreign Intervention, 1858–1900*. New Haven, Conn.: Yale University Southeast Asian Studies, 1967.

———. *Resistance, Rebellion, Revolution: Popular Movements in Vietnamese History*. Singapore: Institute of Southeast Asian Studies, 1984.

Trương Vĩnh Ký. *Cours d'histoire Annamite*. Saigon: Imprimerie du Gouvernement, 1875.

Viet Chung. "Recent Findings on the Tay Son Insurgency." *Vietnamese Studies* 8, no. 11 (1985): 5–29.

Vlastos, Stephen. *Peasant Protests and Uprisings in Tokugawa Japan*. Berkeley: University of California Press, 1986.

Whitmore, John K. "*Chung-hsing* and *Cheng-t'ung* in Texts of and on Sixteenth-Century Việt Nam." In *Essays into Vietnamese Pasts*, edited by K. W. Taylor and John K. Whitmore, 116–136. Ithaca, N.Y.: Cornell University Southeast Asia Program, 1995.

———. "Literati Culture in Dai Viet, 1480–1830." In *Beyond Binary Histories: Reimagining Eurasia to c. 1830*, edited by Victor Lieberman, 221–244. Ann Arbor: University of Michigan Press, 1999.

———. *Vietnam, Hồ Quý Ly, and the Ming (1371–1421)*. New Haven, Conn.: Yale Center for International and Area Studies, 1985.

Wilcox, Wynn. "Allegories of Vietnam: Transculturation and the Origin Myths of Franco-Vietnamese Relations." Ph.D. dissertation, Cornell University, 2002.

Wolters, O. W. "Le Van Huu's Treatment of Ly Thanh Ton's Reign (1127–1137)." In *Southeast Asian History and Historiography*, edited by C. D. Cowan and O. W. Wolters, 203–226. Ithaca, N.Y.: Cornell University Press, 1976.

———. *Two Essays on Đại-Việt in the Fourteenth Century*. New Haven, Conn.:

Council on Southeast Asia Studies, Yale Center for International and Area Studies, Boston, 1988.

Woodside, Alexander. "Buddhism, the Vietnamese Court and China in the 1800s." In *Historical Interaction of China and Vietnam: Institutional and Cultural Themes*, edited by E. Wickberg, 11–24. Lawrence: Center for East Asian Studies, University of Kansas, 1969.

———. "Central Vietnam's Trading World in the Eighteenth Century as Seen in Lê Quý Đôn's 'Frontier Chronicles.'" In *Essays into Vietnamese Pasts*, edited by K. W. Taylor and John K. Whitmore, 157–172. Ithaca, N.Y.: Southeast Asia Program Publication, Cornell University, 1995.

———. "Classical Primordialism and the Historical Agendas of Vietnamese Confucianism." In *Rethinking Confucianism: Past and Present in China, Japan, Korea, and Vietnam*, edited by Benjamin A. Elman, John B. Duncan, and Herman Ooms, 116–143. Los Angeles: UCLA Asian Pacific Monograph Series, 2002.

———. *Community and Revolution in Modern Vietnam*. Boston: Houghton-Mifflin, 1976.

———. "Conceptions of Change and of Human Responsibility for Change in Late Traditional Vietnam." In *Moral Order and the Question of Change: Essays on Southeast Asian Thought*, edited by David A. Wyatt and Alexander Woodside, 104–150. New Haven, Conn.: Yale University Southeast Asia Studies, 1982.

———. "The Tay-son Revolution in Southeast Asian History." Unpublished pamphlet. Cornell University Library, 1976.

———. *Vietnam and the Chinese Model: A Comparative Study of Vietnamese and Chinese Government in the First Half of the Nineteenth Century*. Cambridge: Harvard University Press, 1971.

Wyatt, David. *Thailand: A Short History*. New Haven, Conn.: Yale University Press, 1982.

Yang Baoyun. *Contribution à l'histoire de la principauté des Nguyên au Vietnam méridional (1600–1775)*. Geneva: Editions Olizane, 1992.

Young, Stephen B. "The Law of Property and Elite Prerogatives during Vietnam's Lê Dynasty, 1428–1788." *Journal of Asian History* 10, no. 1 (1976): 1–48.

Yu, Insun. *Law and Society in Seventeenth and Eighteenth Century Vietnam*. Seoul: Asiatic Research Center, 1990.

# INDEX

Page numbers in **boldface** type refer to illustrations.

## ABOUT THE AUTHOR

George Dutton is assistant professor in the UCLA Department of Asian Languages and Cultures, and chair of the UCLA Interdepartmental Program in Southeast Asian Studies. He received an M.A. in international relations from Yale University and a Ph.D. in Southeast Asian history from the University of Washington. He has published articles on Tây Sơn-era poetry, Vietnamese military technology, and on Vietnamese historiography and Tây Sơn society.